THE ENGLISH FARMHOUSE
AND COTTAGE

THE
ENGLISH FARMHOUSE

AND COTTAGE

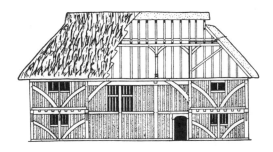

by

M. W. BARLEY

Routledge and Kegan Paul
LONDON and BOSTON

First published 1961
by Routledge & Kegan Paul Limited
Broadway House, 68-74 Carter Lane
London, EC4V 5EL
and 9 Park Street, Boston, Mass. 02108, U.S.A.

Printed in Great Britain
by Lowe & Brydone (Printers) Ltd, London

Second impression 1967
Third impression 1972

ISBN 0 7100 1050 8

To
CYRIL FOX
in admiration and affection

Contents

CONTENTS

Plates

Figures

NOTE: For those who are not accustomed to looking at plans of buildings some explanation of the conventions used may be helpful, especially as they differ from those adopted by architects. Original walls of stone or brick, or the posts of a timber frame, are shown solid black, whatever their age; later alterations and additions which have some historic interest are stippled, while very recent ones are shown open or are omitted altogether. In labelling rooms and other parts, italic lettering has been used for original features and roman for later. Ground plans are taken at the level of window openings, so that doorways are represented as a complete break in the line of walls; window openings have the lines of the inner and outer faces of the wall below, and usually also the lines of the window frame and of the glass. Ceiling beams, and in some cases joists as well, are indicated by broken lines. Door frames are omitted, and so are the arcs of circles by which an architect shows which way a door opens.

Tables

Abbreviations

A.A.S.R.P.	*Associated Architectural Societies' Reports and Papers*
Agr. H.R.	*Agricultural History Review*
Ant. J.	*Antiquaries' Journal*
Arch.	*Archaeologia*
Arch. Camb.	*Archaeologia Cambrensis*
Arch. J.	*Archaeological Journal*
E.H.R.	*English Historical Review*
Econ. H.R.	*Economic History Review*
J.B.A.A.	*Journal of the British Archaeological Association*
J.R.S.A.	*Journal of the Royal Society of Arts*
L.R.O.	Lincoln Record Office
Med. Arch.	*Medieval Archaeology*
Mon. Ho.	*Monmouthshire Houses,* Fox and Raglan
P.R.O.	Public Record Office
Proc. Camb. Ant. Soc.	*Proceedings of the Cambridge Antiquarian Society*
R.C.H.M.	Royal Commission on Historical Monuments
Somerset A.N.H.S. Proc.	*Somerset Archaeological and Natural History Society Proceedings*
Test. Ebor.	*Testamenta Eboracensia* (Surtees Society)
T.C.W.A.A.S.	*Transactions of the Cumberland and Westmorland Archaeological and Antiquarian Society*
V.C.H.	Victoria County History

Acknowledgements

THE collection of material for this book has depended so much on the help of historians, archivists and archaeologists that it could be called a work of collaboration if that were not to place on others a responsibility which the author alone must bear. My interest in records of houses was stimulated by Dr. W. G. Hoskins and he has been generous and helpful at every stage. More specifically, he has placed his own Devonshire notes at my disposal and put me in touch with Mrs. M. C. S. Cruwys, whose transcripts of Devonshire terriers have been of great value. Mrs. V. M. Chesher provided extracts from Cornish terriers, and Mr. G. H. Kenyon his notes of Sussex inventories. I have been singularly fortunate in being able to use some of the material collected by Miss L. F. Midgley for the proposed *Agrarian History of England*, under the editorship of Dr. H. P. R. Finberg and Dr. Joan Thirsk of the University of Leicester. I have received help from archivists at Bedford (Miss A. J. Godber), Chichester (Mr. F. W. Steer), Lincoln (Mrs. Joan Varley and Mrs. D. M. Owen), Maidstone (Dr. Felix Hull), Norwich (Mr. T. F. Barton, honorary archivist to the diocese of Norwich), Stafford (Mr. F. B. Stitt), Ipswich Public Library, Taunton (Mr. Ivor P. Collis), St. Anthony's Hall, York, and at St. Bartholomew's Hospital (Miss M. V. Stokes). To the Principal Registrar at Somerset House and to District Registrars at Birmingham, Nottingham and York, and to their staffs, I am indebted for access to collections of probate inventories at that time in their custody.

To those who have placed plans, drawings or photographs at my disposal acknowledgement is made in the appropriate place. Many of them are fellow members of the Vernacular Architecture Group, in whose company I have seen something of the wealth of houses of every age in rural England. More than that, I have watched their skill in analysing the archaeological problems which nearly every building presents, and although those from whom I have learned are too numerous to mention individually, I must single out Mr. T. W. French, Dr. E. A. Gee, Mr. S. R. Jones, Mr. R. W. McDowall, Mr. T. L. Marsden, Mr. J. T. Smith, Mr. Peter Smith, Dr. Margaret Wood and Dr. R. B. Wood-Jones. Mr. F. Marston and Mr. F. Thomas have provided Derbyshire material. One of the pleasantest, as well as the most profitable, parts of the long task of collecting material took the form of visits to Devonshire and Somerset farmhouses in the company of Mr. A. W. Everett, Sir Robert de Z. Hall and Dr. W. G. Hoskins. Dr. Peter Eden, the Rev. H. A. Dunn and Mr. R. S. Smith read my manuscript and helped to improve it.

The records accumulated by the Royal Commission on Historical Monuments (England) in the course of preparing its inventories, particularly of Essex, Herefordshire, and Westmorland, are an important quarry. I am indebted to the Commission for permission to make use of them, as well as some of the Commission's photographs, and the section of a house at Old Anstey, Leicestershire prepared for the Commission. I am also indebted to Messrs. Batsford for permission to reproduce a plan (fig. 19) from L. Ambler's *Old Halls and Manor Houses of Yorkshire,* and to the National Museum of Wales for Sir Cyril Fox's section of Court Farm, Llandenny, from *Monmouthshire Houses,* vol. I, p. 25.

To the numberless country people—farmers, parsons, farm workers—who scarcely ever refused to allow me, sometimes alone, sometimes in the company of forty others, to see inside their houses, to open every cupboard door, to fetch a ladder for climbing into the roof, my debt is beyond counting. Without their friendliness and hospitality, culminating often in the offer of a wash and an invitation to stay to tea, such a book could not have been written.

Whether the attempt to cover so large and unwieldy a subject has been successful, only further research will show. The most the author can hope is that it will facilitate the further work that will certainly follow, and that it will earn as fair a judgement as that which Thomas Fuller once passed: 'no hand so steady as always to hit the nail on the head'.

M.W.B.

Preface

THIS book attempts to describe the houses of the majority of the rural population of England, particularly in the sixteenth to eighteenth centuries. There are many reasons why the attempt has not been made before, at least in this manner. The first is that the most homely of topics has been regarded as the least important. The books about the English house which are to be found on the shelves of any public library deal, whatever their titles, with the homes of the wealthy and powerful: those who could afford grand designs and whose patronage made architectural history as well as putting the seal on their social eminence. To this generalization there were, until recently, two exceptions only. The first was S. O. Addy's *The English House*, a book which, more than any other, deserved that most general of titles. Its character is explained by the fact that Addy was not a professional historian, but a businessman who devoted his leisure to local studies in an area (the neighbourhood of Sheffield) where the social and economic environment gave less encouragement than elsewhere to the local historian's predisposition to feudal and manorial history. The other was G. F. Innocent's *History of English Building Construction*, the by-product of an academic career as an engineer. It too, significantly, was a northern product. Both writers belonged to a part of England in which, fifty years ago, men of substance felt themselves less distant from the peasantry than did their southern equivalents.

In this study, only the smaller houses of the English countryside will be considered; anything above the rank of the lesser manor house will be excluded. 'Manor house' may at first thought connote some degree of social dignity, but many of them, especially by the end of the Middle Ages and particularly in counties like Lincolnshire where the social structure of the villages included many smaller manors, were farmhouses whose dependent estate was small by modern standards. They were, with the parsonage houses, the largest in those villages which had no resident gentry. Below them, in status and size, came the houses of the rest of the village population. To concentrate attention on the lower ranks of rural society may seem like historical slumming, but is more fairly judged to be an effort to redress a balance which has remained too long at the other extreme.

The second reason for the neglect of this subject has been that the smaller houses have to such a large extent failed to be the subject of the record-accumulating process. The peasant who owned no real property and very little personal property made no records and scarcely provoked others to put pen to parchment or paper, except to record his crimes and misdemeanours, his succession to his father's property and his disappearance from his narrow earthly scene. Hence the difficulty to which Trevelyan could do no more than draw attention, and to be fair to him it must be said that direct historical evidence scarcely exists for the peasant house in the Middle Ages. That being so, other disciplines must fill the gap. The most important of them is archaeology. In the great vogue which archaeology has come to enjoy in the past ten years, most of the emphasis has been placed on excavation. It is only one of several techniques which the archaeologist employs in the study of material remains of the past. Our Victorian grandfathers studied cathedrals and parish churches, castles and monastic buildings, and attempted by comparative methods to elucidate each structure and to provide a chronology for its development. They evolved a method of field study irreproachable in principle, but limited by an insufficient body of accurate data, in the way of measured plans, elevations and records of structural features, and by an antiquarian approach which collected Norman doorways or Easter sepulchres as others collected silver or china. The only significant addition in this century to archaeological method, as far as the subject of this book is concerned, has been appreciation of the importance of studying distributions: that is, not only collecting and classifying information, about Norman doorways, hammer-beam roofs or cruck-built houses, but plotting them on a map, so that their incidence can be connected not only to material factors such as available resources but also to the movement of cultural and political influence.

The study of small houses is then a problem for the archaeologist. It has the advantage over excavation that it is much less arduous; much of it must be done under cover, and householders, if properly approached, are almost invariably hospitable—indeed often pressingly so. Most important it does not involve the removal of evidence. The man who excavates a Roman villa leaves nothing behind, if he does his work competently; he takes on the responsibility (often too little appreciated) for preserving in print what he has taken from the ground. By contrast, examination of a stone farmhouse in Northamptonshire or a timber-framed cottage in Warwickshire leaves the building intact, for others to see, and to confirm or overthrow the findings. These pages will show occasions when a second examination, in the light of greater knowledge, produced a better explanation.

The archaeologist can contribute more than the architect or the architectural historian, for we are concerned with building rather than with architecture. The middle ages would not have understood this distinction, and it did not affect farmhouses until the eighteenth century and cottages until the nineteenth. Till then both remained in essence functional building, in which purpose determined plan and form, and ornament was subordinated to them. That the builder often achieved what an architect now cons-ciously strives for—a satisfactory relation of forms, a harmony of structure and environment, a pleasing variety of finish and ornament—was incidental to his purpose of making a machine for living in. The archaeological approach, as distinct from the aesthetic, makes it easier to relate the form of an artefact, whether it is a flint implement, a pot or a house, to the culture which evolved it and the purpose for which it was made.

But the archaeologist sometimes has to admit that he cannot pass over the gulf between form and function: cannot say whether a pot was made for domestic or ritual purposes, whether a building whose foundations he finds was a house or a barn. Here the historian can step in. Although documentary evidence about medieval houses is very scanty, from the sixteenth century onwards there is an embarrassment of material, in the shape of contemporary accounts of houses and their contents. They consist primarily of household inventories made in connection with obtaining probate of wills. There are also records of a particular class of dwelling, the parsonage house, whose condition was of concern to the church authorities when they began to realize the necessity of finding satisfactory housing for a man compelled to reside in a particular place. Occasionally in the seventeenth century efficient estate management produced large scale surveys of housing. The wealth of material is indeed such that it provokes another problem: that of interpretation. On the one hand is the view that one can point to a particular house as typical of a period or class: a Norman house, a Tudor house, or a yeoman's house. On the other hand, there is the view that the variety of surviving houses and complexity of domestic arrangements revealed in documents are such as to defy classifi-cation: that there are no distinguishable types. The truth lies, as always, between the extremes, and indeed the variety is a challenge; its range can at least be described, in order to lay bare that most intimate segment of human life: the home.

The use of such voluminous material necessarily involves statistical methods, about which something must be said. Given a collection of many thousands of documents, all apparently of the same character, the alter-natives to reading them all, which is physically impossible, are either to make a deliberate selection, or to take a random sample. For practical reasons, the random sample is often the better method; it can be used to find the range or variety of living conditions and the average (or *median*) within.[1] An attempt is made in the following pages, to compare the results from one period and one region with another—a much more dangerous process. The other point on which doubt has been cast[2] is whether the household inventory is a reliable guide to the size of a house and its contents. Any single inventory may be incomplete, but the possibility that the approvers sometimes omitted a room because it was empty, or because its contents had been earmarked for the widow, does not invalidate the conclusions that shape themselves after one has studied a large number of documents.

While one historian, if he is prepared to visit the county towns whose record offices now contain much of this material, can acquaint himself with a substantial part of it, no one person can do the same for the buildings themselves. There are still many regions of England in which vernacular building has not yet been studied. The country houses of the sixteenth to eighteenth centuries have been worked over time and again by architectural historians, but knowledge of farmhouses and cottages is confined to a very few regional studies, and to accounts of particular buildings published in journals of local societies. The Royal Commission for Historical Monuments has in fifty years dealt with only eight out of thirty-nine English counties; its work, and the photographic record compiled by the National Buildings Record, have reflected until recently the common preoccupation with architecture, to the neglect of building. The recent change in the attitude of the Historical Monuments Commission has been due more than anything else to the appearance of *Monmouthshire Houses* by Sir Cyril Fox and Lord Raglan,[3] which in its turn reflected the interest of Welsh archaeologists in the peasant society out of which modern Wales has sprung. Apart from the skill in recording and interpretation which these volumes display, they are untouched by any predisposition to regard small houses as 'debased' or 'not first class'.[4]

Since no English counties have yet been surveyed in similar fashion, this book must rather refer to the scope for field work than digest the

[1]See Joan Thirsk, *English Peasant Farming* (1957), 3, for remarks about sampling and its validity. I would confirm, from my own experience, that median figures are valid and significant, though one needs to find a convenient way of expressing the range and distribution, without overloading the reader with pages of statistics.

[2]By F. W. Steer in 'Smaller Houses and their Furnishings' in *J.B.A.A.*, XX–XXI (1957–8), 143.

[3]National Museum of Wales, 3 vols., 1951–4.

[4]Phrases used by reviewers in *Arch. J.* 109 (1952), 160.

results of it. Immensely valuable work can be done by amateurs, without a training in architecture, and without the equipment and responsibility required by excavation.[1] It can give them the essential satisfaction of archaeology, of finding new facts and fitting them into a logical pattern. The task is both urgent and important: urgent because the houses themselves are being altered and demolished more rapidly than ever before; important because except in the field of music, England still lags behind the other countries of north-western Europe in the study of folk culture. Ireland has a Folk Lore Commission; Britain has Historical Monuments Commissions. The contrast marks the dichotomy in the archaeology of north-western Europe for the past century. British scholars have concentrated on the cultural and artistic influences radiating from the Mediterranean, to the neglect of the native, the traditional, the submerged elements. Scandinavian scholars have led the way in the study of more primitive cultures, since they were surrounded by distinct traces of a peasant society if not by a living form of it. In England that society and the culture it evolved were finally killed by the Industrial and Agrarian Revolutions, and the scraps and fossils from it are more rare. One thing and one alone has survived in quantity—the rural house. Here is an essential part of this older culture: the focus round which many of its activities flourished and the environment in which those who belonged to it spent their leisure. That is what makes the study of the farmhouse and the cottage a topic of such exceptional interest.

[1]For a brief account of what can be done, see Council for British Archaeology, Research Report 3: *The Investigation of Smaller Domestic Buildings;* available from 10 Bolton Gardens, London S.W.5.

Part One

THE LEGACY OF
THE MIDDLE AGES

CHAPTER ONE

Medieval Society and its Housing Needs

BEFORE the ideas and accomplishments of the sixteenth and seventeenth centuries can be examined, we must trace their ancestry, so as to have a point of view from which to assess them. The problem, stated at its crudest, is to see how complex the medieval house had already become: that is, how far building had already responded to the stratification and diversity of society. Providing shelter for his family is one of man's basic needs, so we must not be surprised to find that in western Europe he had arrived at various ways of solving it even before the time when Britain became a province of the Roman empire. Although a search for ultimate origins would carry us back into prehistoric times, we must be content to take up the inquiry a mere thousand years ago, when the elements that went to the making of the medieval house can already be discerned.

The study will necessarily begin with houses of a higher social grade than the farmhouse. Social betterment is simply a process of imitating the ways of wealthier folk, as anyone would agree who noticed the cars parked in the roads of a local authority housing estate. The only source of the Tudor farmer's concept of an ideal home was the medieval manor house.

There is still another reason for taking the houses of the medieval gentry into our view. The successive waves of conquest, starting from the open south-east coasts and only reaching the north and west much later, are just as marked a feature of this domestic branch of history as of political affairs. Throughout the study of small houses of the centuries prior to the Industrial Revolution runs one persistent fact: the difference

3

between Lowland England, south and east of a line from Teesmouth to Torquay, and the Highland Zone beyond it. It is not merely that different building materials are to hand in Cambridgeshire and the Peak District, or that climate still makes the highland farmer more concerned with sheep and cattle than with corn. The lowland zone had advantages of soil, of climate and also of position: that is, of close and easy connexion with the Continent, at more than one time the source of new social and technical concepts.[1] Before invasions from the Continent, each bringing a new ruling class, older ways of life were easily swept away, while in the recesses of Pennine valleys they could linger on. Eventually the Industrial Revolution, by locating sources of power in the highland zone and bringing great new towns into existence, reversed the old relationship. Before that, the only response that northern and western England made to influences from the south-east, as we shall see, was to take over some of the features of the house and absorb them into older forms. At any period, therefore, the culture of the highland zone is found to consist of an amalgam of features of varying age which originated in other and more prosperous regions. The prehistorians were the first to demonstrate this truth; it is equally applicable in the historic period in dealing with a material aspect of highland society.

Tracing characteristics of the Yorkshire or Devonshire house back to origins in south-eastern England is not always a straightforward matter. For one thing, the prototype may have been swept away by technical improvements. One may be compelled, in order to explain the facts, to assume the existence of models that can no longer be found. That is the case, as we shall see, with cruck building and with the long house. The other problem is the contrast in the highland zone between the simplicity of housing standards and the superior building techniques sometimes used to attain them. The aisled hall, originally suitable for bishops and lords of manors, was later erected by Yorkshire yeomen. Unless we look first at the houses of bishops and their like, we shall fail to make sense of the homes of Yorkshire yeomen.

The prime function of the house is to shelter humans, but it may have, and in some societies of north-western Europe it has until very recently, sheltered animals as well, and a farmhouse now implies necessarily barns and other buildings to store farm products and implements. Secondly, the house provides shelter for a family, but what kind of family? Has it always been the simple family of parents and children, or has the rural economy of England at any time had a place for the joint family of three generations or more under one roof—parents, married children and grandchildren? In the third place, how much has the evolution of the house been affected by

[1] C. Fox, *Personality of Britain* (1947), 87–8.

the need for providing shelter for dependents not members of the family—for retainers, for servants working within the house and out of doors? Historical evolution does not mean more of everything; it may mean more television sets and washing machines and at the same time fewer rooms in houses of a certain class and fewer domestic servants. A fourth factor has had its influence at certain times or in certain regions: the need for defence.

It is easier to make such a list of social and economic influences on the form of the house than to give as neat an account of the varieties of building in which they have been expressed.

To take the last and simplest of the above factors, the need for defence. It may help to explain two types of house, separated in time and space, and with so far no proven link between them. The earlier is the first floor hall.[1] In this kind of house the hall or common living-room is on the first floor, entered by an outside staircase, and over a ground floor or basement used only for storage.[2] It is to be found all over England from Northumberland to the Isle of Wight, and from Shropshire to Suffolk. There are examples from town and country in the twelfth century, because no distinction had so far emerged between urban and rural types, but the thirteenth-century examples are nearly all rural. There is a good fourteenth-century example in the Fish House, Meare, Somerset.

The type is also to be found in purely military contexts: that is as the hall of a castle, and protected primarily by its defences.[3] This raises the possibility that this mode of building a house was devised by Norman castle builders, and taken over both by lesser feudal lords for unfortified manor houses such as Boothby Pagnell, Lincolnshire, and by urban merchants.[4] The most elaborate first floor hall house known from literary sources is that built c. 1117 by Lambert of Ardres on the motte of his castle at Ardres. Its ground floor had cellars and granaries; living accomo-

[1]See M. E. Wood, 'Norman Domestic Architecture', *Arch. J.*, XCII (1936), 167–242, and 'Thirteenth Century Domestic Architecture in England', *Arch. J.*, Suppl. to CV(1950). The type is most important in the twelfth century and in the thirteenth declines in proportion to ground floor halls, but it lingers on into the fifteenth.

[2]It has recently been argued (by P. A. Faulkner, 'Domestic Planning from the Twelfth to the Fourteenth Century', in *Arch. J.*, CXV (1958), 150–63) that the basement was in some cases intended for habitation, but the argument seems to require stronger evidence.

[3]The earliest example of all is a military one: at Richmond Castle, Yorks., the hall, known as Scollands Hall, was probably built by Alan, Earl of Brittany, (1071-89) but got its name from Scolland, Lord of Bedale, who was steward to a later Earl Alan (1137–47). 'Norman Domestic Architecture', 207.

[4]The two examples of first floor halls in Lincoln, though one of them was in the possession of a Jewess shortly before the expulsion, cannot be proved to have been built by Jews.

dation was on the first floor along with larders, buttery and pantry, a great chamber and a chapel. The garrets were used as sleeping space for children and servants.[1]

The Bayeux Tapestry contains two pictures of first floor halls. One is Harold's manor house at Bosham, in which he is shown at a meal. The building has open arcading to the ground floor, probably of stone, an external staircase and a tiled roof. The other house is part of a scene for which there is no historical explanation: two Normans are setting fire to a house from the open basement of which a woman is leading a boy. This building is a much simpler affair, with a basement of one bay only. Above it sits a small structure with a central doorway and hipped roof whose shingles are beginning to burn. The superstructure is in fact precisely like two peasant cottages in the background of a scene where a Norman foraging party returns with captured animals.[2] It has been proved by excavation that the rendering in the tapestry of motte and bailey castles is quite faithful, and there is no reason why these houses should not be equally real. The tapestry in fact proves that first floor halls were being built in England before the Norman Conquest both by men of Harold's standing and by peasants.

Such houses must be related closely to those of the late Saxon period and onwards built over a cellar wholly or partly below ground level. They have been found at Oxford, in the area cleared to make way for the Norman castle, and in the Saxon town of Thetford.[3] An essential feature of the Rows at Chester is a vaulted basement which raises the main floor of the houses some three feet above ground level; access was by outside stairs, the space between them occupied by stalls which were eventually incorporated in the houses.[4] This method of building is in turn related to the type of house which has so far figured largest in the pre-Conquest archaeological record in England: the sunk house, its floor perhaps two feet below the surface but without any upper floor. It was the only type found in the early Saxon village at Sutton Courtenay, Berks.,[5] and isolated examples have been found elsewhere. The type is brought to life by the

[1]A translation of the description of the house is given in full in R. A. Brown, *English Medieval Castles* (1954), 31–2.

[2]*The Bayeux Tapestry*, ed. Stenton (Phaidon Press 1957). The Bosham house is on pl. 4, the peasant cottages on pl. 47 and the burning house on pl. 52. See also *Speculum* 34 (1959), 179-83.

[3]E. M. Jope, 'Late Saxon Pits under Oxford Castle Mound', *Oxoniensia*, 17–18 (1952-3), 99. I am indebted to Group Capt. G. M. Knocker for allowing me to see his report on the excavations at Thetford prior to its publication by the Stationery Office.

[4]H. M. Colvin in *Medieval England*, ed. Poole (1958), I, 70.

[5]*Arch.*, 73, 147; 76, 59; *Records of Bucks.*, 9 (1907), 282.

recollections of a Victorian of the houses he had seen at Athelney, Somerset, fifty years before.[1] The pipe-makers who were responsible for them dug a hole about 24 × 15 feet, leaving a balk for sitting and sleeping round the margin and supporting the roof on poles standing within the house. These huts repeat, with minor variations such as the position of the roof supports and the height of the walls, the methods of Saxon peasants, but there is of course no proven historical connexion between the two examples.

Two things are clear: that there was already some variety in types of houses in England before the Norman Conquest and that the first floor house, in view of its structural affinities with cellared houses, was not originally a defensive structure. The variety of forms which a storeyed building had already assumed before the Conquest was further elaborated afterwards. In the town, a storage basement was particularly useful for merchants, and at Lincoln the two surviving Norman first floor houses face respectively the medieval fish market and the old corn market.[2] In the country, first floor hall houses persist throughout the Middle Ages at the social level of the manor house. They are mainly of stone, and one of the most impressive is the fifteenth century manor house of the bishops of Lincoln at Lyddington, Rutland, known now as the Bede House because it was converted to an almshouse by the Cecil family after the Reformation.[3] The convenience of such dry and secure accommodation for a wealthy bishop fits perfectly the historical evidence for men of his status spending their time between several manor houses, staying in each long enough to consume the surplus produce of the estate.

The same form of building suited those who wished to build on a confined site, not only in a thriving town like Lincoln, but also within a monastic precinct. The abbot's lodgings at Kirkstall, Yorks., and Beauvale, Notts., are both storeyed buildings, with basement store, first floor hall and a chamber above.

Once the concept of the first floor hall reached the highland zone, it was there adapted to local needs and persisted after it had gone out of fashion elsewhere. In the fifteenth and sixteenth centuries it was widely adopted in Devonshire for church houses: that is, for the building evolved from the brewhouse in which church ale or scot ale was made. One of the best of these, at South Tawton, Devon, was built c. 1500 of granite, with an outside staircase. It has lost the pentice or covered alley alongside, which

[1]H. Laver, 'Ancient Types of Hut at Athelney', Somerset A.N.H.S. Proc., 55 (1910), 175. The two examples, Saxon and Victorian, are shown side by side in A. L. Poole, Medieval England, I, 79.
[2]J. W. F. Hill, Medieval Lincoln, 153–4, for the position of the various markets.
[3]V.C.H., Rutland, II, 189. It is now in the custody of the Ministry of Works.

is still to be seen at Widecombe in the Moor or South Tawton. Presumably festivities were held in the hall upstairs (if wet), or outside in the sun, and most of these church houses naturally became village inns in modern times.

Devonshire people were thus quite familiar with the first floor hall. In some surviving Dartmoor buildings, it is possible that the ground floor was used as a byre. One of them is at Neadon in Manaton parish; it is now an outbuilding to a more modern farmhouse, but the gable window with wooden tracery of c. 1500 shows that it has come down in the world. The ground floor opening is so wide as to suggest that it was for cattle in the middle ages, as it is today, and the open roof upstairs appears to indicate a division into two rooms.

The most striking evidence of the strength and popularity of the first floor hall tradition, has come from a recent study of priests' houses in the south-west.[1] Some of them had, from their beginnings in the fourteenth or fifteenth centuries, chambers over the hall. In south-eastern England that chamber is, as we shall see, the least important and the last to be added to houses in the main stream of tradition. If Devonshire and Somerset were already in the Middle Ages used to the idea that the chamber over the hall was the best one, the most likely explanation is that this was a local evolution from the first floor hall. Lowland notions and practices were often modified thus when they reached the highland zone.

There is a similar problem in the northern counties: to find links between the first floor hall of the twelfth century and the peel tower of the fourteenth. The name peel refers to the pale or palisade surrounding the site. The peel tower normally consists of three, or very rarely, four storeys; the ground floor is vaulted either with a single barrel vault or with two vaults (serving as buttery and pantry) flanking a through passage. Sometimes a newel stair, or a straight stair in the thickness of the wall, leads to the upper floors; in places considered more exposed to danger a wooden ladder, removable in emergency, provided the only way up. Pendragon Castle, Westmorland, is an isolated tower of the late twelfth century which ought perhaps to be regarded as a tower keep;[2] at Burgh by Sands excavation has revealed a circular tower, typical of the thirteenth century, attached to the corner of a hall.[3]

The peel tower proper appears only in the fourteenth century, when

---

[1]W. A. Pantin, 'Medieval Priests' Houses in South-West England', *Med. Arch.* 1 (1957), 118–46, with descriptions of houses at Dunchideock, Congresbury, Stanton Drew, and references to others.

[2]H.M.C., *Westmorland*, lx, 163.

[3]*T.C.W.A.A.S.* N. S. 54 (1954), 106.

the king began to permit private fortifications near the Scottish border. These houses fall into two groups: those (nearly all in Northumberland) where the tower stands alone as the sole residence, and those more removed from the Scottish danger (mainly in Westmorland) which from the beginning consisted of a tower wing to a ground floor hall. As a class they thus represent the persistence of the first floor hall with its defensive qualities strengthened, and the addition of a defensive tower to a ground floor hall. Examples are not always easy to identify, because in many cases the hall has gone or been rebuilt. Arnside Tower, built in the fifteenth century, seems to be the only Westmorland example of the isolated tower, and it has a turret staircase at one angle. There are free-standing towers in Northumberland such as Chipchase Tower and Cocklaw Hall with a staircase in the thickness of the wall reached only from the basement room, and Chipchase has a portcullis barring the ground floor entrance. Cocklaw is more developed in having a small chamber as well as the hall on the first floor. The chamber walls were covered with painted ornament in the sixteenth century.[1]

The house with a tower as a strong point or lookout is as widespread and persistent as the first floor hall, though surviving examples are less numerous. They range in date from the tower of Stokesay Castle, built in the twelfth century, to the extraordinary tower of Caister Castle near Yarmouth, which looks more like a factory chimney than any other medieval monument. It has been put down to the influence of the Low Countries, and it shows one element, the high look-out, carried to extreme.[2]

A glance at evidence from the Continent shows that the variety we have already traced in England was common to those parts of western Europe with which the English were most closely connected. The sunk house occurs widely, among the Germanic peoples, sometimes as we should expect alongside ground floor houses. The storeyed look-out is found in the tenth century fortified settlement of Stellerburg near the mouth of the Oder in Holstein.[3] The first floor house continued to play an important part in France as it did in England. The typical farmer of Quercy still lives on the first floor of his house. In towns like Cordes (Tarn) there are

---

[1] *History of Northumberland*, IV (1897), 180–4, 333–9.

[2] *Ant. J.*, 32 (1952), 36–51.

[3] W. U. Guyan, 'Einige Karten zur Verbreitung des Grübenhauses in Mitteleuropa im ersten nachchristlichen Jahrtausend', in *Schweiz. Gesellschaft für Urgeschichte*, 42 (1952), 174–97. In France, the sunk houses known to French archaeologists as *mardelles* may be part of the same tradition; see A. Grenier, *Manuel d'Archéologie Gallo-Romaine* (Dechelette), 2, ii, 752–63. For Stellerburg, see M. V. Rudolph, *Germanische Holzbau der Wikingerzeit* (Offa Bucher Band 6) Neumunster, 1942.

superb thirteenth century houses, of stone, built over an open ground floor. A striking feature of the new towns of south-western France founded in the thirteenth century, both by the English and the French is that the market places are commonly surrounded by an open arcading.[1] Under it runs the street round the market place, so that this arrangement may represent originally an encroachment by house owners, but in one or two cases the *cornières* are not confined to the market place.[2] At Figeac (Lot) there is a free standing first floor hall in a square, known locally as the Hotel de la Monnaie; it is of thirteenth century date and may have been the *hôtel de ville;* it has an open basement which served as a market hall. It serves to link the timbered and stone market halls of the sixteenth and seventeenth centuries in such English towns as Ledbury and Tetbury with the earlier domestic tradition. No doubt such French and English building is parallel and largely independent, since there is no evidence for an exchange of craftsmen, but the exchange of ideas in Gascony may have helped to maintain both developments.

The next factor to be considered is the need to provide shelter, under one and the same roof, for animals as well as humans. This way of living has been very widespread in western Europe even in recent times, in the mountains and the plains, in regions where farming is restricted by inferior and insufficient soils and where there is enough soil to support a wealthy peasantry. There is a tremendous contrast between the tiny Irish cabin and those imposing farmhouses of north-west Germany in which, under one great sweeping roof, one finds family accommodation at one end and in the rest a barn, thrashing floor, cattle stalls and pig pens.[3] Scholars of the Celtic fringe have been anxious to find a racial origin for the long house, and particularly to have it developed by the Celtic people but have admitted that they cannot prove this claim. What other reasons can be responsible for its persistence in certain regions? Climate might be thought important, but much of south Wales, in which Peate found many long houses, enjoys a relatively mild winter climate. Such traditional beliefs as that cattle must be kept in sight of the hearth fire, which increased the yield of milk,[4] belong to a poor peasant community, each family dependent on one or two cows.

The evidence from excavation is so far very slight in quantity and most

[1]Turner and Parker, *Dom. Arch. of the Middle Ages*, II, 154, has an engraving of the corner of the market place at Monpazier, founded by Edward I in 1284.

[2]Dr. M. W. Beresford has pointed out to me an example at La Bastide Armagnac in Gascony.

[3]See for example, Otto Lehmann, *Das Bauernhaus in Schleswig Holstein*, Altona, 1927.

[4]An Irish belief quoted by E. Estyn Evans in *Antiquity*, 10 (1936), 210.

of it marginal to our inquiry.[1] At Mawgan Porth, on the west coast of Cornwall south of Tintagel, a village inhabited between the ninth and eleventh centuries included houses consisting of rooms arranged round a small courtyard, one of the rooms holding cattle as well as a family.[2] The long room, measuring in one case 33 × 14 or 15 feet internally, was divided by a wooden partition; the house part had an entrance in the gable end, bed benches against the walls and a central hearth. West of it was a cross passage linking two more entrances in the middle of the side walls; the byre had a drain through the wall at the south-west corner, and the floor level was lower than that of the house part. These people were fisher folk, shell gatherers and pastoralists, not agriculturalists. At the other end of Britain there was at the same time a community of agriculturalists, of Viking origin, at Jarlshof in Shetland. The first settlement consisted of a house and three other farm buildings widely dispersed about a garth, and as the community grew additional houses were built. One of them, first built at about 1200, was in the next century enlarged to accommodate cattle in its new, lower, half.[3] The economic emphasis of the community had by then shifted from farming and stock-rearing to fishing, as abundant finds of line-weights and sinkers indicated. This primary dependence on fishing is the only factor common to Mawgan Porth and Jarlshof, but a wish to maintain a secondary food supply with the minimum of trouble will not explain the similarity of the house plans. It is more likely that Viking society, even in a tiny group like Jarlshof, was already sufficiently diversified to allocate a house to servants in charge of livestock, just as in England until recent times farmservants often slept with or over the livestock.

On the fringes of Dartmoor there are buildings, now ruined or converted to other uses, which may belong to the colonization of the moor in the thirteenth century. They have no fireplace and were no doubt heated by an open hearth, and they may have sheltered animals as well as human beings. Their most striking feature is the way that local granite is used in their construction; more than one is founded on an outcrop, and walls incorporate slabs as much as 49 × 41 × 9 inches thick.[4] At Yardworthy in Chagford

[1] J. T. Hurst in a paper to Section H of the British Association in 1960 stated that excavations have produced evidence (so far unpublished) of such houses in deserted medieval villages in several lowland counties.

[2] R. L. S. Bruce Mitford, 'A Dark Age Settlement at Mawgan Porth, Cornwall' in *Recent Archaeological Excavations in Britain* (1956), 167–96.

[3] J. R. C. Hamilton, *Excavations at Jarlshof* (1956), especially 102–110, 158, 171–2. There is a suggestion that two earlier houses had contained a byre (138) but this is inconclusive.

[4] See R. Hansford Worth, *Dartmoor* (1953), 404–5, for an account of the methods of walling.

a building now used for calves and hens is about 36 feet long by 19 feet externally, with walls 2 feet 6 inches thick; it has a porch in the middle of the east side away from the rainy quarter built of single slabs and roofed with two more. The whole forms a remarkably megalithic construction. The porch sides are rebated for a door that was harr hung, that is, pivoted at the heel. The upper pivot hole can be seen in one of the roof slabs. Other buildings at Challacombe and elsewhere would, if systematically investigated, tell us much about the pastoral farmer in one of England's most conservative regions.

This evidence for long houses, distant as it is in time and place, has been reviewed because it is all that can be put alongside the later houses which seem to have the same ancestry. The Mawgan Porth house can be turned to account when we consider the type of family for which the medieval house was built. Many of the new settlements of the Anglo-Saxon peoples which by the time of Domesday Book had become villages must have started as the venture of family groups. At Mawgan Porth the one house completely excavated had, as well as the long room with its provision for a family and some livestock, other rooms north and south of the court-yard, of which that on the north was also used for habitation. It had a hearth, and a double bed in the north-east corner. The room added to the east at a later stage also had a central hearth, a box bed in the north-west corner and a bench against the east wall. Neither room held livestock. They must have been for members of the family: married sons rather than servants.[1]

English historians have had very little to say about the joint family, of grandparents, married sons and their offspring, because it has left few traces in records. The evidence from Kent and East Anglia for the equal division of a peasant's land among his children carries with it the implica-tion, sometimes confirmed by records, that the land was occasionally held jointly by the heirs and cultivated in common by them. Evidence for partible inheritance has also come from Lincolnshire, but by 1300 traces of this large family, as a social or even an economic group, had vanished everywhere.[2] It may well have been connected with the existence in East Anglia of a unit of family holding (terra unius familiae) as large as 140 acres, while in Wessex the same unit, the hide, is said to have been only 40 acres. It is hard to believe that the two belonged to the same kind of family. In Jugoslavia the joint family disappeared in the nineteenth cen-

[1] Recent Excavations, 181–2.
[2] H. M. Colvin, Medieval England, I, 91; G. C. Homans in Econ. Hist. R., 8 (1937), 48–56; 2nd Series 10 (1957), 190–2; H. E. Hallam, ibid., 10, 340–61; Lincs. Archivists' Report, 9 (1957–8), 29.

tury, when ploughing with two or three pairs of oxen, managed by four or five men, gave way to ploughing with two horses, operated by one man.[1] The economic expansion of thirteenth-century England led to the last traces of the joint family being replaced by the family of parents and immature children only. The Jugoslav evidence suggests the possibility that the eight ox plough team of the English Danelaw, implied by the ploughland of eight oxgangs from other evidence, may also reflect the former existence of the joint family. In Wales even in the sixteenth and seventeenth centuries, members of a family were still in some instances putting up two or more houses close together but with no communication between them: that is, combining to work a farm while maintaining separate households.[2]

This excursion into historical sociology is prompted not only by the Mawgan Porth courtyard house but also by the large size of some peasant houses. The earlier houses at Jarlshof were 70 feet or more in length; the one boat-shaped house at Thetford was 50 feet long, 15 feet wide, divided by cross walls into five rooms. The barrack blocks in the Viking stronghold of Trelleborg were each 98 feet long, divided laterally into a central hall and end chambers,[3] and no doubt they reflect the domestic tradition of the Scandinavians. The evidence from Jarlshof is paralleled from Iceland and appears to indicate a standard type. For nearly two thirds of the length, as far as the opposing side doors, stone kerbs marked the edges of the dais–sleeping bench on either side, facing the long hearth down the centre. The rest of the house contained another central hearth, used mainly to heat stones for an oven, and is usually termed a kitchen. Such an arrangement does not make its way into the English tradition, in which the kitchen is rare, except as a detached part of large houses; and baking bread or cooking meats in an oven is an innovation, in peasant homes, of the sixteenth and seventeenth centuries. At Wharram Percy the houses ranged in size from 20 × 10 feet to 70 × 15 feet,[4] and until positive evidence is forthcoming of the function of the larger buildings, the possibility of their housing joint families seems as tenable as the alternative that they contained both a living part and a byre.

When we turn to the question of the place of servants, retainers and the like in the medieval house, a large part of the picture is very clear, because documentary evidence is abundant and the archaeological evidence easy to

[1]K. Koenig, 'Changes in the Western Family', in *Trans. of Third World Congress of Sociology*, 4 (1956), 65.

[2]W. J. Hemp in *Arch. Camb.* 97(1943), 98–112; C. Fox in *Mon. Ho.*, 2,75; 3,76.

[3]*Arch. J.*, 106(1949), 72; *Aarboger* (1952), 108–162.

[4]*Ex. inf.* Mr. J. G. Hurst.

interpret. Whether the light cast by such evidence illumines a sufficient range of medieval society is another matter.

Among the Germanic and the Scandinavian peoples, both before and after their establishment in England, men of the highest levels of society were accustomed to spending their active and their leisure hours together. The institution of the *comitatus*—the band of warrior companions who accompanied the king in war and who were bound to him by the deepest sense of loyalty—implies a house or palace with a common life for young unmarried men. Later they could expect to be rewarded with an estate of their own, and thenceforward they would be seen less in the hall. One of the most enduring beliefs among the aristocrat of English society has been the notion that upbringing in a household of higher rank was the best education for a young man. Alfred's arrangement that his thanes should serve him in regular rotation, one month at court and two at home,[1] is socially indistinguishable from the feudal practice of knights doing such a rota of castleguard. The household of an English king, before and after the Conquest, was copied by the ranks immediately beneath him; for any such household, the hall alone is clearly insufficient, and we must think rather of a defended enclosure—*burh* in English, *garth* in Scandinavian, *curia* in Latin—containing the hall and also separate buildings for other purposes. The multiplication of detached units is the most striking and the most persistent feature of the large household of the Middle Ages. So the Anglo-Saxon king or noble provided for himself and his wife or mistress,[2] for the women servants about the place, and for the more senior officers. The Anglo-Saxon word for such buildings, *bower*, remained the only word for any addition to the hall, whether detached or not, until it is supplemented in Norman times by the word *chamber*, from the Latin word *camera* (a vault or arched roof).

Such a complex of buildings was revealed by the excavation at Yeavering, Northumberland,[3] of the seventh century palace of the Northumbrian kings. Its most distinctive feature for us was the contrast between the building which was taken to be king Edwin's hall and the remaining buildings. Edwin's hall was about 100 feet long, with a room at each end screened off from the main body of the hall. Other halls of similar design but about half the size are taken to be the bowers for retainers and other superior members of the household. Still smaller buildings characterized

[1] D. Whitelock, *Beginnings of English Society*, 57.

[2] The well-known account in the Anglo-Saxon Chronicle, *sub anno* 786, shows that the surprise attack on King Cynewulf of Wessex was made easy because he was in such a building which had only one door and could be surrounded by his attackers.

[3] By Mr. B. R. Hope Taylor, on behalf of the Ministry of Works.

by sunk floors were perhaps houses of servants, constructed in the peasant tradition.

The provision of separate buildings for service purposes and for sleeping gradually turns the larger medieval house from a hall in its enclosure into a courtyard or yards completely surrounded by buildings and entered by a gatehouse. A parallel process produces the regular layout of monastic or college buildings round a cloister. The intermediate stage of a somewhat haphazard scatter of buildings is well illustrated by the plan of the royal palace at Clarendon, Wilts., in the thirteenth century.[1] Independent buildings were linked by long pentices or covered walks. At a much later time the builder of Gainsborough Old Hall in 1481 provided chambers or bed-sitting-rooms for resident staff in a wing at the service end of the house. The latest stage can be seen at Kirby Hall, Northants., where an Elizabethan grandee provided ranges of lodgings for staff or guests along the sides of the outer court.

In the manor house which was in fact a working farm, and in the house of the yeoman rich enough to employ resident farm workers, most of the men no doubt slept either in the hall or in the farm buildings. The common seventeenth century references to chambers above oxhouses and the like must represent a tradition of great antiquity. The numbers so employed can be gauged from the fourteenth century accounts of the Argentine family which had two manors, at Melbourn in Cambridgeshire, and Great Wymondley in Hertfordshire. The latter was their chief residence but, like others of their class, they spent enough time at each manor to consume its surplus produce. There were at Melbourn six men boarded in and about the house: two ploughmen, two plough drivers, a carter and a shepherd. There was one woman servant about the place, and a boy who helped on the farm.[2]

We now turn to the developments which explain the vast majority of medieval houses: those arising primarily if not entirely from the needs of a single family dependent on a small farm for a livelihood. It is the largest problem because it touches such a large segment of society, and one for which no documentary and little archaeological evidence is available. The critical distinction between larger houses such as Clarendon Palace or Haddon Hall and the ordinary farmhouse is that the former developed by improving the relation between separate rooms or buildings, the latter by enlarging one simple building.

Out of the latter process emerged what is sometimes called the typical

[1] *J.B.A.A.*, XX–XXI (1957–8), pl. XXXII.
[2] W. M. Palmer, 'Argentine's Manor, Melbourn, Cambs.', in *Proc. Cambs. Ant. Soc.*, 28 (1925–6), 16–70.

medieval house: that is, one with a central hall open to the roof, flanked by wings of two storeys roofed at right angles to the run of the hall. The most important requirement was a hall large enough for a variety of purposes. The second was access from the hall directly to whatever specialized rooms were thought necessary. In this development the first floor hall has no place, either from the point of view of plan or of the structural problems involved.

The builder most concerned was not the mason but the carpenter, since the development of the hall depended on his ability to roof it with a stable and convenient cover. The professional carpenter made the pace, for house building, above the level of the cottage and in all but the poorer regions of England, was in the hands of craftsmen from Norman times at least. A charter of William the Conqueror to bishop Odo says that the men of Kent were to build a *domum aestivale quod anglice dicitur sumerhus,* but also gives the sum of money they were to pay in lieu, and the commutation of this duty into *sumerhussilver* shows that the carpenter was taking over even the building of a temporary hunting lodge for a Norman baron.[1] In the north the obligation of the bishop of Durham's villeins of Aucklandshire to build him 'a hall in the forest, of the length of 60 feet and of the breadth within the posts of 16 feet, with a buttery and a hatch and a chamber and a privy, and a chapel' lasts somewhat longer, as one might expect.[2]

The largest type of hall, which already had a remote ancestry at the time of the Norman Conquest, but which was the main type of construction in manor houses and large farmhouses of the next three centuries, was the aisled hall (see fig. 1). It is the starting point of development in south-eastern England.[3] The county of Essex contains the best early examples, if only because it alone of counties in the south-east has been systematically examined.[4] Economic historians have long realized the superior wealth of eastern and south-eastern counties in the Middle Ages. Is that a sufficient explanation? It seems conceivable that carpenters there had also the advantage of centuries of patronage by wealthy and large peasant households, and that halls with one aisle or two were particularly suited to a family of three generations. Fyfield Hall, Essex, had a hall of two bays only, measuring with its aisles 40 × 29 feet 6 inches, and may stand as an

[1]N. Neilson, *Cartulary and Terrier of the Priory of Bislington* (Brit. Academy Records, 1928,) 15.
[2]*Bolden Buke* (Surtees Soc., 1852), 24, 29.
[3]See the fundamental papers by J. T. Smith, 'Aisled Halls and their derivatives' in *Arch. J.*, 112 (1955), 76-93, and 'Medieval Roofs: a Classification', *Arch. J.* 115 (1958), 111-49.
[4]See H.M.C. *Essex*, a four volume inventory published 1920-3.

example of a manor house of *c.* 1300, with perhaps a further wing which has vanished. It had an open hearth in the centre of the hall, from which smoke escaped by the open gablets above the hipped ends of the roof. This type of roof persists in the south-east, and was also used for the ventilation of the large barns which such farms required.

Edw.ᵈBlore delᵗ.   J.H.Le Keux fc.

FIGURE 1. Interior of Nurstead Hall, Kent, a fourteenth century aisled hall built of timber. The smoke from the open hearth escaped through gablets at the ends of the hipped roof (compare fig. 5). The roof has tie-beams, crown posts, a collar purlin, and trussed rafters, as in figs. 3–4.

The second requirement, a private room for the lord or head of the household, is illustrated by the late Norman manor house at Boothby Pagnell, Lincs., incidentally a first floor hall, but divided at first floor level into a hall with a fireplace on the side wall (usual in first floor halls) and beyond it a chamber or solar, unheated[1] and about a third of the size of the hall. Other thirteenth-century houses have the same division,[2] which must have become common in manor houses of that time. A survey of Lincolnshire lands of the barony of Bayeux, 1288, shows the following rooms in manor houses: Thoresby and Calcethorpe, hall and chamber; Stewton, hall, a little chamber and a kitchen; Linwood and Welbourne, hall and two chambers, kitchen and brewhouse. The last two were no doubt detached, as was the Linwood bakehouse with a little chamber, for the flour and the baker himself.

In large houses, such as those of thirteenth-century bishops, the service end of the hall had already been elaborated by having two rooms built there, the buttery for ale and the pantry for bread. The chamber and the buttery remain the commonest additions to the hall until the seventeenth century, and we shall have to see how far down the social scale these improvements had penetrated at any one time and the purposes for which they were used. The kitchen, as soon as we have any evidence of it, is a separate detached building, sometimes beyond the service end of the main building. In such cases access was by a passage between the buttery and the pantry, so that there are three doors, instead of two, at the lower end of the hall. One important topic for us will be to see when the kitchen begins to be incorporated in the house.

We have one opportunity, and one alone, to read from records how far a community had gone by 1300 in developing its housing. That is provided by tax assessments, made in 1296 and again in 1301, for the town of Colchester and villages near by. Medieval taxation was based on personal property, and so required assessors—necessarily local men of standing, since there were no civil servants available—to go round from house to house compiling lists of goods and chattels, and on that basis of the tax payable.[3] The picture they have left is fascinating though difficult to interpret. The lists are plainly incomplete. The jurors did not assess themselves, and may have omitted others as well, either intentionally or by

---

[1] It is possible that such rooms were heated with a brazier, but there is no evidence to that effect.

[2] E.g. Moigne Court, Ower Moigne, Dorset, c. 1270–80: *Arch. J.*, 105, Supplement (1950), 17, 28.

[3] *Rotuli Parliamentorum*, I, 228–38, 243–65. See also J. F. Willard, *Parliamentary Taxes on Personal Property, 1290–1334* (1934), and G. Rickword in *Trans. Essex Arch. Soc.*, 9 (1906), 133.

mistake. The second list, which gives more details of personal property, contains 384 names—a large sample, with a high proportion of merchants, traders and craftsmen, as we should expect. How many poor folk were left out because their goods were not worth valuing we simply do not know. The fact that most of the people were town dwellers, who are supposed to be outside our purview, is not important. The form of the medieval house in town and country alike starts from the same point, and the usual adjustment to urban conditions was to turn the plan at right angles to the frontage, to fit the long and narrow shape of urban proper-ties.[1] The large town house in the west Midlands, presenting a range of gables and three storeys to the street, is a fifteenth and sixteenth century development.

Since these Colchester lists are in fact the earliest inventories of the contents of English houses, they are worth detailed attention. The first on the list is Roger the Dyer, and he had a large house by the standards of his time. It consisted of a hall or living-room, a chamber or bedroom, the kitchen which as well as the hall had its fireplace, and the brewhouse where he carried on his dyeing and also his brewing. He was one of the wealthiest men caught by the assessors—only seventeen others had goods worth more than his—and we can take his as the most commodious kind of house in or near Colchester in 1301. Such men usually had three rooms and a further twenty, not quite so rich, had two: hall and chamber. Most of these occur in the earlier part of the list, for the jury began their house to house visitation in the centre of the town and finished up in the back streets and the neighbouring villages. Some parts of the list can thus be assigned to particular villages,[2] and if this has been done correctly it does not show any distinct variation between town and country standards.

What of the rest of the householders, who had no more than one room? More than half had no household goods at all, and only the clothes they wore. The rest had one or sometimes two beds, and a few cooking imple-ments: a brass posnet, an andiron to support it over the fire, and a tripod.[3] No doubt the jury decided not to bother with pottery vessels, wooden bowls and such trifles, when they found them. On the other hand, the impression given by the list that many of the dwellings were mere hovels containing nothing to which a value could be given is certainly correct.

These lists show that at the turn of the thirteenth and fourteenth

[1]E.g., the Golden Cross at Oxford: W. A. Pantin and E. C. Rouse, *Oxoniensia*, 20 (1955), 46–89.
[2]By G. Rickword, *loc. cit.*
[3]These and similar domestic articles are described and illustrated in the introduction to F. W. Steer's *Farm and Cottage Inventories of Mid-Essex, 1635–1749* (1950).

centuries only a small minority of Essex people had houses of more than one room.[1] Rising standards in the fourteenth and fifteenth centuries have left enough examples to show that for many above the status of peasant two rooms were regarded as the norm. When Ralph, bishop of Salisbury, built, or began to build, the Vicars' Close at Wells in the middle of the fourteenth century, he provided houses of two storeys with one room on each and a newel stair at the back. He thus adapted the two rooms plan to confined urban conditions. The vicars choral were among the lower ranks of the clergy, and at Lincoln they were given only one room each. Since they had their meals in a common hall, the accommodation at Wells appears generous.[2]

[1]Similar to the house found by excavation in the High Street, Oxford, measuring 18 × 9 feet with a hearth in one corner; S. E. Rigold in *Oxoniensia* 16 (1951), 83. Another excavated in Bramble Bottom near Eastbourne measured 30 × 15 feet; R. Musson in *Sussex Arch. Coll.*, 93 (1955), 157.

[2]For a plan of the Vicar's Close, Wells, see *Arch. J.*, 107 (1950), 113; for Vicar's Court, Lincoln, see M. E. Wood in *The Lincs. Historian*, 7 (1951), 282.

CHAPTER TWO

The Evolution of the Medieval House in Plan and Structure

IN the later Middle Ages interest centres first on the carpenter's success in making the timber-framed house more convenient for its users. He was required, before anything else, to clear the hall of the obstruction of the posts supporting the roof. He managed it by resting their feet on a tie-beam across the hall at the level of the top of the walls instead of on the ground. In the north of England the posts down the centre of the hall become king-posts[1] starting at tie-beam level, and this may have happened by the eleventh century.[2] The same step was taken by carpenters farther south when they had to build an aisled hall. They thus produced by the fourteenth century a roof in which the tie-beam supported not one central king-post but two, on the lines of the former arcades. Another solution, to be seen at Tiptoft's Manor, Wimbish, Essex (a small manor house securely dated to the years 1348–67), was to clear the hall by using a hammer-beam truss. The hammer-beam roof is the glory of medieval church roofs in East Anglia, and Westminster Hall, built in 1395–9, has the finest timber roof in western Europe, but it is not usually realized that the same form of construction might be used in a manor house. This south-eastern development takes place, however, in a context fundamentally different from the northern. Medieval roofs in south-eastern England have no ridge beam. Pairs of common rafters are halved and pegged together at the

[1]See Glossary, p. 289.
[2]J. Walton, 'Hogback Tombstones and the Anglo-Danish House' in *Antiquity*, 28 (1954), 72.

apex.[1] At first each pair of rafters was braced by a collar about a third of the way down, and when the tie-beam and crown-post roof appeared the crown-post was short, since its upper end supported a timber which ran the length of the roof under the collar of each pair of rafters (as in fig. 4). This timber was known as the collar purlin, and its structural importance must be emphasized, because it provides a link between types of building apparently quite different.

In the north and west, the problem of clearing the hall was often solved in a totally different fashion, by using large posts based on the line of the outer walls and curving to meet at the ridge and support the ridge-beam on which the ends of the rafters rest (see fig. 14). These posts, often made by splitting one trunk so that they followed the same curve, were most commonly called crucks. Much printers' ink has already been spent on the problem of where and when cruck building originated. It is found in Wales and Scotland; in England it occurs only north and west of a line from Flamborough Head through Sheffield to Southampton Water. It cannot have been imported by the Scandinavian settlers of the ninth and tenth centuries, for no cruck houses have been found in Lincolnshire and East Anglia, which received the strongest influx of Danish folk. The discussion has been bedevilled by Teapot Hall, Scrivelsby, Lincs., a house of one bay with walls sloping inward from ground level to the ridge.[2] It was certainly not a genuine survival of a primitive tradition. Every cruck house has vertical walls to give adequate head room inside. The upright posts of the walls are linked to the cruck blades either by an extension outwards of the tie-beam at wall-plate level, or by a short timber, a spur, from each cruck blade out to the wall-plate (see fig. 2).

It has been suggested that the method is an imitation in wood of the Gothic arch,[3] but that seems out of keeping with what we know of the skill and inventiveness of the medieval carpenter. Any explanation must take into account the very high quality of the carpentry in Welsh cruck building, compared with say the English Midlands. It is possible that it is an ancient mode of building once general but replaced in south-eastern England by more advanced methods. It eventually became something suitable for barns and cottages. A lease of 1474 providing for new buildings at Rawmarsh, Yorks, specifies a framed house of ten posts (*de decem*

---

[1] See J. T. Smith, 'Medieval Roofs: a classification', in *Arch. J.*, 115 (1958), 113.

[2] The building was fired to celebrate VJ Day, 1945, but it had been fully recorded and frequently illustrated, for example in A. L. Poole's *Medieval England*, I, 81, by H. M. Colvin. One tradition, which cannot now be checked, said that it was built early in the nineteenth century by a retired captain of a tea clipper—hence its name.

[3] By Lord Raglan in *Man*, 56 (1956), 101–3.

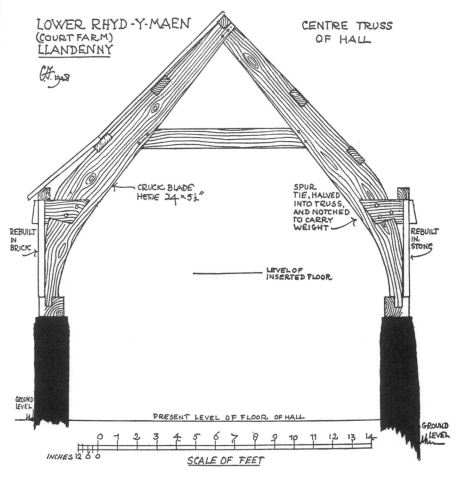

LOWER RHYD-Y-MAEN
(COURT FARM)
LLANDENNY

CF. 1948

CENTRE TRUSS
OF HALL

CRUCK BLADE
HERE 24×5½″

SPUR
TIE, HALVED
INTO TRUSS,
AND NOTCHED
TO CARRY
WEIGHT

REBUILT
IN
BRICK

REBUILT
IN
STONE

LEVEL OF
INSERTED FLOOR

GROUND
LEVEL

PRESENT LEVEL OF FLOOR OF HALL

GROUND
LEVEL

0 1 2 3 4 5 6 7 8 9 10 11 12 13 14

INCHES 12 6 0

SCALE OF FEET

FIGURE 2. Section across a Monmouthshire cruck-framed hall, showing how an open cruck truss was tied to the outer walls. Court Farm, Llandenny, by Sir Cyril Fox.

postibus, that is, five bays) and a barn of the same size but cruck trussed (*unum orrum de decem crokkes*).[1]

Cruck barns as large as that are not uncommon, but most cruck houses were either two or three bays, giving a total length of either 32 or 48 feet in the Midlands. A good example is Church Cottage, Stanley, five miles north-east of Derby. The name suggests that it may once have been the parsonage house, and this seems confirmed when one finds it standing between the church and the Victorian vicarage. Building alterations in 1958 revealed that the modern brick walls concealed a cruck house of

[1]L.R.O., Cragg, 4/34.

three bays. All that is visible now is part of the second truss from one end. The tie-beam and the arched braces up to it from the cruck blades are chamfered, as are the purlins, and one concludes that this truss was once in the middle of a two bay hall, with a third bay at the end whose details are lost. The use of arched braces made it possible to raise the level of the tie-beam to give plenty of clearance below and so to remove the oppressive effect which it would otherwise have had on the hall. All the time, even in such modest houses, structural considerations go along with those of convenience and a consciousness of visual effect.

Once the house has been divided into two portions, whether they are house and byre or hall and service rooms, the most convenient place of entrance is in the side. The middle of the side walls, or if the hall was longer, at its lower end next to the byre or the service wing, was obviously the best. Equally obviously it was better to have two opposed doorways, and then to make some kind of screen between this passage and the hall proper. The cross passage or through passage becomes then a characteristic feature of the medieval house which we shall have to follow through to its eventual disappearance. Fortunately it can often be traced, where it no longer figures in the ground plan, from features of the roof construction. It seems to emerge from two directions independently, in the long house and in the aisled hall. In the large house it gave seclusion from the traffic of servants and the draughts from the two doors, and became an architectural feature of great consequence, dominating the hall of a large Elizabeth mansion like Audley End or Wollaton. In Devonshire farm houses of the sixteenth and seventeenth century the legacy of the long house seems apparent in the great width of the passage.

We have now arrived at the notion of a farmhouse consisting of a range of building under a continuous roof, divided into hall and cross passage, with a further section for service uses. A remarkable example has recently come to light in the village of Clifton, Notts. (fig. 3 and pl. Ia). A small farmhouse, of L plan, with a thatched roof and brick walls, bears on the gable the date 1707 in dark headers. Once inside, an observer with patience[1] will eventually find that he is in a fourteenth-century timber-framed house, enlarged c. 1600 by the addition of a cross wing and given brick walls instead of wood and clay in 1707—the date not of building but the last alteration. Moreover, the carpenter made use of two forms, the aisled hall and the cruck-truss, in his building. The house had originally a hall of two bays with a third bay beyond the cross passage. The aisled construction shows best in the partition west of the cross passage (see

[1] I should add the advantages also of the good nature of the occupier, Mrs. Deaves, and of the help of Mr. J. T. Smith in elucidating the problems.

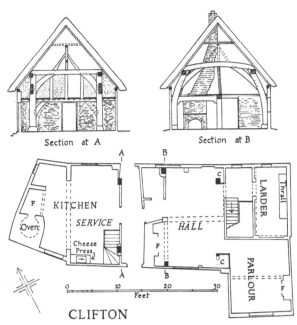

Section at A   Section at B

CLIFTON

FIGURE 3. Plan and sections of a house at Clifton, Nottinghamshire, with a hall range of the fourteenth century. The cross wing was built and the service end extended c. 1600, at which time also the hall was chambered over. The sections show the aisled construction and the 'base crucks' used over the open hall. The section at B shows the inserted floor of the chamber over the hall, and the remains of an earlier chimney hood of timber and mud within which the modern brick chimney has been built. See also fig. 4 and pl. 1A.

fig. 3) where upright posts set 2 feet 6 inches inside the line of the walls support an arcade plate whose present length, visible upstairs, defines the size of the original house.[1] That there was some kind of speer, making a cross passage, is shown by dovetail joints cut in the arcade plate. In the hall, the ground space is cleared of posts by placing their feet on the line of the outer wall; curved posts had to be used to bring them in to the line of the arcade plate, so that they look like beheaded crucks (see fig. 4). This sort of hybrid has been called a base cruck, and it can be seen in the Guildhall, Leicester, and at the Manor House, West Bromwich, where the curving beams have capitals carved on their inner face.[2] There must always have been some kind of hood over the fireplace, for the main truss of the hall roof with its curved tie-beam and arched braces is not blackened by smoke. There is still a rather flimsy hood of timber and mud

[1]Whether the end bay was originally divided into two storeys is in fact uncertain, although it is so shown in fig. 4.

[2]Ex. inf., S. R. Jones.

25

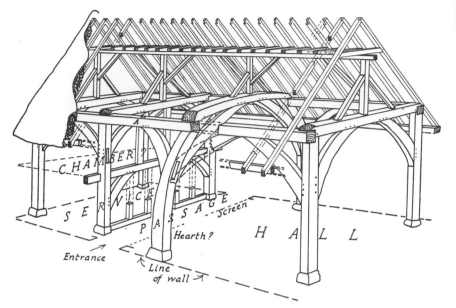

FIGURE 4. Perspective view of the original form of the house at Clifton shown in fig. 3, as far as it can be deduced. Some details have been omitted, or interrupted, for clarity. The plan is shown open at the hall end, since there was certainly another bay (perhaps with a cellar at ground level and a solar over it) which was demolished to make way for the cross wing built in *c.* 1600. A dovetail joint in the arcade plate at A shows that there was always a screen between hall and passage. The service end is shown chambered over, though there is no certain proof of it. See also plate 1A.

through which the modern brick flue rises, but its construction is inferior to that of the original house. One cannot get into the roof over the hall to see whether there is any break in the medieval rafters for a louvre.

The interest of this house is twofold: first, in the two sources from which the carpenter took the forms of construction he used, and second in the discovery of original features under later alterations. No doubt many more as interesting remain to be found. In the Midlands they are likely to elaborate this picture of the merging of different techniques. The south-eastern counties seem to have been the source of innovations.

Some of these new features can, in the present state of our knowledge, be reported with an admission that their source is not apparent. A vital stage which remains so far unexplained is the emergence of what is called the Wealden type of house (fig. 5). It replaced the aisled hall in Kent,[1] and its ample accommodation, by medieval standards, has prompted the sugges-

[1] J. T. Smith, *Arch J.*, 102 (1955), 93. See also A. Oswald, *Country Houses of Kent*, ch. 3. Fig. 5 is based on R. W. Schultz in *Arch. Cant.*, 27 (1905), 193.

tion that it evolved to shelter the joint family of a Kentish yeoman with his married sons and their families, cultivating the holding together.[1] The Wealden house has a central hall open to the roof with a storeyed wing at one end or both. The whole is under a continuous roof, but the storeyed wing is jettied out, to overhang the ground floor by a foot or more. The hall front wall is then recessed, and the eaves plate (on the line of the wing

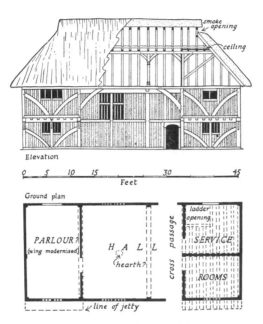

Elevation

Ground plan

FIGURE 5. Plan and elevation of a 'Wealden type' house at Shorne, near Gravesend, Kent. (After R. W. Schultz in *Arch. Cant.* 27 (1905), 193.) It has a hipped roof, with smoke gablets, and the same form of construction as in figs. 1 and 3–4. There is an open hall of one bay and a half, between storeyed wings, the front wall of the hall being recessed. The north window of the hall is high in the wall to keep out draughts; it will have been closed by a sliding shutter inside. In this instance the treatment (and hence the function) of the ground floor room at the left end of the house cannot be ascertained since it has been modernized.

or wings) has to be supported over the hall by arched braces from the wings (see pl. IIa). The hall roof had a tie-beam and a short crown-post under the collar purlin; the ends were hipped, with gablets, and both features link the Wealden house with the aisled hall, the starting point of south-eastern development. The hall had an open hearth in the centre, an old-fashioned arrangement in the fourteenth century, but a better social focus, and a better way of warming a large number of people, than the fireplace backing on the cross-passage which we have seen at Clifton. The central

[1]H. M. Colvin in A. L. Poole, *Medieval England*, I, 91.

hearth was so convenient in a large establishment that it survived into the last century in such places as Lincoln College, Oxford and Westminster School,[1] and until the sixteenth century in most Kent and Essex houses, judging from the fact that so many of them have an inserted brick chimney stack of that date. It was not convenient for cooking, and its persistence implies that the housewife had another hearth, in a kitchen. The wife of a peasant who could only afford to keep one fire going preferred a hearth better screened from draughts, with a reckon or rack to hang the pots on, and room to stand others by the side.

So much for the hall of the Wealden house. What of the rest of it? A cross passage is always to be found; if the hall was small the passage, and so the entrance to the house, was placed within the service wing. The purpose of the rooms on the ground floor across the passage is clear enough: they were service rooms, and often two doorways survive to show that we may call them buttery and pantry, for wet and dry stores respectively. Records have not bequeathed to us so certain a name for the ground floor room at the upper end of the hall. The Anglo-Saxon name bower had gone out of everyday use in southern England by the fourteenth century and to judge from later records most people in the southern and south-eastern counties called it the chamber. The difficulty over nomenclature, which is after all related to function, is that terms like *bower, solar*, and *chamber* were not used consistently in the Middle Ages. Bower and chamber could both be applied either to ground floor or first floor rooms, but chamber became the commonest name among the peasantry for the ground floor sleeping-room.

The coming name for it, in the fourteenth century, was the *parlour*, a name taken over from the medieval monastery for the place set aside for the reception of visitors from the outside world. It was also coming into use in the still current sense of the mayor's parlour.[2] As a room in a house it occurs first in Chaucer's *Troylus* in c. 1374. It is the equivalent of the 'drawing chaumbre' of a London contract of 1410, or the 'chamber commonly called "withdrawing room" ' in Sleaford Castle in 1419,[3] and these references show that by the end of the fourteenth century the upper classes were using the chamber at the upper end of the hall for secluded conversation and entertainment. Among ordinary farmers, it became the principal sleeping-room, and so remained until the seventeenth century in south eastern counties. It is an important change. In the older Wealden

[1] R.C.H.M. *Oxford*, pl. 121; Turner and Parker, 3 (i), 58.

[2] E.g., *Nottingham Borough Records*, 3, 253: 'the Counsell House and the Parlour under it'.

[3] Salzman, *Building in England*, 484; Lincoln Record Office, Register 14, f. 102.

type houses such as Wardes, Otham, the ground floor rooms in both wings have ceilings with beams only roughly finished;[1] the room at the upper end of the hall was not conceived as a parlour. Other fifteenth century houses, of manor house status, reveal by the finish of the ceiling or the existence of a good fireplace its superior status.[2]

When we move upstairs, by a newel or spiral stair in larger houses or by a simple ladder in, say, a Kentish yeoman's house, we may find that the room over the parlour or chamber is another superior room, with its open timber roof moulded, the wooden mullions of the window rising to a traceried head, or the window itself built out on a bracket into an oriel. We have been taught to call this the *solar;* the word means no more than an upper part of the house, supported on beams. Its use as a bedroom seems to have sprung from the dying tradition of the first floor hall house, for there seems no other way of explaining this use of an upstairs room when the weight of common practice, in most classes, favoured living on the ground floor and using upper rooms only for storage.

We are then left with a technical aspect of the wings of a Wealden house: why were they jettied out? Much nonsense has been written about the jetty, which became one of the characteristic features of the medieval timber-framed house and lasted well into the seventeenth century. It was *not* a sensible way of winning more space for upstairs rooms, since it is as common in the country as the town (and incidentally, on the Continent as well as in this country), and there is no evidence that it was taken over by the country carpenter from the town craftsman. It *may* be true that the cantilever function of the upper floor joists prevented them from sagging. It *may* protect foundations and the lower part of the frame from rainwater. The best technical explanation[3] is that the carpenter hit on it as a way of strengthening the frame of the house, for it gave him two places instead of one at which to make the necessary joints for the junction of ground and upper wall posts with the first floor sill beam. He thus avoided having to make mortices from three directions at one point in the horizontal beam. Once he had decided to make a jetty, he had a chance to display his skill in carving the corner posts supporting the ends of the main projecting beams. A pleasure in the appearance of a jettied house, in the eye of the house owner who could afford to pay for it and the carpenter who could build it, must have become powerful factors; how otherwise explain the fact that it may appear on one side or two, or even more, quite at random?

The next and final stage in our typological sequence is the appearance

[1] See illustrations in A. Tipping, *Engl. Houses*, II, 151, figs. 220–1.
[2] E.g. Frampton Manor Farm, Gloucs.; Tipping, *loc. cit.*, 193, fig. 280.
[3] Put forward by Mr. J. T. Smith.

of what has been called the 'typical' medieval house: that with a central hall, still open to the roof, and a storeyed wing at each end longer than the hall is wide, and so, of necessity, roofed at right angles to it. This is another major innovation, and it must have arisen in circumstances where the numbers to be fed in the hall called for larger service rooms, as well as access to a kitchen commonly separate from the house. Since access from the hall was essential, the only solution was to extend the service wing beyond the width of the hall, and that involved turning the axis of its roof. The fourteenth century part of Penshurst, Kent, built about 1341 by Sir John de Pulteney, a wealthy London merchant turned country gentleman, has 'unquestionably the finest fourteenth century hall surviving' which is 35 feet wide. The service wing is 55 feet long, and the other wing, which has the solar above, is 58 feet long. At the service end there are three doors into the wing, to pantry and buttery and, between them, to a passage leading to a kitchen which has disappeared.[1] Those three doors only appear where the kitchen lay beyond the service wing; if it lay to the side of the house one of the doors from the cross passage would lead more directly to it. At the other end of the hall at Penshurst the persistence of the first-floor house tradition can be seen in the fact that the ground floor, under the very long solar, was originally used for storage.

This account of elements in the medieval house is a gross simplification. It is really no more than a catalogue of pieces which were, in one region or another, arranged in various combinations: so much so that it would be easy to throw in one's hand and say that the results defy classification. Some pattern can be discerned. The most distinct is the migration of types. Once the demands of the client and the skill of the carpenter had evolved a particular mode of building, it was widely copied. The best example is what we have called the Wealden house, with its recessed hall, jettied wings and hipped roof. It is not in fact confined to Kent, though it seems to be commonest there, whether it stands in the main street of a Kentish village or away from the village in an isolation which perpetuates the work of some medieval yeoman in clearing woodland and making a farm. But Essex yeomen adopted the same type of building; Bridge Farm, Theydon Bois is a good example, little altered, and preserving the hipped roof with gablets. Others can be seen widely in the counties north of London, and even as far afield as Shropshire or Devonshire usually with a gabled and not a hipped roof. The most surprising thing is to find it in the city of York, turned at right angles to the frontage, as a town site demands.[2] The explanation is easy to find: medieval carpenters were as

[1] A. Oswald, *op. cit.*, 29.
[2] *Ex. inf.*, Dr. E. A. Gee.

much migrant workers as masons, and employment on major works such as cathedrals and castles must have dispersed far and wide the innovations of any region. The labour force assembled by Edward I for his Welsh castles in 1277–84 included 670 carpenters drawn from 15 counties, ranging from Northumberland through the Midlands and East Anglia to Somerset as well as from the Welsh border counties.[1] Those men no doubt went to Carnarvon or Aberystwyth at the pace of the sheriff who rounded them up, but once the contract was over, whether they stayed or worked their way home again the result might be to take new techniques far from their place of origin.

The other distinct migration is that of the aisled hall, and of elements in its design, from the south-eastern counties as far as Lancashire, Yorkshire and the Welsh border, the territory of the cruck house. The earliest dated aisled hall is the Bishop's Palace, Hereford, which is well above the social range we are considering, but provides a date for the introduction of the type into the border counties. Aisled halls have been discovered in the West Riding of Yorkshire[2] and we shall see later that the design still has its influence in houses there in the seventeenth century. Even if the carpenter did not attempt to build an aisled hall, he was ready to take over particular features of it. The cross passage was an essential part of the standard farmhouse plan, and for the screen between it and the hall he often erected a *speer truss:* that is a framed screen with an opening in the centre to the hall. It had principal posts placed inside the lines of the wall, as if piers in an aisled hall (see fig. 6). The speer truss became almost a standard part of midland farmhouse design in the later Middle Ages, and it was being built in Lancashire and Cheshire as late as the early years of the sixteenth century.[3] While cruck building survives as the most convenient way of building a range of single storey building, as soon as a client wanted a storeyed house, the carpenter was ready to combine cruck building with framed construction. A house at Erdington near Birmingham illustrated by Innocent in process of demolition,[4] had a two bay hall, cruck trussed, and a cross wing also of two bays, framed. Other examples may be seen in Herefordshire of crucks in the hall and a storeyed wing of framed construction in the same house. The carpenter adopted whatever method suited best the job in hand.

That resourcefulness of the craftsman which is exemplified by the dispersal of various techniques is also shown by the great variety, in scale

[1] J. G. Edwards, 'Edward I's Castle—Building in Wales', in *Proc. Brit. Academy*, 32 (1946), 60.
[2] E.g. Broad Bottom, Hebden Royd, near Halifax; *ex. inf.* Mr. C. F. Stell.
[3] J. T. Smith, *Arch. J.*, 112 (1955), 93.
[4] P. 29, fig. 8; see also J. T. Smith, *Arch., J.* 109 (1952), 151–2.

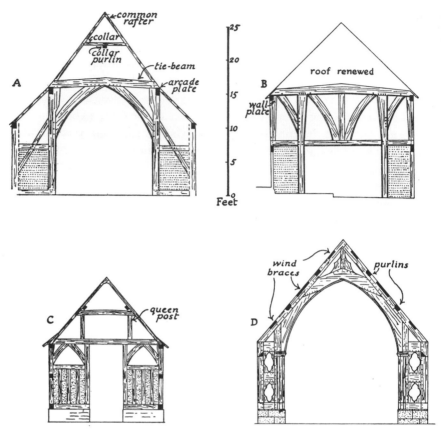

FIGURE 6. Speer trusses in midland houses, showing their derivation from the aisled hall. A: West Bromwich Manor House, Warwickshire (S. R. Jones). B: house at Coleshill, Warwickshire (S. R. Jones). C: The Old Ship, Anstey, Leicestershire (R. W. McDowall). D: Smithell's Hall, Bolton-le-Moors, Lancashire (H. Taylor). A is fourteenth century, B and C first half of fifteenth century, D early sixteenth century. Even the simplest (B and C) have an impressive ornamental character, with curved braces rising into the darkness of the smoke-filled roof.

and in the relation of one part to another, in houses of the later Middle Ages. Two of the elements of the Wealden house, recessed hall and jettied wing, are found in all possible combinations: that is, with a hall of one or two bays, with one storeyed wing of one or two bays and with two storeyed wings. Where there is only one wing, it may be found either at the upper end of the hall, or at the lower end beyond a cross passage. The passage itself may be either within the hall or within the service wing. In such variety, and widespread distribution, the Wealden house almost dissolves as a local type, and so it deserves to do in the interests of truth. If it is well known today, it has been placed in the popular mind by estate agents' literature, and partly by the sixteenth century rhyme about the yeoman of Kent being wealthier than a knight of Calais or a lord of the north country. To the historian, Kent is singular in that the local system of inheritance, gavelkind, gave particular security of tenure to a free class of farmer, and because his patrimony was divided among his heirs, both sons and daughters, it protected and encouraged a large class of yeomen of moderate wealth. To us the importance of the Kentish yeoman is not his wealth but that he made up a class numerous enough to have left behind many houses suitable for conversion into attractive residences for City businessmen. Exactly how many survive we shall know only when the county has been systematically surveyed.

Many a medieval church has only one aisle, so it need not surprise us to find a fifteenth century house with a hall of the same design: Priory Cottage, Bramber, Sussex.[1] No priory built it; it is in fact 'only a modest yeoman's house', remarkable for its one aisle and the finish and elaboration of the workmanship. There is a hall of two bays, the open truss in the centre having the usual tie-beam and crown-post; arched braces had their spandrels pierced by tracery, and in the aisle additional struts and braces had similar ornament, showing that the aisle was open to the hall. We shall see later that halls with one aisle only can be traced in Yorkshire, and an Essex barn of the same type is mentioned in the thirteenth century.[2] The aisled hall must be the origin of the outshot, which does not become a common feature until later times.

When a carpenter was asked to roof a church, he could most conveniently place the main trusses, of tie-beam, king-post, braces and principal rafters, at regular intervals along the walls. In preparing the frame for a house, he adapted the spacing of the trusses to the divisions of the house. A house named Trimmer's Pond, in the Sussex parish of West Hoathley, which was taken down in 1929 and re-erected on another site, had a hall of one and a half bays; the cross passage occupied half a bay and had a speer truss.[3] In Herefordshire there are houses with a cruck trussed hall of one and a half bays. That brings us to another important observation: that although a hall of two bays—not less than 24 feet long—is common enough to be thought typical of a yeoman's house in the fifteenth century, there are some with a hall of only one bay in length. The best example is The

[1]W. H. Godfrey 'St. Mary's and Priory Cottage, Bramber', *Sussex Arch. Coll.*, 87 (1947), 112–17.

[2]*Domesday of St. Paul's*, ed. Hall (Camden Soc., 1856) 123; of a barn at Wickham, Essex: 'nec habet preter i alam'.

[3]I. C. Hannah, 'Medieval Timber Houses at West Hoathley and Forest Row', *Sussex Arch., Coll.* 71 (1930), 107–25.

Old Shop, Bignor, Sussex, because it still reveals all the features of the Wealden type of house; the only alteration has been the insertion of an upper floor to the hall and a brick chimney stack, and the removal of the bay window which once ran the full height of the hall. Notice the jettied wings and recessed hall, with braces from the wings to the eaves plate, and the braces to the angles, slightly curved, sweeping upwards from the sill beam. The roof still has its hipped form, with gablets. The hall measures about 18 feet in width and 12 feet in length, the parlour wing the same, but the service wing, since it contained the entrance and through passage, was made 15 feet long.[1] The Old Shop was probably built in the middle of the fifteenth century, and neither it nor the other houses with a single bay hall are of poor or mean construction; 'it is simply a matter of reduction of size in what is usually regarded as the premier apartment', and the reason must be that with four other rooms the hall had become relatively less important.

Small medieval houses which have been altered as little as The Old Shop at Bignor are the greatest rarity; even if they have eluded the common enemy, decay, they have usually been subject to changing needs of owners and the different standards of later generations. Even in the Middle Ages provision for aged parents sometimes required additions or divisions of the house. Manorial courts took cognisance of the arrangements proposed by the tenant for his parents when he took over the family holding, and so we read of a Worcestershire villein undertaking to build a house for his widowed mother, and another instance at Dunmow, Essex, where the widow was to have a separate room at the end of the house.[2] John Cocksedge of Felsham, Suffolk, gentleman (d. 1467), provided in his will for the division of his house between his son and his widow; she was to have 'the new house called the parlour with the kitchen and the chambers pertaining . . ., and the little garden on the east side of the parlour', with fruit from the trees in it and access to the 'bakehouse in lawful time of brewing, for baking and drying of malt'.[3] The additions to an old house which puzzle those who try to elucidate the structure—a wing added within a short time of its building, or the duplication of service rooms—must sometimes have arisen from such special circumstances.

Hitherto we have been concerned with the free peasant of the Middle Ages, or the men who, if they were legally less than free, occupied none

[1]R. T. Mason, 'Four Single Bay Halls', *Sussex Arch., Coll.* 96 (1958), 12–13. For an illustration, see for instance Batsford and Fry, *The English Cottage*, pl. 32.
[2]*Halesowen Court Rolls*, ed. Amphlett (Worcs. Hist. Soc., 1910), 1, 167; G. C. Homans, *English Villagers of the Thirteenth Century* (1942), 434, n. 2.
[3]*Bury Wills and Inventories* (Camden Soc., 1850), 45.

the less enough land to maintain a family. But English society had always contained a class of men who had no more than the roof over their heads, and since that was their sole distinction they were known to historical records as cottagers. In Domesday Book they were 'cottars' or 'bordars', the one an English, the other a French word, and they formed then almost a third of the recorded population. Neither historical nor archaeological research can yet produce more than trifling pieces of evidence to fill the gap between the Anglo Saxon peasant hut of the Sutton Courtenay type and the well-documented cottage of the seventeenth century. We know for instance that in about 1300 the cost of building cottages on one North-amptonshire estate was between 12s. and 25s. apiece,[1] at a time when craftsmen employed on Welsh castles earned a little more than a shilling a week.

The significant improvement from the Saxon hut to the Stuart cottage is not in size, but in having walls of a man's height, so that head room need no longer be got by sinking the floor below ground level. In Anglo-Saxon Thetford, the one common feature in houses of various plans and different construction is the use of sand or turf for walling. The use of earth for walling is the most ancient and persistent part of the vernacular tradition. It goes back indeed to the Bronze Age, to hut circles on Dartmoor, where the earth walls are retained by stone. In Lincolnshire the older cottages in the limestone belt have walls of two skins of stone with earth between. The carpenter carried the development of the medieval house in the direction of making a timber frame to bear the weight of the roof, and the filling of the box-frame—mud plastered on to a base of splints or wattle sprung into grooves in the sides of timbers—bore no load. The carpenter in Chaucer's *Miller's Tale* who proposed to break through the gable of his house when the flood came would only have had to pierce 5 inches or so of mud infilling. The cottager who, even if he could take a tree from the waste of the manor, could not get much timber of good quality, and could not command the services of a carpenter, developed the art of building mud or clay walls. Building in mud or cob was not confined to cottagers, but it must have been the chief distinction of houses built by their owners, for it was to be found in counties where other materials were available. It simply required the knowledge that earth of the right consistency, which could be found almost everywhere, could form durable walling when mixed with straw, hay or cow dung to bind it, allowed to dry sufficiently during building and afterwards protected from weather. There are medi-eval references to mud walling at Southampton, Bridport, Leicester and

[1] D. Wills, *Estate Book of Henry de Bray of Harleston* (Camden Soc., 1916), 49–51.

Hedon;[1] and we may be sure that when labourers were employed to build mud walls round a churchyard or for a monastic building, they were doing for others what they were used to doing for themselves. There are also hints that turf was used where it was available. In the Isle of Axholme fourteenth century peasants had the right to cut turf for walling as well as for fuel,[2] and later references to a turf coping to a dry stone wall, to a turf cottage on the waste of Leicestershire manors, and to a turf built woad mill in a nineteenth century Fenland village of Lincolnshire, all[3] suggest that its use may have been common. In Cumberland some sixty years ago barkpeelers built themselves huts which consisted of four poles lashed in pairs to support a ridge piece, 2-ft high walls of earth between two skins of wattle, and a sod roof. This temporary house was about 13 feet long and 8 feet wide. Its main refinement was a stone-built hearth and chimney in the side opposite the door.[4] In size and mode of construction it must have been very like a poor medieval cottage in a part of England where good timber and straw for thatching were scarce. It was certainly like most medieval cottages in having only one room for all purposes.

Before we leave these medieval houses, what of their washing and sanitary arrangements? Washing was something to be done after meals, and larger houses had a brass basin and ewer in the hall, or a stone basin (*lavatorium*) in the screens passage. Some people had a hanging jug or ewer (*lavacrum pendens*) with a pierced bottom from which water ran over the hands into a standing bowl of iron, or into a 'sinkstone'.[5] Sinkstones or sinks are rarely mentioned in inventories after 1500 or so, not because they became more unusual but just the contrary. Like window glass and chamber floors in Tudor times, they were valued in inventories while they were novelties and regarded as tenants' fixtures. They must have been new to fifteenth-century Yorkshire. Most countrymen, however had to be content with washing in one of the wooden tubs that stood about the hall.

In larger houses, where first floor rooms were used for sleeping, the garderobe with its stone or wooden seat and chute to ground level was a regular feature. It is not found in houses of peasant farmers. It is rare in

[1]Brought together by L. F. Salzman, *Building in England* (1952), 88, 187; also J. R. Boyle, *Early History of Hedon* (1895), civ.

[2]W. B. Stonehouse, *History of the Isle of Axholme* (1839), 233.

[3]*Household Book of Lord William Howard of Naworth Castle* (Surtees Soc., 1878), 90, 247; at Whitwick, Leics., in 1604 a 'poor man, a wisket maker, made a cote of stickes and turffes', *Trans. Leics. Arch. Soc.*, 15 (1925–7), 248; there is a nineteenth century reference to a turf cottage at Long Whatton, White's *Directory of Leics. and Rutland*, 1846, 364; J. B. Hurry, *The Woad Plant and its Dye* (Oxford, 1930), 22, for description of woad mill.

[4]H. S. Cooper in *T.C.W.A.A.S.*, N.S. 1 (1901), 141–3.

[5]Turner and Parker, II, 44; *Test. Ebor.*, II, 23, 87, 195.

timber houses. The garderobe was in any case mainly for night use, and some houses had only a small stone basin upstairs into which a chamber pot could be emptied, or which a man could use as a urinal. At the Manor House, Appleby Magna, Leics., the stained wall outside shows the use to which the drain was put.[1] The house near Melksham, Wilts., known as Great Chalfield has several such drains. By the middle of the sixteenth century we are entering an age when the wealthy used close stools, which must have been an improvement on the offensive garderobe.

For the peasant—even for the Kentish yeoman—we can only imagine a hole in the garden, some distance from the house: the latrine pit or rubbish pit which any excavator of a medieval habitation site expects to encounter. How often it was made large enough to last for years, or had a roof over it, we cannot guess. It is as well to remember that even in the nineteenth century a very large number of country cottages had no sanitary convenience whatsoever.

[1]The drain is illustrated in Turner and Parker, III, i, 73.

CHAPTER THREE

Men and their Homes in Early Tudor Times

WHEN Elizabeth came to the throne, England was on the brink of a period when new houses were to be a commoner sight than ever before. If we are to see clearly what the changes amounted to, we must look more closely at the way men lived in her father's and grandfather's times, and try to define the classes of rural society whose homes we are to explore. Fortunately, new sources of information are open to us, which make it possible to see houses furnished and in use, and not merely the skeletons of stone or timber exposed by the measuring rod or the spade.

We have seen already that secular methods of taxation might give leading citizens of a medieval community some practice in the business of making inventories of men's goods and chattels from which assessments could be fixed. The medieval church had its own reasons for wishing to see an inventory of a deceased person's goods. The making of a will was enjoined in Christian teaching long before the Conquest. Since a will served religious purposes—that of repairing sins of omission, such as tithes forgotten, as well as paying a mortuary due to the parish priest and making proper provision for a funeral service—the church made itself responsible for the execution of the will, and to do so needed to know what a man had to dispose of.[1]

---

[1] The Council of Lambeth in 1261 included in its ordinances one to the effect that no executor should administer the goods of a deceased person without producing a faithful inventory of them to the ecclesiastical court; Wilkins, *Concilia*, I, 754. Since this was a reforming rather than an innovating Council, this provision cannot have been new.

Surviving inventories of the Middle Ages tell us something about the homes of the gentry, the wealthier clergy and a few merchants and craftsmen,[1] but nothing about peasants. The thin stream of wills and inventories became a flood when the authority of the state was placed behind that of the church. Henry VIII's Reformation Parliament put on the statute book an act[2] limiting the fees to be exacted by the church courts for proving wills; its second clause required executors to find four honest persons to 'make a trewe and perfyte Inventory of all the goodes catells wares merchaundyses as well moveable as not moveable . . . and shall cause the same to be Indented. . . .' Thus begins a form of record which takes us, in the company of the neighbours who made it, through the house, the farm buildings and the fields of Tudor, Stuart and Hanoverian farmers and cottagers. To speak of a flood of inventories is no exaggeration; there are at least 75,000 for the county of Lincoln, ranging in date from c. 1520 to the middle of the eighteenth century, by which time the church courts had begun to reduce the executors' duty of listing goods and chattels to a formality which tells us little. Similar collections are to be found for most counties, though in many the earliest surviving belong only to the later years of the seventeenth century.[3] Into the flood the historian can either plunge his bucket and examine everything that he finds in the sample, or he can use a net, to fish up information about any particular village, or class of men. We shall use both methods as opportunity occurs.

The make-up of rural society emerges more clearly from a study of probate inventories than from any other class of record, for while a will commonly tells us what a man called himself, it is the inventory which shows us how he stood in the eyes of his neighbours. The two are not always the same; just as in our time there are fewer men and women ready to admit that they belong to the working class, so in Tudor times a man might call himself a yeoman while his neighbours regarded him as a tanner. Such differences reflect not only a wish to better oneself but a chance of so doing; such opportunities were to be found in Tudor England in farming and its combination with trade. Leaving aside the gentry, with whom we are not concerned, and for the moment, the village parson, the upper crust of rural society was composed of farmers who in the sixteenth

[1]See *Test. Ebor.* (Surtees Soc., 4 vols.); *Wills and Inventories . . . of the Northern Counties* . . . (Surtees Soc.), etc.

[2]21 Henry VIII, *c.* 5.

[3]For an invaluable guide to surviving collections, and notes on the complex pattern of ecclesiastical jurisdiction, see B. G. Bouwens, *Wills and their whereabouts* (2nd edition, 1951, Society of Genealogists, Chaucer House, Malet Place, W.C.1). For a description of the types of record produced by the probate process see F. W. Steer, *Farm and Cottage Inventories of Mid–Essex, 1635–1749* (1950).

century were coming to be called *yeomen*.[1] The medieval term *franklin*, for landowners of free but not noble birth, had gone out of fashion by the sixteenth century inventories. Below the yeoman came the husbandman, originally an unfree peasant (*bond*) who had his own house and land; his villein status had been forgotten except in the rare instances where a courtier with access to the right ears and the right records might find a chance of exacting payment from a wealthy peasant for the purchase of freedom. Below the husbandman came the large class of men not entirely dependent on the occupation of land: the village ·craftsmen and those engaged in rural industry, shepherds, fishermen and the like. They had their stake in the land, and their way of life reflects both the varied needs of a community and its inability to provide a landholding for all its men. The age of marriage was high, as it must be in a peasant society where a man can only marry and set up a home when the family holding becomes his. Below all these, in wealth and in the eyes of contemporaries, came those who called themselves labourers; no one called himself a cottager in Tudor England.

If we exclude those who were not householders—the servants employed by the aristocracy[2] and by wealthy yeomen; the bachelor whose goods amounted to the clothes he wore and perhaps his bed; the spinster who had only linen in a dowry chest and the few pounds her father had bequeathed—if we exclude those, we have left only the village parson. At what level did he fit into village society? Whether his equals were the richer yeomen or the modest husbandmen depended on the history of his living and his own qualities: whether it was a rectory which gave him all the tithes, or a vicarage which only had lesser tithes; how much glebe land there was and whether he farmed it with energy and skill. The substantial Victorian parsonage house, sold in our time because it is too large and expensive to run, was the end product of two centuries of occasional pluralism, the augmenting of clerical incomes by Queen Anne's Bounty, the hard won profits of keeping a boarding school for young gentlemen, or the resources of a private income. As an official residence, the house was more likely to be rebuilt or enlarged than reduced, and this inflationary process has bequeathed to our age houses which exaggerate the former status and condition of the village priest. So do surviving medieval houses,

[1] See Mildred Campbell, *The English Yeoman* (1942); ch. II discusses the class and its relation with others. The derivation of the name has not been clearly explained, but it meant originally a servant or attendant in a large household; perhaps a 'young man'.

[2] The 'menyall and household servants' of a large establishment in Gloucestershire in 1608 were divided into eight yeomen and six husbandmen; R. H. Tawney, *Econ. H.R.*, 5 (1934), 33, n. 2.

in all probability; the priests' houses of Devon and Somerset (the only area so far studied intensively[1]), none of them less than 50 feet long, must have been the best of their time or they would not have escaped destruction. The living standards of the parochial clergy varied at least as much in the Middle Ages as later. How much they could differ in Jacobean times, when freedom to marry had given every parson a motive for wanting a larger house, we shall see from later evidence.

The south-eastern counties, where the most advanced types of house were to be found in the thirteenth and fourteenth centuries, were still ahead in the sixteenth and that superiority persisted, though it was somewhat reduced, in the seventeenth. Comparison of one region with another shows a progressive simplicity of accommodation as one moves north and west, so that it is best to see first what Kentish houses were like in the early part of Elizabeth I's reign, and to compare with them whatever we can discern elsewhere. Our first glimpse of houses in the eastern half of Kent comes from inventories dated about 1570.[2] The Kentish yeoman does not dominate the picture yet, as he comes to do in the next century; there was a solid majority of small farmers and those who called themselves yeomen and husbandmen rarely occupied more than 50 acres. Freehold estates were still commonly divided among heirs and that had hindered the growth of large estates among Kentish yeomen; the average value of the inventories is only £28, less than in Norfolk or Suffolk at this time. It is not that Kent was poorer, but that wealth was more widely distributed, for that was the effect both of the inheritance system and of the good quality of Kentish soil. A man might live quite well on a small farm, as did Alexander Paramore, yeoman, of Reculver. His goods amounted to £128 in all. He had 25 acres of arable, 16 cattle, 6 horses, 114 sheep and 14 pigs, and his assets included debts to a total of £43. Such debts become common among men of his class at this time and later. Sometimes they are what they appear, the loans of a village moneylender. Sometimes, as here, they are only a necessary reckoning of neighbourliness interrupted by death. 'Item owing me of Thomas Piskill 44s., and I owe him 7 bushels of wheat and 7 bushels and a tolvet of malt'. Such lending and helping is still a part of rural life; debts and favours may go for years, remembered by the lender but not always a matter for open reproach.

Alexander Paramore's household goods were worth less than £7, though his house was comfortable enough. It consisted of a central hall with a

---

[1]By W. A. Pantin, 'Medieval Priests' Houses in South-West England' in *Med. Arch.*, I (1957), 118–46.

[2]Maidstone R.O., PRC 10/5 (Register of Inventories, 1569–71, Archdeaconry Court) and 28/2 (Consistory Court).

storeyed range at each end. Whether it was of the Wealden type, with recessed hall, or had large wings, we cannot tell. In the hall the only ornament was a painted cloth on the wall. Such cloths were to be found in houses of almost every degree in Tudor England. They were a modest substitute for the embroidered 'halling' or tapestry of wealthier folk, for they consisted simply of canvas stretched on a wooden frame and then decorated by the painter-stainer. The only painted cloth still in the house for which it was made is at Sparrow's House, Ipswich, a fifteenth century house with much fine plaster work and panelling of the Elizabethan period and later, including the cloth on the stairs, about 6 feet high, with a picture of Samson and the initials of George Copping who lived there before his death in 1578.[1] Such cloths must have been cheaper than paint applied direct on to wall plaster, which had a distinct regional popularity in the counties north of London, and is found in quite humble houses.[2] Cloths were also removable by the tenant, like window lattices, doors and even ceilings.

Paramore and his family sat for their meals at a table in the hall. There was a chair for him, or for any visitor, but only a form or a 'bench with a mat' for the others. Some cooking was done on the hall fire, which may well have been still on a central hearth. By the fire stood two kettles, two iron pans (one of them a 'stuppen' or stew pan) and three brass pots. Meals were eaten from pewter, with a tin spoon; a dozen wooden trenchers stood on a hanging shelf but they were no longer used now that the family had pewter.

At night three pewter candlesticks lighted the hall, or the family on its way to bed. Husband and wife slept in the better of the two rooms at the end of the hall; it was called a parlour, but held only two feather beds and a couple of chests for linen. Next to it another bedroom, called a chamber, had a flock bed in it, but was used to store the two spinning wheels (for linen and wool), a flour bin ('boulting hutch'), two tubs and two more old chests. Over these two rooms was a loft with a truckle bedstead and a featherbed. At the other end of the hall was a room which they called the kitchen; it contained mainly brewing gear and dairy vessels, but there was a hearth against a wall with two spits and a dripping pan for roasts. Here in fact we catch a family in process of changing their habits; the hearth in the hall is ceasing to be the focus of family life, and cooking

[1] I am indebted to Mr. R. W. McDowall for reminding me of this example. There are fragments of painted cloths in the Victoria and Albert, Luton and Lewes Museums. The painted cloths in Owlpen Old Manor, Glos., done c. 1700, are quite exceptional because in general the vogue for them had ceased by c. 1650.

[2] E.g., the paintings of c. 1500 in a small house at Piccott's End, Herts., illustrated in *The Times* of 22 November 1956. See F. W. Reader in *Arch., J.* 87 (1930), 71–97.

Ia. TIL house, Clifton, Notts., now so called because Thomas Lambert and his wife Joan were responsible for casing the parlour wing in brick in the year 1707; their work is perpetuated in brick headers. This is a useful warning that the date on a house may not be the date of its building. The proportions of the hall range suggest to the experienced eye that it may, in view of the size of the house (which is not a cottage), be an open medieval hall. See pp. 24-6.

Ib. A cottage at Midville, Lincs., of two rooms with axial chimney stack. It stands on the bank of a drain in part of the Lincolnshire fens not drained until c. 1820.

IIa. The entrance to the Old Rectory, Mon
Horton, Kent, a Wealden type house, as
recessed hall and the brace to the eaves indica
The brick infilling and stucco are modern

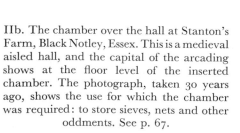

IIb. The chamber over the hall at Stanton's
Farm, Black Notley, Essex. This is a medieval
aisled hall, and the capital of the arcading
shows at the floor level of the inserted
chamber. The photograph, taken 30 years
ago, shows the use for which the chamber
was required: to store sieves, nets and other
oddments. See p. 67.

(and the housewife) are being relegated to the kitchen. How long this change was protracted, and the classes through which it passed, will be a significant point to watch as we examine houses of other regions and periods.

How far was Alexander Paramore's home typical of Kentish yeomen? It was unusual in still having a hall open to the roof; a substantial number of houses in the county already had a chamber over the hall, and a very few smaller houses already had a loft.[1] We shall meet this distinction frequently; it is never defined, but presumably a chamber was superior in having a floor at such a height that there was room in the walls for windows, while a loft was no more than the triangular space made by inserting a floor at eaves level. It is not a distinction imposed by use; any room, either down- or upstairs might be called a chamber in this part of England. It was convenient to have a chamber over the hall, since it was dry from the fire always burning in the hall below, and such chambers were usually used for storage.

Thomas Whitfield of Eastry, whose goods were worth £227 6s. 4d., had a house of similar plan to Paramore's; the chambers in the wings each had beds in them, while that over the hall had wool and russet yarn; hempseed, mustard seed, oats, cheese, butter and apples; an eel share and a rook net, his armour and hunting gear, and fifteen sickles and hooks. This combination of foodstuffs and farm seed with articles used only once in the year is quite typical of the uses to which one at least of the upstairs rooms, and usually the least important of them, is invariably devoted. The wealth of Kent and the way of living that richer farmers had already evolved had made them take a step in improving the accommodation and convenience of their houses which in the rest of England was very rare at this time. The open hall, the characteristic feature of medieval houses, was already on the way out, and the process had begun by 1500, as a contract shows.[2] The concomitant alterations—the insertion of a brick chimney for the hall fire and of a staircase—will be described later.

The ground floor room at one end of these houses invariably served as the principal sleeping-room; where there were two rooms in that wing, a few people called one of them the parlour, but it was a pretentious term. If visitors were entertained there, they must have sat on a bed or a chest, for there were very seldom any chairs. More often these rooms were called chambers: 'the Chamber behind the Hall' and 'the Chamber over

[1] The figures are: seven chambers and two lofts in a random sample of fifty inventories in PRC/10/5.
[2] Maidstone R.O., Ch/4/9; a contract dated 1500 for a house at Coldham, 'all the said house to be lofted over'.

the same Chamber' (John Maycott, gentleman of Ospringe); the 'Loft and the Chamber beneath' (Richard Need of Hinxhill); a physician of Chilham kept his 'apothecary stuff' in a chamber which must have been on the ground floor. Joanna Hemar of Ivychurch had a hall (still used for cooking) and at one end of it the lower bed chamber and the higher bed chamber; at the other, the milk buttery and the drink chamber or beer buttery. This use of 'chamber' for ground floor rooms, including sleeping-rooms, distinguishes the south-eastern counties, as far north as Bedfordshire and Oxfordshire, from the rest of England where functional names (parlour, buttery, etc.) are in general use in Elizabethan times. The difference suggests strongly that the existence of a separate sleeping-room in farm-houses of the Midlands belongs at the earliest to the fourteenth century, when the term parlour was coming into use, while in the south-east it was an innovation of earlier times, to judge from the general use of the Norman-French word chamber.

There are plenty of houses larger than Paramore's in Kent at this time: homes of men of substance, some calling themselves yeomen, occasionally wealthy tradesmen such as tanners and clothiers. They had between six and twelve rooms: two or more service rooms (bakehouse, larder, brew-house), and store- and sleeping-rooms for servants upstairs as well as family bedrooms downstairs. Occasionally one meets a house with 'galetts' or garrets; the Tudor and Stuart period knew no other name for a third floor in the roof. The special crops of Kentish farming are beginning to appear by 1570: Robert Harryson, a yeoman of Tonge, had an oast loft and Stephen Gibbon of Rolvenden had an apple chamber, but malt, hops and fruit growing on a large scale are rare before the seventeenth century. Most people of Paramore's standing had several service rooms: the buttery, where drink and presumably food as well, were kept; the milkhouse and the brewhouse are the commonest. Flour was usually kept in the milk-house, in a boulting hutch, rather than in a separate boulting house. In William Peyr's house at Woodchurch the hutch was in the 'bakhouse', along with malt querns, a kneading trough, milk boards and bowls. It is often difficult to know when 'bakhouse' means *backhouse;* usually at this time it signifies *bakehouse.* William Peyr's had a 'bakehouse loft', containing malt and wheat.

At a lower social level the most distinct type of house is that with three or four rooms.[1] The inventory of Jane Sybley of Lenham may serve as an example; her husband had been a coverlet weaver, to judge from the presence of a coverlet loom in her sleeping chamber. Such people very

[1] It formed a quarter of the 1570 sample of inventories in the archdeaconry collection.

seldom used the name parlour; and since the chamber was only needed at night, there the craftsman usually worked if he was not rich enough to have a shop. Apart from the chamber, she had a hall, very simply furnished, and a kitchen used for cooking. Other folk of similar standing—perhaps husbandmen in the main—often had a fourth room, the buttery. It was no doubt often a mere division within the hall; it is usually named immediately after the hall and once or twice described as 'within the hall'. Perhaps the principal distinction between larger houses and these smaller ones is that, as well as having no upstairs rooms at this time, they had no cross passage. Unless the passage had any furniture—for instance, a chest, as it occasionally had in the next century—it will not be named; hence we have no evidence from documents on a point of great historical interest: how far down the social range can we find houses with a cross passage? However that may be, the combination of chamber, hall, buttery and kitchen is not uncommon; it probably connotes a house of three bays or main units, with a small hall in the centre and a buttery off, a sleeping-room at one end and a kitchen at the other. The remarkable thing is that the kitchen, not only as a general service room but as a cooking room, should have become by this time an integral part of such modest houses; one more respect in which Kent is ahead of the rest of England.

The smallest house which can be clearly distinguished in Kent is that with only two rooms. Here we must face the problem that we shall encounter throughout this attempt to use probate inventories to reveal housing standards. In some cases the four neighbours who were called in to make the list do not punctuate it with the names of the rooms through which the widow took them. Two explanations are possible: either that there was only one room in the house, or that the approvers did not think it necessary to distinguish one room from another. The attitude of the officials of the church court to which they eventually took their inventory must have been that when they were dealing with the estate of a rich yeoman, they could be sure that the inventory was more or less complete if they could read, in Gothic letters, the names of half a dozen or more rooms. With poorer folk it mattered less, and so, here in Kent and in every other county, the inventories which fail to name rooms are predominantly those of the least value.[1]

The inventory of Thomas Whyall of Boughton under Blean is printed in full (Appendix, p. 277) to illustrate the problem. He was probably a labourer; in Kent men calling themselves labourers, or so called by their neighbours, very rarely made a will. Two rooms are named, the hall with

[1] E.g. eleven out of the poorest twenty-three inventories in the sample from Kent Consistory, 1568–9, PRC 28/2.

a cross heading and the parlour incidentally. The group of kitchen gear listed after the linen suggests that this may be really a house of three rooms, the kitchen not being named. Even if that is so, there are certainly other two-roomed houses to be found in inventories of this time. On the other hand, the single-roomed house had disappeared from the Kentish scene; no document allows us either to see it distinctly or even to infer it. This is the final item in the account of the superiority of living standards in south-eastern England.

In the north of England, farm labourers were still living in one-roomed houses in the nineteenth century.[1] The contrast between the south and the north in housing conditions had already grown up by the end of the Middle Ages; houses in Lincolnshire and further north, other than those of the rural upper and middle classes, were smaller in size, simpler in arrangement and seldom had an upper floor. The Lincolnshire marshland, the coastal fringe between the Wolds and the sea, was thickly populated with large villages, containing much the richest peasants in the country. In mid-Tudor times they were, like farmers everywhere, profiting from the inflation of prices; between the 1530's and the 1550's the average farmer's goods more than doubled in money value,[2] and he was about as well off as his counterpart in east Kent. But while his Lincolnshire cattle waxed fat on some of the best grazing in the country, the wealth they represented had scarcely begun to be turned into a comfortable standard of living. Very few inventories of the 1530's mention rooms; usually the valuers were content to list the 'howsshold stuffe', under a figure sometimes as low as a few shillings, and mounting on the average to only eleven per cent of their total wealth.

Here in the east Midlands we meet for the first time the practice of calling the hall, or main living room, the house. It is not merely an archaism; it reflects real historical differences in housing development, and in particular the fact that the one-roomed house must still have been common in mid-Tudor Lincolnshire. In the 1530s, two thirds or more of the inventories fail to mention any rooms; by 1572, the proportion falls to one third, and thenceforward it steadily diminishes until by the end of the seventeenth century one does not expect to encounter such uninformative documents at all. Admittedly, this change could represent the increasing skill of the few literate men in a village at producing an inventory which

[1] W. Howitt, *The Rural Life of England* (1838), I, 167: 'Cottages are of one story, and generally of one room'.

[2] According to a sampling of inventories for the region made by Miss V. Booth, to whom I am indebted for permission to use her transcripts. See Joan Thirsk, *English Peasant Farming* (1957), 54–7, for similar figures for the period 1530 to 1600, and comparisons with other regions of Lincolnshire.

would satisfy the officials to whom it was submitted. Nowadays, filling in forms has become part of our everyday life; it needs an effort of imagination to think of the difficulties of men who started with a blank sheet of paper and had to frame the questions as well as find the answers. There are certainly some signs of more trouble being taken; for instance, the occupation of the deceased is inserted more often as the years go by. Yet the inventories of the poor fail us more often than those of the rich, though they were sometimes made by the same men. It is tantalizing not to be able to give due weight to the two factors—the inadequacy of the documents and the simplicity of the house—but in the last resort, faith in the documentary evidence is confirmed by the study of existing houses. Glancing for the moment as far as Lancashire and counties farther north, the preponderance of uninformative inventories diminishes only at that stage in the late seventeenth century when a substantial number of new and dated houses tells us that standards common in medieval Kent were beginning to appeal to Westmorland farmers.

A search for the largest farmhouses in Lincolnshire takes us to the uplands, particularly to the limestone ridge which forms a spine to the county. There were the richest farmers and the villages were small; land which would produce high quality wool was plentiful. Thomas Cony, a Grantham wool merchant, used the profits from his flock of 1,000 sheep to build himself a house at Bassingthorpe. A small stone house with crow-stepped gables, moulded diagonal chimneys and a small oriel window in a chamber overlooking the churchyard, is marked as his by the rabbit (cony) in a pediment; it is dated 1573. What remains is however no more than the parlour wing;[1] the hall has gone, as have the buildings round the court, with their chambers over for hinds and shepherds. The maid servants slept above the principal chambers in the parlour wing. A fortune from wool was no new thing, as medieval brasses of wool merchants in churches along the limestone belt as far as Gloucestershire can show. Thomas Cony had no heir; his daughter took her fortune into a gentry family,[2] and her father's house, instead of becoming the nucleus for a Georgian country house, relapsed to the level of a small farmhouse. It can stand however as an example of the standards of successful farmers in upland country whether in Lincolnshire or the Cotswolds.

In the clay lands of the east Midlands, large farms were more rare, and the richest yeomen lived more simply than Thomas Cony. Thomas Bradgate of Peatling Parva was the richest yeoman in Leicestershire when

[1]His inventory is printed in *Lincs. N. and Q.*, I, 132.
[2]She married William Sutton of Averham, Notts., and her son became Baron Lexington; *Complete Peerage*, VI.

he died in 1539,[1] but his house was a modest affair; a hall, two service rooms (buttery and kitchen) and a bakehouse; two parlours and one upstairs room. Only the silver spoons and saltcellars and the 'whole garnish of pewter' show that he was a cut above the yeomen of his time. In Leicestershire villages in his time, and for another generation longer, most houses must have had either two rooms (hall and parlour) or only one; a good many of them cruck built, with one, two or three bays.[2] This is strikingly different from Kent, where the single-roomed house had already disappeared, and the two-roomed house was a thing of the past for many husbandmen and labourers.

In the Lincolnshire marshland in the 1530's one of the wealthiest farmers—whether yeoman or husbandman we do not know—was Robert Towte of Skidbrook; he had fourteen acres of arable, fourteen cattle of all sorts and four horses. His house, with its three rooms—hall, parlour and kitchen—was probably one of the largest in this community; compared with Kent it ranks low in the scale. By the 1550's there are slight signs of improving standards; more inventories name rooms in houses, though still less frequently than in Leicestershire at this time. One simple pattern emerges in region after region: the richer the soil, the greater the number of small and medium farmers it would support, and even landless labourers where there was plenty of common land; the more widely dispersed the wealth the simpler the standard of housing.

At the same time there were chances of advancement to a solid competence, if not to the status of rich yeoman. John Lusby of Fulstow, who died in 1556, was called a labourer by his neighbours, but he had enough land and common rights to keep twenty-three sheep, three kine, two horses, pigs and hens; his wife made butter and a hard cheese. He grew, or bought locally, the hemp which a village weaver made up into the harden sheets on which they slept. In their hall there was a painted cloth on one wall, a single chair, a table, a form and some stools; three brass pots and three little pans stood on a dish bench by the fire, and on the table, covered with a cloth at meals, were four pewter dishes, two candlesticks and a salt. Their parlour had only a bed, and three chests and a press for linen; there was a chamber (probably over the parlour) used for storing beans, wool and a spinning wheel. This is the first time we have seen how a labourer might live, but he is not typical of his class.

In the Isle of Axholme, a low-lying area between the Trent and the Yorkshire Ouse, there was a large population of peasants less rich than those of the marshland, living by pasture farming supplemented by some

[1]W. G. Hoskins, *Essays in Leics. History*, 153–4.
[2]See Hoskins, *The Midland Peasant*, 285, for the evidence for Wigston Magna.

crop growing, particularly of flax and hemp for making harden and sacking.[1] Only two out of twenty inventories dated 1557–8 give details of rooms, and many of the houses must have been single cells, possibly built of peat. William Chapman of Crowle had goods worth £39 2s. 8d., three times the average figure; he lived in a house similar to that of Thomas Bradgate of Peatling Parva. Alison Pinder of Amcotts still had her husband's farm stock, including a flock of thirty sheep, and the neighbours called her two rooms *house* and parlour. Most people burned peat for fuel, and had hemp seed, a hemp brake, hemp yarn or 'hemp in the bun', evidence of a major local industry. Salt beef and bacon hung from the roof, and sometimes a loaf or two of rye bread as well.[2] Very few peasant houses at this time had an oven. In John Heywood's play *Johan, Johan*, written c. 1530, when Tyb and her gossip Margery made a pie, Margery paid for the baking: that is, paid what the baker charged for putting it in his oven. Rye bread is no worse stale than fresh, and these Axholme folk, like most people in the northern half of England, had a batch baked from time to time.

Sometimes one can infer from the order in which household goods are listed[3] that although no rooms are named we are in a two-roomed house. What plan did it have, and how had the division between living and sleeping parts been made? In the east and central Midlands, the usual plan in later times had an entrance in the middle of one side, facing a chimney stack which divided the two rooms, whether it had one flue, for the hall only, or two, for hall and parlour. The earliest version of it, without a chimney, appears in the Bayeux Tapestry. In Lincolnshire it survived into the nineteenth century (see fig. 7 and pl. Ib). In stone regions the traditional position for the fireplace was against the gable end, where it would be easy to build out a hood over the hearth and a chimney of timber and earth or of stone. Whether the entrance was in the gable end, alongside the hearth (see fig. 16) or in the middle of the side, the fire would be well shielded from draughts. An open hearth in the centre and opposite the entrance, with living space to one side of it and sleeping space to the other, is inconceivable without a speer or screen between doorway and hearth. If, as seems almost certain, this way of arranging entrance and hearth was already ancient in the Tudor period, it must have been characteristic of cottages rather than farmhouses, for in the latter the entrance always led into the through passage.

[1] Joan Thirsk, 'The Isle of Axholme before Vermuyden', *Agr. Hist. R.*, I (1953), 19.
[2] E.g., 'larder at the Balks and one great cake' in the inventory of Isabel Traves of Haxey, L.R.O., 23/94. Later inventories often refer explicitly to loaves of rye bread.
[3] E.g., L.R.O., 23/91: Richard Wall of Epworth.

FIGURE 7. Three cottages from the Bayeux Tapestry (*c.* 1080), and a sketch of the vicarage at Fulstow, Lincolnshire, made in 1819 to accompany an application for a faculty to build a new one (Lincolnshire R. O., Faculties 12). All have in common a hipped roof and an entrance in the middle of one side (see p. 49).

There are no surviving houses, prior to the adoption of two-storey building in brick, to solve this problem for us, but the answer may one day be found in the excavation of a deserted village in the Midlands. If we assume that the central chimney stack was an innovation of later times, it is easy to imagine a functional division into house and parlour preceding a structural division; the rudimentary partitions in some Welsh cottages of the nineteenth century, made of cloth or wisps of straw, could without violence to history be carried back to peasant houses of the sixteenth century, and we might infer that painted cloths were used for that purpose. Later on, Welsh and Lakeland farmers who could afford a dresser or a tiered cupboard often placed it where it would serve as a division or built it into a partition; then the parlour screened off by furniture lies at the opposite end of the house from the entrance and the gable fireplace.

Once we cross the Humber, into the south-eastern part of Yorkshire, we find standards of housing little different from those of the rest of the lowland zone. Holderness was one of the richest parts of the county; the East Yorkshire Wolds, like the uplands of Lincolnshire, had their wealthy farmers. The name parlour for a ground floor sleeping-room had reached the northern counties, nearly a hundred years after its appearance in the south,[1] and the name cellar for the ground floor store-room, under a solar

[1] E.g. *Test. Ebor.*, II, 99, 164, 172.

or first floor sleeping-room, had by now gone out of fashion, though sometimes men used the newfangled name for a room without changing its use.[1]

By the middle of the sixteenth century the larger farmhouses were remarkable for the number of parlours. The house at Stillington in the Vale of York which had belonged to an Archdeacon of Richmond consisted in 1526 of a hall, three parlours, one towards the garden, another next the hall; a chapel and a kitchen, and four chambers: the great chamber, one over the chapel and two over parlours.[2] A house at Brotherton which in 1552 belonged to John Tyndall, esquire, had in all six parlours as well as five chambers with beds in them; apart from the parlours used by the family, there was one for the maidservants and another for the menservants about the house, while the farm-servants slept in the oxhouse and the stable with the animals they tended. The manor at Elmswell near Driffield, on the edge of the Wolds, whose economy in the seventeenth century was described in such detail by Henry Best,[3] was held at this time by William Lakon, and when he died in 1563 the house had three parlours, one of them for himself and another for servants, and three chambers, one of them called the Lord's Chamber. Although it seems commodious enough, the house was rebuilt by the Best family soon after they acquired the manor in the 1590's. These large Yorkshire farmhouses show at one and the same time the habit of medieval aristocracy and gentry of sleeping upstairs, and the newer practice, proper to the yeoman class, of building more ground floor parlours for greater comfort and privacy in an establishment with servants resident.

A picture begins to emerge of the difference between the south-eastern counties and the north at this time. In the south-east, advantages of soil and climate, together with a busy land market in which, over the centuries, the traditional peasant holding and even the manorial demesne had been broken up, had created a class of wealthy peasant farmer in such numbers that many of the houses they built are still to be seen. In the north such houses are much more rare, and there is a gulf between the few large houses which have survived or which are clearly exposed to view in inventories, and the houses, smaller, simpler in accommodation and more primitive in construction, belonging to the rank and file of the peasantry.

[1]John Cadeby, mason, of Beverley, who died in 1451, kept in his parlour poleaxes, scales, a barrel of salt salmon and a barrel of eels; a York tailor kept in it 'all that longs for making bowstrings'; *ibid.*, 97, 300.

[2]Letters and Papers of Henry VIII, 4, part I, 874–6.

[3]*Henry Best's Farming Book* (Surtees Soc., 1857). The inventory of William Lakon of Elmswell is in the York Probate Registry: Dean and Chapter Box L (1438–1687).

William Lakon's house at Elmswell has gone, but in Lancashire and Cheshire such houses as Bramhall Hall or Moreton Old Hall present a similar picture, much enlarged, of the few wealthy landowners who in the fifteenth and early sixteenth centuries planted fine and elaborate timber houses on a soil too poor to carry many of them, but rich enough in timber to do that well. There is an inventory of Bramhall Hall in 1480, which takes us through the screens passage, where the pewter was kept, either into the hall, or into the service wing, with its kitchen and half a dozen other rooms. Beyond the hall was a wing with a chapel and a parlour downstairs and chambers above. There were ten chambers in all, in the house itself, over the gatehouse and over the buildings round the courtyard at the rear.[1]

There are very few houses to bridge the gap between the style of living at Bramhall Hall and that of the bulk of the population. One of them is the house of Alice Aldbrough of Knaresborough, who died in 1565; she had a hall, a parlour and a kitchen, but the one chamber was used as a hayloft as well as a sleeping-room. In Yorkshire inventories of this time, household goods are in general worth less than ten per cent of the total. The wills made in Durham in the early years of Elizabeth are still medieval in flavour: the bequests consist of lands or rents, farm animals or cash—very rarely the items of house furniture that had appeared often in Suffolk wills a century earlier. Very few people can have possessed such minor comforts as Sir Thomas Aykrigge, a Richmond parson, who had painted cloths on his walls, carpets over the windows to keep out the draughts that pierced the shutters and curtains round his bed as an ultimate protection. A few houses had an 'iron chimney' or a 'range', a novelty which probably implies the use of coal for fuel. George Allenson of Cundall, five miles north of Boroughbridge, was a wealthy husbandman, but his household goods were worth in 1564 only £3 18s. out of a total of £69, made up for the rest of farmstock. His furniture can scarcely have occupied more than one room, and his house must have been a common type. What Stukeley wrote in 1725 of cottages in Longton, Northumberland, must have been true in 1525, and even in 1625, of many northern farmhouses: 'mean beyond imagination . . . without windows, only one storey. . . . We returned through Longton, a market town, whose streets are wholly composed of such kinds of structure: the piles of turf for firing are generally as large and handsome as the houses'.[2] The one link between these hovels and the houses of wealthy Yorkshire people of an earlier age is that household routine was confined to the ground floor. We shall see that

[1] H. Taylor, *Old Halls of Lancashire and Cheshire* (1884), pl. 33; G. J. Piccope, *Lancs. and Chesh. Wills and Inventories* (Chetham Soc.), I, 76–81.
[2] *Itinerarium Curiosum* (2nd edition) 1724, II, 57–8.

this is the most persistent feature of Yorkshire and the other northern counties, and it is gratifying to have traced it back to the middle of the sixteenth century.

How much this situation was due to poverty, and not merely to conservatism, is shown by inventories from Derbyshire in the middle of the century. The average value of men's goods was less than £12, an even lower figure than for the Isle of Axholme, and less than half that for Kent in 1570.[1] There were a few wealthy farmers on the margins of the county, men with mainly arable farms and also large flocks of sheep. Like William Lakon of Elmswell, they were so placed that they could exploit two types of soil, the upland sheep pastures and the heavier soils below. Church Farm, Alvaston, may have been built at this time by whoever leased the glebe land of the parish. It has only two bays, cruck trussed, and it is remarkable for the height of the crucks (about 25 feet) and for the fact that one bay, containing the hall, is much longer than the parlour bay. The house was altered in the next century and the original arrangements are difficult to trace.

In the villages of the central limestone plateau, life was even simpler. Some labourers and husbandmen were certainly living in houses of one room only. John Symons of Longford was rich by Derbyshire standards; his goods were worth £36, and they included three yokes of oxen and another of bullocks; he had land sown with winter and spring corn, and a flock of sheep. His only household goods consisted of his bedding, two little coffers, a trestle table, pewter worth 3s. 8d., a little posnet, a 'brooche' (spit), two pots and two pans. Thomas Spendlove of Wirksworth was perhaps a poor husbandman; he had two kine and a heifer, a mare and a little nag, eight ewes and six pigs; his goods amounted in all to £5 9s. 10d. In the house there were a little board or table, and five wooden doublers from which the family ate; cooking was done in two little pots and a little pan, over a hearth with a pair of pot racks, pot hooks and tongs. Four wooden vessels (looms and 'bowkes') held the milk he got from his two kine; he slept at night between two canvas sheets, kept warm by a blanket and two old coverlets. Such simplicity and lack of comfort cannot be explained by saying that these Peakland folk cheated the church by leaving out some of the household furniture from the inventory; the lists are remarkably consistent in content. There is rarely a good table and even more rarely a chair or even a stool; even if there was a mattress there was no bedstead. Harrison, writing in 1577 of Essex, quoted old people as saying that their fathers had 'lain full often upon straw pallets, or rough

[1]Inventories for Derbyshire, as part of the diocese of Lichfield, are in the Birmingham Probate Registry; those used here are from Box 5, 1547–55.

mats covered only with a sheet' and in Derbyshire those recollections are confirmed. The greatest comfort was to possess a featherbed.

In communities with such standards of life, it is useless to look for the difference between a farmhouse and a cottage; it does not emerge from inventories and it probably meant little to the villager except when he had to attend a meeting of the manor court and listen to legal distinctions. Thomas Stone of Wirksworth had a barn with corn and hay in it, a plough and a harrow, so his house would not have been called a cottage, but his only mark of superiority over Thomas Spendlove, his neighbour, was that he could put four pewter dishes on the table, instead of wooden doublers. We shall see that in 1600 it was already as difficult as it is today to distinguish precisely between a house and a cottage. What mattered was not the size of the dwelling, nor the standards of the occupants, but how much land went with either.

Part Two

THE FIRST PHASE OF THE HOUSING REVOLUTION: 1575-1615

Introduction

BY the middle years of Elizabeth's reign there were clear signs of new developments in domestic building and the fields of social activity from which they sprang. All over lowland England there were brand new country houses to be seen, showing to the world ranges of windows much larger than had been seen before in any building but a church, and finished with the ostentation of pillared porches, parapets of strapwork and ranges of chimneys. Many of these houses flaunted their novelty from a bare hill top site. At Hardwick, near the Nottinghamshire-Derbyshire border, two Elizabethan houses stand on a hill-top whose further slopes are now bared again by opencast coal working. Wollaton, on a hill five miles from Nottingham is surrounded by a park which could only be made as the last traces of the village of Sutton Passeys were demolished. What was going on at Wollaton between 1580 and 1588 must have been widely known over the east Midlands, for the stone came from Ancaster or thereabouts in Kesteven, and tenants of Sir Francis Willoughby were employed to carry building materials from a wide area.[1] Building at Burghley, near Stamford, must have been noticed by travellers on the north road, and the work at Theobalds or at Audley End must have been even more a matter of local remark when it culminated in the royal visit for which such houses were designed.[2]

Lord Compton had built much of Castle Ashby, Northants., before his death in 1589; Sir Thomas Tresham spent that decade in prison for his recusancy, passing the time in speculations on the virtues of the number three, which led him as soon as he was freed to build the Triangular Lodge at Rushden as well as Lyveden New Build. Christopher Hatton was building both at Kirby Hall, where he continued a project started in 1570, and at Holdenby, not far away. Sir Edmund Brudenell before his death in 1585 had largely rebuilt on a grand scale the medieval manor house he had inherited at Deene.[3] These Northamptonshire instances are enough to

[1] I am indebted to Mr. P. E. Rossell for allowing me to see his thesis on 'The Building of Wollaton Hall' based on the building accounts in the Middleton Collection, deposited in the University of Nottingham.
[2] Lawrence Stone, 'The Building of Hatfield House', in *Arch. J.* CXII (1955), 101.
[3] *Arch. J.*, CX (1953), 193, 200, 206–7.

show what was happening, all the way up the limestone belt, from Montacute in Somerset (begun *c.* 1590) northwards; building on a large scale, with stone from quarries reopened after a couple of generations in which the church had had little use for them. The impetus had reached as far north as Derbyshire and the West Riding—Aston Hall, Derby, was built in 1578 and Barlborough Hall, *c.* 1584.[1]

Tudor society was one in which men desired 'not to be rich but to be richer than other men'. Mill wrote those words of the Victorian age,[2] but they apply equally to the Elizabethan, especially if we add that men desired to appear to be richer than others. The difference between the two ages was that in the nineteenth century the opportunities were more rare but the levels of success were vastly higher. In Elizabethan times the mansion on a hill-top built by an Elizabethan *nouveau riche* was matched by the yeoman's new farmhouse and by the labourer's cottage planted at night on the common. By the nineteenth century the common had been enclosed, the freehold farmer was left to go bankrupt and the industrial worker had to accept what housing the mine and mill owner chose to erect for him. In the intervening centuries the concentration of property in fewer hands, and the denial of opportunity which inevitably followed, had begun to create the pattern of dependence, acceptance of a condition of submission and a lack of initiative which we now have to bewail and seek to remedy. In the upper levels of Tudor society violent social change produced just the effects it does now; the few families which passed in two or three generations from the stable environment of the yeoman farmer to a wealth whose proper place was the court of Charles II moved into circles marked by violence and lack of respect for the law. But in the sixteenth and seventeenth centuries such delinquency was confined to a section of the aristocracy and its hangers on. The lower ranks of rural society were still held together by a respect for craftsmanship and established ways of working in a close-knit community.

The gentry were building for show, so that they could entertain their equals or their betters, and visibly keep up the style to which they laid claim. Others could not afford such a luxury, and yet new building went on, in all ranks of rural society. No doubt some yeomen were as much moved as the gentry by a wish to maintain a proper port and impress their neighbours, as they began to build up larger estates in the years 1540–70;

[1]Heath Old Hall, near Wakefield, is very similar to Barlborough and dates from 1584; Swinsty Old Hall, Otley, is 1570. See L. Ambler, *The Old Halls and Manor Houses of Yorkshire*, 53–6.

[2]'Posthumous Essay on Social Freedom', Oxford and Cambridge Review, June 1907, quoted by R. M. Titmuss, *Essays on the Welfare State* (1958), 108.

IIIa. The hall of this 14th century house, known as Kite House or Kite Manor, was chambered over in 1574, the date of the dormer window. A fireplace and chimney to the hall, dated 1578, are necessarily part of the same improvement. The brickwork of the ground floor walls is 18th century.

IIIb. Whiteheads, Hatfield Broadoak, now demolished, was dated 1560, and so one of the earliest dated examples of the rectangular plan with an axial chimney stack. The stack itself had the zig-zag profile which became fashionable in the eastern counties. The fireplace to the third room was almost certainly a later addition. See p. 68.

IVa. A house at Norwell, Notts., which represents very well the scale on which a poor husbandman might build in the 16th and 17th centuries, although the house externally cannot be earlier than *c.* 1700. The steep gables carried high above the roof (now pantiled but formerly thatched) are typical of the region.

IVb. The house of Screveton, Notts., whose plan is shown in fig. 13. The porch, the brick infilling, the tile hanging of the gable and the nearer chimney are all modern.

more land changed hands then than had ever happened since the Norman Conquest, and the yeomen had their share of it. But as one passes down the ranks of society, the motive for new building changes into the plain necessity of satisfying the needs of a rapidly increasing population. The impact of this can be seen best in London. By 1588 the city had more than doubled in size since 1500 and was well on the way to 200,000 people; the mortality rate was so high that a very large immigration from the country is needed to explain the growth. In the next century London swelled to over half a million. In the early years of Elizabeth the total population of rural Leicestershire had still not regained the level reached before the Black Death, but by 1603 it passed it. The increase may have been more than fifty per cent in two generations,[1] and in every village must have led to adjustments of housing accommodation to meet the new pressure: whether building a new house, adding a new bedroom or two or converting a barn into cottages.

Contemporary records suggest that additional building, especially of cottages, reached its peak between 1580 and 1630. In the manor of Epworth, Lincs., which contained a number of villages, 100 additional cottages were built between those years.[2] In Rockingham Forest new cottages were built and stables, kilns and barns converted into cottages, and in Northamptonshire and Oxfordshire there is similar evidence of new building and subletting.[3] The vast majority of the Oxfordshire examples are cottages of one bay, measuring 10 × 12 feet. In Sussex widows and aged labourers sought leave to build cottages for themselves on the lord's waste.[4] A petition by a Suffolk ploughwright, supported by his fellow villagers, is printed in the Appendix (p. 271).

By 1589, this building activity was so obvious that parliament intervened. The preamble to the Cottages Act refers to 'the erecting of great numbers of cottages, which are daily more and more increased in many parts of this Realm'. The Act insisted that each cottage must have assigned to it at least four acres of land; that is, it was intended to check destitution, not the new building.[5]

The countryside was affected indirectly as well as directly; both town and country called for more foodstuffs. London bakers and brewers swarmed into the home counties in order that they might 'greedily buy

[1]V.C.H. *Leics.*, III, 138–40.
[2]Joan Thirsk, *English Peasant Farming*, 117.
[3]P.R.O., E. 176/2/5; S.P 14/120/35; C. 99/60. I am indebted to Mr. P. A. J. Pettit for these references.
[4]V.C.H. *Sussex*, II, 193.
[5]31 Eliz., *c.* 7. The Act did not apply to towns, or to housing for quarry and mine workers and others not connected with agriculture.

great quantities of grain', and the navigation of the Lea valley in Hertford-shire was improved for the purpose.[1] The demands of London were met by an 'important net increase in the output of English agriculture', without foreign imports or even diverting to the capital what hitherto had been exported,[2] and what was true of London applied to a lesser degree to provincial towns.[3]

By the middle years of Elizabeth's reign, elderly and middle-aged farmers had lived through a time of inflation which had raised prices far above the level of their childhood. As primary producers they gained most from that uncomfortable process, for the price of corn rose by considerably more than that of most other things. Their rents, if they had any to pay, were fixed, except when the expiry of a lease or the surrender of a copy-holder gave landlords a chance of levying an increase. Not that things were always easy for them. The Leicestershire village of Cotesbach found itself in 1603 saddled with a new landlord who intended to sell their holdings to tenants, to charge higher rents, or in the last resort to enclose the open fields.[4] Some of the cottages which 'daily more and more increased' were built by men evicted from such villages. At Owersby, Lincs., the Monson family was in the middle of a long and unspectacular process of building up an estate by leasing one manor in 1571, buying another in 1602, and in a century and a half buying out twenty-five small owners, of whom seventeen were yeomen.[5] While the unfortunate were reduced to moving into a town or building for themselves a cottage on the waste, the fortunate and enterprising had a chance to buy or lease more land, branch out into corn dealing or tanning, or to turn to industry.

It has been said that the desire for privacy in domestic life was an important factor in the development which the English house underwent at this time. Once we have the whole range of Elizabethan society in view from the manor house leased by a successful yeoman to the cottage built for himself by an evicted labourer, we can see how limited the notion of privacy must have been. It applied only to the farmer who was able to respond to the economic facts of his time: to acquire more land, grow

[1]The complaint came from rural middlemen of Hertfordshire in 1595. See G. B. G. Bull 'Elizabethan Maps of the Lower Lea Valley', *Geog. Journal*, CCXXIV, pt. 3 (1958), 375–8, for evidence of the Lea being deepened as far as Ware in 1571, in order to take corn and malt to London and coal, pig iron and salt to the country.

[2]F. J. Fisher, 'The Development of the London Food Market, 1540–1640', *Econ. H. R.*, 5 (1935), 51–2.

[3]See for example, a case of Lincolnshire corn going to York, in M. Campbell, *The English Yeoman*, 195–6.

[4]L. A. Parker in studies in *Leics. Agrarian History*, ed. W. G. Hoskins, 59–60.

[5]*Lincs. Historian*, Autumn 1953, 395–6.

more corn, keep more sheep, and to take on more farmworkers to do so. Somewhere in the middle ranks of village society was the divide between the large farmer with hinds living in, and the man who had no more help than his wife and family could give him. The latter might still have enough money in the new conditions to rebuild or enlarge his house, but let us not make the mistake of applying class concepts out of their proper context.

To a contemporary, greater comfort and convenience seemed the most important thing. When William Harrison, an Essex parson, was invited to write a description of England for what was intended to be 'a universal cosmography of the whole world', he thought it worth while to devote a whole chapter to 'the manner of Building and Furniture of our Houses'.[1] Like Leland before him and his contemporary Camden, he was willing to travel for his material; he writes of English society with a vigour born of personal experiences and convictions. He says that timber building was now giving way to stone, that chimneys and glazed windows were by now common, and that, within the houses, all classes enjoyed more comfort.

[1]The Cosmography was eventually reduced to a history of England, the *Chronicle of England* by Ralph Holinshead, in which Harrison's 'Description of England' was incorporated. It was published in 1577 and reprinted in 1587. Harrison's 'Description' is most accessible in the separate edition, ed. F. J. Furnivall, *Elizabethan England*, n.d. but *c.* 1900. Thomas Fuller inserted in this *Church History* a comment, under the year 1587, on the improved new houses which were then being built, but he was writing two generations later and presumably using Holinshead's second edition. See *Church History*, Book IX, Section VI, 67.

CHAPTER ONE

South-eastern England

L ET us now examine houses of the period from 1580 to 1610. It can be a much fuller picture than for earlier times, because there are more surviving houses, some of them dated by the men who built or enlarged them, and also there are more documents. Since the south-eastern counties still had the most advanced conditions, it is logical to start with Kent and proceed north and west. There will be gaps which must be left for others to fill.

In Kent in 1600 the average man left at his death goods worth upwards of £33, compared with about £27 in 1570.[1] It was not a spectacular increase, and the inflation in prices could account for it, but the Kentish inheritance system still put a brake on the accumulation of a large estate. There was a solid core in the villages of east Kent of men with goods worth between £30 and £60. Such men lived in houses of six or seven rooms, rather than the three to five rooms of a generation earlier. Richer men with goods worth from £80 up to £725 (more than twice any figure in 1570), frequently calling themselves yeomen even if they had started a grocer's shop or a wheelwright's business, lived in houses with nine rooms or more. One cannot generalize about the arrangement of these larger houses because many of them must have been old houses, much altered or enlarged, and so varying greatly in arrangement. No one had abandoned the habit of using a ground floor room as the principal bedroom,[2] but a few of them were referring to it as the parlour. The upper rooms are as likely to be called lofts as chambers; John Brett's house at Kinnardington had a loft over the hall containing a bedstead, wheat and malt, and a little chamber over the

[1]According to a sampling of inventories, Maidstone R.O., PRC 10/30, dated 1600–3.

[2]E.g. John Bennett of St. Lawrence, Thanet: 'the chamber where he did lie' and 'the loft over the chamber where he laid'.

hall with a bed alone. He also kept a close stool in the loft; they were still very rare among men of his class and he cannot have used it regularly. All these wealthier men had a kitchen, and usually a buttery, or drink buttery, and a milkhouse.

The homes of the middling men—either husbandmen or craftsmen no doubt—are easier to visualize. All had a hall, but only a few had a kitchen; that is, most of their wives were still cooking in the hall. Nearly all had a buttery, drinkhouse or milkchamber; whether craftsmen or not, many must have had land and cows to milk, and judging from the variety of wooden vessels—tubs, keelers, firkins, churns, pails, milkbowls—beer and milk were usually kept in the one room. Very few had a brewhouse. The other ground floor room was called indifferently parlour or bedchamber. All the houses had upper rooms, a few of them only one, some three, but the majority two. That is, they were houses with three ground floor units, some at least chambered over. Among the poorer folk two out of ten lived in houses of only two rooms—halls and either parlour or chamber. As among wealthier men, ground floor rooms are habitually called chambers— 'chamber on the ground floor', 'milkchamber', 'the chamber next the hall'. Very few had a kitchen or a milkhouse; most of them must have been labourers or poor craftsmen. One of them was a shearman— Jeremiah Austen of Smarden, whose goods were worth £18 10s. 2d.; his house had a hall, a buttery, two chambers with beds in them, presumably on the ground floor, and 'the working loft called his shop'. There he prepared for the clothier the fleeces that came his way; their bulk made the loft over the hall a convenient place for storage. Only one inventory specifically refers to new improvements: Richard Bullock of Smarden, whose house already had chambers over the hall and the buttery, had made a 'new loft', perhaps over his kitchen.

Very few Kentish houses can have retained, as late as 1600, a hall open to the roof. Sometimes the owner has himself provided the evidence. Kite House, Monk's Horton, is a medieval house with a fine dormer gable over the hall dated 1574 (see pl. IIIa), and in the hall a fireplace dated 1578.[1] Sometimes the improvements almost conceal the medieval origin of the house. Hunt Street Farm, Crundale, has a central hall bay protruding beyond the line of the jettied wings, and carried up to a lofty chamber over the hall and an attic over that with a large gable; this was done by William and Mary Chapman in 1595, according to the inscription 'WC 1595 MC' on the porch. The fine brick stack must go with these alterations, and the insertion of a framed staircase, to replace the ladders which had given access to the wings. In Surrey the same process of modernization can be

[1]A. Oswald, *Country Houses of Kent*, 26–7, and illustrations.

observed. Great Tangley Manor, near Guildford, is a medieval hall house with recessed front of the Wealden type; in 1589 it had the hall front built out to the lines of the wings and chambers over the hall; gables were added over hall and cross passage to give more headroom in the chambers. The gables of different size still reveal that the medieval hall consisted of two unequal bays.[1]

In west Sussex standards of wealth were very similar to those of east Kent,[2] but the overall similarity conceals variations due to different soils and methods of farming. Men living in the coastal parishes, between the Downs and the sea, fall into a compact group of middling wealth, contrasting with the much greater diversity—ranging from wealthy yeomen to poor craftsmen and labourers—of the Weald parishes. The wealthiest yeomen are to be found in the Weald, along with a weaver from Horsham and a wood turner from Petworth who were nearer the bottom of the scale than the middle.

These social contrasts have left their mark on the villages to this day. The better soil of the coastal belt sustained a larger number of middling peasants, comparably to those of the Lincolnshire fen and marsh, but such men have never, in any region, left behind them houses of quality and size. Hence the coastal villages today are poor in vernacular building;[3] they had no great tradition in timber construction, and by the early seventeenth century were using inferior materials, such as flint and cobbles, if they had not always done so. In Weald parishes such as Fernhurst, the few wealthy yeomen, glovers and ironmasters have left behind them good stone houses of this age.[4] The contrast we observe today between the houses in woodland and open country was due less to differences in local building materials than to distinct forms of economy and social structure.

Thomas Botting's house at West Grinstead will serve as an example of the larger type. He was only a husbandman, but his goods were worth £81 (nearly three times the average) and few wealthier yeomen had larger farmhouses. His home consisted of a hall with a chamber over it, a ground floor chamber in which he slept, and four service-rooms, kitchen, buttery, milkhouse and cheesehouse. The large number of service-rooms is already a mark of the richer farmer; convenience for work is at least as important

---

[1]C. Baily, 'Remarks on Timber Houses' in *Surrey Arch. Coll.*, 4 (1869), 278 et seq. Other similar changes have been observed at Houghton Place (*ibid.* 63 (1923), 203) and Bell's Farm, Stangham (*ibid.*, 88 (1948), 15).

[2]To judge from a sample of inventories dated 1597–1615 from the archdeaconry of west Sussex; Chichester R.O., Ep. I/29.

[3]See the architectural descriptions in V.C.H. *Sussex*, IV (The Rape of Chichester), *passim*.

[4]E.g. *op. cit.*, 55 (North Park Farm), 82 (farmhouse S.S.W. of Stedham church).

as comfort for leisure. Whatever the rooms were called, they provided space for cooking, brewing, cheese- and butter-making and for the things used for those purposes. John Ayling of Stedham had a kitchen and a cellar. The last must have been a ground floor room, for it held a furnace of brass (for brewing), a brewing vat, two keelers, a boulting hutch, a cheese press, a salting trough, a kneading trough, a churn, two butter tubs, five little 'kevers' (brewing tubs) and some barrels. It is unlikely that the family and servants went up and down a flight of steps scores of times a day about their household jobs. The vicarage at Wisborough Green when Philip Somer died in 1584 had two service-rooms, a kitchen with a very large collection of pewter and another chamber used as a brewhouse; it differed from the farmhouses of his yeomen neighbours in having three chambers furnished as bedrooms, one of which he used as a study. One cannot tell how many of them were first floor rooms, for Sussex folk used the word chamber so widely, not only for a ground floor sleeping-room but also for a buttery ('the Back Chamber next the Hall') or a brewhouse.

The rooms upstairs are often called lofts (either *loate, lofe, loath* or *lought* in Sussex dialect). A loft is a space in the roof, and in the coastal villages, where there were fewer men rich enough to have a two-storeyed house, contriving some storage room in a single-storey house was the most anyone wished to do. In the larger houses most of the upper rooms had beds in them, but usually at least one was used for seed, food, or the articles rarely used. Robert Mills of Westbourne had a loft with fruit, butter, cheese and linen yarn, and another over the kitchen for hops. A Midhurst weaver stored wool in his loft; a husbandman of Kirdford filled it with wheat and cheeses. Usually a house had either lofts *or* chambers, not both, but Henry Miles of Pulborough had chambers over the main rooms of his house, and a loft over the kitchen containing yarn, hemp and wool. His kitchen must have been a single-storey addition to the house; we shall meet that arrangement frequently. An Arundel glover had a house of two and a half storeys, with a 'coplofte' over the chambers.

The difference between the two regions of West Sussex, and the arrangement of smaller houses, can be seen from the following analysis of twenty inventories:

WEST SUSSEX HOUSES *c.* 1600

Rooms	Coast	Weald
Hall and chamber only	4	—
Hall, chamber and kitchen	1	2
Parlour instead of, or as well as, ground floor sleeping chamber	2	5
Hall, chamber and one loft	—	1
Hall, chamber, kitchen and one loft . . .	2	3

The superiority of Wealden standards emerges from the commoner presence of a parlour, as well as the greater accommodation. Conservatism, as well as poverty, might keep men in smaller houses than their neighbours. A yeoman of Angmering, with goods worth £109, lived in a two-roomed house; he was content to sit on a stool by the fireside, and to sleep with the smell of apples and cheese in his chamber.

It was unusual not to have a ground floor sleeping-room, except in the houses of craftsmen who used it for a workshop, as did two weavers of Midhurst and Horsham. We shall find that in most regions at this time the craftsman engaged in domestic industry usually had his loom, his lasts and leather or whatever it might be, in a ground floor room of his house, rather than upstairs or in an outside workshop.

CHAPTER TWO

East Anglia

WHEN we move north of the Thames, it is clear enough, even without the evidence of inventories,[1] that standards in Essex resembled those of Kent. For the richer yeomen, improving a medieval house, rather than complete rebuilding, was the order of the day: the insertion of a chamber over a medieval open hall with its usual concomitants, the insertion of a hall fireplace and brick chimney stack, putting in a staircase, the raising of a gable or two over the hall to light the new chambers. The changes made in the sixteenth century in Stanton's Farm, Black Notley, illustrate admirably how a fourteenth century aisled hall could be adjusted to modern needs. A chimney stack was built in the west bay of the two bay hall, and the upper floor, hitherto confined to the storeyed wing at the west end, was extended over the hall. At the same time a new cross wing was built at the east end. When the house was first visited and photographed, in about 1920, the chamber over the hall was still being used, as it had been since it was made, for the storage of farm equipment not in regular use[2] (see pl. A IIb). The Tiptofts Manor, Wimbish (above, p. 21) is now an even more unusual sight, because a very large fireplace was inserted in the hall without its being chambered over, reducing the hall to a quite small room of towering height.

The position chosen for the new brick stack must have depended in part on the size of the hall. That room was now less important; it was no longer used for cooking in houses as large as these, and it was also being replaced as a sitting-room by the parlour. The cross passage was no longer as

[1]The earliest Essex inventories are those for the peculiar of Writtle, beginning in 1635, and printed in F. W. Steer, *Farm and Cottage Inventories of Mid-Essex* (1950).

[2]It has now been tidied up, but the sieves, baskets and the like on the floor and hanging from beams correspond perfectly to many an inventory of this time.

important as the convenient siting of fireplace and staircase. In some houses the passage is now blocked by the inserted fireplace, or the new staircase is built in it, for now that there is a chamber over the hall the storeyed wings are no longer sundered by the open hall, and the one staircase can serve all the upper floor.

There was not room for both a fireplace and a framed staircase at one end of the hall, so that if a staircase was built into the passage, the fireplace had to go elsewhere. Framed staircases were still rare in farmhouses prior to 1625 or so, and the problem of finding room for both fireplace and stairs was usually solved in less ambitious fashion, by the traditional newel stair, turning through two right angles between ground and first floor. The striking innovation—and it seems to be an innovation of the south eastern counties in the reign of Elizabeth—lay in combining the two: a simple, economical and efficient solution. The chimney stack built on the line of an outside wall, the usual position ever since the twelfth century, gives way to a stack in the middle of the house. This arrangement will henceforth be described as an axial stack (cf. fig. 9). It was not difficult to insert a brick stack in the centre of the house, using this prefabricated material of uniform size and weight, easy to handle. It was convenient in that the newel staircase could be placed alongside it, supported in part by it. It was efficient in that radiant warmth from the stack was not lost on the outside air, and two rooms could be heated by back to back fireplaces, sharing one stack.

One of the earliest dated examples of this new design, which spread throughout the Midlands and as far as the Welsh border by the eighteenth century, was a house named Whiteheads at Hatfield Broadoak.[1] The plan was a simple rectangle of three rooms; that at one end had no original fireplace and was a service-room; on the line between the other two rose a stack with the initials TE and the date 1560 (see pl. IIIb); it served the hall and parlour, and possibly one of the chambers over, for there were three chimneys. No stack on a side wall or a gable end could hold more than two flues. Whiteheads is a timber-framed house, with close set studs, now plastered over, but it is built on a brick plinth; that and the brick stack, in a novel position, mark it out as the product of new conditions and some new thinking.

There must be a transitional type of house, combining the traditional cross passage and an axial chimney stack at the upper end of the hall. It has not been observed in Essex, but a house at Marcham, Berks., known as the Priory, illustrates it perfectly.[2] It is stone built, of two full storeys, with

[1] R.C.H.M. *Essex*, II, 120 (11). The house has been demolished.
[2] See E. M. Jope in *Berks. Arch. J.*, 57 (1959), 1–9.

three rooms on the ground floor. At the lower end of the central hall is a passage with an unheated service-room beyond it. At the upper end of the hall the fireplace shares an axial stack with the parlour, and the stairs go up to one side of the stack, on the parlour side. In addition to this combination of through passage and axial stack, there are three entrances, the two into the passage and a third into a lobby in front of the stack. The house thus has all the features of the old and new designs, and it was built c. 1550–60.

Massive brick axial stacks, rising square above the ridge of the roof, are to be seen widely in the south-east. South of the Thames they are usually finished with over-sailing courses, while in East Anglia the local builder preferred to finish with diagonal chimneys, or with a zig-zag form in which there are more angles than flues.[1]

The farmhouse at Cratley, Suffolk, known as Wydard's (see fig. 8), which was restored in 1940, after being condemned by the local authority as 'unfit for human habitation' (that fatal phrase which has lost us so many old houses) shows the details of this type of house.[2] It was originally built in the early Tudor period, and enlarged later to its present plan, perhaps after 1600, to judge from the new windows with mullions and transoms. The alterations, which included adding the parlour and building a new chimney stack alongside the old, before demolishing the latter, were all of a kind that could be done while the house was lived in. How else could they be done, in most cases? Adding and improving were much commoner than complete rebuilding, except among yeomen and gentry acquiring a new property; the inconveniences of rooms full of dirt and stacked with new timber, doing without a fire, holes in a ceiling and a roof covered with sacking to keep out the rain, were as familiar then as they are now to anyone who has 'had the builders in'.

Wydard's is a timber-framed house, its panels filled with daub laid on rods or splints fixed in holes or grooves in the horizontal and vertical members and tied together with hempen string. The house has brick footings throughout, and the axial stack has four flues for hall and parlour and the chambers over each; three of the original fireplaces were found. The hall fireplace has a bread oven at one side, and at the other the winding staircase. The main entrance is in the usual position for medieval houses with a cross passage, and that is the only respect in which the plan departs from the new form; one would expect it to be opposite the staircase. The

---

[1] E.g. *Essex* II, pl. 128, houses at Felstead, High Easter and Black Notley.
[2] See A. Welford, 'Restoration of a XVI Century Farm House in Suffolk,' *Proc. Suffolk Inst. of Arch.*, 24 (1940–8), 1–19. I am indebted to Mr. Norman Smedley of the Ipswich Museum for information about the house, and to Mrs. Welford for permission to reproduce drawings of it.

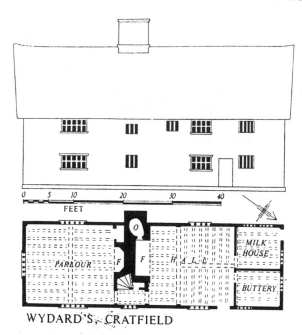

WYDARD'S, CRATFIELD

FIGURE 8. Ground plan and elevation of Wydard's, Cratfield, Suffolk, after enlargement in Elizabethan times, when the axial stack was inserted and the parlour built. The old-fashioned arrangement of the service end survived, with an entrance at the lower end of the hall and two service rooms. (After A. Welford in *Suffolk Inst. of Arch. Proc.* 24 (1940–48), 1–19.)

service wing consists of two unheated rooms, and there is no kitchen. The plan is in fact medieval, except for the position of the chimney stack, and that it has two storeys throughout. The older windows had diamond-shaped oak mullions, with slender oak bars between, both set in the frame of the house and not in a distinct window frame. The oak bars are an old device, to keep out intruders, but they were equally convenient for fixing the glazed windows which were now coming into fashion. A will of 1569 from Bildeston, Suffolk, lays down that the benches in the parlour and hall, the portal and screen, the glass lattices and boards belonging to the hall, and the two stalls in the buttery should remain in the house.[1] That must be the will of a man who had himself put in those items, including a chamber over the hall and glass windows, and so regarded them as his goods and chattels and not as a matter of course as part of the structure.

In the absence of documents we can only discuss storeyed houses; no surviving two-roomed houses have been discovered. The simplest Essex type is that with two rooms on the ground floor, both chambered over, the

[1]*Bury Wills and Inventories*, 155.

chambers reached by a winding stair alongside the axial stack and usually between the stack and the entrance; at the farther side the stack goes through, perhaps sometimes because of its accompanying bread oven, to the rear wall of the house (see fig. 9, type plans, I). Given an axial stack, this arrangement is not inevitable; in Cambridgeshire, Huntingdon and the east Midlands the stack usually stands free, with the stair on the farther side of the stack from the entrance and the door to the parlour. Many of the numerous examples no doubt belong to the later years of the seventeenth century, but the type must have emerged in Tudor times. The rarer examples, in which the stack is lateral, not axial, are presumably among the earliest.

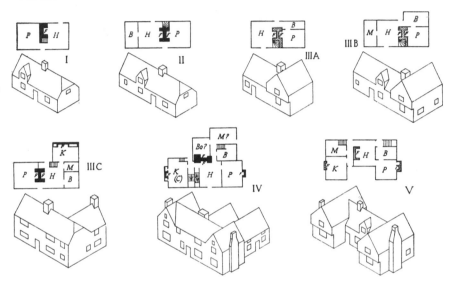

FIGURE 9. Types of Essex house plan in the sixteenth and seventeenth centuries (based on R. C. H. M. *Essex*). Types I, II, III C and IV are new buildings, but IIIA, IIIB and V are medieval houses improved by the insertion of brick chimney stacks and a chamber over the hall. All are of timber construction.

The next type, as one climbs the social scale, has the same form and arrangement, but has, and to judge from the window openings has always had, a third unheated room at the opposite end from the parlour (see plate 3b, Whiteheads, Hatfield Broadoak). It is somewhat less common than the first, but forms a substantial part of the range to be seen throughout Essex and East Anglia. In the smaller versions of the plan the roof is commonly hipped at one or both ends, or half hipped; whatever the structural qualities and history of that type of roof it probably indicates that the chambers over are not important. In a cottage near Priory Farm,

Ickleton, Cambs., the room behind the hall chimney stack has no fireplace and the room over it, which has an unglazed shuttered window, is still reached only through a trapdoor. This is a good example of the kind of storage chamber to which inventories constantly refer.

Essex inventories of a somewhat later date show that the commonest rooms, after hall, parlour, chamber and kitchen, were milkhouse and buttery;[1] in Suffolk these rooms would have been called buttery and back-house. A version of this plan in a traditional manner is Allen's Farm, Elmstead,[2] dated 1584, of two storeys with chamber windows tucked under the eaves, the upper floor being jettied along the front. There is no hint that the roof space could be used at all. The difference between this and Aylmer's, Sheering, perhaps about a generation later in date, is that Aylmer's has the same arrangement of ground floor rooms,[3] but has two storeys and attics throughout, and there is no jetty to the first floor. Instead, the front has three protruding bays, the central one somewhat wider than the others, each carried up to a dormer window, and the outer gables are jettied at eaves level. The symmetrical arrangement of the façade, apart from the doorway, shows the country builder still using traditional materials and traditional devices such as the jetty, but disposing the elements of the design in the orderly manner dictated by Renaissance fashions. The plan was one which suited a wide range of customers, judging from its wide distribution, and was probably most popular in the first half of the seventeenth century, though still used in the second half. Its social range is shown by the variation between one and a half storeys, and two full storeys with attics or garrets. Gables on the façade show that good headroom in the garrets was required in the larger versions, or that part of the roof space was used for the chambers by ceiling them over at the level of collar purlins.[4]

In Norfolk and Suffolk this garret space was known as the 'vance roof', or the 'vance house'. The word only occurs in those two counties, and it is in use as early as 1587.[5]

Aylmer's is placed above the level of the husbandman's house not only by the three storeys and the architectural treatment of the elevation, but also

---

[1]F. W. Steer, *op. cit.*, 8–9.

[2]R.C.H.M. *Essex*, III, 96 (4).

[3]Or had, prior to later additions; *Essex*, II, 211, and pl. 44.

[4]E.g. Bailey's, Mashbury, has a central gable jettied out, without a window in it, *Essex*, II, p. 111. A house at Marwood Green, Hatfield Broadoak, has three gables; the outer ones have no window openings, while the centre one has a small opening so high as to suggest that the chamber ceiling is above eaves level.

[5]The date of the earliest Norwich Consistory Court inventories; see bundles 1587, 24; 1589, 34. See also Glossary.

by the fact that it has a wing at the rear housing a framed staircase. Essex has many such examples of this improvement on the simple rectangular plan, and a staircase wing, always at the rear, becomes a common feature, from this time onwards, in houses of middling size and upwards. Anyone who wanted a framed staircase, and had not inherited a medieval hall with plenty of room to spare, or a cross passage no longer required, was driven to building a special wing at the back of the house—until, after a century or so with this predicament, builders fell back on the unhappy alternative of putting fireplaces at the gable ends, leaving the centre of the house clear for small hall and staircase. Neither the dog-leg design of staircase, rising first in one direction and then reversing at a half landing, nor the well type, rising round three sides of an open well, could be got into less than about three times the space taken by a winding stair.

The majority of Essex farmhouses older than 1640 and larger than Aylmer's are in fact medieval houses, at the most modified or enlarged at this time. There is no great rebuilding in Essex, at least of yeomen's houses, though there is a great deal of improving, so that many houses bear a final stamp of the years 1590–1640. Of the numerous houses with a hall and one chambered cross wing, the majority are no doubt earlier than 1550, but some are new. The current type can be defined in terms of a house at Gore Pit in Feering:[1] hall with chamber over lighted by a dormer window; stack at the junction of hall and cross wing, with the entrance opposite the stack; a gabled wing containing the parlour at the front and another room at the rear which has a fireplace, whether original or not. The houses with hall and two cross wings (the medieval half H plan) are of two types: those in which a lateral stack was added to the hall, usually earlier in the sixteenth century, and those which were built new, later in the sixteenth century, with an axial stack. Badcock's Farm, Easthorpe, a rebuilding in 1585 on a moated site, must be one of the latest Essex examples of this plan, and it has a hall between two cross wings; the hall is chambered over with a jetty and the stack at the lower end of the hall blocks what would earlier have been the cross passage.[2]

There is more evidence in Huntingdonshire than in Essex of new building at this time; it is very apparent in Godmanchester, where there are several new dated houses of a rural type. They are of timber in the traditional manner, with close studding and the timbers exposed; several have the gable of the cross wing jettied out at attic level; stacks are brick with diagonal chimneys. They are all large, with at least three heated rooms, and they illustrate the transitional ideas of the time, particularly the com-

[1]*Essex*, III, 99 (27).
[2]*Essex*, III, 92.

bination of axial stack with cross passage. In every case the rear wing has service-rooms; it was the need for dairy or milkhouse, backhouse, brew-house, bakehouse or the like which provoked the departure from a simple rectangular plan. The L plan must derive at this time from the medieval hall and one cross wing; the modification, in that the cross wing protrudes at the rear but not at the front, is a significant one. It is easy to understand in Godmanchester, a village whose more important houses face the main road to the north. An even more important factor is easier access, from outside, to the service-rooms in the wing; this change is thus part of the process which, in the more advanced lowland zone in particular, reduced traffic through the house, and especially through the hall.

The casual observer can see that Cambridgeshire buildings fit broadly into the known picture. Rectory Farm, Whaddon, for instance, is a good example of a medieval hall house modernized at this time. The walls of the hall were rebuilt to bring it in line with the cross wings; two large brick stacks were built at the junction of the hall and cross wings, and the new chamber over the hall given two dormer windows. The whole makes a house of regular and symmetrical form, in line with new notions.

A map of regional variations in farmhouses and cottages, once we have enough knowledge to compile it, will probably show that Essex has affinities with Kent, just as Somerset and Devon characteristics have their parallels in South Wales. Certainly Suffolk inventories of the late Eliza-bethan years[1] provoke comparison with the east Midlands rather than with counties south of the Thames, as well as having their own individuality. First, ground floor rooms are very rarely called chambers. Upper rooms are most often chambers, occasionally lofts, sometimes *sollers*. Suffolk inventories usually speak of things 'on the chamber' 'on the soller', or 'over the soller'. The solar is, as its contents go, exactly the equivalent of the Sussex loft; it is a store for corn, cheese, unwanted lumber, whether it is over the hall or over the buttery. Its inferiority is shown by the inventory of William Brecket of Freston, who had a hall, and a parlour, with a chamber over the parlour, a solar by it, and a solar over the hall containing rye, cheese, locks of wool, etc. The room over the hall, which is only a secondary part of the house, is often a store-room.

The Suffolk inventories for 1582–4 give a median value of all but £29—

---

[1]Inventories for the archdeaconry of Suffolk, which comprised east Suffolk, as distinct from the archdeaconry of Sudbury, covering west Suffolk, are at Ipswich, where there is a joint scheme for city and county archives. There are bundles of inventories for 1582–4, 1590, 1685 and a continuous series from 1705 onwards. They are separated from the wills, but the latter are also available, and can be used, for instance, to find the occupation of a testator. The inventories for the archdeaconry of Sudbury are in the Record Office at Bury St. Edmunds.

the same as the figure for Kent in 1570—but this is only part of the picture. The habit of making a will extended lower down the ranks of Suffolk society, but there were still real differences: a large middling peasantry in Suffolk, of men whose goods were worth from £40 to £80, as well as a larger group of poorer men, including a labourer, a cloth-worker, a shoe-maker, a sailor and a fisherman. Then with less than £25 come husband-men, weavers, a thatcher and a mariner. In the middle between £40 and £80 come more husbandmen, yeomen, a portman and a tailor. Above them comes an occasional husbandman, and over all in wealth, more yeomen and a fishmerchant of Dunwich. Fishermen, labourers and some weavers are among the poorest, and as poor as any peasants we shall meet.

Some folk had two-roomed houses—a widow at Debenham, a couple of fishermen on the coast, a butcher at Orford, each with hall and parlour-chamber, and a shoemaker at Dunwich living in one room and working in the second. More had three-roomed houses, of hall, parlour-chamber and a solar or upper chamber. They were the homes of a labourer, a cloth-worker, a sailor and a husbandman, and of a weaver at Bungay with a hall, an upper chamber furnished as a bedroom, and the 'house under the chamber' containing his 'loom, the warping bars and the travis thereto'. Wealthier weavers, such as Edward Frewerde of Needham Market, with two pairs of broad looms and two of narrow looms, had a shop, no doubt separate from the house. Those living by the sea, whether they called themselves fishermen, sailors or mariners, often had a towhouse,[1] where ropes (or tows), fishing nets and similar gear were kept. The towhouse of an Orford portman contained among other things barrels of tar and pitch, with pitch and tar kettles, a barrel of herring, spits for herring and sparling, a tow comb, a twisting wheel and a 'waine to braid on'. Inventories of craftsmen are not always informative, unless the neighbours were familiar with the tools and specialized equipment they used, but a patient searcher could provide a complete picture of how such men made a living.

Among people with goods worth more than £20, the next most common room is the backhouse. Of these Suffolk houses, less than a quarter had a kitchen, and two fifths had a backhouse. The term is already on the way out, for a few years later the kitchen becomes more common than the back-house. We shall meet the term again as we move north, in the coastal villages of Lincolnshire; in Yorkshire it seems to be the same as the netherhouse. What is its purpose and origin? It is a service-room, but it is

[1]See particularly Norwich Consistory inventories 1589, 28, and Archdeaconry of Suffolk, 1582–4, 59, 61, 79, 139. Inventories of the Norwich Consistory Court are in the Reynolds Chapel, of the Bishop's Palace there. The relevant wills are in the Norwich Probate Registry.

the only room in the house which lacks a name indicating a specific function. Norfolk and Suffolk, still using the names solar and backhouse, must have had a conservative peasantry, and the suspicion is confirmed when we find a Norfolk inventory with the hall called a 'firehouse'. Elsewhere we shall meet that term only in the highland zone. It may be that we have uncovered an older historical stratum, in which firehouse and backhouse were names for the living and sleeping part of the house at one end of the building, and the storage half at the other end. It is tempting to think that the backhouse or netherhouse had once been used for animals, and that, once the livestock had been turned out, no new name was immediately given to the room because no distinct and pressing purpose for it had yet developed.

This East Anglian house, with its backhouse as the only service-room, is exactly comparable with houses in Monmouthshire in which Fox found it impossible to decide whether the third room beyond the cross passage was originally a cow house or not.[1] We shall find the same type in Westmorland and Cumberland. The argument that the backhouse may once have been a cow house is forced on us by the fact that it is found in the same regions (except for East Anglia) as the long house with dwelling and animals under the same roof. The variants are: long house with access to cattle from cross passage (Dartmoor, Wales, Lake District); long house with separate access to animals (Yorkshire, Derbyshire), and house with backhouse (East Anglia, Lincolnshire, Yorkshire and the northern counties). That they are connected is plain, though for the time being lack of evidence prevents us from defining the relationship.

The backhouse usually held the boulting hutch, the mixing tray, moulding board, pele and rake used in baking, and it looks as though baking bread at home was at this time more common among these arable farmers, growing plenty of wheat, than in regions where pastoral farming was the main concern. The backhouse also held malting and brewing vessels, and the salting trough. Suffolk made a hard cheese, which required a press and vats and a board, as well as milk bowls. Cheesehouses were common, and the cheeses were stored in chambers over them, or over the hall or the dairy. Some inventories group together dairy and backhouse, and then the dairy must have been taken out of the third unit in the plan.

The absence of a kitchen at Wydard's is no matter of surprise, for Suffolk and Essex are part of a region where the kitchen was still regarded as not part of the house. This stemmed from the medieval tradition of the detached kitchen, which was still alive. In Essex, some parsonage houses had detached kitchens,[2] and there are other examples in the Midlands. As

[1] E.g., *Mon. Ho.*, III, 54.
[2] E.g., those of all the three Lavers; V.C.H. *Essex*, III, 93, 101, 107.

for the other end of the house, a few Suffolk houses had two parlours; both contained beds, but one of them is sometimes called the bedchamber, and this serves to distinguish East Anglia and the Midlands from the counties south of London, where the parlour bay was less often divided into two rooms, because the upper rooms were more used for sleeping.

To those familar with local authority housing estates of the past thirty years the 'non-parlour' house is nothing new. It was not invented by modern housing legislation, but represents an ancient strand in the tradition of peasant or working-class housing. We meet it first in Norfolk; a husbandman of Stalham, called John Callowe, died in 1603[1] in a house which was quite commodious, and yet it had no parlour. That is why his neighbours called the one living and sleeping room the firehouse. It was reasonably well furnished, with a post bedstead, complete with a tester of stained cloth, a featherbed, a bolster and a feather pillow. There was another bedstead, a trundle bedstead, also with an old featherbed and bolster; it would be low enough to go under the post bedstead in the day-time, to save room. The rest of the furniture consisted of a table with fifteen pieces of pewter to grace it at mealtimes, a chair for the head of the family and stools and forms for the rest; two coffers and a cupboard. The other ground floor room was called the dairy, and had a cheese press, querns for malt or mustard, four firkins on a stand for ale, milk bowls, trenchers and the like. It also had andirons, spits, kettles and pans, and none of those things are mentioned in the firehouse, so Callowe's wife must have been cooking in the dairy. The house is not so primitive after all, but the family had chosen to make living more convenient by cooking in the dairy rather than by making a separate sleeping-room. There was a chamber upstairs (the phrase is 'upon the chamber') containing an old bedstead, one chest, a coffer, some hemp and other old tubs. Callowe was wealthy enough to have a barn with corn in it, some corn standing on the ground (on November 17th), three milking cows, five other cattle and six pigs, four geese and three hens. This picture is not of an unusual state of affairs, for Norfolk people continue for another century after this to speak of the firehouse when meaning a room used both for living and sleeping. Thomas Callowe's house helps to bridge the gap between medieval one-roomed cottages and improved cottages of later times.

[1]Norwich Consistory, 1603, 197. His goods amounted to £3 10s.

CHAPTER THREE

The Midlands

a. Lincolnshire and Nottinghamshire

THE region between the Wash, the Humber and the eastern slopes of the Pennines is today, on a superficial view, poor in houses of the sixteenth and seventeenth centuries, except for the stone belt of Lincolnshire and the timber houses of its western margin. It would be unhistorical to dismiss two counties for failing to yield a story to visual examination, and not to look for the reasons. One of them is certainly the relative poverty of Lincolnshire in timber. That is reflected in the peasant habit of burning cow dung for fuel, or in a scheme launched in James I's reign for reopening the Fossdyke, the Roman canal from the Trent to Lincoln, to bring Nottinghamshire coal into the county more cheaply. Another reason is the social structure of the region, or part of it. Where land was good enough for small farmers to resist being swallowed up by larger, small houses continued to be built. Some of the smallest houses in England, of nineteenth or even twentieth century date, can be seen in the Lincolnshire Fens. In the third place, farming is an industry as well as a way of life; its farmhouses, barns and dovecotes can tell us when, where and how it flourished just as surely as can a Lancashire cotton mill of the Victorian age or the new factories on the Great West Road making razor blades and toothpaste.

These factors combined explain why so many east Midland villages look as if they belonged entirely to the century 1770 to 1870. The evidence of an earlier revolution in housing standards disappeared in a later one. Happily we are not forced to write off the earlier changes as lost to history, for the buildings which time has taken away are preserved in a greater wealth of documentary material than any other part of England possesses. From them we can see how big (or how small) rural houses were, what materials they were built of, even to the construction of floors upstairs and down, and how they were furnished.

First let us take an overall view of the type and size of house at the end of Elizabeth's reign.[1] Among the poorest folk, the single-roomed house, which had persisted in substantial numbers, began to be abandoned in favour of a house with structural division into house and parlour. It appeared for the first time, among those with goods worth less than £10, by the first decade of the seventeenth century, and it was not confined to the poor; indeed it was by then one of the commonest types of house. Houses with three rooms were as common as those with two, and of two designs: those with a third ground floor room for services, and those with house and parlour but with a chamber over hall or parlour. The latter was more common, if Fenland houses with a loft instead of a chamber are included. Notice that the southern term loft is found as far north as the villages between Spalding and King's Lynn; the dialect of that part of the Fens has distinct affinities with East Anglia. Where there was a service-room, it was as likely to be called a dairy or a milk-house as a kitchen, and kitchens sometimes lacked a fireplace and cooking utensils. No doubt these houses were of the East Anglian plan, with hall and parlour sharing an axial chimney stack, and a third unheated room.

About a fifth of the houses had two chambers, usually over hall and parlour; the use of chambers, for storage and sleeping, was well established in all but the smallest houses, but Lincolnshire people, while they had taken over from the south this particular type of building, still shared with Yorkshire a reluctance to sleep upstairs. More than a third of the houses had two parlours, and some three. Very often they are the outer and inner parlour, upper and nether, or great and little; clearly the parlour unit is subdivided into two rooms, one reached through the other. Sometimes they are servants' rooms—the men's parlour or the maids' parlour. There is no sign that it was thought better for servants to sleep upstairs, or for the family to move up and leave the servants below. To judge from surviving houses of a century later, the parlour commonly had no fireplace; it was a bedroom only and not a sitting-room. Five inventories speak of the *new* parlour. A survey of the manor of Burwell, in the Lincolnshire Wolds, made in 1590, shows how a working farmer would use a medieval manor

---

[1]The inventories used here are in the Lincoln Record Office and in the Notts. County Record Office (for the peculiar of Southwell). See *Econ. H.R.* N.S. 7 (1954–5), 291–306.

house when the lease of it came into his hands: the house contained among other things '2 pretty Rooms at the East end of the parlour used for a dairy and a milkhouse . . . sometimes the chapel', and 'the malt loft over the hall sometimes the great chamber'.[1] The only example of a dining-parlour at this time is in the manor house at Holme by Newark; it was a large house first built late in the fifteenth century out of a fortune made in wool.[2]

Round the Wash lived peasant farmers who, collectively, made Holland the richest part of Lincolnshire, but among whom wealth was more evenly distributed than elsewhere in the county.[3] Smallholdings prevailed, because of the richness of the soil and the structure of the peasant society; houses were correspondingly small. A third of the inventories mention no rooms, or no more than one, and it is more likely here than anywhere else in the region that there was a substantial minority of single-roomed houses. Among middling peasants, with goods worth between £15 and £50, a house with four rooms was normal. Most of them were husbandmen, a few yeomen, and their houses contained hall, parlour, one chamber, and one service-room—either a kitchen, a milkhouse or a buttery. There is a more striking degree of homogeneity in the houses of these villages than any-where else in the county. The only distinction of the few wealthy peasants is that some of them had two parlours, and all of them had two or three service-rooms.

When a contemporary was asked what these houses were built of, in any part of Lincolnshire except the limestone uplands and their margins, the usual answer was either 'post, pan and balks,' or 'timber and clay', 'built of wood and walled with earth', on the one hand, or simply with 'earth walls' or 'walls of clay' on the other.[4] The phrases appear to indicate all the range from timber-framed building, with the frame visible,[5] to build-ing in mud with a subordinate use of timber, or even none at all. The words cannot be taken entirely at their face value, because they were chosen by parsons obliged to fill in a form for an official (diocesan) inquiry, and

[1] *A.A.S.R.P.*, 24 (1897-8), 76.

[2] The house has gone, but a map dated 1735 (Newark Museum) shows its plan; the inscription devised by its builder, John Barton,

> 'I thank God and ever shall
> It is the sheep hath paid for all'

was recorded by Thoroton, *Nottinghamshire* (1677), 349.

[3] See Joan Thirsk, *English Peasant Farming*, 42-47.

[4] See below, pp. 91-2, for a discussion of the records from which these phrases are taken.

[5] Posts were the vertical timbers, pan the horizontal ones such as the wall plate, and the balks were the tie-beams and other members of the roof construction.

parsons then were as inaccurate and careless as form-fillers of any age, but the phrases do indicate the superficial appearance of houses of the time. A few survive, in such Wold villages as Thimbleby and Somersby, and examination shows that although apparently of mud, there is often a slender timber frame, only visible inside if at all (see fig. 10). The mud

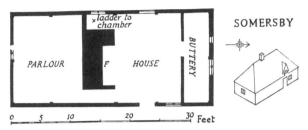

FIGURE 10. House at Somersby, Lincolnshire, built of mud and stud. The studs show in the inside face of the walls, but externally the mud walling is carried over the studs to protect them. There is one chamber, over house part and buttery.

walling was carried over the face of the timber uprights, even at the angles, and that in its turn covered, either originally or later, with a water-proof plaster rendering. The map on p. 82 (fig. 11) shows that houses said to be of mud or earth alone were concentrated somewhat in the southern Wolds. The eastern slopes of the Wolds had always been, and still are, relatively rich in woodland,[1] and the concentration cannot be due to lack of timber. The parishes are small, however, and the villages tiny; many of their churches were rebuilt in the Victorian age, because only poor buildings had come down from the Middle Ages. A few mud-walled houses have escaped rebuilding, because even in the heyday of Georgian farming this part of the county was less able to afford new building than any other. It is clear then that a timber-frame was the beginning of house building, but that the poorer the owner, the slighter and flimsier the wood he could afford to use.

There was very little building in brick as yet. None of the brick farm-houses still to be seen are earlier than the Restoration period, but there must have been a few in the Fenland villages, along the Humber side and the Trent valley as far up as Gainsborough. Those are precisely the areas where brick building had gone on in the Middle Ages; the tradition had not expired, but it had not yet begun to swell. Roof covering was usually thatch, everywhere; there was a little reed thatching in the Fens and the Marshland, but elsewhere wheat, rye and even barley straw were used.

[1]See H. C. Darby, *Domesday Geography of the East Midlands*, 61, for a map of the distribution of woodland in 1086, which agrees tolerably with that shown on the modern O.S. 1 inch map.

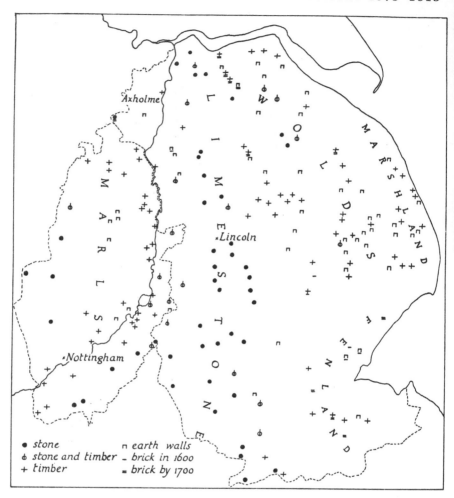

FIGURE II. Lincolnshire and Nottinghamshire, showing building materials in use in the sixteenth and seventeenth centuries according to parsonage terriers.

Reed thatching was a professional craft, but straw thatching was done by farm workers, who could cover a house as well as a stack.[1]

Floors downstairs were usually of earth, even in better houses. It must long ago have been discovered empirically that clay mixed with oxblood and ashes made a hard floor which might even be polished. Floors paved with limestone were to be found mainly where transport of paving slabs from the south Lincolnshire quarries would not be too expensive, and very few farmers were yet using bricks for flooring.

[1]See L. B. and M. W. Barley, 'Craftsmen's Inventories of the Sixteenth and Seventeenth Centuries', *Lincs. Historian*, II, No. 6 (1959), 17–18.

In the houses which had an upper room or two, the floor might be made in a variety of ways. The most superior was a boarded floor. About a third of Lincolnshire parsonage houses had such floors upstairs, and they were probably representative of farmhouses. In the vicarage at Candlesby in 1605, one bay was 'chambered over with a fastened chamber of a somer-tree, joists and boards, the other old bay having a somertree and joists fastened but the boards loose and moveable. . . .' There were two reasons for not fastening the floor-boards of a chamber. One was that these floors had often been inserted by a tenant; the boards were left loose so that he could remove them if he wished. They are, like the glass of windows, not infrequently included in an inventory along with furniture. Secondly, when both joists and floorboards were loose, it was much easier to get bulky goods, such as bales of wool or sacks of corn, into a chamber by removing part of the floor than by struggling up a narrow winding stair. Joists laid on the somertree, or main ceiling beam, and not jointed into it, have occasionally been observed by archaeologists; it may be that the practice was more widespread than has been assumed, and that the chamber floor evolved from a permanent beam (the tie-beam), with loose joists and boards on it, to a completely fixed structure.

Plaster floors for upstairs rooms are no surprise to anyone who knows the east Midlands; they may be taken for granted in houses of every class, from an Elizabethan mansion at Doddington Pigot, built by a successful lawyer in 1600, to the smallest cottage; and in date from Elizabethan times to the nineteenth century.[1] The best material for them was the gypsum, or calcium sulphate, of the Keuper Marl; it was well known in the Middle Ages in its superior form, alabaster, and the figures in the arcading of the timber façade of the fourteenth-century White Hart at Newark, Notts., are of moulded plaster. Gypsum was used for floors in the Isle of Axholme and at least as far south as Leicestershire. The earliest documentary reference to a plaster floor is 1556, when Bess of Hardwick instructed her steward at Chatsworth to 'cause the floor of my bedchamber to be made even either with plaster, clay or lime'.[2] Analysis of samples has shown[3] that lime was used in the floors at Hardwick Hall (completed in 1597), but the keep of Bolsover Castle, c. 1620, has a gypsum floor. In such houses these floors

[1] The suburban villa of c. 1825 in which these pages are being written has attic floors of plaster.
[2] *Arch.*, 64 (1912–3), 351. An estimate for the repair of the prebendal house at N. Newbald, E. Yorks., undated but c. 1580, includes: 'for flooring of two chambers over the parlior iiij tonn of plaister xxd. a tonne everye lode ijs cariage viijis (York Diocesan Record Office, R.G. 913).
[3] At the Building Research Station, by Dr. N. Davey and Mr. H. J. Eldridge. I am indebted to them and to Mr. H. Bagenal for notes on these samples.

would be covered with rush matting. Whether lime or gypsum was the base, clay or burnt brick was usually mixed in as aggregate, and the slow carbonating of a lime plaster floor turned it eventually into limestone. Bess of Hardwick wanted an *even* floor; timber taken from park, wood or hedgerow straight to the sawpit, and then used without long seasoning, must quickly have settled into the uneven condition that we take to be a sign of age. A plaster floor required the usual beams and joists, across which straw or reed was laid, then a layer of plaster about two inches thick. It was economical of timber, as well as more even, and probably more fire-resistant; eventually it might sag with the weight and crack. No doubt the saving of timber was the most powerful reason for plaster floors in farmhouses and cottages, since eastern England was beginning to feel an acute shortage of wood for any purpose. A third of Lincolnshire parsonage houses had such floors upstairs.

The other method was to make earth floors in the chambers, as in Candlesby vicarage: 'all the rest boarded over with chambers moveable made of timber and earth'. Another phrase is 'chambered over with mud floors'. As soon as chambers are needed, it is natural to make them of the same material as floors downstairs, laid on joists and a layer of straw or reeds. The vicar of Candlesby called such a floor moveable, presumably because he thought himself free to take the timbers away if he left for another living, though dismantling an earth floor must have been a task not to be faced more than once or twice in a lifetime. Earth was a cheap alternative to plaster; it was more used in the eastern half of Lincolnshire, farther away from sources of lime and gypsum. Further research will show that it was used in other counties which had neither of those materials (see fig. 33).

An intensive search of the east Midlands has shown that a few houses of this age can still be found. In the hamlet of Little Carlton, near the Trent and two to three miles north of Newark, a house known as 'The Gables' is a good specimen, almost unaltered inside, of a yeoman's house of c. 1600 (see fig. 12). It faces north, as houses of this time commonly do, for the sun was not yet a thing to be welcomed in the house. It is timber-framed, but the ground floor walls are now entirely of brick, the timbers either removed or concealed. It has the medieval plan of hall and storeyed cross wings, with one wing for kitchen and milkhouse, the other for the two parlours. There is no doubt that it once had *two* parlours, and the room now used as a larder was probably the buttery. One parlour still has the framed opening in the joists for a ladder to the chambers in that wing, and one of the stairs in the kitchen must be in the position of the former ladder. The staircase in the angle of hall and wing was added c. 1700, and a low

THE GABLES, L.CARLTON

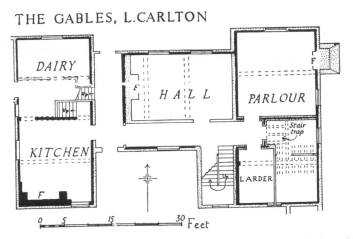

FIGURE 12. Ground plan of The Gables, Little Carlton, Nottinghamshire, a yeoman's house of traditional late medieval design with open hall and storeyed cross wings. Note that the hall fireplace backed on the cross passage, a highland feature also found in the north Midlands. The staircase was added and the hall chambered over *c.* 1700. Half of the parlour wing has been turned into store-rooms, and much of the timber-frame has been replaced by, or cased in, brickwork.

room made over the hall. Notice that the hall fireplace backs on the through passage, and this is a characteristic of houses in the Trent valley which they share with those in northern counties. This was a superior house, for one of these east Midland villages. Its builder cannot be identified, but this was a community of rich yeomen; their inventories show that they were using the good grazing of the Trent valley for sheep and cattle rearing, wool and cheese production. South Muskham, the parish in which the house lies, was enclosed early, possibly at the time when this house was built. There were enough yeomen of means and initiative to get rid of the open fields, a type of farming which hindered men of their resources and ambitions. The house fits perfectly the social environment from which it sprang.

Three miles farther north lies Norwell, which for a thousand years has been part of the endowments of Southwell Minster.[1] In Tudor times the village contained none but husbandmen, tenants of the Minster, and rather poor husbandmen at that. The houses in Norwell today are small (see pl. IVa), apart from two large farmhouses on moated sites which represent the prebendal mansions of the canons. Many of the houses show timber and brick work of several periods, the piecemeal self-help of men of limited

[1] The foundation charter, which included the gift of Norwell and other estates in the neighbourhood, has been dated 956.

means. Norwell was one of the last parishes of the county to be enclosed, because there were few wealthy farmers to take that initiative. The history of the two communities, Norwell and Little Carlton, is apparent in their buildings.

Although some timber houses in these east Midland villages were substantially enough built for them to have survived, the carpenter's work is usually of the plainest. There are no moulded beams in 'The Gables'. There is a house at Screveton, Notts., which has the same lack of pretension in its workmanship, and the typical northern simplicity of plan. It may have been built in 1607,[1] but it has only one storey, and no through passage (see fig. 13 and pl. IVb). The entrance is opposite the speer.

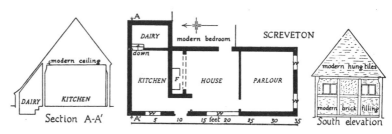

FIGURE 13. Plan and sections of a husbandman's house at Screveton, Nottinghamshire, which may have been built in 1607. It has one storey, and a type of plan very common in the east Midlands at the time. See also pl. IVB.

Beyond the hall lies the one parlour, and on the other side of it is the kitchen. The latter had no fireplace originally, and might have been called the buttery. The milkhouse is a small outshot behind the kitchen, its floor sunk below ground level and its lower walls of local stone. The particular combination of four rooms in a single-storey house makes it a unique example of a type common among Elizabethan husbandmen.

In Lincolnshire one can still find small houses in which the one service-room is a subdivision of the hall. They show that the combination of hall, parlour and buttery so common in inventories need not imply a house of three bays. At Thimbleby there is a row of houses of this kind, each with an axial chimney stack. In one of them the living half of the house has a small kitchen and larder made by a partition about six feet high. They remain open to the roof, but the hall part has been ceiled over, so that it is easy to reach up from the kitchen to put something on top of the hall ceiling, but there is no ladder to make it a proper loft. At Somersby a house

[1] It stands near the church, and has been thought to be the parsonage house, but there is no positive evidence for that. It appears to have the date 1607 carved, very incompetently, on the wall plate.

north of the church is of slightly superior status, because it has loftier walls and a chamber over the hall (see fig. 10). The posts of the slender timber frame can be seen inside, but outside the mud walls conceal them and the angles are rounded. The axial stack is of brick, probably a re-building, and a ladder by it leads to the chamber. The buttery or milk-house is partitioned off the opposite end of the hall. These two houses show how the traditional two-roomed design was being made to suit rising standards. One larger design of medieval origin, the house with hall and one cross wing, seems to be rare in the east Midlands.

Conditions were changing so rapidly at this time that several large landowners arranged for detailed surveys of their estates, to satisfy them-selves that rents were kept in line with increasing values. In 1608 Ralph Treswell, a well known professional surveyor, compiled a survey of the Duchy of Lancaster manors in Lincolnshire, and six years later Henry Valentine surveyed the Willoughby d'Eresby manor at Toynton.[1] Most of the tenants involved were husbandmen and cottagers, though not all, for copyhold had lost the taint of its servile origin, and was merely a form of tenure; hence gentlemen and yeomen are sometimes included in these surveys. For each tenant we are told not only how much land he held, in arable and meadow, but also what farm buildings and even what sort of house. Such surveys had been a commonplace of estate management for centuries, but never till this age did they include the farmhouse. The tenant was responsible for his house, with the right to timber from the manor, and by this time improvement was so widespread that the size and quality of the house was worth considering if rents were to be reassessed. These Lincolnshire surveys can be matched by that of the earl of Pem-broke's manors in Wiltshire, made in 1631–2,[2] but the earlier Wiltshire survey of 1563 does not give any information about houses and cottages, and when Ralph Treswell came to survey the Duchy of Lancaster estate of Pickering, Yorks., he saw no need for such details. Clearly improvements to tenants' houses had become something of importance on southern and midland manors, but in Yorkshire at this time the medieval homogeneity of peasant housing had not yet begun to break down to any significant extent.

The regional variations revealed by the Duchy of Lancaster survey of 1608 can be seen in the table on p. 88. Not all the copyholders' houses are described in detail, especially in Fen and Marshland villages. Why should

[1] P.R.O., D.L. 42/119; L. R.O., 5 Anc. 4A.
[2] Edited for Wilts. Arch. and N.H. Soc. Records Branch by E. Kerridge, *Surveys of the Manors of Philip, First Earl of Pembroke and Montgomery, 1631–2* (1953). See below, p. 160.

the surveyor have said, of one man, that he had a messuage containing a house and parlour, with a barn and 5 acres of land, and of another merely that he had a messuage with a barn and 6 acres of land? Possibly because the former had improved or rebuilt his house. The Fen and Marshland houses are smaller, because holdings were smaller; conservatism and inferior building techniques made farmers and cottagers there less inclined to build an upper storey than those in the upland villages where there was stone. Waddington, on the limestone south of Lincoln had larger and more varied houses; Toynton, at the southern edge of the Wolds and including

HOUSES ON DUCHY OF LANCASTER ESTATES IN LINCOLNSHIRE, 1608

Size of house	Upland Villages		Marshland Villages		Fen Villages	
	No.	%	No.	%	No.	%
House and parlour . .	10	9.3	14	41.2	22	41.7
House, parlour, service-room	12	11.2	14	41.2	15	28.4
House, parlour, chamber .	15	14.0	2	5.9	2	3.7
House, parlour, 2 chambers	9	8.4	—	—	1	1.8
House, parlour, service-room, chamber . .	19	17.8	4	11.7	8	15.1
House, parlour, service-room, 2 chambers .	25	23.4	—	—	1	1.8
Larger houses . .	17	15.9	—	—	4	7.5
Totals . . .	107	100.0	34	100.0	53	100.0

some Fenland, had smaller and much more stereotyped housing. Eleven out of twenty-three Toynton houses comprised hall, parlour and a third (service) room, like the house at Somersby. Sometimes the third room is called 'the room below the entry'; in other cases it is a 'backend', like the backhouse of East Anglia. In two cases it is an 'outend', presumably an outshot. Where it is 'below the entry', the house either has a cross passage or an entrance at the lower end of the hall, like the house at Cratfield, Suffolk. Widow Pinder of Toynton held a cottage at the fen side, consisting of hall and parlour only; on the accompanying map it is drawn as a gabled house with an axial stack, the common plan.

This survey also gives a chance of seeing what in the eyes of a Jacobean surveyor was the difference between a messuage and a cottage. Treswell had three terms: *messuage* for a property which comprised house, garth and barns and stables; *toftstead*, with a house and usually also a garth and a barn, but presumably smaller than the messuage; and *cottage*, which usually had a garth but rarely had farm buildings of any description. Henry Valentine only distinguished between a tenement and a cottage.

The word cottage was already as flexible as it is today; it could comprehend a house of one room, and one with house, parlour, kitchen and a chamber in the Wold villages. Nonetheless it commonly meant a house with two rooms only, or occasionally with a 'backend'. At Toynton most of the cottages had two rooms, though there were two of only one room. These surveys provide the clearest proof of the persistence of the one-roomed house.

COTTAGES ON DUCHY OF LANCASTER ESTATES IN LINCOLNSHIRE, 1608

Size	Upland villages	Marshland villages	Fen villages
House	1	1	3
House and parlour . . .	17	8	7
House, parlour, service-room .	5	12	—
House, parlour, chamber . .	3	—	—
Larger cottages	7	—	—
Totals	33	21	10

We can fill some of these cottages with their household goods. John Osborne of Donington on Bain in 1608 was tenant of a cottage, containing hall and parlour, and a garth of twenty poles, for which he paid a rent of 1s. 4d. Ralph Treswell valued it at 5s., no doubt because of what Osborne had done, and before his death in 1615 he had put in a chamber.[1] He possessed seventeen sheep and two kine, and his goods were worth altogether £12; his neighbours called him a husbandman. In the hall there were a cupboard and two tables, a plank for a form, two chairs and some stools; he had seven pieces of pewter. On the dishbench stood a brass pot, a pan, a pestle and a frying pan, in the hearth a spit, reckons and tongs. The living-room must have been full, for the bowls and kits for milk were there, a tub, a spinning wheel and various small pieces of farm gear—a pitch pan, three forks, a brake, a hatchet and a spade. The parlour contained one bed, three chests and a press, and the salting trough was kept there. The value of the joists of the chamber was included in the inventory, but the chamber was empty.

John Wright of Belchford, who had a two-roomed cottage in 1608, was still only a poor husbandman twenty years later, with corn and hay in the yard, three cattle and six 'rotten sheep',[2] and goods amounting in all to £8 8s. clear. His parlour contained no more than a bed, a chest and 'other trash', and the hall only a cupboard, one chair, a few fireirons and pots and

[1] L.R.O., 117/431.
[2] L.R.O., 134/167.

89

pans. Richard Thynne of Tetney was tenant in 1608 of 'a toft with a croft, which toft conteyneth a hall, a parlour with one chamber over them, with a garth conteyning half an acre'. In 1618 he was called a wool-winder, and he had some arable land and livestock of all kinds. His goods were worth £106 (excluding his debts of about £80) and his house now had a milkhouse as well as hall, parlour and chamber.[1] Thus some of the tenants of cottages, among whom were husbandmen as well as labourers, had managed to enlarge their houses.

Among the larger copyholders there was similar improvement of living standards. This is not surprising for two of them were gentlemen— Edward Lacon of Tetney and Adam Heneage of Donington on Bain. Only one of the others was called a yeoman at death, and most were probably husbandmen. John Lyson of North Coates held in 1608 a messuage with a house containing a hall, a parlour and a kitchen; with it went a barn, a stable and 56 acres of arable. By 1624[2] he had added a buttery, and a chamber to store corn in; he was clearly a successful farmer who might well have called himself a yeoman, for that status was often claimed by men who had no freehold. Perhaps Lincolnshire rural society, in the out of the way villages of the Humber estuary, did not yet encourage such pretentions. Philip Kyrke of South Thoresby was another successful man; in addition to the 24 acres of his holding, of which 12 acres were sown with wheat at the time of his death in 1626, he had rented a further 4 acres.[3] His goods were worth £156, mainly in farmstock; he had made a milk-house, and put glass in the windows of the house. William Caborne, yeoman, of Tetney had added a new parlour to his house, with a chamber over it.[4]

Two of the cottages at Toynton were 'new built' in 1614, and there is other evidence of such new building, even on the Lincolnshire Heath,[5] where enclosure was making most headway. At Glapton, south of Nottingham, the housing shortage made some farmer convert a medieval cruck barn of three bays into a small house, while still leaving one bay and a half of barn space (see fig. 14). The eastern bay of the barn was pulled down, and the new house, timber-framed, made partly within the barn and partly beyond it. The house had hall and parlour on either side of a cross passage which led to service-rooms behind the parlour and in an outshot: not

[1] L.R.O., 121/206.
[2] L.R.O., 128/254.
[3] L.R.O., 131/358. These comparisons are made on the assumption that the man in question had stayed on the same holding.
[4] L.R.O. 128/324.
[5] P.R.O., D.L. 42/119, f. 25, new building by the Disney family at Boothby Graffhoe, Timberland and Bassingham.

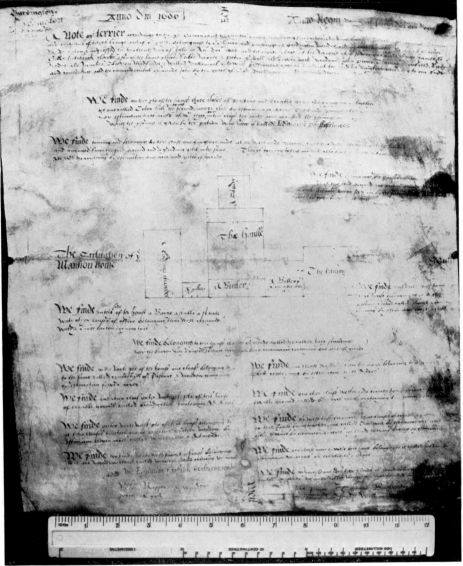

V. The sketch plan of the parsonage house at Hardington, Som., made in 1600, is the earliest plan of its kind. It represents, if it is accurate, an unusual house, no doubt of several dates, each room having an independent axis parallel to the next. If the rooms were under a continuous roof the arrangement would be typical. Note that there is no parlour, but a 'lodging chamber' at the left hand end.

CHATCULL OLD HALL

VI. A drawing made in 1838 of a small manor house of the West Midlands built perhaps c. 1635. The plan, with hall range and one cross wing, is one of the commonest types in the

quite a traditional plan, but a skilful modification of it. The stairs were in
the usual position, alongside the hall fireplace. By 1958, when the house
was pulled down, the mud walls had been replaced by brick, in places only
4½ inches thick, and more space had been taken from the barn, to enlarge
the dairy and to make a bathroom beyond the parlour.

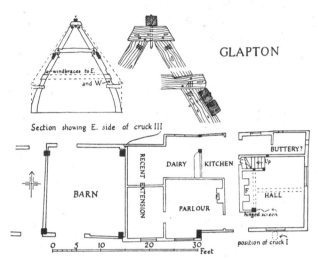

GLAPTON

Section showing E. side of cruck III

FIGURE 14. Plan of a house formerly at Glapton, Nottinghamshire, made c. 1600
by adaptation of an older cruck-framed building, either a house or a barn. The
numbering of the cruck trusses shows that the first truss at the east end was
demolished when the house shown was built. The timber-framed and earth walls
were replaced by brickwork in the eighteenth century. The hall fireplace is c. 1600,
modernized, but the parlour fireplace is a recent insertion. More space had been
taken from the barn in recent times to make an additional room and to enlarge
the dairy.

We have seen how the rise in housing standards made estate owners
aware that as landlords they had a vital interest in knowing precisely what
improvements were being made to the building in their manors. The
church, for its own reasons, was equally concerned to see what parsonage
houses were like. The parochial clergy were faced with a difficult task, for
they were expected to satisfy an increasingly critical congregation, and the
authorities could see that the adequacy of the country parson was threatened by the poverty of many country livings. In order therefore to safe-
guard their endowments from loss, by carelessness or misappropriation,
the clergy and churchwardens of each parish were required, from 1571
onwards, to produce a schedule of the property of the parish church. It
was mainly concerned with real property, and so was called a terrier, the
usual word for an extended description of an estate, field by field or strip
by strip. Plate V has been selected from those compiled in the diocese of

Bath and Wells because it also has what must be the earliest plan of a vernacular house. Usually the bishop or archdeacon who initiated the inquiry was content to ask whether there was an official residence for the parson or not, for that could not be taken for granted after the changes of the Reformation. The bishops of Lincoln seem to have seen that the problem in their large diocese (which still stretched from the Humber to the Thames) was not merely whether there was a house, but whether it could be deemed adequate. From 1605 onwards they asked much more specific questions than did their fellow bishops: about the size of the house, the materials of its walls and roof, and the number and names of the rooms.

The value of these terriers, which had to be returned to the authorities at frequent intervals, is limited only by the parson's occasional failure to make an accurate answer. Nevertheless they present a remarkably full picture, and the vicissitudes of the parsonage house can be followed through the centuries. The form is shown by the extracts printed in the Appendix, pp. 273-6.[1]

What the parsonage house was built of depended on local custom more than on the resources of the individual (see fig. 11). There are occasional exceptions, such as the vicar of Skirbeck, who in the seventeenth century was living, he said, in a large brick house of eight bays with a four square tower covered with lead. The full story is that the corporation of Boston, which was patron of the living, had neglected the vicarage house to the point where it eventually was demolished, and they allowed the parson to live in the medieval manor house of the Hussey family, which was also corporation property, until a new parsonage house was built in 1739.[2] Usually the house must have been typical of the village in which it stood; it remains to see how it compared in size and accommodation with neighbouring farmhouses.

The living standards of Lincolnshire parsons reflected the small size of their parishes and hence the relative poverty of their livings; their houses are somewhat smaller than those in Leicestershire or Worcestershire. The following table shows their size in bays.[3]

[1]Lincoln Record Office possesses between six and twelve terriers for each of the 600 parishes in Lincolnshire. These remarks, and the map on p. 82, are based on examination of terriers for about a quarter of the parishes.

[2]P. Thompson, *History and Antiquities of Boston* (1856), 474.

[3]The stone houses of Lincolnshire are not fully represented, because they could not easily be described in terms of bays, and some parsons did not attempt it. Leicestershire terriers 1611-12 and 1625 (that is for the archdeaconry of Leicester) are also in Lincoln Record Office. Worcestershire figures are given in D. M. Barratt, *The Condition of the Parish Clergy between the Reformation and 1660, with special reference to Oxford, Worcester and Gloucester* (Oxford thesis, 1949, Bodleian Library).

SIZE OF PARSONAGE HOUSES, 1605–25

	Lincolnshire 1605–6	Leicestershire 1611–25
Houses of 2 bays	10.9	6.2
Houses of 3 bays	36.2	25
Houses of 4 bays	21	23.4
Houses of 5 bays	12	20.3
Houses of 6 bays	12.7	9.4
Houses of 7 bays or more . . .	7.2	15.7
Total	100.0%	100.0%
Size of sample	166	64

What did the size in bays mean in terms of rooms? Alford vicarage, of two bays, had a hall, a parlour and two chambers; Kirmington had one chamber. Alkborough, with three bays, consisted of hall, parlour and kitchen, but most houses of this size had chambers. Sometimes the service bay had several rooms, like the kitchen, buttery and little milkhouse at Anderby, and the parlour bay at Bonby with two little parlours. The parsons rarely had a study at this time, and there was often no difference, except for the presence of a few books, between his home and that of the wealthier farmers with whom his house compares. The commonest type of parsonage house, with three bays, and between four and eight rooms, was at its smallest like that of the yeomen of middling status in the Fens, or at its largest like that of wealthier yeomen elsewhere.

At Wyberton, near Boston, the rectory house in 1606 comprised '7 bays, part of brick and part of mud walls, covered with tile, 5 bays being chambered over with plaster'; how much was old mud building and how much new brick we cannot tell. It was a rich living, and when William Symonds, the rector, died in 1615, his goods were worth £254 10s.[1] He had a study and three parlours, as well as hall and kitchen, buttery and milkhouse. Upstairs the great chamber was used as a bedroom; otherwise the inventory mentions only the hay and corn chambers, and the former was probably an outbuilding. Thomas Storre, vicar of Bilsby, had a house 'built of wood and clay and covered with thatch'; it had three bays 'chambered over with mud floors and one boarded'. He lived comfortably, farming his glebe and keeping six cows, but also possessing books valued at £13 6s. 8d. and plate worth £10, out of a total for his goods of £167 18s. The hall of the vicarage contained the usual table, forms and stools, with two chairs and a cupboard 'with the cloths'. There were two parlours, one

[1] L.R.O., Inv. 117/509.

of them probably his bedroom, sitting-room and study, with a living table, a counter table and one chair in it; the other was the 'maidens' parlour', with no more than two beds, two chests with linen and a warming pan. There were three service-rooms—buttery, dairy and kitchen—and cooking was done in the kitchen. Two of the chambers were used as bedrooms, and pains had been taken to make them comfortable; one of them had been 'seel'd', and the ceiling was valued, with two chairs and two stools, at £4; the other was 'the matted chamber', for rush mats covered the earth floor. The third was the 'store chamber', with beans, bacon and barley, a cheese heck, some pewter and various tubs. Outside in the yard were farm implements and a stock of 'dythes', dried cow manure commonly used in the east Midlands and parts of Yorkshire for fuel at this time, for wood was scarce and cows were many in this pastoral farming county. Across the yard was the brewhouse with a chamber over it for storing malt.

The vicarage at Bucknall sounds a modest affair, 'of four bays, walls of earth and covered with straw, two bays being chambered over with plaster and earth'. Arthur Wright, vicar, had livestock worth £58, corn and hay in the barn, and the value of his inventory is inflated by 'bills and bonds' worth £600. If the terrier of 1606 is accurate he had enlarged the service end of the house by 1614, for instead of kitchen alone he had kitchen, milkhouse and brewhouse; the kitchen was used for cooking and his servant (or servants) slept there. The hall was well furnished with five chairs, five stools and cushions, as well as the usual table and forms. Here, as so often, the buttery is mentioned *after* the hall, and not with the other service-rooms; it must have been a small room contrived out of the hall where the pewter was used and the beer drunk. Wright had two parlours. The 'little parlour' had three beds in it; the other, although it had two more beds, was used as a sitting- and perhaps dining-room, for it had a long table, a bench, two forms, a chest, a pair of tables and a warming pan.[1] Such was the way of life of fairly prosperous parsons; no inventories have been found of poorer clergy living in houses of two or three bays.

The words that parsons used enable us to see precisely the status of the kitchen in a house of c. 1600. The service bay of the house had not included a room for cooking in medieval houses, but by this time the process of taking it, or a part of it, over for that purpose had made distinct headway in the south. In many midland houses, especially where there was only one service-room, the name kitchen was now being used for it, although cooking was still done in the hall. The kitchen is in the process of becoming part of the house. Only a few parsons spoke of 'hall, parlour and kitchen' as though the integration had been completed. Usually the kitchen is a

[1] L.R.O., 117/321.

distinct building: 'unto this building is joined a kitchen containing two little low baysteads' (Saltfleetby St. Clements, Lincs.). Occasionally it is free standing and separate: 'Item a kitchen builded four square' (Bottesford, Leics.), and there it must be medieval in date. It is unlikely that detached kitchens were still being built at this time, but even in new houses they might be narrower or lower than the rest of the building, and evidently thought a distinct part of it.[1]

b. Leicestershire

Leicestershire is still distinctly richer than Lincolnshire or even Nottinghamshire in surviving timber-framed houses, because the clay soils which cover much of the county had more woodland and hedgerow trees. The two-roomed cottage was to be found there, as everywhere, at the end of Elizabeth's reign.[2] Thomas Burbigge of Freeby, who died in 1596, was a labourer; he must have had some land, for as well as two kine he had some hay and manure in the yard. In the house (note that the northern term is used) the furniture consisted of a table, an aumbry or cupboard, and some pewter and brass. In the parlour were two bedsteads 'with simple furniture', four coffers containing linen, and other things unspecified. The parlour walls were hung with painted cloths; they were to be found in many east Midland cottages no larger or richer than this, either on the walls or round a bed. Thomas Burbigge's goods were valued at £8.

Very few Leicestershire farmers had the title of yeoman conceded to them by their neighbours; most of them were called husbandmen,[3] although their goods ranged in value up to £244 and averaged £80. The poor ones lived in houses of two or three rooms, but half of them had, as well as the living-room, two or three service-rooms and one or two chambers. A few had two parlours. Edward Shell, the blacksmith at Barleston near Market Bosworth, was comfortably off, with goods worth £67; his home consisted of a hall house, two parlours and chambers over house and parlour. The two chambers were used for sleeping and storage, but he had no service-rooms, because he was using that part of the house as his shop with the smithy or anvil, vice, beckhorn (the beak of the anvil), grindstone, bellows, hammers and other working tools.[4] He was much richer in goods

[1]Manor Farm, Stretton, Rutland, rebuilt early in the seventeenth century, has a kitchen built as the end bay of a stone house, but with only a loft over it, not a chamber.

[2]These remarks are based on a study of inventories dated 1594–8, for the archdeaconry of Leicester, in the Leicester Museum.

[3]Twenty-one out of thirty for whom the inventory gives the occupation, compared with one labourer, four craftsmen, three parsons and one yeoman.

[4]File 1594–8, A59.

and convenience than the parson of Queniborough, William Bradley. His house consisted of four rooms, hall, his lodging parlour, chamber and study. He had books worth £5, and was perhaps glad to escape to the study, for without any buttery or milkhouse, the hall must have been cluttered; as well as two framed tables, a cupboard, four stools, two chairs and a bench, there were the pots and pans needed for cooking and 'looms, pails, barrels, kimnels and two churns'.[1] The hall would have been more convenient if he had not acquired two of the new-fashioned framed tables; they could not be taken down and set aside between meals like the older table top placed on trestles.[2]

c. The West Midlands

North-west of the limestone belt the local sandstone was not good or plentiful enough to be much used at this time. The few stone houses are usually of manor house status. Bellingham Hall, Herefordshire, built in 1602, is of two storeys, with a long hall range, a storeyed porch in the middle of it (i.e., at the lower end of the hall) and a large parlour wing. Before the death of Elizabeth the only use of brick was in large houses like Napley Hall, just as in Nottinghamshire it is only to be found in the basement of Wollaton Hall (1580–8) and in Thrumpton Hall (c. 1608), or in Leicestershire at Sutton Cheney Hall, built in 1613. Otherwise it is confined to chimney stacks in timber-framed buildings in the west midland black and white style.

The contrasts between the east Midland vernacular, as seen in the houses at Screveton and Somersby, and that of the west Midlands is well shown by a cottage at Snitterfield, Warwicks. It is no longer inhabited but its original design is clear (see fig. 15). Instead of the single storey, with or without a loft or chamber in the roof space, it has two full storeys. Instead of an axial stack, the one fireplace is at the gable end; the chimney hood of timber and clay has been replaced in brick. The hall ceiling is quartered by moulded beams. The only anomaly is that there is no service-room, but since the parlour bay is larger than the hall, the parlour may have had a small buttery taken out of it.

Haughton Old Hall, west of Stafford, is a good example of a small manor house of the same age.[3] It has close studding in front and side walls,

---

[1] A 63.

[2] Cf. the play *Johan Johan* by John Heywood, written c. 1530, where John is instructed by his wife to set up the table for the meal. At Jesus College, Cambridge, c. 1600, there was a long table for Fellows' use, but Scholars ate at trestle tables which were removed when the hall was wanted for other purposes.

[3] See V.C.H. *Staffs.*, IV, facing p. 138.

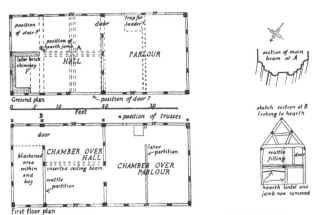

THE SADDLER'S, PARK LANE, SNITTERFIELD

FIGURE 15. Plans and section of a house at Snitterfield, Warwickshire, now an outbuilding (S. R. Jones). It was built in early Elizabethan times, to judge from the moulding of the beams which quarter the hall ceiling. The original arrangement can be deduced, though the apparent absence of any service room is puzzling. The chambers, originally open to the rafters, were later ceiled over at tie-beam level.

with a more ornamental treatment of the panels beneath the windows and in the gables. Apart from that, its plan and arrangement can be found frequently between Derbyshire and Herefordshire, in houses of any date between the sixteenth and the eighteenth centuries. It has a hall range and a cross wing, both of two storeys, the principal variation being in the length of the hall range. At Haughton it contained hall and kitchen, as at Bellingham Hall, and also in Youlgreave Old Hall Farm (below, p. 170). In smaller houses there was no kitchen. At Haughton neither of the two parlours had a fireplace, and the stairs were in the back parlour. On the other hand, Chatcull Old Hall, which must be of similar date, has an elaborate chimney stack on the axis of the parlour wing. It is illustrated here (pl. VI) by a drawing made in the 1830's, one of the remarkable collection entitled *Staffordshire Views* now in the William Salt Library, Stafford.

Many medieval houses in Staffordshire had upper floors and chimney stacks inserted at this time, and the new stack was usually placed on the axis of the building.[1] An early dated example of the axial brick stack is at Baswich, built in 1616.[2] This is half a century after the Essex example already described, but there is documentary evidence of a bricklayer in dispute with his employer over that very job in 1560.[3] The west Midlands

[1] E.g. Moat House Farm, Haughton; V.C.H. *Staffs.*, IV, 136–8.
[2] *Ex. inf.* S. R. Jones.
[3] *Coll. for a History of Staffs.*, N.S. IX, 1906.

took up much more rapidly than the north the innovations of the south-east, and particularly the axial brick stack. Where it was placed depended on the size of the house. In the smallest, of two rooms, it was naturally put in the centre. In the hall and cross wing house it was built at the junction of hall with wing, and the entrance was in the angle facing the stack. This disposition is common in Cheshire houses of the seventeenth century, and no doubt the staircase rose on the further side of the stack. When the hall range had a kitchen as well, as at Haughton, Bellingham, or Youlgreave, the two rooms were served by back to back fireplaces.

Although these traditional plans persisted in the west Midlands, a few houses show that awareness of new fashions was not limited to the practical matter of a chimney stack. Building to two full storeys, or two and a half, with a more or less symmetrical elevation graced by a storeyed porch or bay window (a matter of pure ostentation) appealed to some farmers. The storeyed porch had been popular among the lesser gentry since early Elizabethan times (cf. Handforth Hall, Cheshire, c.1562), and was becoming a feature of houses of parsons and yeomen. There is a storeyed bay window in the Priest's House, Prestbury, c.1581. A house at Gnosall[1] was typical of the new ideas of a Staffordshire yeoman. It must have been built about 1600 at the earliest for it had a frame of square panels. The massive ribbed stack divided the two main rooms, as in many cottages, but there were two full storeys, a storeyed porch, and garrets lighted by small oriel windows in jettied gables. The house is more than reminiscent of Aylmer's, Sheering, but perhaps a generation later.

Even in north-west Herefordshire the new fashion for a storeyed house can be found—another indication of the speed with which the Welsh border counties took up such new ideas. Leys Farm, Weobley, was built in 1589,[2] and in such an exceptional style for its place and time that it has remained virtually unaltered. It must be one of the earliest versions of timber constructions in square panels instead of close studding. The plan is the traditional half H, with one wing extended at the rear, primarily to contain a staircase. The chimney stacks are all external, as one expects in this part of the world; on the rear wall of the hall and the gable end of the parlour wing. The fireplace in the service wing is a later addition. The parlour and hall ceilings are divided by substantial beams into square panels, another western feature which presumably goes with the panelled frame for walls. Timber was still plentiful enough to be used generously. The most novel feature is the treatment of the elevation: symmetry broken

---

[1]Demolished in 1838, but drawn for William Salt at that time; see V.C.H. Staffs. IV, 90.
[2]See R.C.H.M. Herefordshire, III, 196 and pls. 103, 176.

only by the greater width of the parlour bay window and the porch at the lower end of the hall; seven gables in all, not only for the wings and the storeyed porch but also in the hall roof and for the three storeyed bay windows.

The fondness for ranks of gables no doubt spread to the countryside from the towns. Preston Court, in west Gloucestershire, looks as if it could have been built by a housewright from Ledbury, only four miles away. The timber frame, close studded, has a hall with cross wings protruding only at the rear; the elevation is a full three storeys with four gables. Why should a gentleman want such a house in the country? Partly for show, but the chief answer lies in the range of lofty garrets, where there remains a large hoist, with wooden pulley wheels, no doubt used for raising sacks of wool to the loft. There is also a large hanging cheese rack in the loft, but it is probably a later fitting.

In most of Herefordshire timber building persisted through this phase, and through much of the seventeenth century, but in the south-west of the county the local style gradually gives way to that characteristic of Elizabethan Monmouthshire: rubble stone walls and wooden window frames and doorways. It is a very distinctive combination, whose origin is yet to be found.[1] It may lie in Gloucestershire, though stone houses there with wooden frames and lintels appear to be much later in date than this.

Some timber farmhouses have marked similarity of plan to Devonshire houses of cob or stone, showing that lay-out arises from social needs, rather than available materials. Lower Jury Farm, Abbey Dore,[2] has a typically Devonshire plan, with a wide cross passage, a hall to one side of it with dairy beyond and fireplace and staircase on a side wall; the room on the other side of the passage was a parlour. Both hall and parlour have ceilings treated in the western fashion: that is, divided into square panels by heavy moulded beams.

Herefordshire seems to have taken more readily than Devonshire to new ideas entering the county from the Midlands. One of the new designs is the two-roomed plan with an axial chimney stack (in stone, not in brick) and a staircase to the side of it. The same design is also to be found in a three-roomed plan.[3] The result is that by the early years of James I's reign, rural housing in this remote county, as in Devonshire, exhibited great variety. Nonetheless two features seem clear. One is the persistent medieval plan with hall and cross passage, now modified in very diverse fashion by the accepted need for a stone chimney stack. It may be found at

[1] Fox and Raglan, *Mon. Ho.*, II, 101–4.
[2] R.C.H.M. *Herefordshire* I, 11 (15).
[3] *Ibid.*, 61 (Eaton Bishop 6); III, 12 (Aymestry 10, 11; Almeley 16).

the upper end of the hall, at one side, at the passage end, or even inserted in the passage itself. The other feature is the chimney stack between two rooms—usually between hall and parlour, but once at least[1] in a peculiar modification of the intrusive idea. Two parlours in the wing were given fireplaces in adjacent corners, the stack being on the outside wall.

[1]*Ibid.*, III, 6 (Summer House, Almeley).

CHAPTER FOUR

Stone Houses in the Lowlands

A<small>T</small> the present stage of knowledge one approaches with some hesitation the task of describing the houses of the limestone belt. Little intensive field work has been published;[1] masons were so conservative in their methods that dating by such features as the mouldings of window mullions may be misleading and the habit of placing a date on a new building, or on an alteration to an old one, did not become widespread until the seventeenth century. The earliest dated houses so far noticed both belong to the 1570's[2] but many more instances would be needed to make the framework of a chronology. There is a popular impression that Cotswold villages are full of Elizabethan houses. In part this comes from estate agents' advertisements, in part from looking only at manor houses, in part from the persistence of traditional ways among masons. The truth remains to be exemplified, and it will certainly be that the seventeenth century, and the second half of it at that, saw the most building activity in the villages of the stone belt, from south Lincolnshire to Somerset.

The other outstanding problem is to find confirmation, or denial, of Harrison's remarks about a transition from timber to stone in this region in his time. He may have been right, as we shall see, about some counties, but the limestone uplands had been intensively occupied from Neolithic times, and specialized in sheep farming in Roman and medieval times; it is unlikely that their timber resources can have been comparable even with

---

[1]The pioneer work of Fox and Raglan on the transition from timber to stone in Monmouthshire stands alone so far.

[2]A house near Banbury noted by R. B. Wood-Jones, 'The Banbury Region', *Trans. Ancient Mon. Soc.* NS 4 (1956), 2; a small manor house at Fenton in Beckingham, Lincs.

those of East Anglia. It is possible that the medieval timber houses disappeared completely in later rebuilding, especially from 1660–1725, but more likely that they were always exceptional. In the Cotswolds proper, the few surviving timber houses are to be found in market towns like Northleach or Burford, or else to the west of the limestone scarp on the margin of the Severn valley. In the Banbury region they are to be seen only in the lowland valley.[1] The best village in which to observe the transition from timber to stone is Lacock, in the Wiltshire part of the Avon valley (see pl. VII). Lacock is a rich treasury of vernacular building which still awaits detailed examination, but a casual stroll through the streets reveals an impressive cruck-framed house, other framed houses whose studded and braced fronts are still fully visible or traceable under later stone work, and the stone houses which became the normal thing in the years after about 1600. Some of the timber houses have windows with ovolo-moulded mullions, indicating the persistence at least into Elizabeth's reign of the timber tradition. More important than the question of date is the clear hint from these examples that a full study of this problem will require an appreciation of the distinction between upland and valley villages.

In Lincolnshire, the Tudor parson with a parish on the limestone belt usually lived in a house 'walled with stone'. We could guess that it was of coursed rubble, for one reads occasionally of 'rough stones' or 'small stones'. On the margin of the stone belt, both to east and west (see fig. 11) there were houses of 'stone and timber'. Whether they were 'built of wood and walled with stone' (that is, a timber frame filled with stone), like the parsonage house at Bottesford, Lincs., or had ground floor walls of stone and a timber first storey, the parson fails to explain. Most probably they had first floor walls of timber, like the surviving vicarage at Sleaford, and that was the way timber was being used in Cotswold towns at this time. Farther away still from the quarries there were such houses as that at Digby with 'walls of stone, splint and mortar'. This must have meant low stone walls with stakes stuck into the core as frame for earth walls above. Mortar at this time meant simply earth, if it was not called lime mortar.[2]

On the Lincolnshire Wolds, between Louth and Horncastle, there were a few stone houses, built of the ironstone used for churches in the neighbourhood, but further south the soft purple sandstone of the Spilsby area

---

[1] R. B. Wood-Jones, *loc. cit.*

[2] Henry Best, writing in 1634, described how earth was broken up and water added, to make what he called mortar walls; *Farming Book* (Surtees Soc., 1857), 145.

was not used for houses at all. Similarly in Norfolk the equivalent stone, carstone, was not used for houses before the eighteenth century. At Kirmington, Lincs., the parson no longer lived in the vicarage and it was used as a poor house; it consisted of '2 bayes of buildings built of ashwood, post pan and baulkes, the walls stone and daubed with clay'. The stone may have been an infilling of chalk blocks. Chalk, like carstone, was little used before the end of the eighteenth century.[1]

In the Banbury region the characteristic house of this time had very thick stone walls, 2 feet 8 inches or so, compared with about 2 feet in seventeenth century building.[2] Medieval builders had taken over the cruck method of roofing, adapting it to their purpose by resting the feet of the cruck blades at a height of several feet in the thickness of the wall.[3] Houses at King's Sutton and Bloxham have a later form of the same construction: the roof is supported on curved principals whose feet lodged in the upper wall.

Plaster floors were to be found in the Cotswolds, made of lime plaster instead of gypsum; spaces between joists were packed with clay laid on wattle;[4] that is, the technique for filling the panels of a framed building was turned to this purpose.

The limestone uplands stretching through Lincolnshire, east Leicestershire and Northamptonshire to the broad plateau of the Cotswolds must have been characterized throughout by small villages and large farms, with wealthy yeomen and gentry landowners, as rich as the average villager was poor, for on the thin soils of the limestone the average farmer was less wealthy than his opposite number on the clays or the pastoral regions.[5] The cloth industry on the Severn side of the Cotswolds is not likely to have modified this pattern. Hence Cotswold villages are a product of the seventeenth and eighteenth centuries, rather than the sixteenth. Rebuilding by small yeomen and husbandmen took place not in the first flush of the great rebuilding, but in its later phases.

Even so, one can already pick out those distinctive features of house planning in stone areas which were to persist until Georgian times (see fig. 16). For one thing, the axial chimney stack between two rooms never became popular. In houses of three units (hall, parlour and service-room)

[1] There are good chalk cottages at Speeton, Yorks., dated c. 1800.

[2] R. B. Wood Jones, loc. cit.

[3] At Church Enstone, the fourteenth century barn has the feet of the crucks seated in the wall at a height of 5 feet.

[4] W. G. Davie and E. G. Dawber, Old Cottages, Farmhouses and other Buildings in the Cotswold District (1905), 15.

[5] An extension to the Cotswolds of Joan Thirsk's findings about Lincolnshire; English Peasant Farming, 83–4.

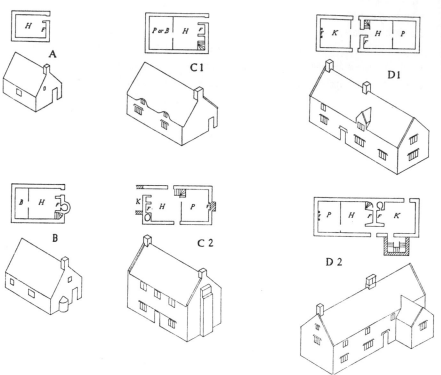

FIGURE 16. Types of house on the southern part of the limestone belt (i.e. the Cotswolds and Somerset). In types A–C, entrance at the gable end is usual until *c.* 1700, and type C2 is based on an Elizabethan house at West Camel altered in 1701. In type A, there must have been a ladder to the loft when that improvement was made. It is difficult to separate types B and C: that is, to distinguish Buttery from unheated bed-chamber or parlour. Type D1 is particularly common in the Ham Hill area of Somerset and lasted from the sixteenth century until *c.* 1700 or later. Type D2 (based on a house at Rodcombe, Aston Subedge, Gloucestershire, after G. L. Worsley) is not earlier than *c.* 1600, since it has taken over the axial chimney stack from the eastern region and in this instance the staircase wing was added *c.* 1665.

the cross passage with a hall fireplace backing on the passage is found in the Cotswolds and the south-west; whether it extends north through Northamptonshire to Kesteven is doubtful. The Cotswolds share this type of arrangement with the northern and western parts of the highland zone; dated examples in the Cotswolds have been noted at Laverton near Broadway (1582) and Stanton (1615),[1] but this adaptation of the lowland cross passage plan to a stone tradition probably took place in the Middle Ages. The fireplace is set in a stone partition wall; the other internal

[1] G. L. Worsley, *Traditional Domestic Architecture in the Cotswold Region* (Manchester thesis 1956), 88–9.

divisions, such as that between hall and parlour, are usually timber-framed. In the smaller Monmouthshire house the stone stack precedes the insertion of upper floors: 'the changeover from the smoke-filled interior of the Middle Ages to the comparative comfort of a smokeless room—however draughty through lack of glass in the windows—took place while the custom of living in a hall open to the roof was still current.'[1] No doubt the same was true in other stone regions. When an upper floor becomes a necessity, the staircase is built near the chimney stack, just as it is incorporated with the axial brick stack in eastern counties. The limestone uplands were too prosperous in later times to tolerate the survival of the small two-bay open hall which continued to be good enough for Monmouthshire, and which was improved by putting in a gable-end fireplace with stairs alongside to the new chamber.

The smallest type of new house sufficiently convenient to have stood for the succeeding centuries without major alteration is the medieval type with a hall and cross wings. The chief novelty at this time is that there is a chamber over the hall from the beginning. For the yeoman who had bought or leased a manor, rebuilding in that improved version of a traditional plan put the hall-mark of success on his ambitions. Moat Farm at Barford St. John, Oxon., was rebuilt in 1606 on the moated site of the medieval manor house; one window of thirteenth century date, reset in the south wing of the new house, is the only trace of its predecessors. When a yeoman took over the demesne land of a former manor the manor house began to be known as manor farm, whether or not a new manor house was built elsewhere. Manor Farm, Orton Waterville, Hunts., is a new house, with hall and cross wings, dated 1571 (pl. VIIIa). It was no doubt such buildings, built of stone in a county where timber had been the usual material, that Harrison had in mind when he spoke of stone replacing timber. The Old Rectory, Elton, Hunts., was rebuilt at a slightly later time, and the rectory at Sherrington, Bucks., in 1606. Both are of stone, with hall and cross wings: two full storeys on a medieval plan. At Sherrington the internal partition walls are timber-framed and the fireplaces on outside walls. The parson who built it described it as 'conteyninge five bays, all of stone, a hall, a parlor, a kitchen, a buttery and a boultinge howse, with chambers over everye roome well and sufficiently boarded'.[2] He must have regarded the hall as one bay and each of the wings two. Today one wing contains drawing- and dining-rooms and the other study and kitchen (apart from modern additions), but the original arrangement was probably parlour and buttery in one wing, and kitchen and boulting house in the other.

[1]Fox and Raglan, *Mon. Ho.*, I, 45.
[2]L.R.O., Terriers, Vol. 8.

The dormer window, as a device for making more headroom within the roof space, had been invented in the Middle Ages. In larger stone houses the line of the wall was carried up at intervals to provide for window openings with gables over them, and such gabled dormers flush with the façade became from this time a regular part of the vernacular building of limestone regions. With it went the practice of making the upper floor at a level lower than the eaves, so that the chambers were only half in the roof (see pl. IXa). A farmhouse at Laverton, near Broadway, dated 1582, has this arrangement. In smaller houses the windows were made in much simpler fashion, entirely within the roof, by raising a few rafters to clear a small opening over which the thatch curved like an eyebrow (pl. IXb). It is impossible to tell in general whether such small dormers are a later insertion or whether they are original. Many of them must be original, the work of builders who made the least possible change in customary ways to incorporate this improvement.

At Yetminster, south-east of Yeovil, there is a good example of a yeoman's house of late Elizabethan date, characteristic of its age and the region. The walls are of local rubble stone, coursed but rough; the roof is thatched. The long rectangle is low in proportion, for the upper rooms are within the roof space, lighted by low eyebrow dormers. At the one end is the hall, with its open fireplace in the gable, and alongside the staircase, buttressed out. The hall ceiling is divided into square panels, in the West Country tradition, by a main beam 12 inches deep and 11 inches thick, with a deep chamfer, and smaller beams of the same proportions morticed into it and into wall beams and the beam of the passage partition. Beyond the hall is a wide through passage, and on the other side of it a buttery which is less than the width of the house, leaving room for a way through to the third room, the parlour. The latter was not heated originally, since it was only a bedroom. The only alteration in modern times has been the insertion of a range in the open hearth of the hall, and of a staircase from the parlour which is straight and somewhat less steep than that in the hall.

That part of Somerset within five miles or so of the Ham Hill quarries has villages with a wealth of stone houses which offer the same problems as the Cotswolds. It is easier to pick out types of plan than to put a date to them. The mullioned window continues in vogue well into the eighteenth century with no change of proportions; early in the seventeenth century the mullion with a plain or hollow chamfer gives way to the ovolo moulding. The lights of windows still have four centred heads, of Tudor style, for some time after 1600, and door openings of similar shape with a moulded label, again of essentially Tudor style, are to be seen on houses dated after 1660. Most of the houses no doubt belong to that late period, but at Chisel-

VIIa. This one view in Lacock, Wilts., shows a cruck-framed house, a later timber-framed house with jettied first floor, and stone building of still more recent times.

VIIb. The further part of this house at Rodley, Glos., was built of timber in the 17th century, and the nearer part added in lias limestone, perhaps early in the 18th century, when the timber frame was also filled with brick.

VIIIa. Manor Farm, Orton Waterville, Hants, built in 1571, has the traditional H plan; the only new element is the chamber over the hall. The wings are of two full storeys, compared with three in Manor Farm, Clipsham, Rutland, built in 1639 (plate XIIIb). The photograph shows that there is a through passage with the hall fireplace backing on it.

VIIIb. A drawing of a Middlesex farm-yard in 1715, showing timber-framed and weather-boarded buildings making a tight group round a farmyard.

borough and elsewhere there are houses of two unit plan which may be fifty or sixty years earlier (see pl. Xa). They have two rooms, hall and parlour, with an upper storey and small dormers under the thatch. The hall has a gable-end fireplace and the parlour is unheated; the entrance is either in the gable end, alongside the fireplace, as in the Monmouthshire houses of this sort, or in the centre of one side. The two-roomed house of the Cotswolds thus differs only in detail from that of the Welsh Marches or the north of England.

CHAPTER FIVE

The Highland Zone

a. The West Country

ALTHOUGH there is as much evidence from Devonshire as any other county of intensified activity from *c.* 1575 onwards, it is more than usually difficult to distinguish phases within a process of rebuilding which lasted until the eighteenth century. There was no pronounced change in materials. Cob may by the end of that time have been less highly thought of, but was as much used. Some stone farmhouses bear a date, but that is rarely so in the case of cob, and a chronology must depend mainly on a detailed study of mouldings, which remains to be attempted.

Throughout the period the cross passage remained in west country minds an essential feature of the house plan. The reasons are obvious. Over the greater part of Devon, the farmer was more interested in cattle than in sheep or corn, though there were considerable districts noted for their arable husbandry even in the sixteenth century. For perhaps three farmers out of four, however, the lay-out of farm buildings and of the house itself was determined by the need for daily attention to cattle and their produce, rather than the more seasonal requirements of arable farming. For that reason the byre and the dairy were more important than the corn chamber. The term *dairy,* as distinct from the eastern term milk-house, is found in the sixteenth century all the way down the west of England from Lancashire to Devon, and is an ancient mark of the pasture farming half of the country. The need for access from the dairy to the court or yard at the rear, every day and many times a day, perpetuated the usefulness of the cross passage. The other reason for its persistence is that many west country farmhouses had a detached kitchen. Now that this has been made plain from records,[1] outbuildings which might be thought to be older houses which were not demolished in a rebuilding assume a new significance. At Exminster vicarage, for instance, there is a building of fifteenth century date which answers perfectly to a description of 1679: 'an old house built with stone and covered with reed, one oven to bake standing in the chimney, and place to brew. . . .'[2] There is a detached kitchen among the farm buildings at Woodlands, in the parish of Bridford. It is built of cob on stone footings; it consists of one room with a chamber over it, and a fireplace, and it is distinguished from the adjoining barn by the range of three mullioned windows to the kitchen. They are of wood, each with two lights; the mullions have a plain, steep chamfer which could indicate a date of c. 1550–75. The openings have never been glazed, but had the usual slender oak bar between the mullions. The house itself will be discussed later.

Alongside these persistent and old fashioned elements in the Devonshire tradition there is one other: the use of a chamber as the principal sleeping-room, whether it was the chamber over the hall or that over some other room; that is, the medieval solar. In no other part of England can sixteenth century houses be found in which so much attention was paid to the open roof of the chambers, showing what a high status they had. One example is the Old Rectory, Sampford Peverell, which may have been built c. 1535; the first floor room in the cross wing has a fine waggon-roof of eight bays.[3] The hamlet of Nettacott, 4½ miles north of Exeter, consists of three houses, of which the largest, which we may call Upper Nettacott, was perhaps a franklin's house of c. 1500. It was[4] built of cob, of two storeys in a long rectangle, and the roof over the hall and parlour chambers was of the same style. Such buildings in a developed medieval tradition were clearly a source of inspiration in arrangement, if not in finish, to less wealthy farmers of a generation later.

On the fringes of Dartmoor, where the long house had persisted, the process of separating the living part from the byre began at this time. The first stage was to make some kind of partition, turning the cross *walk* into a cross *passage*. When Robert Furse of Morshead, in the parish of Dean Prior, spoke of making a porch and an entry, that is what he meant.[5] The simpler division, and no doubt the earlier, was of wood (see fig. 17).

[1]Terriers, particularly of 1678–80, which are discussed below p. 222.
[2]Terrier 1679, Exeter R.O.
[3]W. A. Pantin, 'Medieval Priests' Houses', *Med. Arch.*, I (1957), 139–40. For an illustration of the type of roof, common in Devon churches, see Howard and Crossley, *Engl. Church Woodwork*, 98.
[4]The past tense is appropriate, since in 1958 the house was in the last stages of decay.
[5]R. Hansford Worth, *Dartmoor*, 410.

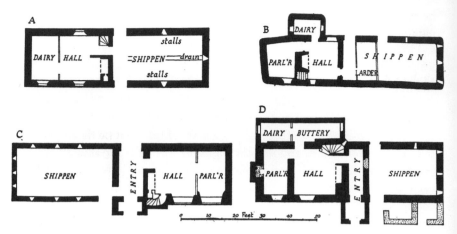

FIGURE 17. The development of the Dartmoor long house. A: the simplest type, with dwelling entered from the cross walk (after R. H. Worth, and based on Colliehole Cottage, Chagford). B: cross walk turned into cross passage by a wooden partition (Tor Farm, Widecombe, after R. W. McDowall). C: stone wall between passage and shippen, with separate entrance to shippen (R. H. Worth, based on Shilston, Throwleigh, dated 1656). D: dwelling and shippen still further separated, and dwelling developed (R. W. McDowall, Lower Tor, Widecombe, dated 1707). The parlour is only identified with certainty in D, where it has a fireplace.

The cross passage in the average Devon and Somerset house is distinctly wider than elsewhere in England. At Pinn Farm, Otterton, it is 6 feet 6 inches; at Prowse, Sandford, Devon, it is 7 feet 9 inches. One suspects that this width is due to its origin as a way through which cattle were brought into the byre, rather than from a passage within the hall for strictly domestic traffic. With this goes naturally a very wide doorway— 3 feet 10 inches at Prowse. The floor of the passage there is still of cobbles, an interesting survival and no indication of inferior building, for the passage ceiling has moulded beams and joists. At Brook Farm, Clapton in Gordano, Somerset, both the doorways already mentioned were at some time widened by cutting the jambs into a curve at about three feet above the ground, in order to get large cider barrels into the house and *through the hall.*

The traditional position for the fireplace in the highland zone is against the wall of the cross passage, so that in one sense[1] the passage is outside the house (see pl. XIb). This arrangement persisted in Devonshire throughout our period, but as in so many other respects, this county departs from the general rule. When it came to making a chamber upstairs and a staircase

[1]As Fox and Raglan pointed out, *Mon. Ho.*, I, 87–8.

to it, fireplace and stairs are seldom found side by side, possibly because there was not room for both in a length of wall less than the width of the house. The newel staircase, with treads of stone or solid oak balks, is placed on the back wall in its own projection of stone or cob.

In what appear to be the simplest houses the only other room one expects to find is a dairy, on the other side of the hall from the passage (see fig. 18). There are examples, of sixteenth century date, of houses so

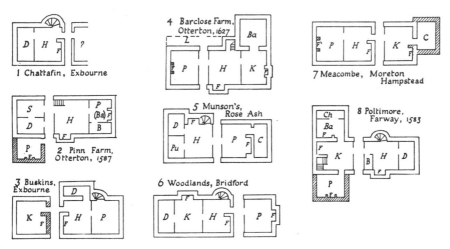

FIGURE 18. Examples of Devon farmhouse plans outside the Dartmoor region. They vary in more than one respect, and so cannot be arranged in type series; they show how many ways rich but conservative farmers could find of adapting a plan derived from the long house. Nos. 2, 7 and 8 are of stone, the others of cob. Nos. 2, 4 and 8 have the West Country front chimney stack. Parts certainly added are hatched, but a plan such as No. 6 may be the result of piecemeal development. H, Hall; P, Parlour; K, Kitchen; D, Dairy; C, Cider Cellar; B, Buttery; Ba, Backhouse; Ch, Cheese room; S, Store.

small as not to have a through passage, in which the two-bay house was divided into hall and dairy with a chamber over the dairy.[1] Perhaps this arrangement stemmed from the type of farmhouse in which the third unit, across the passage, was still used for cattle, but it was followed in at least one new house of this period—Poltimore, Farway, built in 1583. Chattafin in Exbourne parish is a good example. On the other side of the passage there is now a nineteenth century extension, but the hall with its three doorways is unaltered. They all have heavy oak frames with a flat pointed head, and all are chamfered on the hall side. A doorway in the back wall opens on to the staircase; by its side is a cream oven (see below p. 168).

[1]See *Mon. Ho.*, I, fig. 22, for a section through New House Farm, Christon, S. Devon, and a similar Monmouthshire house.

The third door, in the far wall, leads to the dairy. This was also the arrangement in the house of Robert Furze.[1]

The most striking innovation of this age was the house, in stone or cob, with a chimney stack on the front wall serving both hall and chamber over it. The yeoman farmer took the idea from larger houses.[2] The most easterly example is a medieval farmhouse at Hinton St. George where such a stack was added in a remodelling which included a range of gabled dormers for chambers in the roof. The type is found all over Devon and in Cornwall; in east Devon and between Exmoor and the north coast of Somerset it is the standard type (see pl. XIa). The earliest are late Elizabethan (e.g. Pinn Farm, Otterton, dated 1587) and the fashion lasts for a century; an example in brick at Otterton dated 1707 is exceptional. Why should it have found such favour? Pride in the sight of such a novel feature, often carried out in contrasting materials, such as grey limestone and red sandstone, or limestone with flint and stone chequer-work, must have dictated placing it where every passer-by must notice it. What is novel is that when improved heating arrangements came into fashion, the two rooms so provided were the hall and the chamber over it, rather than hall and parlour alongside. Local tradition conquered convenience, for it was not as economical as an axial stack, since at the most it could serve only hall and chamber. The stack is usually placed in the corner of the hall, adjacent to the through passage, which invariably accompanies it; the main window is then at the other side of the fireplace, but there is sometimes a smaller window in the chimney corner through which callers can be observed.

At Poltimore in Farway parish, where the fireplace in the chamber over the hall is dated 1583, there was originally a newel staircase, entirely of wood, in the corner of the hall by the entrance from the passage. Other features of the house remain unchanged such as the open hearth fire in the hall. The partition between hall and passage at Poltimore is of stud and plank construction, and the studs have chamfered edges stopping at the level of the bench fixed along the partition, showing that the bench is an original fitting. The windows at Poltimore and at Blamphayne in Widworthy parish, which is dated 1588, have ovolo moulded mullions. The ovolo replaces the plain chamfer at this time, and with it go doorways made up of three large timbers, joined and pegged at the shoulders, cut into a flat triangular head and chamfered on one face. Such points of finish were in part a matter of cost in relation to function, as well as of fashion. At

[1] R. Hansford Worth, *Dartmoor*, 406.
[2] Such as Boycombe in Farway parish, of which a plan is published by W. G. Hoskins in his *Local History in England* (1959), 125.

Brook Farm, Clapton in Gordano, near Bristol, the doorway into the cross passage (that is, the 'front' door) has an ovolo moulded frame and a square head, while that from passage to hall has a pointed head and plain chamfer.

One cannot assume that Devon houses of this age had a parlour, because the chamber over the hall must often have filled that need.[1] Pinn Farm, Otterton, a front chimney house built in 1587, now has beyond the hall a room with a gable end fireplace which may originally have been a parlour, with a small buttery in it. In the eighteenth century this room was demoted to a backhouse or kitchen, because the working room in this position still seemed more useful. At Brook Farm, Clapton in Gordano, the only room beyond the hall was a service room which became a cider cellar, whatever its original purpose.

There is a contemporary comment on what Cornish husbandmen were doing to their houses which is all the more valuable because Cornish inventories, like those for other parts of the highland zone, rarely give details of rooms. Richard Carew, writing in the 1580's,[2] said that husbandmen 'in times not past the remembrance of some yet living' dwelt in houses with 'walles of earth, low thatched roofes, few partitions, no planchings or glasse windows, and scarcely any chimnies, other than a hole in the wall to let out the smoke: their bed, straw and a blanket: as for sheets, so much linnen cloth had not yet stepped over the narrow channel betweene them and Brittaine. To conclude, a mazer and a panne or two, comprised all their substance: but now most of these fashions are universally banished, and the Cornish husbandman conformeth himself with a better supplied civilitie to the Easterne patterne.' There is no mistaking the unanimity of the remarks of Harrison of Essex, Carew of Cornwall and King of Cheshire. The one novel phrase used by Carew is that earlier houses had few partitions. We shall see that in Yorkshire houses of the seventeenth century the most significant improvement is not in the size of the small farmhouse but in a growing desire for the convenience of separate rooms.

b. Yorkshire and the North

Between 1585 and 1615 a number of Yorkshire manor houses were rebuilt, and on the western slopes of the Pennines the lesser gentry of Lancashire were busy.[3] The Shuttleworth family rebuilt Gawthorpe, Lancs., in

[1] It is particularly unfortunate that inventories for the diocese of Exeter were destroyed in the German raid of 1943, so that documentary evidence of furnishings and function is not available.

[2] In his *Survey of Cornwall* (edition of 1769), 66 b.

[3] L. Ambler, *Old Halls and Manor Houses of Yorkshire*, 56–72; H. Taylor, *Old Halls of Lancashire and Cheshire*, pls. XXII–XXIV.

1599–1605; the house and farm accounts[1] give details of payments for quarrying stone and roofing slates; for laying foundations, building walls and paying a piper when the roof was reared; to the mason for cutting mouldings and to the blacksmith for making iron casements; for the Irish timber imported to make ceilings and panelling. The yeomen here and there were able to follow suit: Adam Martindale, a yeoman's son of High Hayes, Mossbank, in the parish of Prescot, recorded in his autobiography[2] that some time before 1613 his father had built a new house beside the old one, in order to have more comfort and more 'stowage for corn', the two reasons for rebuilding everywhere.

Further north, every decade saw some new building, but not more than had gone on in the earlier years of Elizabeth. The gentry and the rising middle class were steadily widening the gulf between their living standards and those of the peasantry. The houses alongside medieval peel towers at Blencoe Hall and Cliburn Hall were rebuilt.[3] There was still room for eccentricity in Westmorland, such as the new first floor hall built by Sir William Hutton, known as Shank Castle,[4] or for experiment, such as Smardale Hall, Waitby, which consists of a long rectangle with a round tower at each angle, two of them housing a staircase.[5] At Gaythorne Hall, Asby, the problem of access to upper floors was solved by building a square tower on either flank of a house of rectangular plan;[6] each tower had a stair of the new well type but rising round a solid pier of masonry. In the Eden valley several large houses were built with a two- or three-storey porch containing a newel stair.[7] Thus one can see that among the Westmorland gentry older ideas about the house were dissolving, and in the flux new notions were applied in either novel or traditional fashion.

Some of the new building was, however, on a scale modest enough to set a style for the 'statesmen' of two or three generations later. Orton Hall, rebuilt in 1604, is a simple rectangle of two full storeys; Winder Hall, Barton (1612), has a newel stair in a projection at the rear, to the side of the further door of the through passage; so has Kirkbarrow in the same parish, a rebuilding in 1583 of a cruck-framed house.[8] The projecting newel stair and the gable end chimney, corbelled out, can be found in the local

[1] Ed. J. Harland (Chetham Soc., 1856), 125–70.
[2] Ed. R. Parkinson (Chetham Soc., 1845), 1–2.
[3] T.C.W.A.A.S., 12 (1893), 126; N.S. 7 (1907), 120.
[4] Ibid., 54 (1954), 144.
[5] R.C.H.M. Westm., 233, pl. 18.
[6] Ibid., 16. This plan must have come from London, for it is common among the Thorpe drawings in the Soane Museum.
[7] R. W. Brunskill, 'The Development of the Larger House in the Eden Valley', T.C.W.A.A.S., 57 (1957), 83–86.
[8] Ibid., 189 (6); 37 (4) and (3).

vernacular of 1600. They became after 1660 regular features of the new houses of the small Lakeland farmers who, as they threw off the last shackles of medieval villeinage, became known as statesmen.

Even when rebuilding was not contemplated, minor improvements were made. In the East Riding a wealthy parson, George Haye, rector of Huggate, put wainscotting and a boarded floor in his parlour. Many parsons were to do the same in the seventeenth century, as the parlour began to be used as a sitting-room. Henry Peckston, a farmer at Meaux, put glass in his windows and a chamber over the hall; Herbert Hanley, yeoman, of Gt. Driffield, put 'new inn (i.e. inside) doores and the glasse' into his house. Elsewhere, 'sealing worke', the loose boards and joists over the hall, or 'a chamber over the house' valued at 6s. 8d., are evidence of new ideas about convenience and comfort. Apart from these structural alterations, houses of the gentry and yeomanry began to have an iron range or an iron chimney in at least one room.[1] They are as common in Lancashire as Yorkshire and farther north, and no doubt they imply that coal was being generally used. In Cumberland and Westmorland, the gentry and successful merchants began to have ornamental plasterwork done: moulded plaster beams, friezes, ceilings and overmantels.[2]

In Yorkshire houses of moderate size there are clear signs of rebuilding in stone and the abandonment of timber as the chief material. Some of these houses are being proved, now that they are studied closely, to have been aisled halls in their first form; moreover west Yorkshire was familiar with halls having only a single aisle. Guiseley Rectory, a plan of which was published fifty years ago,[3] has a range of rooms in the main block and a parallel range behind it about half the width (see fig. 19). The arrangement is comprehensible as soon as one thinks of it as a hall with one aisle, and the wooden piers of the arcade, of five bays, actually appear on the plan. The main range was rebuilt in 1601, and the service wing at the rear, making an L plan, is probably eighteenth-century. The result was a house of the newest style; the symmetrical façade has balanced gables and a storeyed porch giving on the medieval through passage.

The house known as 'The Nunnery', Arthington,[4] was built in 1585 on the site of a monastic house and with the stone from it. Its plan shows that the continuous outshot or lean-to, derived from the aisle, had become

---

[1] E.g. Lancs. and Cheshire Wills and Inventories (Chetham Soc.), II, 174, 207, 277; III, 29. The earliest noted is 1562, in the Yorkshire inventory of John Tyndall, esquire, of Brotherton.

[2] H.M.C. Westm., 244 and pls. 48, 50–51 (Calgarth Hall, Windermere); 117 (Blease Hall, Old Hutton).

[3] In L. Ambler, Old Halls and Manor Houses of Yorkshire, pl. LIX.

[4] Ibid., pl. XLIX.

part of the local idiom. There are three rooms in the main range with a kitchen behind the hall, making a T plan; smaller service-rooms are placed in the angles of the T, and behind the rest of the range, aisle fashion. It has three full storeys and there is no trace of any earlier timber building; the partition wall is of stone. Both Guiseley Rectory and The Nunnery have a through passage at the end of the hall, with the hall fireplace backing on it, in the northern manner.

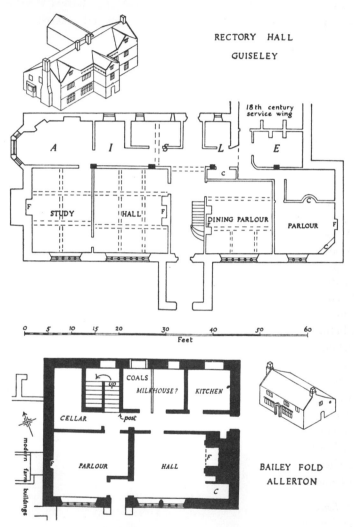

FIGURE 19. Two Yorkshire houses of the seventeenth century, showing the effect of the aisled hall tradition. Guiseley Rectory, a manor house, is a thirteenth century aisled hall of timber, with five bays, rebuilt in stone in 1601. Bailey Fold, a small farmhouse, has at most one surviving post of its earlier arcading.

In addition to these houses with respectively four and three rooms in the main block, Bailey Fold in the Bradford township of Allerton has only two (see fig. 19). It stands, like so many seventeenth century houses in the West Riding, isolated on the slope of a dale at a height of about 800 feet. It is well built, of coursed rubble with mullioned windows; that in the hall has a transom, making it about 9 inches higher than the parlour window. Only the hall had a fireplace at first. Along the rear is a continuous range of outshot, clearly contemporary; it contains service-rooms and, at one end, the stone staircase. The one remarkable feature is a wooden post at the corner of the staircase opening, rising to the wall plate or arcade (whichever one chooses to consider it) and having a curved brace up to the plate. Neither post nor brace is necessary to the structure. They are either the sole relics of a timber hall with one aisle, completely rebuilt in stone, or a hangover from the aisled hall technique. The latter is more likely, for the roof seems to be of the same age as the rest of the building; it is of the usual Yorkshire style, with tie-beams and principal rafters at 8-foot intervals. The king-post to each truss carries the square ridge piece and has three struts on each side out to the principals. The plan matches perfectly what a contemporary called a house 'of three bays with aisling'[1] and shows that in the Pennine valleys the tradition of the aisled hall, which had gone out of fashion in the south in the fourteenth century, was still alive in 1600 and after. That is not to suggest that the aisle was still open to the hall in any of these houses. What survives is a particular constructional method, for the sake of the convenience of a compact plan with the service rooms immediately behind the main rooms.

Bailey Fold, in spite of its simple and limited accommodation, was a relatively superior house. Lesser men were still content with the cruck house. A survey of the manors in Craco (north of Skipton) and Silsden (north of Keighley) shows how busy those lesser men were; even in remote dales the pressure of population and increased means were driving men to build on the common land, with or without the lord's consent.[2] In Lancashire, Rossendale, which had been part of the forest of Blackburnshire, was disafforested by Henry VII, and soon enclosure and encroachment on the waste were proceeding so rapidly that commissions of inquiry were held in 1561 and 1616 to make sure that the new holdings were recognized as copyhold of the lordship of Clitheroe. The commissions found new houses, cottages, smithies, kilns, turf-houses

[1]Survey of 1569 of lands in Worden and elsewhere in Lancs., Preston R.O., DDF/52.
[2]Yorks. Arch. Soc. Library, Leeds: DDI 21/31. The survey is not dated, but belongs either to 1586 or 1603.

and barns.[1] Most Lancashire copyholders' houses had between two and four bays; that is, were anything from twenty-five to fifty feet in length. One of them, as has been said, had aisling as well, but they were all houses of one storey, most of them with only one room. Each house is called a firehouse, but about a quarter of them had a chamber as well: 'one chamber on the east side' or 'two chambers at the north end'.[2] Whether the chambers provided 'stowage for corn' of the kind that Martindale's father needed, or were sleeping rooms, we cannot tell, for Lancashire inventories of this time very rarely mention the rooms of a house. One thing can safely be said: the tradition of the single-storey house was yet unshaken among the countrymen of Lancashire, condemned, unless they were rearing sheep and cattle on the Pennine spurs, to farm some of the poorest land in England. Houses of this sort can still be found in parts of Lancashire, though they are disappearing rapidly now. The common type in the Fylde is cruck built, with 'clat and clay' walls, often replaced with cobbles or bricks.[3]

Harrison had said that men were now content only to use oak for building; at Craco and Silsden most of the new work was in oak, though some ash and elm had been sold, as well as being felled by tenants under warrants 'to make and repair their ancient firehouses and barns'.[4] One man had built a barn of two bays of oak; another a barn of four bays and a hayhouse of three, both of oak and 'lately builded'. Nicholas Ricroft had built 'one firehouse and a lath (barn) of three pair of crucks and one kiln'; Richard Cockson had built a 'firehouse of four pair of crucks—oak'; he also had a barn and a hayhouse each of two pairs of crucks and of 'ill timber'. Five of these cruck houses were of ash and two of oak; of the former, one must have been old, for it was 'ready to fall'. Two of them had chambers; Thomas Toppam's firehouse of three bays, built of ash, had a chamber of one bay, also of ash; William Howson's house, the only one with an upper floor, was of three bays, built of ash (and 'ready to fall') with a 'chamber over the wall plate'. Most of the dwellings were of three bays.

A survey of houses belonging to the manor of Sheffield in 1611 includes dwellings of all sizes upwards from a dwelling with a house of one bay and a chamber of one bay. They very rarely had a kitchen and no other service-rooms are mentioned by name. Most of them had at least a parlour or a chamber as well as the dwelling house. Nicholas Sampson's can be clearly visualized. There was a house of one bay, with a parlour at one end

[1] G. H. Tupling, *Econ. Hist. of Rossendale* (1927), 58–66.
[2] Preston R.O., DDF/52.
[3] See R. Watson, *Proc. Lancs. and Cheshire Hist. Soc.*, 109 (1957) figs. 24 and 25 for a three-bay cruck house possibly of this period.
[4] Leeds; DDI 21/31.

of it and at the other '2 bays for beast houses'. It was a long house, but he had recently added, in a position not specified, two more parlours, as well as two new barns and another beast house. Most of the chambers are clearly on the ground floor. These houses are mostly larger than those in Craco and Silsden, presumably because they went with larger holdings.[1]

Here at last we have a picture of the traditional peasant house in West Yorkshire and Lancashire: cruck built, of between two and four bays in length and most commonly of three bays; called a firehouse because it had a hearth and to distinguish it from a barn or a hayhouse; consisting of one room only unless there is specific evidence to the contrary. Such a dwelling was good enough for a man who could afford to build a barn of four bays and a hayhouse of three. The most remarkable feature is not the size, but that there were in older houses and more remote parts no structural divisions into living-, sleeping- and service-rooms. In the city of York there are houses of the fourteenth and fifteenth centuries with no screen or partition on the ground floor between the through passage and the hall. A house of the late sixteenth century in Patrick Pool, York, is of three storeys and attic, three bays in length and jettied on both the long sides, but there are no structural divisions inside.[2] York builders had thus adopted building techniques, such as the frame building and the jetty, and used them in houses of traditional plan; the new practices of the Lowland zone are absorbed in the north without breaking the essential continuity of highland culture.[3]

Although some northern farmers were still content to have one room for all living purposes, and very rarely had a chamber upstairs even for storage, they began at this time to make a revolutionary break with the past by separating living quarters from the byre. Daniel King, writing during the time of the Commonwealth,[4] said that Cheshire farmers until the early seventeenth century still 'had their fire in the midst of the house, against a hob of clay, and their Oxen also under the same roof'. In parts of Lancashire the long house tradition was still alive, and farther north it lasted even longer. In Yorkshire at this time probate inventories, when they mention rooms, often speak of the netherhouse, the nether end of the house, the low end, or the lower end.[5] It is a service-room, but it has no very distinct

---

[1]S. O. Addy, *Evolution of the English House* (1905), 207–10.
[2]I am indebted to Mr. T. W. French for these York examples, found in the course of the work of the R.C.H.M.
[3]C. Fox, *Personality of Britain*, 88, propositions xi and xii.
[4]*The Vale-Royall of England* (1656), 19.
[5]Cf. E. E. Evans, *Irish Folk Ways* (1957), 43: 'the end of the house farthest from the hearth is commonly referred to as "the bottom end", a relic of the time when it housed the cattle'.

use. It may contain ploughs, or sheep bars, troughs or coal, but it has not been turned to any regular or special domestic purpose. The explanation must be that the cattle had only recently been driven out of it, and that they might be brought back in a hard winter, as they still are in some of the Dartmoor long houses today. In East Anglia by this time the backhouse had become a combination of kitchen, milkhouse and buttery; in Yorkshire it had not yet been taken over for such uses. Occasionally the living part was called the forehouse,[1] and firehouse and forehouse eventually become the commonest names for the hall living-room in a dwelling with several rooms.

Cruck building probably lasted as long in Cleveland as in any part of England, but in such a simple style that surviving houses are difficult to date. One of the most primitive, now a ruin, is Rigg House, Glaisdale Head.[2] It is of two bays with a cruck truss in the centre. There is no chimney, but traces of burning suggest a hearth against the gable, with the entrance to one side of it and the salt box (a hole in the wall near the hearth where salt could be kept dry) to the other. Another example is Stangend, Danby,[3] a yeoman's house by its size, with house and byre under the one roof, entered separately. Stangend has seen some rebuilding and in essence belongs to a century later.

In Durham county we meet the backhouse, the common alternative to netherhouse. John Carter of Shincliffe, yeoman, whose goods amounted at his death to the respectable total of £128, and who had a large farm stock, had only two parts to his dwelling—the hall house and the backhouse. Where the dwelling house is said, as in the manor of Sheffield, to be as much as four bays in length, it was no doubt divided in the same way into living and service ends.

The inventory of William Marshall, husbandman, of Billingham on Tees, is very illuminating, because in it the appraisers spoke of the 'forehouse or firehouse'.[4] It was a living-room of the usual sort, with a long table and forms, and this is the earliest use of forehouse as an alternative to firehouse. It must have been in antithesis to backhouse; the term was already well established in Durham, and in the seventeenth century it was common in Yorkshire as well. Richard Eltringham's house at Aukland in 1616 is clearly described: a forehouse with a table, one chair and two cupboards, pewter, brass and fireirons; a low house with more furniture but presumably a service-room; a parlour with a standing bed and a clothes

[1]E.g. York Registry, A 1536–90 (Eastern Deaneries), inventory of William Adamson of E. Cowton, 1584.
[2]Grid reference SE/748022. I am indebted to Mrs. Mary Nattrass for information about the house.
[3]Mary Nattrass in *Y.A.J.*, 39, part 183 (1956), 140–2.
[4]Durham R.O., Durham Wills and Inventories, bundle 1590.

press, and over it the high chamber, containing another bed and five bushels of rye.

This simple way of life, changing slowly even in an age when new amenities were readily adopted in the south, is reflected in the contents of Yorkshire houses as well as in their plan. In the Vale of York, especially towards the Isle of Axholme, many people still ate rye bread, at a time when as far as one can see it had gone out of fashion in the rest of England. Neither rye nor oats, used alone, will make a dough that rises like fermented wheaten flour. For that reason both rye bread and oatcake will keep indefinitely, and the rye loaves listed in inventories are a durable store. The wheaten loaf was equally unknown in Lancashire and the Pennines, where every house had its bakestone for making oatcake.[1] The vicar of Brayton near Selby still had in his buttery 'three dozen square trenchers, eighteen case trenchers with a case', at a time when others of his class had put the trenchers on the fire and used pewter on the table. Even in quite large farmhouses the living-room might contain, as well as beef and bacon 'at the balks', cheeses ripening or all the variety of milk vessels. This is not mere untidiness, or even lack of other space for such things. The Yorkshire family had not moved so far away from the stage of working, as well as eating, in the hall house.

In the West Riding, the growth of the cloth industry must have been a rapid solvent of traditional ways, not only because of the money that it brought into the homes of those engaged in it but also for the close and regular contact between the clothing towns like Bradford and the townships growing round them, and between both and the larger world which came to want their products. Soon after 1600 there begins a series of inventories for the Bradford area;[2] the earliest is that of John Hudson of Cottingley (dated 1599),[3] a small farmer carrying on weaving in the living-room of his house. His goods were worth £65 10s., of which £10 worth of corn and hay in a barn, four kine and six other cattle, twenty-four sheep made up nearly £36. He had one mare to carry his cloth to market. Household goods worth nearly £30 implies prosperity, but his way of life was simple. The house seems to have consisted of hall and parlour, with the parlour ceiled

[1] In West Cumberland, oatcake was until recently made in sufficient quantity to last for a year; see W. M. Williams, *The Sociology of an English Village: Gosforth* (1956), 20–1.

[2] The Knights Hospitallers had estates centred on their preceptory of Newland, and possessed the right of probate; the post-Reformation owners maintained this profitable privilege, and the surviving records of it have been published as *Wills proved in the Court of the Manors of Crosley, Bingley, Cottingley and Pudsey, with Inventories* (Bradford Hist. and Ant. Soc., Local Record Series I, 1929). The documents in question are in the York Registry.

[3] *Ibid.*, 2–3.

over, possibly for a chamber, though none is named. The living-room had a window curtain, and the pots, pans and a chafing dish, as well as 'one shearboard, one prasse, lowmes, and all other thinges in the howse to clothinge apperteyninge'. The parlour bedroom held an ark and a chest, oatmeal and groats, as well as a bed, one great new chest, one old ark, and woollen yarn; it must have had a fireplace, for 'one chimblinge' is mentioned.

Such houses as John Hudson's at Cottingley, or John Bailey's at Allerton, show that medieval standards had begun to disappear in this lively and prosperous part of the north. Although there is a world of difference between the yeoman's house in Yorkshire and in Kent at the end of the Tudor period, there is still another world, dimly seen, in such remote parts of the north as High Furness. John Swaynson of the Graying in Cartmel, who died in 1600,[1] lived in a house with a living-room, two chambers (the middle chamber and the outchamber) and a *bower*. The word bower had lingered on in northern dialect for an inner room, and Swaynson, with goods worth £30, was not poor, but it is well to be reminded that ways of thought current in the fourteenth century were still alive in Furness in 1600.

[1] Preston R.O. WCW/F/S: 1599–1600.

IXa. A house at Bledlington, Glos., with chambers half in the roof and the Cotswold type of dormer.

IXb. The further part of the Post Office, Hemington, Leics., is a cruck-framed structure at right angles to the road. The nearer part was added in box frame construction, perhaps in the 17th century. The timber has nearly all been replaced by modern brick. Note the dormer windows for chambers within the roof space, and the Yorkshire or sliding sashes to all the windows.

Xa. This cottage at Chiselborough, Som., has gable end entrance and fireplace. All the windows on the front have stone mullions, with varying mouldings; those at the rear have wooden frames. Compare figure 16, C1.

Xb. This house at Ryhall, Rutland, bears the initials G.T.A. and the date 1679. Whatever the history of the house, nothing outside belies that date, and it is certainly acceptable for the storeyed bay window to the hall.

Conclusion

After a wide-ranging tour, which has taken in houses of many kinds, certain clear impressions emerge. Conditions of soil and climate, together with local opportunities for marketing surplus produce, determined farming methods, and they in turn were reflected in the housing standards of the countryside. The effect of material conditions might be modified, as they were in Kent, by local traditions such as the law of inheritance. The simple distinction between highland and lowland England might be blurred when a remote county with much high and infertile ground also contained, as did Devon and Hereford, large tracts of rich soil. Such local features do no more than diversify the overall picture of rural communities busily adapting their living ways to changed economic conditions.

Traditional ideas of the plan and arrangement of the house still dominated the countryman's thinking. In Essex, where medieval standards had been very advanced, the modernization of medieval structures seems to have been as marked as new work. More fieldwork in the south-east may show that the same is true of Kent and other counties. Farther away from London there is more evidence of new building, especially among the yeoman class and other successful members of the agricultural community. On the limestone belt and its margins the last traces of building in wood, until now common in the valleys where timber had been reasonably plentiful, were replaced by building in stone. At the bottom of the social scale the one-roomed cottage was still very common but began now to give way to a house of two rooms, hall and parlour. In eastern England such houses now had an axial chimney stack between the two rooms. The widespread popularity of this plan was new, but it is unlikely that, in an age when traditional forms of plan were as much approved as ever, this type was a novelty.

In the highland zone, buildings of this age, whether actually surviving, or recorded in documents, emphasize the persisting gulf in wealth and living standards between the gentry and the rank and file of the peasantry. The rural middle class, of yeomen and husbandmen with enough money to lease a manor or otherwise enlarge their sphere of activity, had not become numerous enough to make a mark on housing standards. There were exceptions only where opportunity came more readily as in the West Riding of Yorkshire, where a class of yeoman weaver was coming into existence, or in Devon and Hereford, where good soil had for centuries supported a minor gentry and wealthy freehold farmers.

In Yorkshire there was a change at the level of the manor house from timber to stone building, but the new stone houses were a natural growth from local traditions, not an imported fashion supplanting them. The cruck house and the aisled hall were still living elements of the local vernacular. In the west the tradition of fine timber building, both in cruck and box frame forms, was as vigorous as ever. In Devon, where farmers had long since developed their own form out of an ancient prototype, the first floor hall, as well as preserving the primitive long house in the Dartmoor region, they continued to pursue native lines of improvement.

What was happening to rural society to provoke these changes? Growth of population was certainly the most far reaching factor. Nothing else could have set off new building at every level of society. Better prices for primary producers put more money at the disposal of every class. The labourer, in so far as he had some livestock and at least his common rights, was also a primary producer. He was in part dependent on wages, but it would be a mistake to think of him simply as a wage-earner.[1] Even at a time when the pace of engrossment was quickening and common rights might be restricted, some labourers could afford to improve their way of life. Others, less determined or fortunate, deserted the land for the nearest town, and our account of changes in the countryside would be incomplete if we did not take note of their departure.

Ties of blood must often have linked the yeoman and husbandman with the labourer, and even when the latter was not in fact a younger brother or a cousin he was treated as a member of the family.[2] If he lived in the house he was nursed as affectionately when sick; helped to find or build a cottage when he married, and reckoned as a full member of the community. In the face of this, it is profoundly unhistorical to regard the gradual

[1]See R. H. Tawney, 'An Occupational Census of the Seventeenth Century' in *Econ. H.R.*, 5 (1934), 53: 'The picture (of Gloucestershire in 1608) which emerges from these figures . . . is one of a system of family farms worked with the aid of relatives—more than half the sons and brothers in the return are those of yeomen and husbandmen—and only to a small extent with hired labour'.

[2]As he was in West Cumberland until the early years of this century; see W. M. Williams, *Social Survey of an English Village: Gosforth* (1956) for a picture of small farms, largely self-sufficient until the advent of the tractor, and worked by family groups.

growth of privacy in domestic life as one of the prime aspects of housing development in this age, because it was true only of the gentry, who were outside the complex of economic interplay and of kinship which made the community. Anyone who has lived in a twentieth-century village long enough to have become part of it will have discovered that the ties which once held it together have not all been ruptured. There are unwritten codes of behaviour, such as that which prescribes that a gift in kind must be immediately returned in equivalent kind, and unsuspected relationships which explain why, for instance, a family moves into a particular house. They are the last traces of a pattern which we must find if we are to understand the Elizabethan village.

In such a society, expanding both in numbers and wealth but not yet bursting the seams of its habitual ways, more comfort was desirable and attainable. How much was purchased depended on money and ideas, and London was to a surprising degree the source of both. Harrison's comment on the increase of houses with a chimney applied equally to Essex and Lancashire. Another improvement was the glazing of windows, which became so common in this period that no attempt has been made to document it in these pages. As for the minor comforts to which Harrison referred—a feather bed and a pillow instead of a straw pallet and a wooden head support, for instance—there was still a contrast between, say, Suffolk and Yorkshire of the kind shown in inventories of a century earlier. In such respects the north of England was at least a hundred years behind the south.

This contrast probably reflects the degree to which the family farm was giving way, in more advanced regions, to enterprise on a larger scale conducted with paid labour. Beyond the range of the London market, the farmhouse, although its produce went to the local market, was a home for folk whose personal habits were still attuned to subsistence farming. Beef, bacon and even rye bread hung from the roof. Chests in the parlour were full of homespun. On a winter evening when the housewife fetched down the spinning wheel from the chamber, her husband set himself to make a new ox yoke, or fix new teeth in a rake, as Fitzherbert had advised him to do.[1] In such respects words written in Henry VIII's time are certainly applicable to the last years of Elizabeth's reign.

[1] A. Fitzherbert, *Book of Husbandry* (Engl. Dialect Soc. 1882), ch. 24: 'and when the husband sitteth by the fire and hath nothing to do, then may he make his forks and rakes ready . . .' Ch. 5: 'it is necessary for him to turn to make his yokes, ox bows, stools, and all manner of plough gear'.

Part Three

THE SECOND PHASE OF THE HOUSING REVOLUTION
1615-1642

Introduction

THE pace of new building seems to have slackened during the thirty years before the outbreak of the Civil War. Growth of population was curbed by serious outbreaks of plague, especially in the 1620's. Parish registers in counties as far apart as East Yorkshire and Bedfordshire show large increases in the numbers of burials, and they often for a time exceed the numbers of baptisms. The east Midlands seems to have been the worst affected area,[1] and the pressure on housing accommodation must have been relaxed, for between 1630 and 1660 Leicestershire village populations 'were scarcely replacing themselves'.[2] London was growing even more rapidly than it had in Tudor times, and must have drained off much of the natural increase of rural England, while some part of it flowed into provincial towns.[3] There was no doubt even more mobility among the rural population than there had been in the past century; the notion of farming and labouring families as fixed in one village and on one farm for generation after generation is the opposite of the truth, for much of the population of each village moved elsewhere in a generation or so, and the enduring families are most exceptional.[4]

In open field country, though enclosures may not have caused serious depopulation or the disappearance of villages, yet they certainly reduced the number of holdings and the opportunities of getting a livelihood, and the displaced families moved into market towns or larger villages where there was a chance of getting work and a house, or of renting part of a house. The local authorities in such places began to legislate against 'undersetts or undertenants',[5] to check any increase in the numbers of claimants to

[1]J. W. F. Hill, *Tudor and Stuart Lincoln*, 136–7. The east Midlands was not the only region to suffer; there were outbreaks in Wiltshire in 1603–11; G. D. Ramsay, *The Wiltshire Woollen Industry* (1943) 71.

[2]V.C.H. *Leics.*, III, 142.

[3]See C. Gill, *History of Birmingham*, I, 42; J. W. F. Hill, *Tudor and Stuart Lincoln*, 138. Dr. Hoskins mentions similar increases in Devonshire towns in 'The Rebuilding of Rural England', *Past and Present*, 4 (1953), 55.

[4]*Econ. H.R.* 16 (1947), 127–9.

[5]M. W. Barley, 'East Yorkshire Manorial By-Laws', in *Yorks. Arch. J.*, XXXV (1940), 39–40.

common rights and hence in pressure on the commons. Common land and pasture were growing more scarce, and the stinting of the commons in the East Yorkshire village of Burton Agnes, so that no man was to allow 'his servant to keep more than four shorn sheep and four lambs, and no husbandman to keep on the fallow field more than twenty shorn sheep for every oxgang of land and twenty for his house and every cottager twenty sheep for his house, provided that the cottagers shall not let their common rights',[1] goes parallel with the schemes of the Crown and the gentry to drain and enclose the commons in the fens of Lincolnshire and elsewhere. The stinting of commons—even if it was only a reduction of earlier stints— also goes with the steady consolidation of holdings and the growing dominance of the larger farmer in upland country such as the Yorkshire and Lincolnshire Wolds or the Wiltshire Cotswolds.[2] It was the gentry or the large farmers who had the land and the capital to increase hay production by floating or irrigating water meadows, as the Savile family did at Rufford, Notts., or Robert Loder at Harwell, Berks.[3] Even in dairy farming and grazing country the prosperity of small farmers might be checked, as it was in the Lincolnshire coastal marshland, through the invasion of their local economy by larger farmers from outside the region.[4]

The increase in prices continued in the first half of the seventeenth century, though in a more subdued and erratic fashion. It probably operated more in favour of the larger farmer than the small; indeed it has been suggested that it failed to keep pace with the rise of rents.[5] Only increasing difficulties for the small and the part-time farmer can explain the reports of unemployment, distress and revolt. The craftsman suffered as much as the husbandman from an enclosure of commons, for it severed an essential string of his bow; in the Midland Revolt of 1607 it was reported that the rebels were craftsmen, as well as husbandmen and labourers.[6] A Lincolnshire gentleman wrote in 1623 of 'many thousands in these parts (the Lincolnshire Wolds) who have sold all they have even to their bed- straw, and cannot get work to earn any money', and 'many insufficient tenants who have given up their farms and sheepwalks'.[7] No decade passed prior to the outbreak of war without revolts against enclosure, in

[1]*Ibid.*, 38–9.
[2]For Wiltshire, see E. Kerridge in *Bull. Inst. Hist. Research*, 25 (1952) 80–4.
[3]M. W. Barley, 'Cistercian Land Clearances in Notts.' in *Nottingham Medieval Studies*, I (1957), 88, for evidence of such work between 1613 and 1637; G. E. Fussell, *Robert Loder's Farm Accounts* (Camden Soc. 1956), 14.
[4]Joan Thirsk, *English Peasant Farming*, ch. 6.
[5]E. Kerridge, *loc. cit.*, 82.
[6]Lipson, *Econ. Hist. of England*, II (1947), 403.
[7]*Lincs. N. and Q.*, I (1888–9), 16.

Gloucestershire or Huntingdonshire, Dorset or Durham,[1] and most of the counties between.

In some regions the growing stream of bitterness was fed from a new spring: decline in the cloth industry. The Suffolk cloth industry had by now passed the peak of its prosperity,[2] in spite of the stimulus of the new draperies. In Wiltshire the broadcloth industry, lacking the advantage of East Anglia or Devon of coastal ports from which cloth could be shipped direct to the Continent, and hence more in the hands of large capitalists and subject to the political vicissitudes of marketing through London, was suffering from acute distress between 1614 and 1625.[3] The Kentish cloth industry had passed its peak by this time, and by the 1620's its straits were only less desperate than those of Essex and Suffolk. There must have been less money coming into the homes of weavers in Lavenham, Cranbrook or Melksham, and less money brought in from the spinning and carding done by wives and daughters of husbandmen, craftsmen and labourers. Domestic workers who were dependent on a fluctuating foreign market or on diminishing supplies of raw material were in a more precarious position than the weavers of Lincolnshire or the nail makers and scythe makers of the Midlands, who went on playing a steady tune on their two-stringed fiddle.

If this picture of rural England between 1610 and 1642 is approximately true, then the steady progress of engrossment of farms and enclosure, the continual increase of large scale sheep and cattle production, the improved exploitation of resources such as coal and timber, all accompanied by a larger gulf between rich and successful on the one hand and poor and unfortunate on the other, will be reflected in the sphere of personal activity with which we are concerned. So it appears to be: 'a fabulous number of large and medium sized houses were built in the Jacobean age'.[4] Our concern, however, is to find out what lesser folk were doing. The task is easier now than it was in Elizabeth's time; not only have inventories survived from some counties not represented in our first survey, but the habit of making a will was even more widespread than before, and in particular reached farther down the social scale. This is apparent in several ways. Inventories are more numerous, and not only because the mortality from plague was so high; inventories of labourers are to be found, and not because a labouring class was only now coming into existence. The final proof is that archaic

[1] Lipson, *op. cit.*, 406; D. G. C. Allen 'The Rising of the West, 1628–31', in *Econ. H.R.*, 2nd Ser., 5 (1952), 76–85.
[2] G. Unwin, *Studies in Econ. Hist.* (1927), 268, 291.
[3] G. D. Ramsay, *The Wiltshire Woollen Industry* (1943), ch. V.
[4] J. Summerson, *Architecture in Britain 1530–1830* (1953), 52.

terms, such as firehouse and solar, appear for the first time in regions where they had not been recorded before; it is unlikely that these old concepts were being revived, and much more probable that for the first time the historian is allowed to see into homes which had been invisible to him hitherto.

CHAPTER ONE

South-eastern England

THE two-roomed house is still to be found in Kent and Sussex in Charles I's time.[1] John Bevill, labourer, of Thanet, had such a home; the hall was simply furnished with a table and a bench, two chairs and two cupboards, and the chamber beside it had two beds and four chests for linen. Since he had no other room, there were a shovel, two sickles and an axe in the hall, and a kneading trough and two little pins in the chamber. Walter Everden, a shoemaker of Benenden, called his hall the fire-room, and so did Robert Allison, a husbandman of Lidd living in a much larger house. Even in Kent the term had not yet gone out of use among such people as these. Some Sussex husbandmen were living in two-roomed houses, and there is a great variety of wealth among the few householders in this group.

Such houses could be made more convenient in two ways: either by putting in a loft over the hall, as did two Sussex husbandmen, or by making a service-room, as three Kentish husbandmen and a carpenter of modest means had done. The service-room was sometimes no more than a partitioned end of the hall, as in the east Midlands.[2] Craftsmen needed a room down stairs as a workshop, but many of them could not afford to have an additional room. John Medhurst, a cooper of Bathurst, Sussex, had a hall, buttery and shop; the hall was used for cooking and sleeping, for the chamber held his 'buckets, bottoms and coopers' stuff'. Henry Smith, tailor, of Rogate, used the hall as a workroom; his inventory lists parlour,

---

[1]Maidstone R.O. PRC 10/55 and 64 (Archdeaconry Court), PRC 28/1, 28/17 (Consistory Court), 1624 and 1631; Chichester R.O., Ep. I/29, 1631–4.

[2]See for example the plan of a cottage at Blackheath, in R. Nevill, *Old Cottage and Domestic Architecture in South-West Surrey*, (1891), 10.

buttery, kitchen, shop and upper chamber. Edward Collins, a basket maker of South Stoke, seems to have used the parlour-chamber, for it contained not only three flock beds and linen but also 'Item in this shop two rods: were made at his death and his tooles £6'. Two shoemakers' inventories mention no rooms at all, and their furniture would scarcely have occupied more than two rooms. These men are typical of craftsmen working for the domestic market and a very localized one at that. Few Sussex craftsmen left goods and chattels worth more than £20.

Beyond these simple and doubtless very common types of house, with two or three ground-floor rooms and perhaps one loft or chamber, no generalization can be framed without too many qualifications, but it is clear that all classes were now living in more elaborate, if not larger, houses. Most Kentish husbandmen had two service-rooms—milkhouse and kitchen, or milkhouse and buttery—and some had all three. This extension of the working part of the farmhouse took priority over adding to the upstairs rooms. The home of Robert Allison of Lidd, husbandman, who died in 1632 with goods worth £40 11s. 8d., is a good example of how such men lived. The hall, which he called the fire-room, had two joined tables, three small chairs, a form, a joined cupboard and a child's cradle; the fireirons are listed, and cooking was done there, but pots, pans, kettles, a brass 'stuppenet' (stew pan) and a chafing dish were kept in the buttery when not in use, along with the pewter for the table, trenchers, wooden spoons and various wooden tubs. 'His lodging chamber' was downstairs, with its featherbed, two old chests and an old chair. The other service-room was a milkhouse containing thirteen small bowls. There were three chambers upstairs; that over his lodging chamber had the best bed and the store of linen (four pairs of sheets, seven table cloths, twelve napkins, a pillow case and a hand towel); the chamber over the fire-room had two beds and various little-used items such as a pike, a helmet and a sword, and the chamber over the buttery the linen and woollen wheels, old tubs and a pillion saddle (see Appendix, p. 277).

In smaller houses the buttery, the commonest service-room, was sometimes in an outshot. Two inventories, from Tilmanstone and Gt. Mongeham, Kent, speak of 'the little Cove' and 'the Cove adjoining the Hall'.[1] Cove in Kentish dialect meant a shed or lean-to, and no doubt it was descended originally from the single aisle of a hall house.

In Kent at this time the one entirely novel service-room is the washhouse. It is not to be found in west Sussex or Essex, and presumably spread from London. It was simply another service-room, distinguished by having a water supply in it; Thomas Baldock, yeoman, of Leeds, Kent,

[1]Maidstone R.O., PRC 10/64, nos. 71 and 75.

had a wash-house containing a bucket and chain (i.e. for the well), one old quern, two washing-keelers, a washing stool, and a few dairy and cheese-making vessels. The boulting house (often called the 'bunting house') is now more common; in it was kept the flour which had to be boulted, or sieved through a linen boulting cloth whose fineness determined the quality and colour of the bread or pastry. More facilities for baking, brewing and washing are the order of the day. Some of them are no doubt in separate buildings, not subdivisions or extensions of the house; the more there were, and the larger the house, the more likely that they extended round a yard at the back of the house. A kitchen is still not essential, and it is very significant that in two small Sussex houses the room that one would expect to be called the hall, and is the one room for living and cooking, is called the kitchen.[1] These are the earliest instances of what later became a widespread practice, to downgrade the hall to a kitchen where it continued to be used for cooking. This change goes along with turning the parlour into a sitting-room and the hall into an entrance lobby; those who could do neither were ready enough to think of themselves as eating, and sitting, in a kitchen. In larger houses, the kitchen was used for more than one purpose; in Sussex it was commonly used as a brewhouse, for the furnace (of brass or lead) was there. The quernhouse occurs sometimes, and home brewing was certainly on the increase, to judge from the houses with malt lofts, malt querns, or even a supply of oaten malt. A few more Kentish farmers now had an oasthouse.

In the coastal villages of Sussex, the rather poor single-storey houses of Elizabeth's reign must have been disappearing rapidly at this time, for the mixed farming economy there was thriving, and two-storey houses were now more common than those with only lofts upstairs. Such improvements are easier to observe in the better built timber houses of the Weald. When ground-floor timbers decayed the jettied wings were underpinned with brick, or the house refronted on the line of the jetty, so that both overhang and recessed hall disappeared.[2] Work of this sort, or inserting a brick stack in a medieval hall, provided sufficient work for a few brickmakers and bricklayers.[3]

The typical yeoman's house of 1630 had, then, a hall with a long table, a few chairs and plenty of joined stools (the benches had been discarded) and another small table or two; several service-rooms within the house,

[1]Chichester R.O., William Greene of Kingston, husbandman (1632) and Randolf Bower of North Mundham, husbandman (1632).
[2]See R. T. Mason, 'Four Single Bay Halls' in *Sussex Arch. Coll.* 96 (1958), 14.
[3]Inventory of Thomas Cuffe of Sittingbourne, Kent, bricklayer, PRC 10/55, no. 154. His shop contained 'six pole basons, two washing basons, a work pann with a malt kettle, one bearing post and two charres'.

including a kitchen where cooking was done, and others in the yard behind the house; a couple of ground-floor rooms at the other end of the house, one of which was now known as the parlour, for it had chairs and a small table or two as well as a bed, while the other was merely a chamber or sleeping-room. These two last rooms were often heated by fireplaces back to back, an adaptation of the midland type of axial stack to one wing. Upstairs, there might be a couple of rooms used as bedrooms for the family or for servants, while the others as well perhaps as a garret in the roof space provided separate storage for corn, wool, cheese or apples.

In larger houses than this, the roof space was more often used. Rake House, in the parish of Witley near Godalming (see below p. 137), had boards laid along the centre line of the garret floor leading to boarded spaces in the centre of each gable. No doubt this practice spread from the towns, where the three-storey house had long been common. Even a mariner of Thanet, Richard Horne, whose house was quite small and had only one chamber (over the hall), had a garret full of nets and ropes; in his case one cannot be sure where the garret was, but the term usually meant what would now be called an attic. Few Kentish houses had as many ground-floor sleeping-rooms as one finds in the Midlands, and they had no less need of storage space in chambers or lofts, so that further enlargement in the vertical rather than the horizontal plane is not surprising. William Brooke, esquire, of Hartlip, had two or three parlours, two chambers for sleeping and separate lofts for cheese, wool, oats and wheat. Few men had as many rooms as this, and so roof space began to be used, not only in market towns like Faversham but in villages as well.

All the craftsmen, whether rich or poor, had their stake in the land and lived by country standards rather than those of the town. A poor shoemaker of Storrington had 'six sheep abroad in the Common and an old mare and two little colts in the Common'; a Worthing fisherman had eleven sheep, a heifer and a bullock. The houses of such men were indistinguishable from those of labourers or husbandmen, apart from the one room turned over to their craft. More successful craftsmen lived like farmers, for such they were. William Poble, a weaver of Easter, had a barn and a workshop with two looms in it; his house consisted of hall, sleeping chamber and buttery, with a chamber over the hall used as a bedroom and a loft over the other chamber in which he was storing beans. Henry Scutt of Kirdford called himself a wheelwright, but he had six oxen, fifteen cattle, seventeen acres of wheat and another twenty acres of peas and oats. His farmstock was much more valuable than 'his working tools and timber belonging to his trade'.

Robert Quinton of Shipley, ironfounder, had perhaps retired from his foundry business, for he had only farming and household goods. His inventory is a remarkable document, made by 'praisers' who thought that every iron object was worth naming; it mentions the cheese-press with a cast iron weight and iron pins; in the kitchen three iron plates, iron mortars and posnets, a toasting iron and a pressing iron, an iron ringer; in the hall the plate behind the fire and the plates upon the hearth and so on.

Rake House, Witley, was probably once as well furnished in ironware, for its owner, Henry Bell, also had an ironworks on Thursley Heath from 1617 onwards.[1] Since it has been little altered until recently we can see what Henry Bell made of it before his death in 1634. He bought the property before the end of Elizabeth's reign, with money made from minor office at the royal court, a very common pattern of advancement for those with the right connexions, and later acquired the manor of Witley as well as the new ironworks near by. He must have enlarged and improved the existing house, principally by adding the parlour wing and a staircase in the angle of the L (see plan, fig. 20). The plan has several features of

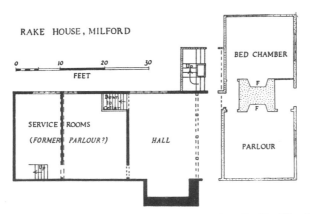

FIGURE 20. Plan of Rake House, Witley, Surrey (after R. Nevill), showing the relative simplicity, especially at the service end, of the house of a Surrey iron-master who was not involved in farming. The house is timber framed and of two storeys throughout; the plan is unusual, e.g. in having a cross passage at the upper end of the hall, and this may be explained as a radical alteration made when the parlour wing and staircase were built.

interest. First there were only two service-rooms, for this was not a farm-house, and so did not need a large range of working rooms. Second, the cooking must have been done in the hall for there was no other hearth in the main range.[2] It was from houses such as this, where the family lived

[1]*Surrey Arch. Coll.*, 18 (1904), 24–33, 61–6.
[2]A kitchen wing was added by Sir Edwin Lutyens.

137

in the parlour wing, that farmers and others got the new habit of calling the hall a kitchen. The parlour wing has the axial stack common to the main range of midland houses, and occasionally to be seen in Surrey, as here, in the wing of a larger house.[1] The family no doubt used the side entrance. Upstairs, one of the chambers has a fine carved overmantel put in by Henry Bell in 1602, and perhaps dating the wing. Another room has a fireback from the family's ironworks, and dated 1630. The staircase is a rather primitive example of a new type; it rises round a square well, which instead of being open and ornamented with carved newel posts and turned balusters has plain posts, the well being filled with stud and plaster work.

[1]The stack was so wide that in alterations of 1882, a passage was driven through it without interfering with either flue. The same thing has been done in modern times in the main stack of some East Anglian houses.

XIa. Barclose Farm, Otterton, Devon, was built in 1627 of cob with the West Country type of front chimney to the hall carried out in two kinds of stone. See figure 18.

XIb. Buskins, Exbourne, Devon, is presumably not all of one date, to judge from the roof line. Note that there are fireplaces backing on the through passage both for the hall (in the centre) and the kitchen (at the lower end).

XIIa. William Lilly's house at Diseworth, Leics., for which an inventory is printed on p. 278. The surviving cruck truss from an earlier house is at the further end marked by the washing line, and is on the line of the nearer wall of the through passage. The main range contains principally the hall and two parlours; the cross range beyond the passage is now a separate house.

XIIb. Great Woodend, Dymock, Glos., has a hall range and one cross wing, with external stone chimney stacks on the gables of both.

CHAPTER TWO

Essex and East Anglia

IN the 1630's we can get, for the first time, a clear view of housing conditions in an Essex village: Writtle, near Chelmsford.[1] The range of standards and wealth shows clearly from the following analysis.

HOUSES IN WRITTLE, ESSEX, 1635–40

No.	Value	Occupation	Rooms
3.	£2.11.9	husbandman	—
10.	£3.7.10	—	Hall, Chamber, Buttery
13.	£3.10.10	—	—
1.	£6.11.8	mason	Hall, Shop, Buttery, Chambers over Hall and Shop.
17.	£12.4.0	husbandman	—
15.	£22.6.5	widow	—
16.	£22.14.4	weaver	Hall, Parlour, Buttery, Chamber over Hall, Shop.
2.	£23.12.0	—	Hall, Parlour, Buttery, Chamber
20.	£29.18.4	—	Hall, Palour, Milkhouse, Chamber over Parlour.
14.	£46.16.5	yeoman	Hall, 2 Butteries, 2 other Service rooms, Chambers over Hall, Buttery.
21.	£53.6.0	husbandman	Hall, Parlour, Milkhouse, Chambers over Parlour, Buttery.
9.	£53.17.0	husbandman	Hall, Parlour, Milkhouse, Buttery, Chamber over Parlour.
22.	£59.6.2	—	(Buttery) Milkhouse, Kitchen, Chambers over Buttery, Kitchen, Cornchamber.
6.	£66.1.6	widow	Hall, Parlour, Milkhouse, Buttery, Chambers over Parlour, Buttery.

[1] The first twenty-two inventories in F. W. Steer, *Farmhouse and Cottage Inventories of Mid-Essex*, are dated 1635–40. The median value is £53 17s., compared with £55 18s. in Sussex.

No.	Value	Occupation	Rooms
5.	£90.12.8	yeoman (?)	Hall, Milkhouse, Buttery, New and Old Kitchen, Quernhouse, Chambers over Hall, Buttery, New Kitchen, Cheese Chamber, Gallery.
12.	£94.5.6	—	Hall, Milkhouse, Buttery, Kitchen, Chambers over Hall, Kitchen.
11.	£96.8.2	—	Hall, Parlour, Buttery, Boulting House, Chambers over Hall, Parlour.
18.	£110.19.10	husbandman	Hall, Parlour, Milkhouse, Buttery, A Room.
7.	£131.6.0	yeoman	Hall, Parlour, 2 Milkhouses, 2 Butteries, Kitchen, Chambers over Hall, Parlour and Buttery (?), Servants' Chambers.
8.	£203.8.4	—	Hall, Parlour, Milkhouse, Poultry House, Kitchen, Quernhouse, Chamber over Parlour, Cheese Chamber.
19.	£389.4.6	yeoman	Hall, Parlour, Milkhouse, 2 Butteries, Brewhouse, Kitchen, Chambers over Parlour, Buttery, Kitchen, Brewhouse, 2 Servants' Chambers, Cheesechamber.

Some of the houses may well have been single-roomed, but the smallest type which emerges clearly has two rooms and a second floor. John Burrows (no. 10) had a hall with a buttery (no doubt a small space partitioned off) and a chamber upstairs. His chamber must have been on the first floor, because Essex people never used that name for a ground-floor room. His house is the only example in these Writtle records of that important non-parlour type of house. The only other house without a parlour was that of a mason who was, like so many craftsmen, using it as a shop (no. 1).

The Essex countryside still has many houses corresponding with those revealed by documents. At Colne Engaine there is a cottage dated 1620[1] with two rooms on the ground floor divided by an axial stack with four flues: that is, both chambers have fireplaces. The stairs rise behind the stack. Inventories rarely mention fireplaces in chambers, because they seldom have fireirons, and they must from the beginning have been meant for use only when someone was ill. The parlour in this house has a bay window with moulded mullions and transom. Although the Royal Commission called it a cottage, the parlour must in this case have been used as a sitting-room.

Even the smallest houses had one service-room—usually a buttery— and the larger houses had between two and five. Brewing involved using large vessels, and the brew had to stand in the vat for several days, so that the Essex housewife, brewing once a month or so,[2] needed a brewhouse

[1]R.C.H.M. *Essex*, III, 76 (4).
[2]Harrison stated that his wife brewed once a month.

more than a kitchen. Most farmhouses made cheese, and Essex cheeses were proverbially large. The cheese-press was kept in the milkhouse, the quernhouse (where malt was ground) or in the kitchen, but a cheese chamber was needed for ripening and storing. Less than a third of these houses had a kitchen, and only two housewives were using them for cooking.[1]

This development of the service quarters, by adding a new wing at the rear of a medieval house, can be seen at Earl's Colne,[2] where there is a fifteenth-century house at the opposite end of the High Street from the church; it has a wing at one end extended at this time. New houses often have still larger wings, and the L plan, which became the commonest type over much of England in this century and the next, emerged most distinctly between the death of Elizabeth and the outbreak of the Civil War. Many Essex houses, especially those of medium size, had the rear wing in the centre, making a T plan. This arrangement must have made access from the hall to the service-rooms somewhat more convenient.

None of these Writtle houses had more than one parlour.[3] Sometimes it had a chair, a table and some stools, as well as a bed. It was being used, at least occasionally, as a sitting-room, and might, as we have seen, have a bay window.

Except for the poorest cottages, Writtle must by now have been a village of two-storey houses, for all new houses were made of that design and the few remaining medieval houses with an open hall had a chamber and a chimney stack built into it by the middle of the seventeenth century. There is a medieval house in How Street, Great Waltham, of hall and cross wings plan, with the date 1623 on the doorway from the cross passage into the hall.[4] The chamber over the hall was the favourite place for keeping linen, because it was a well-aired room. The Great Waltham house had at the same time a new staircase in the south wing to replace a ladder. In new houses it was more usual to build a wing at the rear to contain the staircase, as at Parvill's, Hatfield Broadoak, or a farmhouse at Manwood Green.[5] Turned balusters for a staircase must have been expensive, or perhaps the carpenter in the village had no lathe, for he frequently cut the balusters from oak planks, shaping them to imitate turning and even cutting openings in them for good ornamental measure.

Tiled roofs must by now have been general in Essex, but building in

[1]The best description of the process and the vessels used in brewing and cheese-making is in F. W. Steer, 32–9.

[2]*Essex*, III, 90 (12).

[3]Six inventories fail to mention a parlour at all, for reasons which are not apparent.

[4]*Essex*, II, 111 (73) and plate facing 110.

[5]*Ibid.*, 120 (13), 122 (31).

brick made little headway. There are in the county ten houses known as Brickhouse Farm, and most of them were built in north-east Essex in about 1600 or later. They must have been so named because they were an unusual sight at the time.[1] The tradition of timber building was by now modified to the extent that the frame was usually plastered over. This may seem a trifling change, affecting only the appearance of the house, but it concealed economic and technical changes. The value of a load of timber had risen from 16s. 6d. in 1592 to as much as 21s. 2d. in the first decade of the next century.[2] The housewright adjusted his work by using less timber. A contemporary said that in Suffolk a new way of 'compacting, uniting, coupling, framing and building with almost half the timber that was wont to be used and far stronger' had been devised.[3] The economy was concealed by the plaster rendering. The jetty was still being used for a first floor, and it was supported either on a bracket in the form of a console, a shape which the carpenter had picked up from the repertoire of classical building, or by a bracket in the form of a grotesque human figure. The two can be seen on one house at Waltham Holy Cross.[4] The folk beliefs which conceived such grotesques, or which inspired the horses' heads in terracotta sometimes found on the angle of a Suffolk brick chimney stack, are still an unexplored field.

In the spring of 1633 there was a visitation of the plague at Castle Acre, and within a month it carried off, among others, three labourers. They had each made a will, and their inventories were written out by one and the same man, John High.[5] In one of them he mentioned no rooms except an outhouse; in the next he referred to the firehouse and a little chamber; in the third to a hall and a kitchen. He must have been putting down the names used by the widow or relative of the deceased. The first house had only one living-room and a lean-to or some such for storage purposes; the third was essentially the same, though its second room was larger. The second must have been a single-roomed cottage with a chamber upstairs. These three documents give a clear picture of the living conditions of the East Anglian labouring classes.

The term firehouse was still in regular use to denote a single-roomed cottage, which in perhaps half the cases now had a chamber over it. Such

[1]E.g. Brickhouse Farm, Shenfield, *ibid.*, 270. See index to *Essex*, IV, s.v. Brickhouse.

[2]J. E. Thorold Rogers, *History of Agriculture and Prices in England*, VI, 544–5.

[3]Robert Reyce *Suffolk in the Seventeenth Century* (London 1902), 51. Reyce's MS. is dated 1618.

[4]*Ibid.*, II, 245 (5), pl. facing 80.

[5]Bundle Goodram 1633, nos. 77, 78, 79, Norwich Consistory, Bishop Reynolds Chapel.

were the homes of labourers, poor husbandmen, or even a fairly prosperous butcher.[1] Edward Bell of Broughton, Norfolk, was typical of the labourers. His goods were worth £4 11s. 8d., and his only livestock was a sow with five pigs. In the firehouse there was a standing bed, worth 13s. 4d. furnished, and linen valued at 8s. The only other furniture was a cupboard and three chests, two little tables, a seat with four feet, two chairs and two stools, but he had brass and pewter worth £1 3s. 4d. In the hearth were a frying pan, a spit, dog irons, a hale and a pair of tongs, and the dishes, spoons and other trifles were included at 5s. His labouring tools of all sorts were somewhere in the room, but we are not told what they were.

The new habit of calling the hall a kitchen when it was still used for cooking was now widespread in Norfolk. Few houses had a separate kitchen,[2] and many wealthy yeomen were still content to have cooking done in the hall, but in some cases[3] that room is now called the kitchen. One of them was the home of Richard Coliard, yeoman, of Thornage near Holt. He was probably an old man who had given up most of his farmstock. The contents of his house and their disposition—the hall living- and cooking room, with the milk vessels in it, the parlour bedroom with a fireplace and enough furniture to entertain visitors, the chambers with more beds for the large family, corn, bacon, new cloth and articles seldom or never used but never thrown away—make a picture which in both scale and detail would stand for many a middling yeoman of his time. It also has vivid details more rarely found—the child's cradle, the old-fashioned livery cupboard, the curtains and rods for windows as well as beds, the wooden trenchers and even the earthen pots, and the cow too old and weak to rise.

Although Norfolk society had at least as much variety as we have already found further south, some generalizations are possible. There are labourers, with goods worth up to £16, living in houses with at most three rooms—hall, buttery and chamber. Most of the craftsmen—weavers, tailors, joiners and carpenters, glovers, a cordwainer, a bricklayer—had between £10 and £30 in goods and chattels; their houses usually had one ground floor room as a workshop, and the poorest had three rooms—a glover's had hall, buttery and chamber—while their largest houses had three ground floor rooms and two chambers. One of the richest, a weaver of Grimston, had a house with at most three rooms downstairs, in one of which stood his 'two looms with slays and other things about his trade',

---

[1]Nos. 54, 74, 78, 107, 278 in bundle Goodram 1633. Of these 74 and 78 consisted of firehouse and chamber.
[2]13 out of 94.
[3]Nos. 5, 33, 69, 79, 90, 136, 289, 365, 376.

and a store chamber. His farmstock was worth £23 out of the total of £50. The average yeoman's goods were worth between £60 and £90, and the average husbandman's £30 only, but both classes, and especially the husbandmen, exhibit a wide range in standards: a husbandman might be wealthier than any yeoman. Their wealth could be exceeded by a baker of Attleborough, or a grocer of North Mundham with 'wares in his shop' worth £546 and £223 in ready money. The largest houses (not of course necessarily with the wealthiest occupants) had hall and parlour, between two and four service-rooms and two or three chambers. We meet the dairy, but never the milkhouse, occasionally a backhouse but never a brewhouse by name. More than one parlour is rare although the occasional parlour chamber (as distinct from the chamber over the parlour) is perhaps a second sleeping room downstairs. Two of the largest houses have goods stored in the vance roof.

Before we leave the south-eastern quarter of England, a glance at houses built by the English settlers in north America serves to clarify the picture on both sides of the Atlantic.[1] It also proves that these English counties, and Essex in particular, provided the largest element in the Great Migration. That is enough for any English reader to dispose of the idea that the earliest settlers built log cabins. They belong to the Scandinavian tradition, and were introduced by Swedes to Delaware after 1638. Timber-framing was all but universal in the colonies in the seventeenth century, and the filling was wattle and daub, clay and straw rolled into 'cats' and laid between studs, or unfired bricks laid on edge.[2] Weather-boarding was the commonest finish, and this suggests that weather boarding goes back to the seventeenth century (rather than the eighteenth) in Essex.

Some of the earliest settlers had only time or means to build a house of one room, with a chamber over. A stone fireplace at the gable end had the newel staircase alongside, between the hearth and the entrance. The staircase in that position, rather than on the farther side of the hearth from the entrance is another essential link between the south-eastern counties and the new settlements (see fig. 9, type I). Within a generation or two the commonest transatlantic type was that with a massive axial chimney stack, with back to back fireplaces for the two main rooms, hall and parlour. This new arrangement which had such widespread popularity in lowland England was an equally good answer to New England needs. The one innovation there was the eventual addition of a kitchen at the rear, its fireplace having a third flue at the back of the axial stack. The jettied

[1]See H. Morrison *Early American Architecture* (1952) and A. Garvan, *Architecture and Town Planning in Colonial Connecticut* (1951).
[2]Morrison, 12–13, 16, 30.

upper storey was a common sight in the New England village, and popular thinking has invented still another explanation—that it was for defence against Indians![1] The colonists in Connecticut found themselves compelled to use somewhat smaller timbers than those considered suitable in England, but otherwise made no changes in the methods they had used at home.[2]

Brick kilns were working regularly in Connecticut by c. 1675, although the Dutch settlers in New Amsterdam had made bricks since 1628. All the Dutch features of crow-stepped and curved gables, iron ties in gable ends bearing the date or initials, tumbled gables and pantiles were to be seen in their settlements. There was some brick building at Henrico, on the James River above Jamestown, as early as 1611, but most of the English colonists in the south built in timber. The commonest feature of farmhouses there was the large gable end chimney, of stone with offsets. It suggests a strong west midland element in the southern settlements. There were houses in New England with a front porch containing a framed staircase—either a modification of the common staircase wing to serve as entrance as well, or else the adoption of a northern practice, for storeyed porches with a staircase are a peculiarity of the Lake District.[3] The origins of such diverse features will, one hopes, be easier to place when regional characteristics in England have been more clearly plotted.

[1]Morrison, 28.
[2]Garvan, 87–8.
[3]See above. I am indebted to Professor Hugh Morrison for information in correspondence about the staircase porches at Saugus, Mass. (the Scotch-Boardman House, 1651), Boston (Bridgham House, 1670) and Salem (Jonathan Corwin House, 1675).

CHAPTER THREE

The Midlands

a. The South Midlands

IN the counties between the Thames and the Welland there is ample evidence of new building and improving in the reign of James I and his son. Some Buckinghamshire parsons had been busy. The vicar of Simpson had recently boarded over his hall.[1] At Stapleton, Herts., the parson had rebuilt the service end of his house with timber and tile.[2] Even those whose benefice had a large medieval house found something to add. The parsonage house at Therfield, Herts., was described as follows in 1625: 'one hall on the west side of the entry; beyond the hall two parlours, one study, one other little new built parlour. Above stairs four chambers, one study, a turret. On the east side of the hall one little lower chamber, a cellar, a kitchen, a larder, a scullery. Above stairs four lodging chambers. Item, without, on the south side, one little walking Cloister, one other kitchen, a brew house, a bolting house, a dairy house, a coal house, a little garden plot.'[3] Apart from the new parlour, the service wing must have been rebuilt after the Reformation—one cannot be more precise—to replace the medieval kitchen, detached and reached by the little walking cloister or covered way.

How much it cost to carry out the commonest kind of improvement to an old house—inserting a new chimney stack, with a ceiling for the chamber over, together with a new staircase—we learn from the farm accounts

[1]L.R.O., Terriers, Box 12.
[2]*Ibid.*, Terriers, vol. 8.
[3]See R.C.H.M. *Herts.*, 218; the plate facing shows the surviving fifteenth century wing with the stair turret named in the inventory.

of Robert Loder of Harwell, Berks.[1] He lived at Prince's Manor Farm, and farmed about 300 acres; he succeeded his father in 1610, and for the first ten years kept accounts in which he tried to assess the costs and profits of each branch of his practice. By 1618 he was ready to spend £6 10s. 'about my chimney', including 'making my stairs, my window and ceiling and plastering &c'; the account covered not only masons' and carpenters' work, but painters' as well.[2] His was a large household, with between seven and eleven people being fed daily, including a shepherd, a carter and maids living in.

The autobiography of Thomas Ellwood, the Oxfordshire Quaker, gives us invaluable glimpses of the way of life in such a home in the middle of the seventeenth century.[3] He was born and brought up at Crowell, Oxon., a small hamlet at the foot of the Chilterns; the manor house, known today as Ellwood House, with two large barns behind it, is now the centre of a farm of about 500 acres, which was perhaps about as large as Loder's in the seventeenth century.[4] The house is of brick with a modern tiled roof; its history is not easy to unravel, but it seems to have consisted of a hall and cross wing, in timber, the hall being rebuilt in the Elizabethan period, and the walls of the whole later replaced with brick (see sketch plan and elevation fig. 21). There are large lateral chimney stacks of brick to hall and kitchen, but there is no old fireplace in what must have been the parlour wing. The hall ceiling has moulded beams, but those of kitchen and parlour have a plain chamfer. There are now, and probably always have been, service-rooms in outshots at the rear, but their age cannot be determined. There are still five windows with stone mullions, with ovolo moulding; those in the hall, of two lights, are about six feet above ground level and show no sign of having been glazed originally, and if so they must have been placed high to give fresh air without a draught. The first floor rooms correspond to the ground floor, and are reached by a staircase in the cross passage of which the lower part has been rebuilt, but the upper part, going up to the garret level, has a square newel with elaborate top, a moulded hand rail and turned balusters. The chambers all communicate now, but cannot have done so in 1650. After Ellwood's time, an elaborate bay window was added at the north end which until recently served as a scullery.

[1]Ed. G. E. Fussell (Camden Soc. 1936), 157–8.
[2]The manor house still stands, but none of Loder's work can be discerned, nor is there any inventory in the Bodleian Library.
[3]*The History of the Life of Thomas Ellwood . . . written by his own hand* (4th edition, London, 1791).
[4]I am indebted to Mr. J. Hill, the present owner, for allowing me to see the house and for information about it.

MANOR HOUSE, CROWELL

FIGURE 21. Plan and elevation of the manor house at Crowell, Oxfordshire, now known as Ellwood house, after Thomas Ellwood, the Quaker, who was born in it. It is a timber-framed house, now walled with brick, with some stone mullioned windows remaining; all the windows with transoms are (in their present form) modern. The room at the south end, here called the parlour, was not originally heated. Notice the unusual extension to the kitchen, in the form of a storeyed bay window, which was used until recently as a scullery. The lower part of the staircase has been rebuilt in its original position.

The Ellwood household was small: Thomas, his father and sister, and, after his father had 'put off husbandry' and so most of his servants, only a maid and one man. The family dined in the parlour, and there the father sat in the evening; the servants dined in the kitchen. There were four outer doors, and the keys of all of them were kept on one chain and taken up to the father's chamber at night, for he and Thomas both slept upstairs. The father's extreme, nay violent, disapproval of Quakers and the boy's precocious quietism made it a very unhappy household. While relations were at their worst, the boy sat upstairs in his chamber until his father called him down for fear he caught cold. During the day, Thomas sat in the kitchen, to avoid his father; when his father came from the hall to the kitchen and saw the boy there with his hat on, he 'first violently snatched off my hat, and threw it away; then giving me some buffets on my head, he

148

said "Sirrah, get you up to your chamber". I forthwith went; he following . . . and now and then giving me a whirret on the ear . . . the way
to my chamber lying through the hall. . . .' Thomas must have slept over
the parlour, and reached his room by a staircase which has now gone; no
doubt his father had the best chamber over the hall.

Separate stairs, or ladders, from each ground floor room to the one
above became during this century and the next a common feature of most
houses of this size. Finding the best chamber over the hall, as at Ellwood
House, shows its superior status, and that it is either a new house, or an
old one with the hall roof raised. Studying a page of illustrations to one of
the Royal Commission's Essex volumes, it is easy to pick out those medieval
houses whose hall now has a lofty chamber over.[1] In smaller houses, the
chamber over the hall might be no more than a box round a chimney
stack, ill lit but ideal for storing linen. The kitchen chamber is usually
either a store-room or a servants' chamber.

Parsonage houses varied as much in size as the homes of yeomen and
husbandmen. At Wraysbury there was only a house of '2 bayes built of
timber covered with tile containing 4 rooms (viz) 2 low rooms and 2
chambers boarded . . .', while at Milton Keynes the house had '20
Bayes=Built partly with stone and partly with timber=in a square form,
with a paved Court in the midst thereof, all which is contrived in two
storeys and Disposed into 32 Roomes. . . .' That makes it sound larger
than it was; it had a hall; one parlour; buttery, pantry, pastry, kitchen,
larder, dairy house, brewhouse, backhouse, boulting house; 'all the Rest
are for lodging and store Houses'. The order in which rooms are named is
significant. The buttery is often named after the hall, for it contained the
beer, drinking vessels and table ware used in the hall, and is obviously
ancillary to the hall. More than once however it appears that the buttery is
at the parlour end, not the service end, of the hall. At Amersham we read
of the hall, parlour and buttery, and then move apparently to the other end
of the hall; at Burnham the buttery and cellar are named with the hall;
at Adstock we find 'the parlour and buttery . . . the hall and nether
house'.[2]

The variety in the scale of parsonage houses shows that while some
clergy found the means to keep pace with rising standards, others had to be
content with the simpler ways of their poorer parishioners. The average
Bedfordshire parson had in his parish two yeomen and two husbandmen to
three craftsmen and three labourers, a proportion very similar to that of
the Trent Valley at this period, and probably characteristic of open field

[1] E.g. II, plate facing p. 110; Nazeing (14) and Chignall (7).
[2] Ibid.

England at this time.[1] Bedfordshire was not a rich county,[2] and open field farming hindered the accumulation of yeomen's fortunes. The Bedfordshire yeoman was very little better off than the husbandman, but each left goods worth six times as much as the craftsman, and eight times as much as the labourer.

Housing standards were in keeping with the relatively low level of prosperity, and today no one would regard Bedfordshire as a county rich in farmhouse and cottage building.[3] Among all classes there were to be found single-storey houses of two or three rooms, some no doubt built of timber, others certainly built of mud, for mud building never ceased entirely even in regions of good timber building.[4] Most yeomen and husbandmen lived in homes with three, four or five ground floor rooms and some lofts or chambers; lofts were as common as chambers, and they are usually a pointer to poor building. Houses of such a standard had a hall, a kitchen and one or two other service-rooms—a buttery and milkhouse or boulting house, never a brewhouse or wash-house. The downstairs sleeping-room is usually called a chamber. Standards thus resemble those of Sussex rather than Kent or Essex.

Nearly half the labourers' inventories fail to mention any rooms, and most of these probably lived in single-roomed cottages. The rest had either two rooms—hall and chamber alongside—or a service-room as well with a loft over part of the house. Craftsmen had similar standards, for in such a society as this village, weavers, tailors, carpenters and masons rarely got a much better living than a labourer. One weaver had his loom in the 'working shop or hall'.

Nevertheless, at all levels there is evidence of new building and amenity. A yeoman has built a new parlour with a chamber over it; his old parlour had only a loft above.[5] A shoemaker has put glass windows in his house.[6]

[1] The Bedfordshire figures are derived from F. G. Emmison, 'Jacobean Household Inventories' in *Beds. Hist. Record Soc.*, XX (1938), 50–143. This collection of 166 inventories is substantially all that survives from the collection for the Archdeaconry of Bedfordshire. A third of the inventories do not give any occupation. For the Nottinghamshire figures, based on Southwell inventories, see *Econ. Hist. R.*, 7 (1954–5), 293, table 1.

[2] The median value of 145 inventories is only £26 19s. The median value of sixteen yeomen's inventories is about £130; of seventeen husbandmen £121; of twenty-three craftsmen £22, of twenty-two labourers £16.

[3] The National Buildings Record has very little Bedfordshire material, which reflects the little interest that has been taken in the county.

[4] E.g. the churchwardens of Gt. Bromley, Essex, built a parish poorhouse in 1627–40 which seems to have had mud walls, *J. of Soc. of Arch. Hist.*, XI (1952), 4; a 'small mean cottage' at Burnham, Bucks., with two rooms below and two chambers over had mud walls, P.R.O., Parl. Surveys, Bucks., 9, fo. 1.

[5] *Ibid.*, no. 175.

[6] No. 155.

A poor husbandman was living in a house with hall, chamber and a loft over, and the contents of the loft were barley, rye, boards and old blankets. We can deduce that he must have put in the boarded loft himself, and the blankets were spread on the floor so that the grain would not dribble on to him as he lay in bed in the chamber below.[1]

b. The East Midlands

A broad survey of houses in Lincolnshire and the Trent and Yorkshire Ouse valleys shows that there is a substantial growth by 1635 in the number of four-roomed houses, which usually had hall, parlour, one service-room (called indifferently either kitchen, dairy, milkhouse or buttery) and one chamber. We have met the type among Bedfordshire labourers and craftsmen, and three quarters of the population of rural Lincolnshire lived in houses no bigger than that. The number of single-roomed houses was steadily dwindling, and the two-roomed house was no longer the largest single category, though it must have remained common in some regions, such as the lower parts of the Trent and Ouse valleys.[2] One cannot escape the impression that society in these lowlands remained more homogeneous and conservative than any we have yet encountered in Carolean times. Poverty was not the reason, for there was much more wealth than in Bedfordshire, and as much as in Kent.[3] The increase in personal wealth from 1605 to 1635 was less than in Elizabeth's reign, but the impetus of earlier times was sustained enough to make many people who had been content with two rooms wish to have a service-room and a chamber as well. Physical isolation and the restrictive effect of open field farming were breaking down in face of a steadily growing demand for agricultural goods, and the need, whether prices were good or bad, to increase output and improve methods of handling corn and dairy produce. These may seem excessively powerful concepts to apply to such a simple affair as a small holding consisting of a barn, a hovel for cattle and a house of three or four rooms, but it was certainly in this period, more than any other, that subsistence farming of a still medieval kind began to give way, at the level of the small husbandman, to farming for profit. The house with a service-room for dealing with milk, butter and cheese, and a chamber above for storing corn, wool or hemp, was significantly more efficient than one with only living- and sleeping-rooms.

[1]Lincoln R.O., Inventories Box 129 (1624–5), no. 320; one of a small number of Bedfordshire inventories in the Lincoln collection.

[2]*Econ. H. R.*, VII (1954–5), 294–7. The Yorkshire evidence comes from inventories of the Snaith Peculiar, York Probate Registry.

[3]The median value of inventories dated 1635 is £34 7s.; *ibid.*, 293.

Those who were content with a two-roomed house had to put up with what seems to us muddle and inconvenience, for there were more things to be disposed of. A labourer of North Muskham, Notts., who died in 1623 with goods worth £65, went to his bed in a parlour where, as well as two beds and four chests, there were two spinning wheels (for wool and linen), nine yards of hempen cloth, twenty-seven lbs. of linen and hempen yarn, seven strikes of barley, rye and peas, a cheese press, milk vessels and other wooden ware.[1] A labourer in the Lincolnshire Marshland sat in the evening surrounded by pots and pans on the dishbench, a churn and a tub, while wife and daughter spun linen and wool. Such men rarely possessed a chair or a cupboard, and wood for fuel was so scarce that the fire was kept alight with dried cow-dung, called 'dyths', supplemented with coal when necessary.[2] Self sufficiency was still the key to family habits of consumption, whether it be fuel or home-spun clothing and linen. Husbandmen in the Marshland usually had one or two service-rooms and a chamber, as well as hall and parlour; yeomen had two or three service-rooms and at most two chambers upstairs. There is not much sign of the parlour being used as a sitting-room and the chambers are used mainly for storage.[3]

When someone has time and patience to examine more closely some of the small natural regions in the east Midlands, or better still to isolate particular villages and relate conditions of land tenure and soil to housing standards,[4] some vivid and sharp pictures will emerge, to supersede the generalizations which are all that can be made at this stage. In the Trent valley villages north of Newark there is a clear distinction at this time between labourers and craftsmen on the one hand, few of whom had more than two rooms, and on the other the few richer farmers, mostly yeomen, with two parlours, three or more service-rooms, and special chambers upstairs for corn or cheese. Poor, hungry soil[5] and a scarcity of freehold land kept ambition in a check that few were able to break.

In north Leicestershire there is ample evidence, since there was a good tradition of timber building in the area, of how a successful yeoman could remodel a medieval house. The Boot and Shoe Inn, Long Whatton, no doubt belonged to a yeoman, and its H plan is made up of a long and low

[1]Notts. R.O., Southwell Peculiar inventories.
[2]Such a phrase as 'all the coals and dyths' is not uncommon in Marshland inventories in the Lincoln Record Office.
[3]E.g. the inventory of John Yarburgh, yeoman, of Cockerington St. Mary; Lincoln R.O. Inventories 148/121.
[4]As W. G. Hoskins has done for Wigston Magna in *The Midland Peasant* (1957).
[5]Arthur Young commented of North Muskham that only the sheep had made farming there profitable, and the local saying today is that the soil needs a 'shower of rain and a shower of shit' every day.

hall range with storeyed wings; the timber frame is still visible though the filling is eighteenth-century brick. What is not visible outside, and was invisible inside until recently, is that the hall range is a cruck building of two bays.

At Diseworth, near by, still stands the birthplace of William Lilly, the seventeenth century astrologer (see pl. XIIa). He was born in 1602, the son of a Leicestershire yeoman of the same name, and the father's inventory survives, made in 1635 by a Robert Lilly and Robert Clarke, both yeomen.[1] William left home in 1620, for there was no inheritance for him, but his intellectual interests had already been shaped, at the grammar school at Ashby de la Zouch, and also at home: his father possessed a Bible and 'The Practise of Piety'. His interest in fortune telling must have also started early, for if young William was not responsible for the astonishing pattern of hands with outstretched fingers and other *graffiti* which still cover the walls of the through passage of the house, then they bear witness to a family leaning towards such things.

The house as it stands does not correspond absolutely with the inventory, for there have been changes at the service end. There is a pair of crucks incorporated in the structure, which must have been rebuilt before William was born. It is a two-storeyed rectangle, and its most unusual feature is that the chambers over the house and parlour, although they were being used as bedrooms when the inventory was made, have no original windows on the north side. Instead there was provision for ventilation of the goods stored there by means of small openings, close under the eaves, in the filling of the close studded frame. The accommodation and furniture downstairs were comfortable enough, with two parlours, one of which had a chair in it, but there was no social pretension about the home. Cooking was still done in the hall, and the kitchen was only used for baking.

c. The West Midlands

Like the Essex farmers on the London Clay, the husbandmen and yeomen of Warwickshire and Worcestershire had found pasture farming and cheese making most suited to their heavy red marl and liassic clays. Village industry is not much in evidence, for population was much thinner than in East Anglia, and farmers were less wealthy.[2] Most of the land must have been copyhold, for there were many husbandmen and few yeomen. Although farmers everywhere in open field country were now

[1]Leicester R.O.
[2]Birmingham Probate Registry, Inventories of the diocese of Worcester, bundle 1613–4. Nos. 3236–3406 give a median value of £30 11s. 6d.

turning more of their arable strips into long leys, especially where soil conditions favoured dairy farming, the husbandman was more likely to be content with traditional ways, since he had less to gain from innovation. He had one advantage that although he was bound to keep his house in repair, he could take timber for the purpose from his own hedgerows. This countryside even in our time has much more woodland, and particularly hedgerow timber, than the east Midlands, some parts of which have been stripped bare by generations of arable farmers anxious to get rid of any perch for a crow. In Warwickshire, hedgerow trees provided shade for cattle and 'housebote' for the tenant.[1] Building in timber was still the usual thing. A Warwickshire miller had 'timber for two bays and a cut end of housing' when he died, as well as material for a new windmill.[2] Houses open to the roof were not uncommon, for inventories speak sometimes of beef and bacon 'at the roof'.[3]

One house had a 'hundred and a half of boards loose upon the floor (of the Chamber over the Hall), and a window', showing that both floor and window were tenant's property, and so presumably new.[4] Now that such houses with an upper floor were becoming more usual, the old-fashioned word solar was revived. Robert Leadon of Great Comberton, Worcestershire,[5] was a fairly wealthy farmer of an enterprising turn; his store-room over the hall contained onions and garlic as well as linen, malt, barley, wheat, wool, hops, various tools and a cheeserack. The arrangement of his house is clearly laid out, though it is impossible to be certain whether it consisted of a single range of rooms, or had a cross wing. There was a hall in the centre, and beyond it a kitchen, a nether buttery and a boulting house. The nether buttery was really a larder, so called to distinguish it from the beer buttery at the other end of the house. The service wing was of one storey. At the other side of the hall were the parlour, the middle chamber and the buttery. Both parlour and middle chamber had beds in them. Upstairs there were solars over the chamber, the buttery and the hall; the two former with beds in them but all used as store-rooms.

Robert Leadon's house is a valuable pointer to customs and conditions in the west Midlands. His parlour must have been used as a sitting-room, but the ground floor room used for sleeping only was called a chamber. All the solars are more important as store-rooms than bedrooms, and that

[1]The custom of taking 'botes' is stated in 1649 and clearly still operative: T. Cave and R. A. Wilson, *Parliamentary Survey of . . . the Dean and Chapter of Worcester, 1649* (Worcs. Hist. Soc., 1929), 15, 60, 112, 136.
[2]*Ibid.*, No. 3336. *Cut* is used for a lean-to in this county, Wilts., etc.
[3]E.g. Nos. 3250, 3303, 3350.
[4]No. 3237.
[5]No. 3278.

over the hall, since it was the most novel element in the house, was the principal store. His house and others in Warwickshire and Worcestershire[1] show that these counties were part of the region in which the hall house with a storeyed wing had become a regular part of the medieval village scene (see pl. VI). They link the west Midlands with East Anglia,[2] where the same tradition is still evident at this time. The north Midlands and Lincolnshire are outside this region, for in those parts no one used the name solar, and a ground floor sleeping-room was always a parlour. There the tradition of the hall combined with storeyed wing was much less influential; in north Leicestershire, as we have seen, the cruck house was a dominant feature, and Lincolnshire had more in common with the northern counties than with the south Midlands.

Another feature which the Severn valley and East Anglia had in common was the netherhouse or backhouse. The backhouse was liable to turn into the bakehouse because baking was one of the purposes to which it was now being put. A Warwick baker was doing so, for his backhouse contained the boulting hutches, the dough trough and the moulding boards. But the original purpose—a service-room with no special function—is unmistakable in the home of Thomas Collett, a husbandman at Evenlode, Gloucestershire. There the nether house contained a cheese press, vats, churns and various other wooden receptacles; tools such as axes, bills and augers, and even a bedstead, as well as a flour bin and a moulding board. William Windle called this room simply 'the house beyond the hall' (see Appendix, p. 286).

Until more attention has been paid to these counties it is scarcely possible to paint a clear portrait of their social structure and housing conditions. A beginning has been made in Warwickshire,[3] but little is known of Worcestershire, although the county is rich in houses and in documents. It looks as though rural society was more diversified than in the east Midlands. The few yeomen seem to have been somewhat richer than those in East Anglia. Most Worcestershire husbandmen, who had now become leaseholders, were of modest status,[4] and about labourers we learn nothing from inventories for they rarely made a will at this time.

[1] The solar occurs in Nos. 3252, 3271, 3278, 3289, 3328. No. 3289 is printed in full, Appendix E9, p. 285. Chamber for ground floor sleeping-room occurs in Nos. 3251, 3253, 3256, 3257, 3278.
[2] Two small houses at Godmanchester, Hunts., are described in 1625 as solared over; Lincoln R.O., Terriers vol. 8, Godmanchester 1625.
[3] By Mr. S. R. Jones, whose work will be incorporated in forthcoming volumes of the V.C.H.
[4] The median value of sixteen inventories is about £24. In an unusually large number of cases the inventory includes the value of the lease; e.g., Nos. 3268, 3293, 3369.

One labourer, as rich as the average husbandman, was living in a two-roomed cottage, consisting of hall and chamber. There were cottagers in Newnham, Worcester, who had built themselves houses in Cornwood, which was waste belonging to the Dean and Chapter of Worcester, and they were paying no rent in 1649.[1] No doubt they were equally reluctant to make a will, for to do so would only have drawn attention to themselves. Such scattered indications help to build up a picture of a highly manorialized society, at any rate on the former lands of the abbey of Worcester, whose ancient and imposing authority had given a distinct cast to rural life, as well as to the record-making habits of its people. The iron industry had not developed enough to make a distinct contribution to rural prosperity.

On both sides of the Severn valley the stone chimney stack, built outside the gable wall of a timber frame, continued to be the popular way of heating the living- and cooking-room of a small house. Greater Woodend, an outlying farm in the parish of Dymock in West Gloucestershire, is a small yeoman's type of house, with a hall and cross wing, each of two storeys, and built early in the seventeenth century.[2] The hall has a stone stack on the end gable. The parlour, with a buttery behind it, was originally unheated, and the cider cellar underneath the parlour is an original part of the design (see pl. XIIb). Just as brewing and baking at home were now becoming much more common among yeomen, so the spread of cider making in the West Country belongs to the period 1590 onwards.[3]

[1]*Parliamentary Survey of Worcester*, ed. T. Cave and R. A. Wilson, (Worcs. Hist. Soc. 1924), 110.

[2]The parlour ceiling beams have moulding and stops identical with example vii in Fox and Raglan, *Mon. Ho.*, III, fig. 22.

[3]*Mon. Ho.*, III, 19.

CHAPTER FOUR

The Limestone Uplands

IN the stone-built villages of Kesteven there are a few houses built between 1620 and 1640 which are modest enough to come within our proper scope. They are still rare, however, and though little is known of Northamptonshire stone villages the same is probably true there, just as it is in the Cotswolds and Somerset.

One of the few is Moor Farm, in the village of Humby, south-east of Grantham. It was built in 1631, according to the date over the door head, but the W. B. who built it cannot be identified. It has been much altered inside, and reroofed, but the arrangement originally seems to have been two main rooms on the ground floor, hall and parlour, with two chambers and above them attics lighted by large dormer windows. The front is symmetrical—the earliest example in Kesteven of this Renaissance influence, which did not become dominant until the eighteenth century. Since the doorway is central, the hall on which it gave must have been larger than the parlour. Both rooms are heated by fireplaces at the gable end. The central portion of the hall was cut off in the nineteenth century, to make an entrance hall with a new staircase in it, and the kitchen at the end of the hall was probably added at the same time. It is impossible to tell whether the larder or buttery which is behind this part of the hall was an original feature or not. Even if it was, the standards of the unknown W.B. were extremely simple.

A few yards away is another house of similar date: an unusual proximity and one would like to know more of the history of the estate, to explain these new buildings. The second house, according to local tradition, is the old manor house, and it is just as simple as the first (see fig. 22). It is not dated, but its mullioned windows have the same hollow chamfer as in the first house; it must be of similar age. It is quite lofty, with two full storeys and a garret lighted from the gable, not by dormers. The plan has the familiar eastern arrangement of an axial stack dividing hall from parlour, with a newel staircase to one side of the stack.[1] There is however,

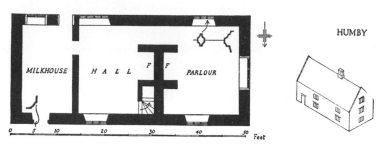

FIGURE 22. House at Humby, Lincolnshire, of three units without a cross passage. The window mullions have a hollow chamfer, identical with those on a near-by house dated 1631. Although superficially similar to the Cotswold vernacular, there is a considerable difference in the plan.

a small service-room (no doubt a milkhouse) at the hall end, and it is on to this room that the entrance gives, so that the doorway, with its hood mould and opening of traditional shape, is at one end of the front. There was no other entrance at first. It is a most unusual variant of the common eastern arrangement of parlour, hall and service-room, and it must have been intended to keep workaday traffic out of the hall.

The third house of this period in Kesteven is that known (without any cause) as The Priory, Heydour (pl. XIIIa). It was probably from the quarries here that the better stonework came,[2] for doorways, windows, copings, etc., in all three buildings. The Priory also has its entrance into the service end of the house, which has three rooms more or less of equal size, and an axial stack between hall and parlour. Here we meet another novelty in the shape of a staircase wing, entered from the hall and carried up to attic level. It contains a stone newel staircase, a remarkably old-fashioned feature at this time, but stone was no doubt cheaper here, next door to the quarry, than anywhere else. The stone newel stair persisted in the Cotswolds for the same reason. The mason's work is of good quality throughout—the spandrels above the four centred arch of the doorway are carved with a cat and a salmon—and much superior to the ideas of design incorporated in the building. All these houses belong firmly to the east

[1]The interior was much altered in 1957, but these notes were, fortunately, made before that time.
[2]All three have coursed rubble walls.

midland tradition of two or three rooms in a rectangular block; the third, where it occurs, being an unheated service-room.

The subordinate status of the kitchen, even where it is made part of a new building, is illustrated by Manor Farm, Stretton, Rutland. It consists of a rectangular range, with a central hall flanked by parlour and kitchen. The kitchen is as wide as hall and parlour, but has only a servant's chamber over it. Its roof is lower than the main range, which is of two full storeys with a panelled chamber over the hall. The parlour has no fireplace; a new drawing-room was built in the eighteenth century and the old one degraded to a larder.

Even when we find a house with cross wings, it is of a particular design: there is no cross passage. This is in fact the main difference between houses at the northern and southern ends of the limestone belt. Manor Farm, Clipsham, Rutland, was built in 1639 by one A. T., according to a carved wooden panel built into a new window shutter (see pl. XIIIb and fig. 23). The house has two floors with garrets, and has scarcely been altered. The original main entrance led into the fireplace end of the hall; although the screen making a passage alongside the hall is modern, there was doubtless some kind of speer to explain the small window lighting the passage from hall to kitchen. Immediately to the right is another original doorway into the service wing; the hall living-room as well as being small in proportion to the rest of the house, is thus relieved of the traffic of people about the work of the house, as at Humby. The

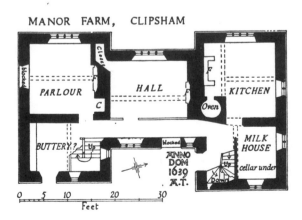

MANOR FARM, CLIPSHAM

FIGURE 23. Plan of Manor Farm, Clipsham, Rutland, dated (by a panel of a window shutter) to 1639. It has the traditional hall and cross wings plan, but in two storeys throughout, and with no cross passage. Both staircases were of newel type; that at the kitchen end led to chambers over the service rooms, and to the garret above, but not originally to the rest of the house. The window in the buttery has been made into a doorway.

service wing has kitchen and milkhouse, with a cellar under; the oven in the kitchen is no doubt original. The partition between milkhouse and staircase is of wood, to facilitate building the staircase, which is of a somewhat flimsy newel construction. On the first floor there was originally no access from the chambers over kitchen and milkhouse into the rest of the house. They must have been servants' chambers, and this, with the existence of a second stair makes Manor Farm, Clipsham, the sole instance in this region of the desire for privacy which has been claimed as a prime motive for the changes we are studying. The other wing, which is slightly shorter, has two rooms, one of them now and always a parlour, the other now a service-room. Another newel stair rises from it, for family use. The window on the east side has been made into a doorway, and there is a stone shelf or gantry. It is probable that this room has always been a buttery, and the salting trough has been there a long time, to judge from the effect of salt on the masonry of the wall.

It is a long way from Kesteven to southern Wiltshire, but similarities of economy are a link between the two. A survey of the Wiltshire manors of the earl of Pembroke and Montgomery made in 1631-2 provides the largest body of information about farmhouses and cottages available in print.[1] The earlier surveys of the same estates[2] had not mentioned any details of the houses that went with the agrarian holdings, but the later survey, like those for Lincolnshire manors of the Duchy of Lancaster, describes buildings in explicit and precise terms. The manors lie in the south of the county, round Wilton; the majority of the tenants are copyholders by law, and no doubt either husbandmen or labourers by social definition; some were perhaps weavers, for this was a cloth-making area, and the estate included three tucking or fulling mills. For each manor the first item is the manor house, described once as 'a fair dwelling house with many rooms' or 'the capital messuage'. The term 'farm' is just coming into use for such a tenement held by lease: we read of 'the capital messuage or farm house of Bulbridge consistinge of twelve lower rooms and thirteen upper rooms, one barn containing seven rooms, two stables . . . one carthouse . . . two pigsties, one dove house, two backsides, one garden, one hopgarden, one orchard'. This usage now leads very occasionally to the designation 'farmer' instead of yeoman; one of the earliest instances occurs in Warwickshire in 1614.[3]

[1] E. Kerridge, *Surveys of the Manors of Philip, First Earl of Pembroke, 1631-2*, (Wilts. A.N.H.S. Records Branch, X) 1953.
[2] C. R. Straton, *Surveys of the Lands of William, First Earl of Pembroke* (Roxburghe Club), London, 1909.
[3] Birmingham Probate Registry, Bundle 1613-4, No. 3281: Christopher More of Norton in the Forest of Arden.

In all, 370 houses are described, nearly all in detail, of which about 8 are manor houses, 320 are dwelling houses and 42 cottages held by copy. Some of them were new. There was a dwelling at Wylie 'of four ground rooms, lofted over, newly built, and a stable newly built'. Jane, wife of John Turner held 'a dwelling house newly built in Barford (10 × 8 feet) . . . at the end of Walter Sloyde's dwelling house', and there were some new cottages on the waste at Fovant. The manor farm at Wylie had been divided into eight parts and the house was a Carolean tenement, each family having two or three rooms. In such statements we see suspended for a moment of time the piecemeal and unceremonious processes— the division of a large house, the building of a tiny cottage built up against another house—which have made villages at once the delight of the artist and the despair of the investigator.

Houses are described in terms of 'ground rooms', and since the size of barns is also given in rooms they must be bays as well as rooms in the domestic sense. Outshots are very rare; only three houses had a 'cut' as the term went. Even more rare is the house which, instead of being 'lofted over', had 'upper rooms'. The typical Wiltshire farmhouse was, then, still a simple rectangular structure, built usually of timber, its upper rooms lighted by dormers. Three houses were 'double lofted': that is, had garrets over the upper rooms. The only information lacking is the names of the rooms.

The number of houses of different sizes, and the numbers with lofts, is shown in the following table.

HOUSES IN WILTSHIRE, 1631–2, SHOWING NUMBERS WITH GROUND ROOMS AND LOFTS

| A. Ground Rooms | | | | | | B. Lofts | Totals |
One	Two	Three	Four	Five	Six or more		
1	9	21	5	–	–	None	36
4	17	18	3	–	–	One	42
	38	41	9	–	–	Two	88
		65	6	–	–	Three	71
			39	–	–	Four	39
				13	–	Five	13
					10	Six or more	10
5	64	145	62	13	10		299

There is only one single-roomed house, held by a married woman at Bishopstone. It is not just a widow's cottage, for the holding includes a barn of two bays, a cowhouse, a backside, an orchard, meadow ground and a yardland of arable. Her husband was tenant of another three quarters of a yardland, and a house of 'one ground room lofted over'.[1]

Houses of two rooms, one lofted over—the complex of hall, parlour and chamber common in Lincolnshire—are the first substantial group, but no more common than those with three or four rooms, most of them lofted. Standards in Wiltshire seem to be somewhat higher than in Lincolnshire.

The table following shows the size of the cottages in the same terms.

COTTAGES IN WILTSHIRE, 1631–2, SHOWING
NUMBERS WITH GROUND ROOMS AND LOFTS

A. Ground Rooms				B. Lofts	Totals
One	Two	Three	Four		
1	6	6		None	13
2	3	1		One	6
	10	3		Two	13
		6		Three	6
			1	Four	1
3	19	16	1		39

Of the last cottage with four rooms, the surveyor, as doubtful as we must be, wrote 'reputed a cottage'; it was held by Susan Smith 'by her widowhood according to the custom of the manor'[2] and was really a farmhouse divorced from its land. The commonest type of cottage was one with hall, chamber and loft, to use Wiltshire terms. The one single-roomed cottage was held by Joan Taylor, aged 22, and her two sisters each aged 10; it had been built on the waste but since 1630 they had begun to pay a rent of 6d. a year.[3] Did their father build it? Or the neighbours put it up for them when both parents were carried off by plague? Or did the estate put it at their disposal when the father died and his holding had to be surrendered? John Hannam and his two sons held a cottage of two rooms which they had 'newly erected' but the copy, which included a little garden and orchard adjoining, was dated 1607.[4] His two sons were 26 and 24 years old; perhaps he had built it when he married, and a vigilant estate had promptly made it copyhold. An ancient cottager's holding consisted of 'a little dwelling house of one ground room lofted over', with six acres of arable

[1]Nos. 378–9.
[2]No. 329.
[3]No. 332.
[4]No. 158.

and common rights for one beast and twenty-six sheep; it was 'reputed a farthing land'.[1] There we must leave these Wiltshire people, and hope that some student will identify from other records any houses that survive and the inventories to furnish them.

[1]No. 305.

CHAPTER FIVE

The Highland Zone

a. The West Country

WE have seen that the clearest type of small Devon farmhouse in Elizabeth's reign had two storeys, with either two or three rooms on a floor. Where there were only two, the second was commonly a dairy; where there were three and a cross passage, the hall might have either a parlour beyond it or a dairy; if there was a parlour the third room across the passage was usually a dairy, or was divided into a dairy and a cellar store. To judge from parsonage houses,[1] most houses had a kitchen, but in many cases it was a detached building.[2] There were also surviving long houses, particularly in the Dartmoor parishes and no doubt elsewhere, in which the third room was still used for cattle.

These Devon farmhouses already exhibited that variety which is a common feature of the highland zone. Apart from the impact of outside forces, the West Country contained greater extremes of farming conditions than most regions of similar size. Even today, it is reckoned that the productivity of agricultural capital employed on the marginal land of Exmoor is only half that of the rest of the country. There must have been similar differences in the seventeenth century. Hence the variety, which became still more complex as farmers of all conditions tried to make their homes more compact and convenient for their wives and themselves by adopting the new amenities. In the long house, the one change which belongs to the

[1]Terriers dated 1613–27, Exeter R.O.

[2]E.g. Alphington in 1601 had '4 houses, hall and parlour under one roof, kitchen and malt house under another, the 3rd a barn, the fourth a shippon with a new stable and a corn chamber'.

first half of the seventeenth century, rather than any other age, was building a stone wall between passage and stable; it made the passage more distinctly part of the house, especially because a chamber could then be made over it. The passage itself was still essential, and in farmhouses of every size it remained the common feature round which rooms could be arranged in various ways.

The improvements affected both the private and the working parts of the house. For one thing, everyone now wished to have a kitchen under the main roof, rather than across the court. When George Hoskins of Exmouth died in 1625, the inventory shows[1] that his house consisted of a hall, an entry or cross passage, a buttery, and two kitchens, the old and the new. There was plenty of room upstairs—five chambers, two over the hall, two over a kitchen and one over the passage. Woodlands, Bridford, shows the results of such a process (fig. 18). We have already described the outside kitchen, built perhaps two generations earlier. The house probably assumed its present plan c. 1640. The oldest part is the hall with the chamber over, which has a roof with curved scarfed principals, and could be contemporary with the detached kitchen. The kitchen beyond the hall, and entered only through the hall, is an addition of c. 1640; there is a dairy beyond the kitchen, so that both hall and kitchen are passage rooms. The Devon farmer made little attempt to rid the hall of workaday traffic, perhaps because he now had a parlour in which he could get away from it.

In other cases the kitchen was made by taking over the third room across the passage, a more natural development one might think, although it was not invariable. Barclose Farm, Otterton, built in 1627 with a front chimney, now has the kitchen across the passage, though its fireplace is not original, and that room must have started as a dairy or store. Buskins, Exbourne (pl. XIb and fig. 18), has no precise dating features, but the half pyramid stop to the beams of the hall ceiling suggests the middle of the seventeenth century. Hall and kitchen on either side of the passage each have a fireplace backing on it; here too the kitchen fireplace may be of later date. The dairy is a lean-to behind the hall, and the third room is a parlour with a newel staircase rising from it in the back wall.[2]

In the hamlet of Nettacott (see above p. 109) the middle sized of the three houses, of small yeoman status, was enlarged in the first half of the seventeenth century (fig. 24). Lower Nettacott comprises four units and a cross passage. To the right of the passage is a hall, with a front chimney stack

---

[1]From notes made by Dr. W. G. Hoskins.
[2]The story may not be so straightforward as it is made here, for the stair projection partly obscures a dairy window. It may be simply that the staircase has been rebuilt.

but no staircase. The window has ovolo moulded mullions of *c.* 1580–1630.
One calls this the hall, because it is unusual for a front chimney stack
to be found in the parlour. There is a stud and plank partition between it
and the end room, which is not used by the present occupants. Is it a
buttery converted into (unheated) parlour? There is a framed opening in
it for a ladder to the chamber. The roof at the end has curved and scarfed
principals of the familiar west country type. On the other side of the
passage is the kitchen, with a fireplace on the rear wall and a newel stair
beside it, both housed in one projection. The end room is the dairy,
narrower than the other rooms and so possibly a later addition.

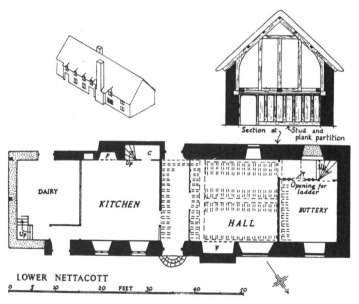

FIGURE 24. One of three houses comprising the hamlet of Nettacott, Upton Pyne,
Devon; this alone being still inhabited. It is built of cob, not all at one time, and
the stages are not easy to elucidate, since the house is now symmetrical (as it were)
about the cross passage. The partition between hall and buttery, with moulded
studs and plank infilling downstairs and scarfed principals above, suggest that
this is the older and superior end of the house. It could well have belonged to a
Devon yeoman of early Stuart times. (After A. W. Everett.)

Anyone who preferred to think that what has been called the hall was
really the parlour, with a hall on the other side of the passage, would be
echoing an uncertainty which began in the seventeenth century. Two
parsons, called on to describe their houses, spoke of 'the hall or parlour'.[1]
This ambivalence was the result of grafting two new rooms, a kitchen and

[1] Terriers of Ashford and Beer Ferrers, 1678, Exeter R.O.

a parlour, on to the old tradition. That must explain the unmistakable cases where the parlour is the room across the passage, at first thought a most improbable arrangement. It can be seen at Woodlands, Bridford, where the ceiling beams have an ogee moulding. At Munson, Rose Ash, the house is more or less equally divided by the passage, with parlour and cider cellar to one side and hall and dairy to the other (fig. 18). There is no kitchen, but the pump house alongside the dairy is used as a back kitchen or backhouse.

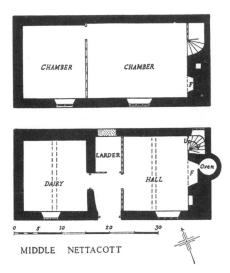

MIDDLE NETTACOTT

FIGURE 25. Middle Nettacott, Upton Pyne, Devon; a small house serving as farm building to the house shown in fig. 24. The function of such a room as the dairy is therefore hypothetical, and with the cob partition between dairy and hall the house is not certainly of one build. The through passage (unusual in a two-unit house) was at some time closed and the space used as a larder. (After A. W. Everett.)

The third house at Nettacott is equally interesting (see fig. 25) and may serve as an example of a husbandman's house.[1] It has only two rooms below, divided by a cross passage so wide that at some later time it was turned into a larder by blocking the farther door. Whether the unheated room was a parlour or a service-room is uncertain; the chambers are reached by a stair flanking the gable fireplace. The bread oven is no doubt original. A growing demand for fresh bread is implied by the oven which bulges from the wall of many a small seventeenth-century house. Instead of daubing the inside of the stone-built oven with clay, the Devonshire or Cornish householder could buy from a potter what the West Country

[1]It is no longer inhabited, but serves as outbuildings to Lower Nettacott.

called a cloam oven. These ovens were made until recently at Truro and Barnstaple. They are by nature undatable, but are most probably an improvement of this century. They were made of clay $\frac{3}{8}$ to $\frac{1}{2}$ inch thick, with large grits in it, in the manner of some medieval and earlier pottery.[1]

Another Devonshire innovation of this time is the smoking chamber, for smoking bacon. It consists of a chamber alongside the fireplace, usually in the gable end, with an opening from the fireplace at a low level and from its corbelled roof a flue returns to the main chimney. One may be seen, in ruined condition, in Heath Cottage, Dunsford, perhaps a husbandman's house of this period.[2] They have been called smugglers' chambers but they are certainly one more example of improving facilities for storing and processing food. Still another, to be expected in Devon, is the cream oven, for scalding cream to make it clot. It is found in the hall, away from the fireplace (for there the cream might get dirty) and it has no flue. At Chattafin, Exbourne, the cob wall near the dairy end of the hall is cut back to make a level surface in which there is a basin-shaped hollow. Charcoal must have been burned in the basin, on which rested the cream bowl. Some housewives no doubt made Devonshire cream over the open fire, but there is no doubt about the function of this contrivance at Chattafin. It can also be seen in the hall at Bartonbury, Down St. Mary.

Many yeoman farmers had enough money for luxurious fittings, as well as for new rooms. The fashion for ornamental plasterwork, hitherto confined to the aristocracy and the gentry, reached the farmer here, as it did elsewhere in the highland zone. Local firms of plasterers sprang up whose work can still be seen in farmhouses of the better sort. Dira in the parish of Sandford was rebuilt at this time to an H plan, which is uncommon in Devon. The central range contains the hall and a dining parlour separated by the through passage. The service wing has a kitchen with a cobbled floor, and the other wing a second parlour.[3] Both this parlour and the chamber over it, which are connected by the principal staircase, have elaborate plaster friezes, and upstairs the ceiling beam has plaster roses on the soffit.

[1] I am indebted to Mrs. R. M. Lake, of W. H. Lake and Son Ltd., for information about the making of cloam ovens. In recent times the rectangular base, about 2 feet $\times$ 1 foot 6 inches, was made in a wooden mould. The sloping slides, supported during moulding by clay pitchers, were eventually gathered into a dome. The oven was fired in the kiln to a temperature of about 1,000° Centigrade. The last cloam oven was made in Lake's Chapel Hill Pottery in 1935.

[2] I am indebted to A. W. Everett for this description and explanation. He quotes other examples at Lower Beara, S. Brent; Addiscombe, Dean; Kilhayne, and Holm Bush, Colliton; Waycroft Manor, Axminster, and Weeke Barton, Bridport.

[3] It is typical of the fluctuation of Devonshire ideas that this parlour should at present be a dairy.

b. The northern counties

Derbyshire in the time of Charles I presents a picture of a society with an upland type of economy, its lineaments sharpened by the poverty of its resources. There were a few wealthy farmers and many poor peasants, and the wealthy were less numerous and the poor were even more humble in their standards of living than on downland in the south or the limestone of the Midlands. Population was growing,[1] perhaps more rapidly than the economy could expand. The lead-mining industry seems to have fallen into the hands of richer men, and some who called themselves miners were employed for wages by wealthier undertakers; they had lost the status of 'free miners'.

At the same time men of all classes were involved in lead mining, without which their living would have been even poorer. The poorest were labourers, like William Aston of Monyash[2] (see Appendix, p. 276), who possessed a few mining tools and a cow and a calf. A husbandman of Grindleford Bridge had 'nine dishes of lead ore lying in Stoke leadmill', and a yeoman of Wardlow had one fother of lead at Hoaley lead mill, and another six fother of lead at Bawtry in north Nottinghamshire, whence lead was shipped down the Idle to Stockwith on Trent. A local craft of minor importance was millstone-making. John Brightmore of Baslow had twelve pairs of millstone worth £13 10s.

The evident poverty appears from distraints for rent or debts, which have not been noticed in inventories from any other region. William Bramall, a miner of Little Longstone had 'one brass pot taken away by Henry Villows of Ashford being bailiff. This pot was taken for the use of Henry Blackwell of Wardlow who took it away and it keepeth'. John Bradbury of Great Longstone had 'a Chest, a truckle bed and a form worth fourteen shillings which Mr. Longsdon hath taken for Rent for one year owing by the Testator'.

The wealthiest men were farmers like Laurence Barber of Ashope, with 640 sheep and 70 cattle, or Robert Barber of Rowlee, an isolated farm in the High Peak north of Hope.[3] Barber had 213 sheep, and the lease of the large farm was valued at £500. He had built a new parlour, so that there were three in all. It is easy to find new building by men such as these.

[1] Parliamentary Surveys of 1649 refer to cottages on the waste in Chapel en le Frith, Gt. Hucklow, Bowden Edge, Eckington, Castleton: P.R.O., Parl. Surveys, Derbyshire 12, 13, 17, 19, 20, 30.
[2] Birmingham Probate Registry, Inventories of the Lichfield Peculiar of the Peak District, A (1562–1709) and B (1569–1636). Inventories are filed with wills, in bundles and boxes according to alphabetical order.
[3] Rowlee Farm and Rowlee Pasture are shown on the 1 inch map, west of Hope Reservoir.

Old Hall Farm, Youlgreave, is one such, dated 1630, and what is now called the Old Hall was rebuilt in 1650. Sheep farming was expanding in this century, but one would like to have estate accounts to show whence money came for these two new houses. Old Hall Farm (see pl. XIVa and fig. 26) consists of hall and cross wing, both of two storeys. This modifica-

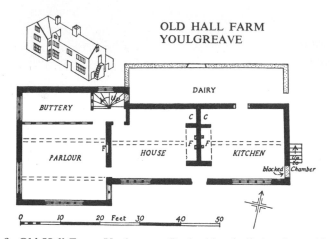

FIGURE 26. Old Hall Farm, Youlgreave, Derbyshire, built in 1630, with the hall and cross wing plan common in the north and west Midlands. Note that the wing contains a parlour, a buttery and a staircase, another common combination in the north Midlands. It is doubtful whether the parlour had a fireplace originally. Although chambers were used throughout the country for storage, external access (as here) is unusual even in stone country. (After F. Marston.)

tion of a medieval design was still popular in the north and north west. The main block of Old Hall Farm contains hall and kitchen divided by an axial stack, opposite which is the quite plain doorway. It is built of well coursed limestone with millstone grit for quoins and windows. The mullions have a plain, deep chamfer, and the main ground floor windows are lofty enough to have a transom. A dairy was built somewhat later, behind the hall range. There is a second, somewhat smaller, version of the same plan at Hargatewall dated 1623, and another at Wormhill near by must be contemporary. The wing contained either one or two parlours; William Butler, yeoman, of Hargreave had two, the outer and the inner parlour, both with beds, but at Youlgreave there is only one, with a buttery behind it. The main staircase of newel type with wooden treads, goes up in the corner of the buttery, but was approached from the hall, not through the parlour. The chambers in the hall block were used as servants' bedrooms and store-rooms, and there is an outside stair to the kitchen chamber at Youlgreave.

XIIIa. 'The Priory', Haydor, Lincs., had no connections with any religious house, but such snobbery on the part of former owners is not uncommon. The modern porch hides the entrance. Notice the protruding wing containing a stone newel staircase. See p. 158.

XIIIb. Manor Farm, Clipsham, Rutland, built in 1639, may be compared with plate VIIIa; notice the loftier proportions current by Charles I's time. See p. 159.

XIVa. Old Farm, Youlgreave, is dated 1630 and is plainly of one build; see the plan, fig. 26.

XIVb. Dean House, Allerton, Bradford, bears the initials of Robert and Susan Deane and the dates 1615 and 1625. It is a long range of building with three gables of typically Yorkshire proportions. See p. 173.

XVa. (*left*). Elaborate plaster ornament for ceilings, along with carved overmantels of wood or stone, was fashionable among the gentry from Elizabethan times onwards. Wealthier farmers, especially in the highland zone, copied their betters, but in a simpler and more rustic fashion, as in this plaster overmantel in Tolson Hall, Strickland Ketel, Westmorland. XVb. (*right*). The small farmers of the Lake District eventually followed the same vogue for elaborate ornament in fixed fittings as in this spice cupboard from Strickland Roger, Westmorland.

School Farm, Ash, next Sandwich, Kent, is dated 1691, and its gables show the Flemish influence common in eastern and south-eastern England. (The house is illustrated in N. Lloyd, *History of English Brickwork*, p. 204, under the caption of 'Cottage at Guilton, Kent'.) See p. 191.

The King's Head, Kirton in Holland, Lincs., is dated 1661 and combines vernacular features, such as the hood mould over the gable window, with English Renaissance elements such as rusticated quoins and strapwork. See p. 200.

XVIa, b. Two examples of the elaborate brickwork popular after 1660.

There are a few new houses of simple two unit plan and two storeys. They have fireplaces at the gable ends. One example is to be seen at Litton, dated 1639. A deep gulf divides the larger houses, such as Youlgreave Old Hall Farm and even the cottage at Litton, from the homes of the majority of Derbyshire people; for although very few houses are fully described in inventories (even that of Laurence Barber of Ashope is not), very few people had enough furniture for more than one or two rooms. The inventory of William Aston is a good example. The uniform simplicity of peasant life is not less marked in Derbyshire in the 1630's than it was in Elizabethan times, though new building, instead of being confined as it was then to the gentry, has now spread to the yeomanry and, in a few instances, even lower down the scale.

In East Yorkshire, the economy of the chalk Wolds resembled that of similar soils elsewhere. There was a growing shortage of land—witness the stinting of commons referred to above—but poor husbandmen and labourers could keep poverty at bay with the increase of their small flocks of sheep, while men like Henry Best, lord of the manor of Elmswell, prospered by the application of skill and resource to an expanding market. There is too little evidence to present a complete picture of the Wold village,[1] beyond the fact that household standards there resembled those of the rest of Yorkshire rather than the lowland zone. Roger Milner of Langtoft, whose goods were worth £33, lived in a house with a firehouse, a parlour and a lower end. Langtoft was an isolated village, set in chalk uplands which had been cleared of timber in prehistoric times, and still cut off from supplies of West Riding coal; Milner was burning cow dung (*cassons* in Yorkshire dialect) on his hearth.

It is difficult to gauge the prosperity of Yorkshire on the eve of the Civil War, for more men made a will now than hitherto, and any sampling of inventories digs deeper into rural society, so that comparisons are dangerous. Nonetheless, housing conditions were not static.

Throughout the north some rich farmers were now speaking of the hall as the forehouse.[2] Such men always had a parlour, and more often two. Although the term had probably arisen in distinction from the backhouse or lowhouse, it is now a stage in the abandonment of the hall as a living room; it is merely the entrance, and the focus of family life—among the wealthy—was moving to the parlour. Christopher Nicholson, a wealthy

---

[1]Only eleven inventories relating to the Wolds were found for the period 1630–40, of which only three described the houses.

[2]Among fifty-six inventories from the Vale of York, sixteen speak of the hall, seventeen the house, eighteen the hallhouse, three the firehouse and two the forehouse.

yeoman of Bedale in the North Riding, had a forehouse, a parlour next to it and a new parlour as well; a new chamber over the new parlour; four other chambers, of which two were for servants, and only two service-rooms, a kitchen and a buttery. More simple folk copied this usage. Thomas Bowman, a yeoman of Haukswell, whose house had only two rooms, called them forehouse and parlour. This change is parallel to the new southern practice of calling the hall a kitchen when it was still the only place in which cooking could be done. In Lancashire, the same change was proceeding, for though the term forehouse was not used there, some houses had both house and firehouse. Presumably the latter is the cooking kitchen, and the house is the hall living-room.

There are now many more houses with two, or even more, parlours. Henry Baker, the parson of Wycliffe, referred in his will in 1640 to 'one parlour which I have laid to my new dwelling house'. A prosperous miller had a garden parlour and a shovelboard parlour. In the Dales they were sometimes called the sun parlour and the north parlour. Wealthier Dalesmen were beginning to build cupboards into the partitions between rooms, which were still usually timber-framed. Thomas Flint of Ripley had in the parlour above (i.e. to one side of) the house 'one little cupboard in the partition and one cupboard in the wall'. Farther north, fitted cupboards, which became such a feature of Westmorland houses after 1660, are rare before 1642. Houses which in 1600 had one or two service-rooms now had three or more, including occasionally a washing house or a larder house: that is, a room in which the larder or stored food was kept. Brewing was now common in such houses, usually in a separate building containing the malt kiln.

In Lancashire new building is still largely the prerogative of the gentry. Society fell into two groups. First the wealthy, such as Dr. Edward Massage, rector of Wigan, who died in a rectory with twenty rooms leaving goods worth £702, or a clothier of Bolton, whose goods amounted to £2,220, including cloth valued at £420; second, men of modest or humble condition. A middle class, of small yeomen clothiers, had hardly begun to emerge.

Men in the first class were busy adding to their houses new parlours and chambers. The alterations to Kenyon Pele Hall illustrate their ideas. It had come into the possession of a successful Wigan attorney, and it was his son who improved the Elizabethan house, for the second generation of such families was always readier to spend money than the first. He added two parlour wings, built a storeyed porch at the centre of the hall façade and made a gallery. He also improved the service quarters, though he was clearly much less interested in that part of the house, and later added a stone gatehouse.[1] Lesser men, whose wives could not leave all the house-work to servants, were content to rebuild the service wing of a medieval house, as did the occupier of Old Manor Farm, Marple, Cheshire.[2] Such work was usually done now in stone, not timber.

Further north, one of the few new houses of this period is Tolson Hall, Strickland Ketel, built in 1638 (see pl. XVa) by a successful tobacco merchant, who thanked God for tobacco in the same manner as a Notting-hamshire wool merchant a century and a half earlier had admitted that sheep had 'paid for all'.[3]

One of the larger West Riding houses described in an inventory is still standing: Dean House, Allerton (pl. XIVb), the home of Robert Deane who died in 1636,[4] leaving goods worth £184. He called himself a yeoman, and had corn and hay in the barn, and ploughs, harrows, a cart and a 'muck wain', and fourteen cattle (including three oxen), three horses and a pig somewhere outside. The house (now divided) stands on the slope, its triple-gabled front looking over the valley, and one end gable bears the date 1605 with the initials R[obert and] S[usan] D[eane], while the other has a sun-dial dated 1625. The plan forms a U, the space at the rear between the wings being now filled with an outshot; the west wing, dated 1605, has different masonry from the rest, and the east wing, under the sundial, has on both floors larger windows, with mullion and transom. There is nothing to disprove the notion that Robert Deane within twenty years first built and then enlarged the house. The inventory includes the house body (a common Yorkshire term for the hall), three parlours, kitchen and the old milkhouse; upstairs, four chambers. The west or older wing, judging from the ground floor windows, probably had a parlour at the front and kitchen and milkhouse behind; in the centre was the house or hall, with a chamber over, and the other wing had the east and north parlours downstairs with the great chamber and north chamber over them. The original entrance leads into the east parlour, which is consonant with the fact that York-shire inventories of this date sometimes begin with the parlour and only reach the hall house later. This is another reflection of the declining status of the hall-kitchen, even in unpretentious Yorkshire circles. Robert

---

[1]H. Taylor, *Old Halls in Lancashire and Cheshire*, 56–7; the contract for new work is printed by W. A. Singleton in *Trans. of Hist. Soc. of Lancs. and Cheshire*, 104 (1952), 89-91.

[2]W. A. Singleton, *loc. cit.*, 89.

[3]H. M. C. *Westm.*; 220–1 (3). The house still contains the remains of windows with painted glass of pipes, plugs of tobacco and 'God by this meanes hath sent, what I on this house have spent. T.T. 1638'.

[4]*Crosley Wills*, 83–89; W. B. Crump, 'The Yeoman Clothier of the Seventeenth Century' in *Bradford Antiquary*, 7 (1933), 222–6.

and his wife were untidy folk, and certainly did not need three parlours. The visitor went into a room which contained three tables, a bed and a desk, but it also held a cheese press, an old ark, two barrows and various farming gear; somewhere in it—perhaps in the desk—were fifteen silver spoons and £14 15s. in cash. Both it and the north parlour behind had little ranges; were fires ever lit in them? The north parlour was also filled with typical farmer's oddments. The west parlour must have been the best bedroom, with its featherbed, cupboard, chests and tables, but someone had put down '2 pounds of wool, one bridle rein, stirrup leather, thread, spice and inkle', and never tidied them away. The house body was orderly enough, with its great table and forms, stools with cushions and chairs; beef and bacon hung from the ceiling and a musket stood in a corner; round the range with its spits were brass ladles, 'striking knives and chopping bills', dripping pan and broiling irons, two chafing dishes, two brass mortars. Light at night came from candles in 'two greater brass candlesticks', and anyone retiring to bed took one of the '3 lesser candlesticks'. The kitchen and milkhouse between them held oatmeal (in a great ark) and malt, a spinning wheel, churns, tubs, bowls, trenchers and the like, and a lot more small tools, as well as hackney saddles, load saddles and other gear appropriate to a yeoman clothier. Robert Deane certainly had been a clothier, for upstairs, among the lumber which mainly filled the chambers, were a 'paire of walker sheares' and also 'one quishion loome', probably no longer used. Now that cushions were so popular, since upholstered chairs were a luxury, there was a growing market for cushion cloths, in which Bradford had had a share for the past forty years,[1] alongside the main manufacture of kersey.

The sort of new building that Robert Deane had done is illustrated in a contract, dated 1648, for a house at Edge End, Ovenden, north of Halifax. The mason was to take down part of two bays of the existing house and to rebuild it as a parlour with a chamber over, each with a fireplace, the masonry to have 'a competent number of throughs in the same'.[2] The parlour was to have a seven light window, the chamber one of five, each light 3 feet high and 1 foot wide. He also built an oven in the kitchen, and made some alterations to all the fireplaces in the house, kitchen, parlour and chamber.[3]

[1] W. B. Crump, loc. cit., 237.

[2] The through stones can often be picked out, especially in barns, because they are left protruding from the wall face.

[3] Yorks. Arch. J., 16 (1902), 108; Halifax Ant. Soc., 1928, 353. I am indebted to Mr. J. Wilson for taking me to see this house, which appears to have been rebuilt in the eighteenth century.

Houses like this were still uncommon, for enlargement had been more often by way of added parlours and service-rooms. In the Bradford area, however, the weavers were now beginning to have the loom upstairs.[1] They were usually men of middling, or ample, means. The evolving industrial society now divided itself distinctly into three more or less equal classes: those with goods less than about £35, a middle class with between £50 and £75, and an upper class with anything from £100 to £500. All of them were engaged in mixed farming, but the lowest class, of labourers and poor husbandmen, rarely possessed a loom. One man had the loom in the parlour of his two-roomed house, six others were using a chamber upstairs, and four had a shop, presumably on the ground floor.

In such houses as these, cooking was usually done in the house body. There, along with the iron range and the reckon hook, were the bakestone and the wooden boards (the bagbread and the spittle) with which oatcakes were made.[2] The kneading trough was often kept upstairs in a chamber when not in use.

The overriding impression from northern counties, especially Durham, is of the relative poverty and simplicity of home life, compared with the south. Men of gentle birth, like William Clavering of Gateside in Durham, or Joseph Cradock of Bishop Auckland,[3] lived in quite simple style, outdone by many a yeoman of the Midlands or south. Clavering's home consisted of hall, parlour, kitchen and cellar, with chambers over all three rooms. Cradock had a forehouse, with a little room beside it serving as a buttery; a parlour and a kitchen, with one upper chamber which he slept in. There was a malt loft over the kitchen, and a stable and coalhouse outside.

As for the rank and file of northern society, houses are rarely described room by room in the inventories of the four northern dioceses of York, Chester, Carlisle and Durham. Appraisers were in the habit of lumping together articles of a kind, wherever they were found in the house—two iron ranges, seven chests, and so on.[4] We learn only that most people had no more than one hearth, which is just as true in other parts of England. The iron range is the significant innovation. Its appearance bears out the words of Daniel King about Cheshire that instead of a hob of clay in the midst of the house the peasantry had since about 1616 'builded chimnies,

[1]*Crosley Wills, passim.*
[2]W. B. Crump, *loc. cit.*, 233 for a description of these utensils.
[3]Their wills are printed in *Durham Wills and Inventories* (Surtees Soc.) IV, 267 and 248; the inventories not printed are in the Durham Record Office.
[4]This is the case, for instance, in eleven of the Crosley inventories of this period.

and furnished other parts of their houses accordingly'.[1] In the Cleveland hills the firehouse consisting of a single room, commonly of two bays with a cruck trussed roof, and heated by an open hearth, was still to be found up to 1660.[2]

[1]Daniel King, *The Vale Royal of England* (London, 1656), 19.
[2]J. C. Atkinson, *Forty Years in a Moorland Parish* (1923), 453–6.

Conclusion

IN the generation 1610 to 1640 documentary evidence is much more plentiful than hitherto. It comes from counties about which nothing could be said, from that source, of the Elizabethan period. Not only that, but a will was often made now by a class of men who had hitherto rarely ventured to do so. To this kind of record a new one was added by estate stewards and professional surveyors: a version of the usual type of manorial survey including in some instances details of tenants' houses as well as of their land. The main limitation in our view of early Stuart society is not the gaps in the material, some of which may still be filled by further work on local archives, but the character of inventories from Lancashire and some northern counties, where the church courts had not yet begun to insist that appraisers must show what rooms a house contained.

The greater social range of inventories shows that archaic terms such as firehouse and netherhouse had a wider currency in the seventeenth century than had been suspected. The farmhouse whose third room was called simply a backhouse or netherhouse was to be found not only in parts of the highland zone but also in conservative regions in the lowlands. In the latter it was beginning to assume the more specialized function of kitchen or milkhouse. The origin and evolution of the third room is indeed the most obscure aspect of the evolution of the farmhouse. Fox and Raglan found that 'the views of the Monmouthshire farming community as to the function of the third room in their larger houses were confused and variable'.[1] We have found a similar state of mind elsewhere. It must have been due not only to the mutually inconsistent ideas involved—that the third room was pantry and buttery, as in larger medieval houses, and that it was the end of a long house—but also to the length of time over which the confusion had had its play. Since the long house has left no other possible trace in the lowlands than the backhouse, it must have disappeared in the course of the Middle Ages. The byre of a long house must in any case have been empty for most of the year, and there are only a few weeks in the year

[1]*Mon. Ho.*, II, 105.

when cattle in the lowlands cannot remain out of doors. For much of the time then the farmer and his wife could use the low house or whatever they called it for storing any oddments. Only when standards rose rapidly and domestic needs were clarified did they make up their minds how to use it.

The apparent slackening in the pace of new building after 1615 or so would seem after closer study to be rather a shift in its social distribution. The pressure of increasing population had relaxed, but the engrossment of land in larger farms, and the greater scale on which their owners and tenants were working, continued to demand expansion of the farmhouse. If a distinction can be drawn between the motives of Elizabethan and early Stuart farmers, it is that the former could afford more comfort and the latter needed more convenience about the house. Hence the emphasis on service-rooms: the malthouse and the storage buildings round the yard of a large house; the two service-rooms—buttery and milkhouse or kitchen —in even the home of a small husbandman. For the same reason special storage chambers were needed upstairs: a corn chamber and a cheese chamber, a room for malt and another for apples.

New building was still entirely within the medieval tradition of a rectangular plan, one room deep and one cross wing or more. The outshot was a way of making a more compact plan, two rooms deep, but does not seem yet to have been common. The now general demand for chambers, either a full storey in height or making use of roof space, could be met by customary methods of building. But the vernacular tradition was, for the first time, showing signs of weakness under the pressure of new social ideas. The effect of architectural concepts was still trifling. Some masons in the stone belt conceded that window openings in a gable end might be symmetrically arranged, and both masons and carpenters were ready to adopt new forms of moulding for window mullions or door openings. Such innovations have an entirely different significance from changes dictated by the householder. For one thing, the through passage, which had for centuries been an integral part of the lowland plan, was no longer thought essential. In some old houses a chimney stack or a fireplace was inserted in it. Even in Devonshire, a highly conservative county, one sometimes finds that it has been closed at the farther end and turned into a buttery. A change of this sort is impossible to date closely, but it may well have begun at this time. In the Cotswolds and Somerset the passage was still a normal part of new houses, but in Kesteven some new houses of stone were built without it.

The integration of the kitchen into the house did more to upset the householder's customary ideas of the functions of rooms than any other development of this age. If, in a Devonshire farmhouse or parsonage, a new kitchen was made in the house to replace an older one across the court, the hall could now be thought of as a parlour or sitting-room. In a small East Anglian farmhouse, if the hall was still used for cooking, it might now be called the kitchen. Inventories show that a room in which milk vessels were kept and washed, bacon salted and beer brewed, might be called a kitchen or a milkhouse, a dairy or a backhouse. This irresolution in the mind of the countryman was the first sign of conditions in which, a generation later, new forms of plan and new methods of building might sweep across the country more rapidly and easily.

Part Four

THE VERNACULAR TRADITION UNDER ATTACK 1642–1690

Introduction

WITH the outbreak of the civil war in 1642, men's thoughts turned perforce to other things than building. Some of the new mansions and manor houses of the Midlands were turned into military strong points, and though many changed hands or surrendered eventually without serious damage, the more bitter struggle of the later stages sometimes led to destruction. A fine new house on the Trent bank at Torksey, first abandoned by its Royalist owner and then garrisoned by Parliamentarians from Lincoln, was destroyed in a foray of the Newark Royalists. Such a fate was reserved usually for the strongholds and symbols of party. Farmhouses and cottages were destroyed only in the accident of skirmishing, or if they interfered with static defences round a town or castle. Sir John Hotham, Parliamentary governor of Hull, burned houses outside the town's Beverley Gate, and the Royalists did the same outside Newark, to deprive the enemy of cover. A few parsonage houses were destroyed,[1] for parsons who insisted on using the church for services unpalatable to the dominant party were liable to threats, or worse. For most villages, this time of war meant keeping up the farming routine without the help of men who had gone to fight, and finding money enough to satisfy whichever side controlled them. The unluckiest were those within reach of both sides, such as Parliamentary Leicester and Royalist Belvoir and Ashby.[2]

Very few houses can be dated to the years 1642–9, and even after that building was slow to resume, though it seems to have got under way most quickly in the south east. In the 1660's there was a spate of new building,

---

[1] E.g. Skinnand, Lincs. (terrier of 1679, L.R.O.), Driby Lincs. (L.R.S., *Speculum Diocesios Lincolncensis*, 42), and Ashby de la Zouch, Leics. (terrier 1674, Leicester Museum), no doubt destroyed by the Royalists out of spite against a notable Puritan parson. The house at Stanwix was demolished in an attack on Carlisle; R. S. Ferguson, *Misc. Accounts of the Diocese of Carlisle* (1877), 105. At least two Exeter parsonage houses were destroyed: those of St. Sidwell and St. Thomas.

[2] For a description based on parish accounts, of Upton near Newark, of how constable and churchwardens carried the responsibilities of such a time, see F. H. West, *Rude Forefathers* (London, 1949).

and it is apparent that the vernacular tradition was now, for the first time, being seriously undermined.

Hitherto new ideas, whether they were a natural development out of existing forms and arrangements, such as the axial brick chimney stack, or the gift of Renaissance scholarship, such as symmetrical tiers of windows in a stone gable, had been taken into a cultural tradition which was robust enough to support them. After the Restoration the tradition was noticeably weaker, because the classes which carried it no longer had the same stability. Their sense of regional propriety had been weakened by travels throughout England in the armies of one side or the other. The sales of Royalist and other estates during the Commonwealth, the third great transfer of land in English history, had the same consequences as the Norman Conquest and the Reformation. Each revolution in land ownership hastened the growth of large estates and of the number of landless men in the villages. Those who now found themselves in a position to build discovered that the former pattern of prices had been transformed, and old sources of material were closed. When Royalist owners recovered their lands they found that timber resources had been squandered by the ex-officers, lawyers and merchants who had acquired them but were not sure how long they would keep them.

In more than one respect, then, the years between 1642 and 1660 produced a more emphatic break with the past than any since the Reformation. In what had been regions of timber building, old ideas were necessarily in retreat before growing scarcity of suitable materials and their rising cost. Timber was used more frugally; slighter and inferior posts were concealed behind a façade of ornamental pargetting. Alternatively, brick took the place of timber. In the stone-using regions masons were now in a stronger position than ever, and their mark on the villages of the jurassic region and of most of the northern counties is most apparent at this time. In many parts of England the use of the simplest and cheapest materials—mud or turf for walls, untrimmed timbers for a roof—was in no danger of disappearing, for the poor were more numerous, and so perpetuated the most primitive methods of building.

CHAPTER ONE

The South-eastern Counties

IN Kent the social scene revealed by inventories is dominated by the yeoman, whose wealth now bears out the boast of a century before. It looks as though the effect of the inheritance system had now been circumvented by the Kentish freeholder. Scarcely any labourers made a will,[1] and only one person in ten had goods worth less than £20. Nearly half the wills are of men with goods worth £100 or more, and those who were called yeomen by their neighbours usually had no less than £150. The only other distinct class were those described as clothiers, clothworkers or weavers; they too were usually comfortably off.

There are, then, plenty of descriptions of larger farmhouses in east Kent, though they defy classification and reduction to a pattern even more markedly than those of earlier times. In all classes, but particularly among the less prosperous, cooking may still be done in the hall. In a few cases, as we have found earlier, it is now called the kitchen, but this process in the decline of the hall at the expense of the kitchen had not made much headway in the past generation.

On the other hand, the service element in these larger houses is still developing, and the new emphasis seems to be on domestic convenience, rather than on places for the by-products of the farm. The old-fashioned term buttery is disappearing, in favour of the name drink house, or drink buttery, and several houses have two. Walter Basucke's house at Fritten-den had an outer and an inner buttery. Thomas Gibson, clothier, of Hawkhurst had a buttery by the parlour, a small drink buttery, and a third buttery by the kitchen. The most specific instances of this change, which

[1]To judge from a sample of inventories dated 1663; Maidstone R.O., P.R.C. 11/21. The median value of the sample is £70 15s. 2d.

must mean some alteration in habits, are the three houses which had a best drink buttery and a small drink buttery. They each belonged to wealthy people—Thomas Furner, yeoman, of Marden; Margaret Baker, widow, of Stone, and Peter Edmet, yeoman, of High Halden. Perhaps the best drink buttery was an adjunct to the parlour—a situation we have already found frequently, and which becomes still more common in the second half of this century—and the other an adjunct to the kitchen.

These changes in family life and in the pattern of hospitality go along with further advances in the status of the parlour. Only one householder in five in east Kent still spoke of it as the chamber. Though two parlours out of three still contained a bed, one never meets now a phrase like 'in the parlour where he lay'. Yeomen and wealthy clothiers had nearly all turned the bed out of the parlour; only when they had two parlours was one of them used as a bedroom. Rooms upstairs were now correspondingly more numerous, and nearly always furnished as bedrooms. A few people, especially those who in their trade or craft used a lot of material, still used rooms upstairs. A baker in Thanet used three lofts, one for wheat, one for bread and the third called the pastry loft: very inconvenient it must have been to have to climb a ladder or even a flight of stairs dozens of times a day. A clothworker at Staplehurst kept some of his stock in a chamber over the shop, and more (nine stone of flocks and 1,000 teazels) in the high chamber. A few farmers still used the loft over the hall or the chamber over the parlour for storing corn, but some of them now used the garret for that purpose. The rest must have found room in one of the farm buildings.

Let us now look more closely at particular houses. Bartholomew Burch of Shadoxhurst near Ashford was a labourer, the owner of three cows and one pig, together with goods amounting in all to £13 19s. when he died (see App. p. 278). He had a house with four rooms, but that no doubt exaggerates its scale, for there was a hall with a sleeping chamber over it and two service-rooms which may well have been no more than small places partitioned off the hall. Such an arrangement, evolved during this century from the one-roomed house, can be found in many parts of lowland England in this period. Burch called his service-rooms milkhouse and drink house; there were three barrels in the drinkhouse, but no brewing vessels, so perhaps he was able to buy ale from the farmer who employed him.

Elizabeth Bassett's house at Sandwich may well have been of the same plan. She called her hall 'the low room', which means that it was not open to the roof, so her chamber must have been over it. She had a buttery, and a cove as well, where she kept one old pail, a basket, a keeler and other old lumber.

One of the signs that rural society had begun to lose its stability more rapidly than ever before is that wealthy men can now be found living in small houses. Peter Edmet of High Halden, yeoman, the wealthiest man in a casual sample of sixty, lived in quite simple style. His hall was the cooking room, and hence called the kitchen; there were chambers over kitchen and parlour, and three service-rooms—milkhouse, a best drink buttery and a small drink buttery. He had a brewhouse with a chamber over it where no doubt servants slept. Like him, Robert Dodd, yeoman of Littlebourne, was rich in farm stock: it was valued at nearly £300, compared with household goods worth only £62. He had seven rooms: hall, kitchen, buttery, milkhouse; best chamber (presumably downstairs since no parlour is mentioned) and chambers over hall and kitchen used as bedrooms.

Stone Street Farm, Petham,[1] is a medieval house altered at this time in a way which shows the kinds of improvement which an old house seemed to need in the eyes of a Londoner (see sketch plan, fig. 27). It is said to have been

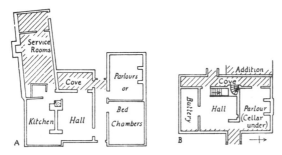

FIGURE 27. Sketch plans of two Kentish houses, to show alterations made after 1660 to older houses. A (The Windmill Inn, Hollingbourne) is a medieval timber-framed house, which now has a *cove* or lean-to added to the hall, and one wing extended at the rear. B (Stone Street Farm, Petham, after E. W. Parkin) had the jettied front underbuilt, the porch added, a cellar excavated under the parlour, and a *cove* and other extensions added at the rear.

bought in 1666 by a merchant escaping from the plague. He put in the hall fireplace, and a cellar under the parlour. A cellar below ground (as distinct from the medieval cellar on ground level) was now becoming popular, and it will most often be found under the parlour; a boarded floor made the parlour warmer. The stairs flanking the axial hall stack go down to the cellar, and a framed staircase to the bedrooms now rises alongside the hall fireplace. At the same time the front wall was built out in brick to the line of the jetty, and a cove or lean-to was added along the whole of the rear,

[1]Now a teahouse known as 'Slippery Sam's'. after a smuggler who owned it in the eighteenth century. I am indebted to Mr. E. W. Parkin for a sketch plan of it.

perhaps to make a second buttery behind the parlour in addition to the original one by the hall.

The use of bricks to rebuild the ground floor walls of a house like Stone Street Farm, or the gable wall of another house now known as The Abbot's Fireside (formerly The Smithies Arms) at Elham, involved no radical departure from traditional ideas. When a bricklayer was given the contract for an entirely new house, he was most likely to adopt an entirely new idiom: that which came from Flanders. The reasons for this invasion we must now explore. Though there must have been plenty of native brickmakers and bricklayers, men who wanted to build in brick had sometimes gone across the North Sea to recruit them. Down to the middle of the seventeenth century, and possibly later, the men who were so hired could make bricks and then build.[1] Even if there is no evidence, from documents or design, of a foreign influence, smaller buildings in brick prior to 1642 can very often be traced to the arrival of an outsider, or to some special circumstances which made it appropriate to break the local link of client and builder. In Wiltshire, Woolmore House was built on the Devizes Road at Bowerhull, Melksham, by Sir George Herbert, a London vintner who had acquired property there in 1629. It has brick walling with stone quoins, string courses and window frames, and apart from the novel material, its design, with a symmetrical façade, stands right outside the local vernacular style of the time.[2] Dorfold Hall, Cheshire, was built in 1616 by a wealthy Nantwich merchant, in a style which suggests that he made use of an East Anglian builder.[3] Several other Cheshire manor houses of the early seventeenth century show that the lesser gentry were beginning to accept the idea of building in brick, with stone quoins. Gray's Almshouses, Taunton, dating from 1635-40, are the earliest brick building in the neighbourhood,[4] and the material was no doubt selected by the benefactor or his executors. In Rye, Sussex, brick was used for the façade of Peacock's School in 1636.[5] All these examples—schools, almshouses, inns (see below p. 201) as well as manor houses—show a strong contrast between, on the one hand, the ideas of those responsible for a public building or for one whose eye-catching contemporary look would be a source of pride or advantage to its owner, and, on the other hand, that strong and unwritten alliance between client and builder in the sphere of domestic building which we call the vernacular tradition.

[1] The Flemish workers employed at Loseley early in Elizabeth's reign were called indifferently brickmakers and bricklayers; *Arch.* 36 (1856), 297-301.
[2] V.C.H. *Wilts.*, 7 (1953), 103.
[3] *Country Life*, 31 Oct. 1908.
[4] *Somerset A.N.H.S. Proc.*, 98 (1953), 79, 95.
[5] *Sussex Arch. Coll.*, 68 (1927), 199.

Near the east and south coasts one must take into account the possibility of building materials imported from the Continent. Whether Sir William More's Flemish brickmakers—Dyrrke, Crawks, Mabbanke, Chetey, Hoke —went home when Loseley Hall was finished we do not know, and it is not easy to decide what kind of foreign influence produced the new brick styles of south-eastern England in this period put up after 1660. A building like Bourne Mill on the outskirts of Colchester, built in 1591 with gables, volutes and pinnacles entirely in the Dutch manner[1] stands alone both in style and date. The average country bricklayer, competent to lay a foundation for a timber-house, to rear a brick stack or even to fill the panels of a timber house with brick nogging, had much to learn before he could build a house. While better workers could use English bond (alternate courses of headers and stretchers), much brick walling of the seventeenth century is laid in a bond that defies classification. A new bond was devised, English garden wall bond, in which three courses of stretchers are succeeded by one of headers.[2] Flemish bond, with headers and stretchers alternately in each course, appeared first in Kew Palace (1631) and St. Catherine's, Cambridge (1634).[3] It was being used in midland farmhouses from 1700 onwards. The English builder also learned to reduce the thickness of walls. Those earlier than 1660 are usually one and a half bricks thick (14 inches). The adoption of the new material is a tentative process, in which gable walls may be thicker than side walls, and have timber tiebeams in them, until eventually mounting skill and experience leads the builder to dispense with timber and rely on walls only one brick or even (in small cottages) half a brick (4½ inches) thick. But that process is not completed everywhere before the end of the eighteenth century, and is parallel to the effect of Flemish influence.

How did it arrive? Dutch building materials began to be imported from about 1625. An English boat came into Boston in 1628 with 3,500 tiles aboard, and the earliest references to pantiles, the S-curved roofing tile, occur in the 1630s.[4] Sir William Brereton travelled in Holland in 1634, and brought home tiles and flooring stones for his house at Handforth in

---

[1] R.C.H.M. *Essex*, III, 71–3, pl. 68.

[2] It can be seen, for instance, in buildings as widely dispersed as Church Farm, Oxton, Notts., and The Pant, Raglan, Mon., the former about 1675, the latter a generation or more later.

[3] D. S. Spittle, *Historical Study of Brickwork in Cambridge* (R.I.B.A. dissertation 1949), 34. I am indebted to Mr. Spittle for allowing me to read his dissertation.

[4] R. W. K. Hinton, *Port Books of Boston, 1601–40* (Lincoln Record Soc.), 171. Pantiles were used on a building in St. Clement's, London, in 1635; N. G. Brett-James, *Growth of Stuart London* (1935), 155. 'Flanders tyle' were purchased by the Savile family, presumably in London, in 1638; Notts. C.R.O., A4/11.

Cheshire.[1] Any traveller could bring back a bag of tulip bulbs, or even a wagonload of tiles, and plenty of Englishmen made the journey across the North Sea: gentlemen and their servants off to fight in Germany; merchants; financiers and their agents going to Antwerp or Rotterdam; ship owners and their crews trading with the Low Countries. But a curved or tumbled brick gable, or a wall laid in Flemish bond, needed more than the materials and a sketch handed to an English bricklayer. Many towns such as Colchester or Maidstone had a sizeable Dutch colony in their midst by the early seventeenth century, and the immigrants must have included builders, as well as those who contributed to the textile, glassmaking and printing industries, to mining and draining undertakings.[2] The earliest evidence of Dutch influence in design, apart from Bourne Mill, appears in Cambridge in the 1630's. The colleges had for at least two generations been ready to build in brick, and by 1625 the choice of materials seems to have been a matter of explicit choice of finish, rather than of cost. The curved gables of Emmanuel date from 1631, and Peterhouse Chapel, intended to be done in brick but eventually carried out in stone, from c. 1633.[3]

Flemish influence was, then, established in the 1630's, but it had no effect on the countryside until after 1660. By that time the import of building materials had spread to the south coast. Dover was most familiar with boats bringing wrought silk or other high class textiles from France and occasionally oranges and lemons from farther south, but a few brought bricks, pantiles and paving stones from Rotterdam, Middelburg or Flushing.[4] Usually such materials were imported by the master of the vessel, as ballast for which he knew there would be a ready sale. Buck's *Prospect of Dover* (1735) shows many curved gables. Even if close study of surviving examples would show whether they were built of imported bricks (and that is very doubtful), we should not know whether they were designed by immigrant builders, by Englishmen apprenticed to Dutch, or merely by imitative native workers. The last seems most likely. The one thing that is clear is that Kentish examples belong to the years after 1660, not before: e.g., a house at Ickham dated 1663, or Jenkin's Well, Old Deal, 1694. Dutch immigrants had been received in Kent a generation and more earlier, but no buildings in their style were put up before foreign materials began to be available, even though the quantities recorded in the Port

[1] *Travels in Holland, etc.* (Chetham Soc. 1844), 59, 69.
[2] G. N. Clarke, *The Seventeenth Century* (1947), 15–18.
[3] D. S. Spittle, *op. cit.* 23–33.
[4] E.g. Dover Port Book, 1663–4, P.R.O., E190/661/19. Cargoes of bricks occasionally entered Southampton; E190/827/2.

Books for Dover are insignificant. By that time, as a matter of fact, Dutch immigration to England was discouraged by both the governments concerned.

The new brick houses departed from tradition in appearance and proportion rather than interior design (see pl. XVIa). Gabled roofs instead of hipped were somewhat of a novelty in the Kentish countryside but had the advantage of providing usable garrets. A string course marked the height of ground and first floor ceilings. The upper one may be higher than the eaves and appear only in the gable end, as at Ickham. They are the best superficial proof that chambers were now required to be as lofty as ground floor rooms, and the Ickham house is a forerunner of innumerable brick farmhouses, especially in the Midlands, whose lofty proportions mark them off so distinctly from the medieval and sub-medieval tradition. At Ickham there are large gable end chimney stacks, another feature that was to become general in the eighteenth century. They go with an internal division into three rooms, of which the central one, the hall, is no more than entrance lobby, unheated, containing the staircase.[1]

West Sussex villages were changing as distinctly as those of Kent, but the contrasts between conditions now and a generation earlier were due to local factors rather than external influences such as the purchase of farms and estates by Londoners. Sussex, cut off by the Weald and the bad roads which exhausted Defoe when he came to pass through it, still hid from outside eyes the resources of its 'deep dirty but rich part'.[2] The Wealden villages which had formerly been poorer than those on the coastal fringe were now richer; there the wealthy yeomen were to be found, while the husbandmen, less prosperous in any case, more often lived in coastal villages.[3] This sort of reversal of fortunes—for farming in coastal villages had been more profitable in the 1630's—was probably happening elsewhere; agricultural techniques were now able to get better results out of the stiffer soils, and the centuries of labour in clearing them and bringing them under the plough were beginning at last to pay large

[1]Assuming that the small central lobby has not been made by partitioning off part of a hall which originally occupied more than half the ground floor. That arrangement is found in houses of *c.* 1700 in the Midlands and elsewhere of non-regional design, but according to R. T. Mason the small hall evolved in Sussex in the seventeenth century, and so the arrangement at Ickham may be original.

[2]Defoe, *Tour through England and Wales* (Everyman), I, 125.

[3]Chichester R.O., Ep. I/29; box of inventories beginning in 1662. Median value (69 inventories) £63 8s. Median value for Weald (42 inventories) £73 or £78. Median value for Coast (22 inventories) £43 or £63. Median value for 18 yeomen (4 from Coast) £76 or £109. Median value for 12 husbandmen (5 from Coast) £57 or £62. Median value for 13 craftsmen £20 or £31.

There are not enough inventories from Down villages to present any conclusion.

dividends. Until historians of agriculture show the exact source of this change—whether in new crops, better implements, or new techniques such as using lime—we can only note that it is taking place, and try to trace its effect on housing conditions.

Although the view presented in inventories excludes the lower levels of village society—no labourers' houses are included—it is clear enough that small single-storey houses were more common among coastal villages than farther inland. Two-roomed houses can be picked out, like that of John Geattere, husbandman, of Clideham, whose goods were worth only £8 1s. It consisted of his bedchamber, with its high bedstead, four chests, and linen, and the hall, with its trestle table, one form and two chairs, an old cupboard. There was a small furnace for brewing, but he only had four pieces of pewter. Such people had still not adopted the name parlour for a ground floor sleeping-room, but houses as small as this usually had a service-room of some sort. In two cases it is called an outlet or outroom: that is, an outshot or lean-to (see Appendix, p. 285). None of the houses appear to be of the one-roomed type with a chamber over. Some of them are of three units, such as Joan Geffery's house at Selsey, with a hall, a kitchen and two chambers, the outer and the inner; these last were subdivisions of the end bay and led one into the other.

It is not surprising that after a century of rapid change the older names for parts of the house were losing their hold on the countryman's mind. William Collins' hall at Horsham was called the fireroom, which may be an old term, but is more probably a new one for the only room with a fire. The inventory of Henry Mitchell, yeoman of Warnham, speaks of 'a low room' which is really a chamber, 'a little room next the hall chamber' used as a store chamber, and the 'room over the buttery' which is a bedroom. Henry Carver's house at Pulborough had a 'room within the hall' which was in fact a buttery, and an 'inner room' where cheeses were made. These changes are more than the loss of traditional names; they reveal the breakdown of traditional modes of life.

Nevertheless West Sussex was conservative in another significant respect: the principal bedchamber, even in houses of substantial yeomen, seems to be downstairs. Houses with a parlour are still in a small minority, and in this respect Sussex and Kent have distinctly parted company in the past generation. The house of a wealthy farmer at Tillington will illustrate Sussex standards at a high level. Laurence Alcock, gentleman, had goods worth £606, of which half was in farm stock. His hall, now no more than an entrance lobby with a fireplace, had in it a table, a form, four joined stools and a cupboard. The parlour was furnished with two tables, three great chairs, six chairs covered in Russia leather, and three joined stools, but next to it was a low chamber with a table, a chair and a stool, and also a bed with a canopy and curtains. Whether it was in regular use, or served as a guest chamber the inventory cannot tell us. At the other end of the house was a kitchen (with incidentally 114 lbs. of pewter), a brewhouse and a milkhouse. Upstairs, chambers over hall, parlour, low chamber and kitchen were used as bedrooms and that over the parlour was the best; the hall chamber was also used for storing hops, and the kitchen chamber for linen. Such a way of life is still firmly rooted in tradition. Apart from this relation of rooms upstairs and down, the Weald houses, products of a superior building technique now reinforced by superior wealth, have usually more rooms upstairs, and more chambers at that, as distinct from the lofts which were still common near the coast.

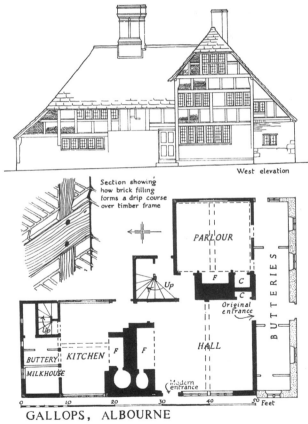

GALLOPS, ALBOURNE

FIGURE 28. Gallops, Albourne, Sussex, a timber-framed house with brick infilling of 1661. Such a technique is very unusual in Sussex, and belongs principally to the Midlands. The lean-to service rooms on the south side appear to be an addition, probably also of 1661, to provide butteries conveniently near to the hall and the parlour. (After W. H. Godfrey.)

The period from 1660 is, more than any other, that of brick infilling or nogging in timber-framed houses. It is often an original element, though it may be difficult to be sure of that in particular cases. A house at Albourne, named Gallops,[1] illustrates this stage, though it is a somewhat exotic house for Sussex, because its filling of bricks laid herring-bone fashion is a midland fashion which is rare in the south. Another unusual refinement is that a course of bricks was laid above each horizontal timber, protruding and chamfered to throw rain clear of the frame. The house has a simple L plan (see fig. 28) with a staircase within the angle, and was perhaps built in late Elizabethan times. Later, and the door to the hall with 1661 in nails on a panel may indicate the date, it was improved and renovated. The plaster filling was replaced with brick and the butteries added alongside hall and parlour.

[1] W. H. Godfrey, 'Gallops, Albourne', *Sussex Arch. Coll.*, 83 (1942–3), 3–14. Godfrey adopted the conclusion that the house was a new building of 1661. I put forward here the alternative view that the date refers to alterations, including the brick infilling.

CHAPTER TWO

Essex and East Anglia

THE advantage of a large collection of inventories from a single village in laying bare the range of rural housing is even more apparent in this period than before. There are forty-two from Writtle and Roxwell in the years 1658–70,[1] and while they seem to do less than justice to the larger houses (mainly of medieval origin), and include none of the smallest, the clear and orderly descriptions give an accurate picture of homes of village craftsmen and medium farmers. Very few had precisely the same accommodation, and all variations and combinations could be found in one house or another, but there was an underlying uniformity which is confirmed by observed conditions not only here but in many parts of England. Only now can one see how much the great expansion in living standards in the past century had achieved, and how universal were the stimuli which had set it off.

If these records are to be believed, the non-parlour type of cottage had entirely disappeared from these Essex villages. This is not likely to be true, for we have no labourers' houses in the group, but the house with a hall (and perhaps a store-room) downstairs and a chamber above, of a kind which we have noticed south of the Thames and elsewhere, was not reported by the Royal Commission among Essex houses built before 1714.

More than half the houses were certainly of two or three unit design. It is not safe to try to distinguish the two from documents alone, because one cannot be sure whether the third (service) room was a full unit or

[1]*Essex Inventories*, 87–117. Four of the persons concerned were not householders (nos. 31, 40, 42, 44). Of the rest, only two lived in houses not fully described (nos. 39, 54). The median value of goods is £44 14s., a lower figure than for the years 1635–40, and lower also than contemporary figures from Kent and Sussex.

merely a subdivision of the hall. Where there were two service-rooms (i.e., milkhouse as well as buttery) then three full units are almost certain. Among the two unit houses, those with one chamber only, over the parlour, and a hall open to the roof were the most common. Some of these arrangements are shown in the type plans and elevations in fig. 9, particularly types I to III, but their variety is not exhausted. Any child with building blocks could make still more patterns out of the essential elements; roofs gabled and half-hipped, chimneys on the axis of the house or at the side or gable end, entrances in front of a stack or elsewhere; single- and two-storey ranges. The small Essex farmhouse was just as diverse in its details, not from childish ingenuity, but because it grew out of varied social conditions over at least a couple of centuries. The most distinct change since the Tudor period is that new houses were no longer built with anything but an axial chimney stack, and if they had more than two units the cross passage was no longer considered a useful part of the design.[1]

Underlying this variety, even among small farmhouses, the community of need which documents reveal is apparent as soon as one compares surviving examples with larger houses. The essence of the great rebuilding in Essex is that alongside the larger houses of wealthy yeomen of the fifteenth and sixteenth centuries, lesser yeomen and husbandmen had now raised a much larger number of simple but convenient dwellings. At least seven of them still stand in Writtle and Roxwell, some of them sixteenth century in origin, but mostly of the seventeenth.[2] One of them, the farmhouse called Benedict Oates in Writtle, has the date 1644 and the initials of T. and S.C. on the chimney stack, but it is tantalizing that T.C.'s inventory cannot be identified. The Chequers Inn at Roxwell, a converted farmhouse now somewhat disguised by modern extensions, is an example of type II in figure 9.

Among the houses of the wealthiest quarter of the community, men with goods worth more than £120 and called yeomen when they are given any designation, that clarity and simplicity of arrangement seems to dissolve. There are more service-rooms: not only two butteries, and even two milkhouses,[3] but a boulting house, a quernhouse or a milkhouse. Writtle and Roxwell in fact still have sixteen houses built before 1660, which could have belonged to men of this class. Nine of them stand on moated sites. This remarkable wealth of material is sufficient to show that the wealthy

---

[1]No doubt exceptions could be found even to these very limited generalizations. For instance Park Farm, Gestingthorpe, which the Commission dated to the second half of this century, has a cross passage.

[2]R.C.H.M. *Essex*, II, 276–7 (Writtle 9, 21, 22), 206 (Roxwell 10, 14, 20, 21).

[2]*Essex Inventories*, No. 136; H.M.C. *Essex*, II, 206 (17), pl. 129.

yeoman had a house of L, or in a few cases, of T plan, with either service rooms or a kitchen in the rear wing. Some houses, even among those of medieval date such as Aubyn's, a fine house on the Green at Writtle, had plenty of space in the rear wing; others were enlarged in the seventeenth century. Duke's at Roxwell was built in the sixteenth century (see fig. 9, IV) with two rooms behind the main range, but it was nevertheless enlarged by Thomas Crush, who died in it in 1686. A wooden panel over the front door bears the date 1666 and the initials T.A.C., of Thomas and his wife. The main range consists of the usual hall, parlour and kitchen, with a cross passage into which a staircase has now been built. The hall fireplace, on the back wall, shares a stack with the room behind, which may be the brewhouse of the inventory. The buttery, and perhaps the milkhouse as well, are in the range behind the parlour, which was lengthened by Thomas Crush, perhaps to make the boulting house and malthouse. The service-rooms described in the inventory cannot be fitted to the plan with complete certainty in each case, but the general arrangement is clear enough. The house had two cellars, well stacked with beer. One of the garrets was used as a cheese chamber; there were 100 cheeses in it when he died, for he was one of the wealthiest farmers in the parish with 135 acres of arable, including 60 acres given to hop growing, as well as 11 cows and other livestock.

At least half the householders still kept a bed in the parlour, and still continued to do so for at least a century after this. A distinction which is still a part of family life had already grown up. On the one hand were those who had cleared the hall of all but a table perhaps, left there for ornament and with the family Bible reposing on it, and who sat in the parlour of an evening with curtains drawn and a grandfather clock ticking in a corner. On the other hand were those who still lived in the hall and had made no effort to make the parlour into a living-room.

Writtle and Roxwell appear as tight and homogeneous communities when one sees how much more varied elements could be found in some parts of East Anglia.[1] The cloth industry was still a significant factor, although it was in decline. There were weavers of every condition, from a poor man like John Wilson of Badingham, whose goods were worth only £13 16s. 6d., and who lived in a three-roomed house with hall, parlour and a chamber over the parlour, to Nicholas Rogers, worsted weaver of Gisleham, or Robert Mingay of Chedgrave, whose goods amounted to £314. The difference in wealth represented a real distinction, between those who worked for others (John Wilson had no loom in his house) or

[1]Norwich inventories, Consistory Court, bundles Burnell (1666) and Withers (1668), Reynolds Chapel, Norwich. The median value of the sample is £115 17s.

catered merely for village demands for homespun,[1] and those who employed others in making better quality goods, principally for export. Robert Mingay had three looms in his workshop at Chedgrave, Norfolk, and no doubt produced some of the men's and children's worsted stockings, short cloths and undefined 'worsted stuffs' which went, along with red herrings, butter and coal, from Yarmouth to Rotterdam. Mingay was exceptionally rich among East Anglian weavers, and unusual also in that he got his living solely from industry. He called himself a yeoman in his will, while to his neighbours he was merely a weaver. He had no farming interests. His house consisted of a hall, now called the kitchen because his wife still cooked there, a parlour and a low bed chamber (both with beds), a larder and a buttery. It is not clear whether the shop was attached to or part of the house, or a separate structure. There were chambers over kitchen, parlour and shop, each with beds, and that over the shop used also to store yarn. This is one more example of the house with few service-rooms because it had no farming products to process or store.

The cloth industry depended on wool merchants, who went at least as far as Lincolnshire for wool, and on other middle men. Robert Pease of Stoke Ash, Suffolk, described himself as a cemmer or comber. He was a farmer, for he had stored in the vance roof 6½ wey of cheeses, eight firkins of butter, six combs of wheat and nine of rye, but the chamber over the dairy contained two loads of wool valued at £200, along with scales and wool weights.

The way that wealthy farmers had geared their farming to new demands is shown by the case of Thomas Waynforth, whose goods at his death were worth £454 (see Appendix, p. 281). He lived in the small village of Roydon, near Castle Rising, but he called himself a maltster, and he owned 'part of a ship at sea' which took his malt to London. His house was of two dates, for one of the rooms is the old hall, now used as a boulting house. The newer part was a complete house, with hall, parlour, kitchen, dairy, storehouse and two butteries. The brewhouse with a malt chamber over it was in a separate building, and there was a 'little house in the foreyard' where one of his workers slept. The new house was of two storeys, with the vance roof or garret used for storage. The chambers over the hall, parlour and butteries were family bedrooms, and servants slept over the kitchen. The vance roof over the kitchen chamber was used for linen, yarn, hemp etc., and that above the hall chamber for wheat, rye and cheese. In the first phase of the great rebuilding, one of the major needs was for chambers which could be used as storage, especially in this mixed farming country

[1]The goods of Thomas Tomson of Brooke, amounting to only £14 2s. 4d., included 'the loom and all the material belonging £1 10s.'

where room had to be found for corn, cheeses, wool and yarn. Now the second floor has to be used, since living standards have altered and production has increased. The use of the vance roof was no novelty in 1660, but has only recently become common. It occurs in one or two cases which suggest lofts over single-storey buildings, but in the main in houses with three, four or five chambers. Some of the chambers were needed for storage as well—Richard Long, yeoman, of Tyvetshall St. Mary's had seventy-five cheeses in the chamber over the dairy, and used the vance roof for corn and wool. The cheeses no doubt needed more frequent attention, but it is remarkable that men were ready to take such heavy and bulky commodities as corn up to the attic. It shows why the staircase of a house of this period usually continues in the same design from ground floor to bedrooms. If the garrets had been merely servants' bedrooms, as they became in the next century, a ladder would have sufficed.

The habit of using the garret space spread as far north as the villages to the south of the Wash, which were at least as closely linked with East Anglia as with the rest of Lincolnshire, though the name vance roof has not been found there. John Woodcock of Sutton St. Mary's was described as a wheelwright but was in fact the village undertaker—a job which still falls on the village craftsman working in wood. He had in his garret a stock of ten great coffins and four little coffins, as well as fifty tod of wool.[1]

Some of these larger houses with ample attic space may well have been of brick in the Flemish manner, for such building became a significant feature of East Anglia villages after 1660. Scarcely a year went by without some ship bringing into King's Lynn and Yarmouth some Flanders brick, pantiles, paving tiles, ridge tiles, or millstones, quernstones, dogstones—even grave stones.[2] In 1661–2 alone, 57,000 bricks and 57,300 pantiles were imported to Yarmouth, in vessels which had set out with worsteds, Yarmouth herrings and coal for ballast. The quantities are insignificant—enough bricks for a pair of modern semi-detached houses with garages—but enough to show that there was a good market for them. Some boats brought as many as 8,000 bricks or 4,000 pantiles and they were not always imported by the master. If bringing bricks to Yarmouth was *not* like coals to Newcastle, that was because demand outran local supplies. In 1680–1, imports of bricks fell to 4,000 but 78,000 pantiles came in. Yarmouth had seen much new building before the Civil War, and it had been resumed by 1651. At first bricks were used only for quoins, or as headers along with squared flints. The earliest small houses built entirely

[1] L.R.O., 194/110.
[2] P.R.O., Port Books, Yarmouth E190, 493/5, 499/1. I am indebted to P. E. Fordham for notes on the King's Lynn Port Books.

of brick were put up in 1636–8.[1] By 1680, local brickyards could satisfy the demand for bricks, but not for pantiles.

By then the fashion, started no doubt by members of the Dutch communities in towns like Yarmouth, had spread throughout East Anglia and beyond; curved gables are found commonly in every county east of a line from York to London, and occasionally beyond it. They have great variety of design but eventually settle down to a simple pattern of a semi-circle at the top flanked by quadrants, either convex or concave.[2] Particular variations often have a local concentration which shows the preference of an individual builder.

Another Dutch device was the *tumbled* gable, used mainly in smaller houses and farm buildings, for it was the best way to give a smooth finish to a straight gable without adding a brick or stone coping. Courses of bricks were laid at right angles to the line of the gable, in a series of triangular wedges (see pl. XVIIa). These eastern gables were of course always carried up above the level of the roof, for the builder's problem was to prevent thatch or tile being lifted by the wind, rather than to stop rain getting in. As soon as pantiles came into fashion this device was even more necessary for they were hung on to laths, without nailing. The earliest dated example of this tumbled gable is in outbuildings to the hall at Westerfield, near Ipswich, dated 1656.[3] Since it is appropriate to humble building it became and remained more popular in Lincolnshire and Yorkshire than in East Anglia, and as far as I know it was not used on the south coast. It penetrated as far inland as Norman Cross, near Peterborough—about as far, that is, as the curved gable. It remained popular in villages round the Wash as late as the early nineteenth century. There it can be seen in small cottages, as a single wedge at the base of a gable, supporting a coping course.

It would be quite wrong to suggest that all the new ornamented brick houses sprang from Flemish influence. The country builder was feeling two forces: the example of men of his own class who had picked up the more homely and simple devices of Dutch building, and that of men responsible for small country houses in the Renaissance manner. The two forces were of the same ultimate origin, and the former was already reduced to his level of capacity, but the latter he had to adapt for himself. Renaissance buildings in brick, on a scale which made them possible models for a farmhouse, were springing up from the 1630's onwards[4] in most counties of

[1] B. H. St. J. O'Neil, 'Some Seventeenth Century Houses in Gt. Yarmouth', *Arch.*, 95 (1953), 141–80, especially 146–9.
[2] C. L. Cudworth, 'Dutch Influence in East Anglian Architecture', *Proc. Cambs. Ant. Soc.*, 37 (1937), and also in the *Architectural Review*, March, 1939.
[3] C. L. Cudworth, *Arch. Review*.
[4] See for example, N. Lloyd, *History of English Brickwork* (1925), 179–81, 184, etc.

south-eastern England. From them the country builder got such elements of design as the string course, the rusticated quoin, the triangular pediment, and sometimes made strange and very unscholarly use of them. They became ways of covering the surface with ornament, as the Elizabethan mason had done in houses like Wollaton nearly a century earlier.

Some of the most prominent new brick buildings in East Anglia and the Fens are inns, built in the newest style to catch the traveller. There is the Swan and Salmon, on the old north road at Little Stukeley, north of Huntingdon, built by 'DCE' in 1676. It has curved gables, rusticated quoins and pilasters, and a swan and salmon in plaster panels set in the gable end chimney facing the road (see fig. 29). Another is the Addison

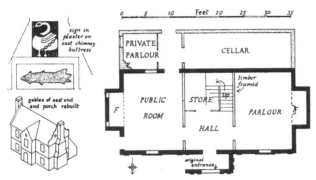

SWAN AND SALMON, LITTLE STUKELEY

FIGURE 29. A new inn of 1676: The Old Swan and Salmon, Little Stukeley, Huntingdonshire. It is remarkable chiefly for the elaborate brickwork then in vogue. The outshot or lean-to on the south side appears to be an addition, but cannot be much later than the house. The inn differed from a private house mainly in having a room, usually large, given over to the public.

Arms, Glatton, Hunts., with curved gables and a plain string course. The most splendid new inn is the White Hart at Scole, Suffolk, presenting a range of five curved gables to the Ipswich-Norwich road. Tradition says that it was built by a London Merchant at a cost of £1,500.[1] It could well be true. Certainly the Civil War had taken men of all classes along roads they had never travelled before, and those with money to invest could see new opportunities. These buildings in the contemporary manner were the result. In the Fens men were much more modest, but still did their best, as much as do the neon signs lighting up neo-Tudor beams today, to catch the growing custom. The King's Head at Kirton-in-Holland, dated 1661, has rusticated quoins and openings, string courses both plain and dentilled, and two features out of the native tradition: a hood mould over a gable

[1] S. Lewis, *Topographical Dictionary* (1831), *s.v.* Scole.

window and diagonally set chimney stacks (see pl. XVIb). The Old Red Lion at Bicker, dated 1665, has rusticated quoins. There must be enough of these new inns to make them worth a special study. Those at Bicker and Little Stukeley have a simple plan, with a storeyed porch; the large kitchen, for local customers, is no doubt a traditional feature. Gilbert Wyatt of Ludham, Norfolk, beer brewer and innholder, had a 'slidegroat room': that is, a bar parlour equipped for shove halfpenny.

The new vogue for brick building had already provoked in East Anglia a realization that firing bricks was not essential. When John Fales of Tivetshall St. Margaret died, he possessed a stock of clay bricks and burnt bricks, paving bricks, lime and timber; he must have intended some new building. What his appraisers called clay brick became known as clay lump, a common medium in Cambridgeshire, Norfolk and Suffolk down to the nineteenth century. Like cob walling, its durability depended on its being kept weatherproof, and so it is now rarely visible unless its plaster rendering has been neglected (see pl. XVIIb). Clay lump came into use early in the seventeenth century,[1] but it had less influence on design than did burnt brick. The bricks were naturally much larger than those fired. Apart from their regular use in East Anglia, which must imply professional manufacture, experimental or amateur attempts cropped up elsewhere from time to time. Sutton Rectory, Sussex, has some walling in clay bricks, 1 foot long by 9 inches thick, probably of nineteenth century date.[2] There was until recently a farm building at Baston, Lincs., of unfired bricks about $9 \times 4\frac{1}{2}$ inches.[3] They may of course have come out of a clamp that failed. Innocent illustrated a cottage at Scarrington, Notts., with walls 'about two feet thick made of slabs of dried mud'.[4]

It is as well to remind ourselves, however, that timber building was still the commonest method of East Anglia. The inventory of William Manshop of Carsham will serve to point the remark: his neighbours called him a house carpenter, and he had a timber stock worth £98, though he was also a farmer in a considerable way. Behind his two-storeyed house with a brewhouse at the rear there was a yard with a barn, a carthouse and a stable, as well as his shop with a chamber over it full of hemp. Although he no longer had a monopoly of local building, he made a good living from the two sources.

[1] There are dated examples such as Mary's Farm, Tacolneston, 1628. See C. W. Messent, *Old Cottages and Farmhouses of Norfolk* (1928), 72; Innocent, 154–5. The inventory of Robert Stokes of Erlham, who died in 1610, includes 'unburnt brick' (NDR, 24/166).

[2] W. D. Peckham in *Sussex Arch. Coll.*, 65 (1924), 24.

[3] *Ex. inf.* Mr. N. Teulon Porter.

[4] Op. cit., fig. 49.

XVIIa. An example of a tumbled gable at Kirton, in Lindsey, Lincs. the only place where it is done in a stone building. This example has been chosen for its clarity. See p. 200.

XVIIb. Clay lump in a house at Hinxton, Cambs., visible only where the protective rendering has come away. The size of the unfired bricks can be judged by comparison with the window. See p. 202.

XVIIIa. A Monmouthsire medieval house, Pant, Llanvihangel-ystern-llewern, with a wing built in brick after the Restoration. The wing was used as a Quaker chapel, but exemplifies the contrast in scale between the vernacular and the new style of brick building. Note the string courses which are both ornamental and functional. See p. 212.

XVIIIb. A timber-framed cottage at Eardisland, Hertfordshire, with the typical gable and chimney in stone. The bedrooms were improved in the 18th century by raising the roof.

CHAPTER THREE

The Midlands

a. Lincolnshire and Nottinghamshire

IN Lincolnshire and east Nottinghamshire, leaving aside the upland country, housing standards exhibit the same consistency as in Essex, but at a somewhat simpler level: that is, there were more small houses, and wealthier farmers still showed their preference for living on the ground floor. New ideas commanded much less widespread acceptance, and houses in the new brick idiom seem, from their scale, their elaborate ornament and their very scarcity, to be farther away from the local idiom. The rural conservatism which this state of affairs implies made Lincolnshire labourers and poor craftsmen as ready as their fathers had been to make a will, to spend half a day helping to make an inventory, and to take will and inventory some twenty miles to a session of the archdeacon's court. The flow of record material is thus about as broad as before the Civil War, and although it does not include more than perhaps a third of the population, it is far more representative than for Kent, for example, where the wealthy yeoman had the archdeacon's court to himself.

This conservatism was not a mark of poverty and stagnation of living conditions. Wealth was steadily increasing, because agricultural production was expanding. It is probable that better farming and the continual rise in the demand for foodstuffs and wool was now beginning to work to the advantage of the small man, as well as the rich yeoman. Personal wealth now begins, for the first time, to rise more rapidly than the current price index.[1] Along with this goes the fact that in many parts of the east Midlands the small farmer, because he was lucky enough to have such good

---

[1] *Econ. Hist. R.*, VII (1954–5), 294, table 3.

soil, was able to hold his own and keep the acquisitive squire or yeoman at bay.

How completely the seal had been set on the developments of the preceding seventy-five years is clearly shown by inventories of 1660–80. Only a negligible proportion of houses is not described clearly, in the main because fewer labourers made a will.[1] Some of them must still have been living in houses of one or two rooms. The most distinctive development is the steady rise of houses with between five and seven rooms, which are now more common than in Essex; they are of two or three units or bays, as in Essex, but they have somewhat less accomodation because they are not invariably of two storeys. The most usual arrangement of three rooms is hall, parlour and one service-room—either milkhouse or kitchen, but not a cooking room in any case. A less common but still widespread combination is hall, parlour and a single chamber over the parlour. Next comes the house with hall and parlour and milkhouse, with a chamber above, and that with two service-rooms, almost invariably milkhouse and kitchen. Such houses belonged mainly to craftsmen and husbandmen, and in a village like Norwell, Notts., where there were no yeomen, houses with five rooms (hall, parlour, two service-rooms, one chamber) must have been almost the standard type of the period.

Even among such men new additions to the house were still being made. In inventories from East Anglia after 1660 one seldom finds any reference to new rooms, but in the Trent valley they figure in some numbers, and in most cases it is a new parlour that is added, with a chamber over it. The parlour is still a bedroom, and seldom furnished for sitting. A blacksmith at North Muskham, with goods worth only £40, has two parlours, and so have a joiner and a husbandman at Norwell; they are also to be found in small farmhouses in the Isle of Axholme and the lower valley of the Yorkshire Ouse. The continued expansion of standards has not broken the traditional framework of family behaviour in the house. The few rooms upstairs are still used primarily for storage. John Hill, carpenter, of North Muskham, who had one chamber, kept there only '2 great saws' and some corn. The blacksmith, who was farming as well, had a cheese chamber, and in nearly every house with more than one chamber one of them is specifically a store-room. The local cheese industry was now entering on its most important phase, and Newark and Gainsborough cheese markets were the outlet for it. Peter Rollinson of Little Carlton, husbandman, had 400 cheeses in the chamber over his house. The difference between one village and another lay not in variations in standards, but in the proportions that a visitor could have observed, in walking down the main street, of houses of one class or another. Whether

[1] *Loc. cit.*, 293 (table 1), 294 (table 4).

he saw large yeomen's houses or more modest ones depended on whether the land was already engrossed by a few wealthy farmers, as it was at South Muskham and Little Carlton, or more widely held, as it was in villages which still had their open fields. Under the roofs of even the larger houses the pattern of life differed remarkably from that of south-eastern England. If we can imagine the visitor not only walking the main street but staying for a time, he would have found himself taking part in an old fashioned way of life—sitting at night in the hall where the smell of cooking still lingered, moving into the parlour alongside to sleep, and only going upstairs if taken to admire the small cheeses sitting, in row upon row, on the cheeseheck.

In the Lincolnshire Fenland the wealth of the soil allowed the small farmer to hold his own, but it also gave ambitious men a chance to build up large flocks of cattle and sheep. Thomas Waters, husbandman, of Tydd St. Mary's who died in 1678,[1] had 282 sheep, 41 cattle, 12 horses, as well as pigs, turkeys, geese and 'dunghill fowls', and hay and corn— a good example of the mixed farming, with concentration on live-stock, which made the Fens so wealthy. His goods, worth £357, included only £27 for his household things. His house had a hall, one parlour, three service-rooms and one chamber only, used for storage. It was unusual in having no more than one parlour, for most men of substance followed the northern fashion of having two. In this respect villages round the Wash belong to the north Midlands, though they were open, as we have seen, to influences from East Anglia.

How the use of brick was invading, without at this stage overwhelming the vernacular tradition, can clearly be seen. The craft of brickmaking had spread slowly, in spite of the use of bricks by wealthy owners and even the encouragement of the authorities.[2] There was enough demand for bricks in the Isle of Axholme to encourage men to make them anywhere, anyhow. William Occarbie of Crowle, Lincs., was presented to the manor court in 1649 'for making bricks on the common and selling them out of the manor'. Such illicit activity was still going on in 1718, when two men at Misterton were compelled to 'promise to fill up the pit they have dug to make bricks at Haxey Gate Smeeth'.[3] The houses of the Isle of Axholme are singularly undistinguished, but all built of the local dark brown brick characteristic of the lower Trent valley. They betoken an isolated community where few

[1]L.R.O., 180/535.
[2]In 1615 the Nottinghamshire justices made an order under the Cottages Act of 1589 to erect a cottage at Sneinton for John Griffin, who the Court was informed 'is an expert in the art of making Bricks and Tile'. They wished to facilitate his settling on the outskirts of Nottingham, where brickmaking seems to have begun at this time. *Notts. County Records*, ed. H. H. Copnall (1915), 125.
[3]L.R.O., CM 4/4/7, and Misterton parish documents.

men have had resources enough to make a show of a new house until this last thirty years. The attitude of the manor court, resentful both of improper use of the common and of its products going outside the parish, offers a faithful parentage for the older houses, built of local material by men with limited capital and ideas. The bricks made by Occarbie were probably used for new chimneys or foundations rather than a whole house, for no buildings of the seventeenth century have survived.

At the other end of the county, in upland country where large estates were coming to be the rule, we can witness remarkably enterprising ideas of estate management, of a kind that must have been very rare in this century. Drayner Massingberd belonged to an ancient family which had moved, like many ambitious families, out of the coastal marshland. There land was so rich that aggrandizement was blocked, because anyone could make a living from it. They moved up to the Wolds, and Drayner Massingberd bought South Ormsby, where his businesslike ideas had more scope. After a spell in the Parliamentary army, he returned to his estate. He enclosed the open fields of Ormsby and Ketsby in 1650, ran a very profitable flock of 1,700 sheep on the new sheep walks, and soon had enough money to think of building. Every transaction made over twenty-five years by a meticulous and enlightened man has been preserved for us in his account and memorandum books.[1]

A decision to rebuild a country mansion or even a farmhouse still involved, as it had in the Middle Ages, finding a brickmaker, to dig the brick earth and make bricks on the estate. An agreement of 1644 relating to Syon House, Middlesex, shows the kind of agreement made. John Hawkes of Hounslow was to have £5 towards digging the earth, £3 for each week when it came to working, £5 15s. at the end of working half a million bricks, and finally 6s. 8d. for each 10,000 'well and sufficiently burnt and delivered out of the kiln'.[2] Brickmaking was a slow process: hence the interim payments. The clay was dug during the winter, allowed to lie so that frost could break it up, then in spring it was wetted and trodden to a uniform consistency.[3] After being made in wooden moulds the bricks were dried for a month before firing, which might take another month or more.

Nearly every parish in the east Midlands had some land suitable for brickmaking, and landowners could usually find a field within a short distance of the site. Most of the bricks for Tattershall Castle were made at

[1] L.R.O.
[2] C. R. Batho, *Trans. Anc. Mon. Soc.*, N. S. 4 (1956), 107–8.
[3] 1752 'Mr. Smith our Rector is now here and purposes to make Ormesby Parsonage an exceeding good house, is to make Bricks early in the spring and build next summer'. Massingberd family letters in *A.A.S.R.P.*, 23 (1895–6), 305.

near-by Edlington Moor, and those for Doddington Hall, near Lincoln, built between 1593 and 1600, were made two fields away from the house.[1] In 1749 the owner of Winkburn Hall, Notts., agreed with 'John Hobson of Sheffield for to make 200,000 of bricks in the paddock at 4s. 6d. per thousand. He to find all tools etc. to work with. I to find coal sand and water for 2 months and nothing else, all to be well burnt and full 10 inches long when burnt, five broad and 2½ inches broad'.[2] For such a contract most brickmakers made a temporary clamp, rather than a permanent kiln. The clamp was built for one firing only, and produced bricks of varied colour and quality; a kiln used as much fuel, but yielded a lower proportion of inferior or unusable bricks. The use of a clamp is as old as brickmaking itself,[3] and every brickmaker had his own best way of building it, but could not avoid some over-fired or under-fired bricks.[4] Turning necessity into virtue, he used the over-fired bricks, vitrified and purple in tone, to make a diaper pattern, or a chequer pattern if he was using Flemish bond.

Few of these contracts are precise enough to tell us the price of such brickmaking, but it was certainly cheaper than buying imported bricks, or going to one of the few brickyards. Bricks bought for Soham church in 1686 cost 16s. 9d. a thousand, and Drayner Massingberd paid 18s. in 1678 when he bought some from his brother.[5] Those made by direct labour probably cost at most a third of that price. There were no brickyards capable of accepting orders for enough bricks to build a country mansion.

Massingberd had dealings with brickmakers for over twenty years, and though he had finished rebuilding his own house by 1660 or so, he went on employing them for work on his estate. As long as large quantities were needed, two men could make as many as 48,000 in one firing, and for some years made about 80,000 a year. Their kilns were used twice, the second firing being about 33,000. Massingberd made no bricks after 1674, but small building jobs, for which he bought materials, occur in his account

[1]Hist. MSS. Comm., *De L'Isle and Dudley*, I, 98, 213; R. E. G. Cole, *History of Doddington* (1897), 59.

[2]Pegge Burnell's Diary, *ex. inf.* J. H. Meeds.

[3]See R.C.H.M. *Essex*, III, 32, for remains of a brick clamp of Roman date. For clamps generally, see A. B. Searle, *Encyclopaedia of the Ceramic Industry*. See also Memoirs of the Geol. Survey, *Geology of the Borders of the Wash*, 110, for references to brickmaking in clamps on isolated farmhouse sites in the nineteenth century.

[4]At Loseley in 1561 a clamp of 120,000 bricks was fired twice, first with 100 loads of fuel, then with 60 loads more, because they were 'not well fired before'; *Arch.* 36, 294. At Gosberton, Lincs., in 1744, 6,000 bricks 'illburned' had to be fired a second time in a new clamp; L.R.O., Tennyson D'Eyncourt Coll., G 16/17.

[5]See *Lincs. Archivists' Report*, 8 (1956-7), 11-15. Sir Henry Massingberd was making bricks at Gunby Hall, near by, between 1666 and 1686.

books down to 1683, and in thirty years he must have helped to transform the villages where he owned land. When it came to the 'finishing brick' for the front of his own house he employed John Adamson, bricklayer, of Barton on Humber, to buy them at Hull, but for the rest of his house, and all the other work, local bricks were used. He 'put away' local bricklayers when they asked 1s. 6d. a day instead of the usual 1s. 4d., but paid the out-siders 1s. 8d. a day without complaint.

In 1668 he paid for 'making a chimney and an oven in the back kitchen at the parsonage house'; since he also paid Robert Blakey, a generally handy man but primarily a carpenter, for making the back kitchen, it must have been of mud and stud. He had also paid Blakey, by agreement dated 1655, for making 'three new chimneys in the town house (i.e. the poor house) and one chimney in the little house belonging to it, and to make the new doors which wanteth to each room and the partitions betwixt every room: viz. all the carpenter's work . . . for thirty shillings and every day he worked a quart of small drink.' The poorhouse must have been a ram-shackle affair, for the end room fell down in the winter of 1672–3, and 'four of the smallest poles felled last year' were allocated for its repair. Other landowners in the county who were busy in this sort of rebuilding also put up a new parsonage house, or a row of almshouses. Lord John Bellasys of Worlaby built himself a new brick mansion and also erected almshouses for four widows in 1663.[1]

There was no such ostentation in Massingberd's make-up; his employ-ment of a carpenter to build a poorhouse of mud and stud, even for the chimneys, goes in keeping with his careful notes of contracts made, prices given and received.[2] When his tenants got a new house, or repairs or improvements to an old one, it was usually after bargaining on the occasion of renewal of a lease. What they wanted was a brick chimney, or a new parlour with a chamber over it, if a new house was out of the question. 'Dec. 29th 1656. Will Wickham is to have all the pasture and arable and other things which he had in his former lease at the same rent. . . . And he is to have a brick chimney built for him this spring, and is to be allowed new barn couples for his house roof.'[3] That is, the landlord was to build

[1] L.R.O., terrier Worlaby 1690. The house has gone, but the almshouses remain. Unhappily they have been reroofed, and the elaborate façade with brick pilasters looks strange without the original curved gables.

[2] A memorandum of 1666 states that corn sold was to be 'by my own strike or Calceby strike, which I shall chose'. Another of 1676 condemns John Smith and his father, wool merchants of Wakefield, as 'foul weighers', after he had noticed a discrepancy.

[3] A note six months later records that the new chimney, 'built by Pedigree Witton and John Pape of Partney with two little boys, took 5,000 bricks and 11 seam of lime mixed with 3 parts sand, being a double chimney from the ground'.

the chimney and the tenant reroof the house, with some timber from the estate. 'Robert Toppin is to have in his new lease his house and onset and close . . . and I must give him wood to build him a parlour'. Every year two or three such bargains were made—for an addition 'with an entry' to one farmhouse in Calceby, a draught or ox house for another, of second-hand timber; for widow Stapleton's house at Calceby to be taken down 'as carefully as may be to prevent the breaking of any wood or tenures', so that a barn could be built of them in John Hodgson's yard. Most of the work is in mud and stud, even at this date. In 1652 Robert Blakey, carpenter, 'agreed to mend Pickles his house and Lyon Bell's house the chimneys so as to make them firm and strong, and each house to have two rooms, one chimney and one dairy taken out of the larger room; one of the new bays of Bell's house to be 28 foot square, for which I am to give him 40s., and he is to bay the chamber in Bell's house again, and I must find labourers to help him sour the thack ere he strings it down, and to remove the mud or earth of the walls'. These sound like houses of a design we have already met, with hall and parlour, the dairy being partitioned out of the hall. Massingberd even made a note, when a tenant's barn and house were being repaired, that he was to let the man 'have a horse to tread clay and slead [sledge] it to the house'. He recorded with frugal satisfaction that a barn was thatched 'with sainfoin straw (except a good horse load of rushes)'.

Two people got new brick houses, one of them being William Wickam, only five years after the double brick chimney was built for him. The landlord provided bricks ('provided the house takes no more brick than is in the brick-kiln now burnt') and transported them to the site; Wickam was to fetch ten loads of sand 'from Matthew Maugham's yard for which I am to allow him 30s. and I am to dig the sand and fling it on a heap ready for him to take away. . . .' Massingberd spent about £20 on labour, for transport, building walls (including a new chimney), an oven and an outshot, and for running the plaster floors. How much the materials were worth we do not know but the total cost must have been less than the £40 estimated by an Essex husbandman in 1654 for rebuilding his home after a fire,[1] and perhaps not more than £25. In 1686 the parish of Saleby near by built a mud and stud cottage for an old man at a cost of £18. The figures suggest that a landlord who was prepared to have bricks made and could use timber and thatch from his own estate could build much more economically from a long-term point of view. Few people were prepared to follow his example prior to the eighteenth century.

There we must leave Drayner Massingberd, although the wealth of his

[1] *Essex Inventories*, 11.

memorandum book has only been skimmed. It gives a picture of day to day repairs and improvements which is remarkably vivid, and is in any case unique, for no records of the kind have so far been found in any other part of England. It is unfortunate that his own house was rebuilt in the eighteenth century. Most new brick houses of this period contain ornate work in the Renaissance manner, such as two at Coningsby and another at Aslackby clearly by the same builder, and others have a Flemish cast. The manor house at North Wheatley, Notts., built in 1673, is a remarkable piece of extravagance, using Renaissance ideas in a quite unclassical manner. It has Ionic pilasters flanking the porch which stop short of the cornice, and a range of lunettes above which are not fitted in scale to the façade, and so are chopped off at the angles. The curved gables have gone, and likewise most of the brick mullions and transoms in the windows.[1] In the villages between Nottingham and Leicester such lunettes, or curved pediments, whichever they are in origin, appear in farmhouses above each window opening, breaking the string course. Sometimes this eyebrow effect goes with a diaper pattern in dark headers.

The influence of trade with the Low Countries is patent in the distribution of curved gables. They follow the Trent valley—Kelfield, Stockwith, Marton and Gainsborough itself. A ship's captain bringing his vessel up to Gainsborough, the limit for sea-going ships, sailed past houses very similar to those he had left at Rotterdam. One of the most imposing is a farmhouse at Bole, two miles south-east of Gainsborough and in sight of the river, with gables rising in a splendid ogee curve.[2] Other simpler examples line the Trent valley, at Newton on Trent (1695) and Newark (Mill Gate, 1663). The tumbled gable arrived at the same time: the earliest dated example being South Leverton School, founded in 1691. The use of pantiles, the third mark of the Dutch influence, belongs to this period; the outhouses of the parsonage at Wroot near the lower Trent were covered with pantiles by 1707.[3]

b. The West Midlands

Although the customs and standards of rural housing have been discussed as though they were determined mainly by variations in local geology, which conditioned methods of farming and also supplies of building material, yet some regions show persistent conventions which refuse to fit into that pattern; indeed, in the present state of knowledge, they defy explanation. Much of Staffordshire and Worcestershire has

[1]See N. Pevsner, *Buildings of Notts.*, 122 and plate 55b.
[2]I am indebted to Mr. T. L. Marsden for drawing my attention to this example.
[3]L.R.O., terrier 1707.

heavy soil, derived from the Keuper Marl, which encourages dairy farming. Cheese and butter making and the production of fat cattle must have been the prime concern of farmers there by the seventeenth century, if not before. Conditions in the two counties diverged at either extremity, north-east Staffordshire having its share of the margins of the Peak District, south-west Worcestershire its part of the Severn valley and the highlands beyond. The arable farmers of the vale of Evesham with its nucleated villages must have been much more prosperous than those who lived in the scattered farmsteads west of the Severn. Whatever the reasons, differences between the two counties are, by the Restoration period, more striking than the similarities. Much more intensive study, especially of Worcestershire, may discover, in the local patterns of farming and industry, building materials, communications and marketing arrangements, the explanation of these variations.

In both counties the yeoman farmer now dominated the scene,[1] as he did elsewhere. Husbandmen were much poorer and even less successful than men engaged in metal working (scythesmiths, gunsmiths, etc.) and textiles (weavers and clothiers), and the few inventories they have left are quite uninformative.[2] The labourer had ceased to make a will and so has disappeared from our view. Nonetheless the conservatism of Worcester-shire ways emerges even from descriptions of yeomen's houses, most of them large. More than half still have ground floor rooms used for sleeping and called chambers. That is, Worcestershire belongs like the east Midlands to the large zone in which sleeping downstairs was still common, but it differs in that the name parlour was used only for rooms which really were furnished for sitting. The parlour had arrived in Worcestershire by the 1660's, not merely as a name taken over out of its true context, but as a sitting-room.

At its simplest, this way of life is unchanged from the sixteenth century. Anthony Glover, a yeoman of Hollowe, Worcs., had a hall, a bedchamber which must have been alongside, and a chamber over the hall used for storing oats, cheese and spare linen. In larger houses, names like 'nether chamber' (Humphrey Heywood, yeoman of Abbot's Salford, Warws.), the 'inner chamber' named after the parlour and with a chamber over it (Henry Turner of Grimley, Worcs.) make it plain that innovations of a century earlier still answered to the needs of most classes.

A few householders still used the name solar for rooms upstairs. One

[1]These paragraphs are based on inventories of the diocese of Worcester, bundle 1661–2, and of the peculiar of Lichfield boxes A and B (Derbyshire and parts of Staffordshire) all in Birmingham Probate Registry. The median value for Worcestershire is £90 5s., compared with £52 10s. for Staffordshire.

[2]Of seven husbandmen from Worcestershire and four from Staffordshire, only two houses are described in detail.

of them was Richard Mucklowe of Napal in Halesowen parish (see Appendix p. 283 for his inventory). The hall house (an unusual name in Worcestershire, but not further north), the parlour and the dairy each had a 'soller' over, and so had the entry. The room names, especially the solar over the entry, make it more than likely that this was a house with hall and cross passage and one cross wing with kitchen, dairy and two butteries in it. Richard Mason's house at Harborne, only four miles away, also had 'sollers' over the hall, parlour and kitchen.

The west Midland weavers had not yet moved their workrooms upstairs. William Powell of Kidderminster possessed four looms, of which two were in his own workshop and two others out in houses of workmen to whom he had let them. The chamber over the shop had a warping bar and trough in it, but otherwise work went on downstairs.[1]

Upland Worcestershire west of the Severn must have had much in common with Hereford and Monmouth, and the conservatism of an economy based on pasture farming and expressed in cruck construction at an earlier time did not very readily absorb the modern notion of a parlour-sitting-room. The gap between old and new ways is strikingly illustrated in Monmouthshire houses. At an earlier time a parlour added *c.* 1600 to a small house of the usual local design was so remarkable a phenomenon that it gave a name to the house—Parlour in the parish of Dingestow.[2] Near the end of the seventeenth century, a lofty wing in brick was added to the medieval farmhouse called Pant, Llanvihangel-ystern-llewern.[3] Since the site sloped away steeply, the wing had a basement level, and the two storeys tower above the older part of the house (see pl. XVIIIa). Tradition speaks of it as a Quaker chapel, and it was certainly used as such, but in design it was a parlour wing with a cellar below and chamber and attic over, no less remarkable than Parlour itself. Between these two, separated by nearly a century, there are several others enlarged at either the service end or the parlour end in ways which demonstrate, in scale or arrangement, how difficult it was to marry the medieval to the modern. The farmers who still used medieval terms like chamber (for parlour) or solar (for chamber) may have been living in medieval houses or at least in communities where standards evolved in the sixteenth century still determined the family life of half the population.

[1]The looms are described by men who knew what they were talking about: e.g. 'one 8/4 loom gear and slay, six shuttles and four treddles, stocks and pulleys at £1 15s.; one 7/4 loom with 12/4 gear and slay . . .; one 6 gear loom next Richard Billingley's house with a 10/4 gear and slay . . .; one 6/4 loom next to John Jones his house with a 7/4 gear . . .'; bundle 1661–2, no. 325.

[2]*Mon. Ho.*, II, 56–7.

[3]*Mon. Ho.*, I, 52; III, 115 and plate XXD.

Near Raglan Castle, Mon., stands Castle Farm, an entire new building of the Restoration,[1] and the earliest example in the county of a complete departure from the local vernacular. It must have been built by Henry Somerset, later created Duke of Beaufort, 'the richest subject that the King hath', for the farmer of the estate immediately belonging to the castle, at a time when the idea of restoring the castle had been given up in favour of a new residence, at Badminton.[2] Castle Farm is of brick, with large segmental-headed windows downstairs, and two-light mullioned openings upstairs. The novelty lies, as usual, in proportions more than in detail. The upper floor has quite lofty rooms, but the attic rooms, marked by a string course only a foot or so above the mullioned windows, were equally spacious, their floor being about 3 feet below eaves level.

Staffordshire went with the north Midlands, rather than the south, for most people still talked of the hall as the house, or occasionally as the dwelling house or house place. No one had yet begun to call it the kitchen. Even the smallest house had a parlour, rather than a chamber downstairs, and any medium sized farmhouse had two; Geoffrey Grymes, yeoman, of Cold Meere in Eccleshall, a very wealthy yeoman with goods worth £954, had three parlours. In two houses a new combination occurs: a parlour in the usual position at one end, entered first by the appraisers, and another 'below the kitchen' (see p. 227 for a Yorkshire example). Presumably this was a servants' parlour. This suggests that Staffordshire standards were very much like those of Lincolnshire at this time, and indeed brick was making headway at about the same rate. A few farmhouses, of brick with stone quoins, went up before the war, and with the return of an acceptable form of government such work was resumed. A house at Forton[3] was built in 1665, at a cost of £100, with four storeys including basement and attics; its plan is a rectangle of three main units, with a projecting staircase wing at the rear. The staircase built out had become a common feature in the south and east half a century before, but in the Midlands its vogue belonged to the years 1660–1700. The Forton house has a symmetrical front with dormers and stone dressings; the restrained Renaissance style is typical of Staffordshire, where builders were not touched by the exuberance of their fellows in eastern counties. The barrier of the limestone belt kept eastern influence away and perhaps helped to build up a time-lag not confined to such new features of design as the built-out staircase.

[1] Illustrated in *Mon. Ho.*, III, pl. XIIID.
[2] Mr. A. J. Taylor in the Ministry of Works guide to Raglan Castle (H.M.S.O. 1950), 44, suggests that Castle Farm was built *c.* 1640, but *c.* 1675 is much more likely.
[3] V.C.H. *Staffs.*, IV, 104, pl. facing 110.

These new houses, so large by pre-war standards, reflect the steady concentration of land in fewer hands. In the manor of Gnosall the number of leaseholders fell from twenty-eight to twelve between 1647 and 1677, while copyholders (most of whom had only a few acres) and cottagers together increased from fifty-seven to sixty-eight. The cottages on the lord's waste paid no rent because they belonged to poor folk, and they were built of any timber that could be got on the commons. The cottages at Wheaton Aston and elsewhere which after about 1675 began to be cased in brick[1] must have been occupied by employees or tenants of a landowner like Drayner Massingberd. The surviving examples have two storeys, and one of them could have belonged to Thomas Arnett, carpenter of Hednesford, who had a house place, a parlour, a buttery and a chamber. Such comparisons cannot be carried any farther because these yeomen and husbandmen were poor by standards of other regions,[2] and their houses were smaller. The surviving cottages of Wheaton Aston, with two main rooms downstairs, match the inventories of yeomen, rather than of labourers or husbandmen. Although farmers on the poorer soils, such as Cannock Chase, were making great strides at this time by concentrating on mutton and wool production, their living standards had not yet begun to reflect their increasing wealth.

Shropshire and Cheshire have more in common with Worcestershire than north Staffordshire in that the timber tradition was still flourishing there, though the house carpenter had by now simplified his task to a somewhat mechanical form. The jettied overhang has disappeared, and the two-storeyed houses he was now required to build consist of a repetition of panels, 3 to 4 feet square, with small braces at intervals to the wall plate. Building on a stone or brick plinth, three panels provided enough height for two floors with chamber windows in the top panel under the eaves; five panels fitted the width at the gable, and four panels went to a bay along the length. This style of building can be seen in houses of all sizes, and it continued unchanged into the eighteenth century. Stanley Hall, Cheshire, is dated 1662, and consists of a simple rectangle with one gable. A house at Churton dated 1679 is of the popular hall and cross wing design. At Flixton in south Lancashire a house built in 1675 with a rectangular plan had the upper storey raised in brick during the next century.

[1] V.C.H. Staffs., IV, 115, 145.
[2] The median value of yeomen's wealth was about £75, compared with £123 in Worcestershire and £188 in the Trent valley. It indicates that Staffordshire yeomen had the same standard of living as husbandmen in Nottinghamshire.

CHAPTER FOUR

The Limestone Belt

THE strength of the vernacular tradition among masons working in the good limestone of the jurassic zone is more marked between 1660 and 1725 than before or after; whatever the importance of the timber tradition in earlier times, there is no question now that stone was the only material used for external walls. Partition walls are sometimes timber framed, but it is not even certain that this is a hangover from building altogether in wood, for in the Banbury region at any rate internal walls of stone seem to be older than those of timber.[1] Both the supremacy of the mason and his conservatism place an astonishingly Gothic mark on the villages along the band of upland country from Kesteven to north Somerset (see pl. XIXa). The conservatism resides in his ideas of the proportions of a building, the size and proportion of window openings, the ornament of a door frame. There is even conservatism of plan, so there is more here than the monopoly of an ancient craft; the upland farmer's way of life, based on mixed farming with sheep as a substantial interest, still suited his land and the market.

On the margins of the stone belt, the mason naturally had to admit useful innovations which had started outside his territory. In the few Huntingdonshire parishes, such as Elton, which belong to the upland zone, the double chimney stack in the centre of the house was taken over by the stone mason (see fig. 16, D2). The result is a hybrid type, indistinguishable in plan from those of the south-east, but carried out in stone; that sort of hybridization, on either side of a line between two regions, is common at every period.

The one novelty which became a common feature of stone houses all

[1] *Ex. inf.* R. B. Wood Jones.

the way from Stamford to Somerset was the storeyed bay window. It belongs to the period after 1660, rather than earlier.[1] It is quite uniform in design from one end of the zone to the other: sloping sides flanking a three- or four-light window at each storey, and the sides corbelled out above to carry the gable (pl. Xb). No doubt the whole could be bought ready made from the quarry. The only variation is in position; it may be found either in the hall or in the parlour. Its purpose is plain: though it had been invented to admit more light to a room, it became popular and has remained so ever since because it gave those inside a better chance to see what was happening up and down the street. There is a good instance in the tiny Rutland village of Clipsham. At a road junction in the centre stands Bidwell Farm, a three unit house with its gable end to the road (see fig. 30). Although there can have been precious little to see, a bay

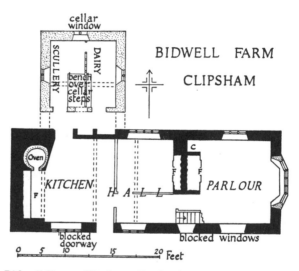

FIGURE 30. Bidwell Farm, Clipsham, Rutland, a house of simple three-unit plan improved by the insertion of a bay window in the parlour and the addition of a service wing with a dairy, scullery and cellar.

window was inserted at this period in the end room, the parlour. It would have given more light if put on the south side, but that view looked only on to the garden.

The uniformity and conservatism of design and treatment is a notable feature of north Somerset villages within range of the quarries at Ham Hill.

[1]One example in St. Leonard's Street, Stamford, is dated 1666; another at Ryhall, Rutland, is 1679; a third at Stoke sub Hamdon, Somerset, is 1674. There is, however, one at Oundle (The White Lion) dated 1641. The earliest in the Cotswolds is 1650; G. L. Worsley, *op. cit.*, 139.

Even a superficial search shows how many houses there are of two full storeys, with three main rooms, a cross passage and the hall fireplace backing on the passage—not a new design but obviously as popular as ever. To put them all into a tight chronology, of the kind that Fox and Raglan evolved from stone houses in Monmouthshire, would call for closer study than they have yet been given. Here are some of the variables. Windows may have frames and mullions of stone or wood. Wooden frames upstairs and stone below may be a late phenomenon, say after the year 1700. Stone mullions have a hollow chamfer, or alternatively an ovolo moulding (see fig. 31). The hollow chamfer came first—about 1580 perhaps—and was replaced c. 1615 by the ovolo moulding, but it seems to reappear either instead of the ovolo or alongside it towards the end of the seventeenth century, and so can be a potent source of confusion in dating.[1] The plain chamfer or splay may be found at any date, and is useless for chronological purposes. Window proportions remain unchanged until after about 1700; only then are lights made loftier. Ground floor openings nearly always have an angled hood mould; the single hood embracing a door and a window, or even all the openings, is a late development.

Although the simple rectangular plan, mostly of three rooms, seems to be the commonest design to anyone who walks down a village street and sees only the fronts of houses, there are of course plenty of farmhouses of L or T plan, with a service wing at the rear. Nevertheless, they do not seem to have become as common as in south-eastern England. Manor Farm, Merriott, Somerset, which has a main range dated 1663, has not been altered recently, but it is difficult to say whether the kitchen and scullery at the rear are original. In this instance the room across the passage is the parlour, and the dairy is entered through the hall. This is a Devonshire type of plan, proper to pasture farming country, though the Ham Hill region is now one of mixed farming. The hall has a storeyed bay window of the usual design.

The field worker always has to be alive to the possibility that a service wing may be older than the main range of a house because it has escaped rebuilding, or is an old house degraded in status. Although villages in the limestone belt may have examples of the three room and cross passage plan which has been called typical of the region, they have many more which defy classification, because they are the result of piecemeal rebuilding. Often the new part was at right angles to the old. More than one observer

[1] I understand from Mr. J. T. Smith that the hollow chamfer also reappears in Dorset. What Fox and Raglan called the reserved chamfer and dated to c. 1590–1620 in Monmouthshire (*Mon. Ho.*, III, fig. 48) does not figure much in the Cotswolds, though I have noticed one example at Lacock, Wilts.

has noted how often a house of this age is at right angles to the road, a situation which remained fashionable into the eighteenth century, when it disappeared in the new notion that a symmetrically designed front must present its main elevation to the viewer, and so to the road. It is tempting to associate the through passage plan with the need for access to the farm-yard and fields belonging to the house, but in the present stage of know-ledge one can do no more than assert that the seventeenth-century house is *commonly* placed at right angles to the road.

Bidwell Farm, Clipsham, was improved at this time by the addition not only of the parlour bay window, but also of the service wing, with two rooms over a half cellar (see fig. 30). Builders were now prepared (and this can be seen in both brick and stone houses) to make a cellar by raising the floor of a service-room over it to an intermediate level in relation to other floors. The service wing at Bidwell Farm is a simple stone box with a plaster floor over the cellar and a wooden partition between the two rooms over. To get head room for the cellar steps, the builder ingeniously put in a wooden bench or table half in each room. Other changes in the main range cannot now be elucidated. There are blocked windows inside in the chamber over the parlour, yet the walling outside shows no sign of them, and must have been completely refaced. This is one of the difficulties facing the student of these small buildings. The same quarries lasted for centuries; at any time a mason could match or repeat the coursed rubble walling of his predecessors, and in a short time it weathered to the same character.

For larger houses the hall and cross wings design had gone out of fashion by this time. In its place there begins to appear something com-pletely outside the medieval tradition: the double house (see pl. XXa). Country builders, whatever their material, had not thought of building a range more than one room in depth from front to rear, and although they had long since solved the problem of putting two such ranges at right angles, they had never attempted to put them side by side. A roof span of more than about 18 feet was not attempted, and two pitched roofs in parallel required a lead channel in the valley between. The valley was difficult to keep clear, and a fall of snow was almost certain to cause a leak. Nonetheless, builders now began to design large farm houses two rooms deep, covered by a double span roof. The design was commended by Sir Roger Pratt, the architect,[1] and reached a few country masons from some such source. The earliest dated example in stone is a farmhouse at Brant Broughton, Lincs., now used as the rectory; the manor house at

---

[1] N. Lloyd, *History of the English House*, 103. Little Park Farm, Ampthill, Beds., a brick house of 1629, seems to be the earliest example, but it has not been studied.

XIXa. A Kesteven three-unit stone house of *c.* 1660 with an axial stack opposite the entrance, serving hall and parlour, and kitchen at the near end. The original windows have ovolo-moulded mullions.

XIXb. The most picturesque of the Dartmoor long houses, with its storeyed porch dated 1707, separate entrance to the shippon and well house. See figure 17D.

XXa. Manor Farm, Ratcliffe on Soar, Notts., was built in 1715 as a double house, exactly square on plan.

XXb. A cottage at Farndon, Notts. The wing protruding towards the camera contains only a well-type staircase with date 1703 on the bottom newel post.

Allington, not far away, must be of similar date. The two differ completely in arrangement. The Allington house, with two parallel ridges of roof and curved gables,[1] is really simple in design. The front range has three rooms—a lobby hall with a fireplace, flanked by two parlours. The back range contains service-rooms and a dog-leg staircase of singularly generous proportions. The windows are upright in proportion, with mullion and transom, so that there is really nothing vernacular about it.

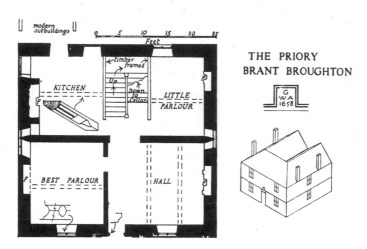

FIGURE 31. House at Brant Broughton, Lincolnshire, known as 'The Priory', now the Rectory. An early example of a double house, for which an inventory has been found (Appendix, p. 279). Later internal alterations have been omitted. An entrance passage has been made, cutting off the hall from the front door (a common improvement to houses of this arrangement); the little parlour has been divided along the line of the ceiling beam, making a small study and a buttery or larder with a cellar under. Note that the fashion for symmetry in window openings leads to windows divided between rooms.

The plan of Brant Broughton rectory is shown in fig. 31 and the inventory for the house in Appendix, p. 279. It was built in 1658 by William Garnon, gentleman, and wherever he got the design, a local mason carried it out. The roof is of square ⊔ shape, hipped at the front and gabled at the rear; both front and side elevations are strictly symmetrical and the main internal division is a cross or spine wall of stone, so that the plan is quartered. This involved dividing the side windows between rooms. The hall takes up two thirds of the front range and from it a wide opening leads to a remarkably fine staircase. It has openwork newel posts, carved out of the solid, a heavily moulded rail, and instead of a baluster, an oak

[1]Of the kind christened Holborn gables by John Summerson.

plank 2 feet wide and nearly 2 inches thick, carved with a scrolled design.[1] It is a fine feature, but the hall must have been intolerably draughty in winter.

The best parlour is panelled throughout in oak, and William Garnon had it furnished with a table (with a carpet or table cloth on it), eleven chairs and two stools. The little parlour behind the hall was not much used, to judge from its sparse contents. Garnon paid hearth tax on six hearths: in the hall, both parlours, the kitchen, and upstairs in the great chamber (over the hall) and the chamber over the best parlour. The house was not well equipped with service-rooms;[2] the dairy and brewhouse, which abutted the kitchen, had been preserved from the earlier house. They have since been rebuilt, with a back kitchen and other outhouses. The staircase goes up to the garrets, where a servant slept along with corn, wool and cheeses.

The main interest of the house lies in the adoption by a gentleman farmer of the Commonwealth of what was then the newest design in country houses. The square plan divided by a spine wall parallel to the façade is a cut-down version of the standard design for country houses from 1660 onwards.[3]

[1]The staircase is identical with that at Auburn Hall, five miles away, and must have been made by the same carpenter. See *Country Life*, 14 February, 1957, for Auburn Hall.

[2]The little parlour was divided early in the eighteenth century along the line of its ceiling beam (see plan), and the part nearer the hall was turned into another cellar with a buttery over it. Perhaps this coincided with the demolition or rebuilding of the service wing at the rear which had been preserved in the rebuilding of the main house.

[3]See J. Summerson, 'The Classical Country House in 18th Century England', *J.R.S.A.*, CVII (1959), 541.

CHAPTER FIVE

The Highland Zone

a. The West Country

WE have seen that in the Ham Hill area of Somerset the traditional type of house was still being put up, with the addition, sometimes, of service rooms at the rear. In north-west Somerset and throughout Devon and Cornwall the front chimney type (see above, p. 112) was just as popular after 1660 as before. Devon and Cornwall were cut off by a broad belt of stone building (Dorset, Wiltshire, Somerset) from the innovations originating in the timber and brick regions farther east. Descriptions of parsonage houses in the diocese of Exeter (Devon and Cornwall), which are more informative than those for any other counties in south-western England,[1] show how western farmers were still pursuing their own old-fashioned but prosperous ways. In the eastern counties so many parsons had built new family houses in the two generations after the Reformation that few of their successors in the seventeenth century were moved to do much more. Perhaps in Devonshire parsons had not got off the mark so quickly, for there seems to have been steady rebuilding and enlargement between 1613, the date of the first series of terriers which describe the houses, and 1678–80 when another return was made.

By that time, cob building was beginning to lose its esteem. Stone houses were commonest on the fringes of Dartmoor and Exmoor, but elsewhere stone was coming into use, and it was not unusual for a house to be so

[1] I am deeply indebted to Mrs. C. S. Cruwys for transcribing for me the relevant parts of more than 100 terriers for Devonshire, and to Mrs. V. M. Chesher for lending me extracts from Cornish terriers. These terriers are interesting enough to deserve publication in full; they are in the Devon County Record Office, The Castle, Exeter, and in the Cornwall County Record Office at Truro.

built while outbuildings were of earth. Although the term *cob* was already known, no parson used it; 'walls of mud or earth' was the general description. Roofing material was either thatch or 'shindles'—that is, stone slates, or shindlestone.

Even the bald descriptions of the terriers manage to convey the way the Devonshire parsonage house (and farmhouse)[1] was snugly fitted into the landscape. Its owner was more anxious to find shelter from the warm south-westerly wind, because it so often brought rain, than the farmer of eastern England was to shelter from the cold but dry winds which were part of his life. Very often there was a walled court or farmyard both at front and back. At Axminster 'a walled forecourt led into the dwelling house'; Bondleigh had 'two close courts'. Sometimes, as at Bratton Fleming and Cullompton, there was a gatehouse. Such houses may well be of medieval date, but no documentary evidence can tell us when they were built, and apart from W. A. Pantin's pioneer article,[2] detailed field work remains to be done. Many of these descriptions of 1678–80 have an essentially medieval flavour, of separate and unrelated buildings round a courtyard. At Alphington there were '4 houses: hall and parlour under one roof, kitchen and malt house under another, the third a barn, the fourth a shippon with a new stable and a corn chamber which I have built'. About three houses out of twenty had still a detached kitchen. Again, one does not know when they were built, but some of them were still in use. At Axmouth, in addition to the walled forecourt, there was 'one little back court leading to an outbuilding where is one kitchen, one larder and another small room, over which there are two chambers'. The kitchen at Combeinteignhead was 'without' the house and had a larder adjoining. Cheriton Fitzpaine had 'one great out kitchen' and another kitchen within the house, and at Bondleigh the very last thing mentioned, after the woodhouse, the cider house, a 'house of office' or privy (obviously one is getting farther away from the dwelling house) is 'an old kitchen floored with earth'.

Sometimes the court at the back of the house had an open lean-to or 'linney', which is an open cart shed, but is also descended from the medieval pentice providing covered access from one building to another. Like the spinning gallery of the Lake District, it was particularly useful in a wet climate.[3] At Coleridge 'the back court between hall and kitchen was enclosed, with a convenient linney in the same'. At Awliscombe the linney had a pump in it, and at Phillack, Cornwall, it sheltered the poultry.

[1]See C. H. Laycock, 'The Old Devon Farmhouse' in *Trans. Devonshire Ass.*, 52 (1920), 54 (1922), and 55 (1923).
[2]'Medieval Priests' Houses in south-west England' in *Med. Arch.*, I (1957), 118.
[3]*Eng. Dialect Dictionary s. v.* linhay. It was used for drying serges, for instance.

As for the houses themselves, the cross passage plan was still universal where there were more than two rooms. It was always known as the entry. Alphington, which consisted of only a hall and parlour in 1601, with a detached kitchen, had grown by 1678 to a complex of buildings round a court, with at least one cross passage (see Appendix p. 274). The hall, to one side of the passage, was in some cases still open to the roof: Bigbury had '1 open hall excellently well timbered' and Bratton Clovelly '1 hall openroofed'. Beyond it was the one parlour, with a buttery 'within'— that is, partitioned from it. The smallest houses had no more than that accommodation, together with a room across the passage; Dunterton, Combeinteignhead and Comberaleigh were of this size and plan, with chambers over.

Although there had been as yet no departure from the traditional Devonshire plan, the general increase in size was leading to a change in the function of rooms. First the hall, since it was no longer used for cooking, was occasionally thought of as a parlour. At Ashford and Beer Ferrers the parson spoke of 'the hall or parlour'. The kitchen was not only a cooking room but a dining-room during the week, where the parson or the farmer sat down to eat at the same long table as his servants and farm hands. The old farmhouse described as typical by a Devonshire man who knew his county well[1] had such a kitchen, and a second kitchen used for preparing and cooking, as well as a backhouse or scullery where pots and pans were kept. His typical house had then four hearths—parlour, hall and two kitchens—each with an open hearth fireplace. This multiplication of hearths in rooms serving very similar purposes—after all none of them is used as a bedroom, as in the Midlands and north—is the most marked feature of these Devon houses.

The second kitchen and the backhouse are relatively modern developments, for few houses had them in 1680. Instead, there was frequently more than one buttery (as elsewhere at this time), and there was rarely a hearth in either of the service-rooms across the passage, unless a kitchen had been added at that end (see plans on p. 111). Sometimes these service rooms were still called cellars, as they had been in the Middle Ages, although they were on ground level.

A water supply in or near the house was a new feature of a few houses at this time. One of the outbuildings at Beer Ferrers was a 'water kitchen', and Beaworthy had a 'water house'. The parson at Arlington had arranged to bring 'into the house the potwater which doth arise in a little meadow adjoining the aforesaid Parsonage Meadows', and although it was not his meadow he had 'the privilege to go and turn in the water at any time

[1]C. H. Laycock, *loc. cit.*, 54 (1922), plan on 227.

without asking leave or paying anything'. There was at Deptford a 'pool where potwater runs out of Churchparl Meadow', and at East Down 'the room to brew and wash in is continually supplied with water which is conveyed thither from a little meadow.'[1] No doubt Devonshire farmers' wives have ceased to wash pots in such a fashion, but the supply of running water is still useful for cooling milk. If no stream could be diverted, then a well was dug; there was at Blegberry in Hartland a well house dated 1657.[2] Another Devonshire peculiarity was the ash house, in which ash from the peat and wood fires was saved for spreading as a fertilizer. The ash house was 'before the back door' of Coryton parsonage in 1686, and there it may be found in many farmhouses today.

Although most of these farmers were dependent on livestock, as the pattern of buildings round the court clearly shows, those who had suitable land grew corn for their own needs and for the market. One chamber was then used for storing corn, and the others for sleeping. We now think of cider as the one and only farmhouse drink in the west, but far more Devon farmers brewed ale than made cider in Charles II's time—another indication of the amount of arable farming—and a few did both. Then there was a brewhouse in the court, with a kiln or 'dry' in it, and a chamber for storing malt.

In Cornwall the parsonage house of c. 1680 (and the farmhouse of which it was only a special form) differed from the types on p. 111 in two respects; far more of them still had detached kitchens, and the third room within the house was more often a dairy or service-room of some sort. This Cornish evidence confirms the inference drawn from Devon that this is the most ancient type of dwelling in the west.

b. The Pennines

Living conditions in Yorkshire after 1660 can be pictured more clearly and fully than before, because nearly every inventory now describes the house in detail. The somewhat tentative inferences drawn about earlier times can now be confirmed. Yorkshire folk had not changed their ideas about the conveniences that a house ought to possess; they were still moving steadily towards an ideal already present in their minds for a generation or two, and were not merely copying new fashions from other parts. The homogeneity of ideas in most classes of Restoration Yorkshire is very striking, especially when we remember that it had already dis-

---

[1]Laycock describes this as a common feature (*loc. cit.*, 52 (1920), 166) as it is in other parts of the highland zone.
[2]Laycock, *loc. cit.*, pl. VI.

appeared from southern and south-eastern society in the Tudor period, and had been a mark of Midland society in the earlier part of the seventeenth century.

The use of brick was spreading inland from the Humber and the Ouse valley. York and the villages of its hinterland are the most northerly extension of the region of ornamental brickwork. The import of bricks into Hull was not significant, for Hull's trade was mainly with Scandinavia and brick-making was an ancient industry in the area, but there was a lively demand for pantiles. Guy Browne of the *Truelove*, who came in from Rotterdam on 6 July 1670, himself imported some Norway deals, 500 laths and 4,000 pantiles,[1] and in 1669–70 thirteen vessels each brought between 200 and 4,000 pantiles. Imported softwoods were already being used in building.[2]

Apart from the beginning of this intrusion which was to transform the East Riding, the larger stone houses which can be dated to 1660–90 agree entirely with the conclusions drawn from documents. Medieval timber houses were still being rebuilt in stone, in the style which Yorkshire had adopted a century before: two full storeys with attics, and three rather flat gables on the façade. The only apparent change is that the long mullioned windows are now somewhat loftier in their proportions, and more often incorporate a horizontal transom.[3]

Documentary evidence takes us to a lower social level than these surviving houses, which represent the most substantial homes of the time. A large proportion of houses of the 1660's can be classified into a few simple types. The table on p. 226 includes in each period about four fifths of those contained in a sample of inventories. The very fact that an analysis can be constructed to include such a large majority is a measure of the simplicity and homogeneity. It could not be done for say Kentish or Essex houses at any period. It is probably also, if the contrast with Kent is valid, a measure of widespread rebuilding in recent times. The great rebuilding has certainly reached Yorkshire by this time.

Houses from all parts of the county have been included in the analysis, because uniformity is more marked than regional variations.[4] The East

---

[1]P.R.O., E190/320/6 and 10.

[2]William Blyth's house at Barlow in the parish of Brayton, near Selby, had '1 loose chamber lying upon strings laid with fir deals' in 1665; York Probate Registry, Peculiar of Selby, bundle B.

[3]L. Ambler, *Old Halls and Manor Houses of Yorkshire*, 84–94. Norland Hall (Halifax), Horton Hall (Bradford) and West Riddlesden Hall (Keighley) were timber houses rebuilt in stone at this time.

[4]The inventories came mainly from the West Riding and the Vale of York, and the East Riding is under-represented.

YORKSHIRE HOUSES, 1660–1720

Type	1660–70		1690–1700		1720–30	
	No.	%	No.	%	No.	%
1. House and parlour	9	9.9	12	10.7	12	15.4
2. House, parlour, chamber	11	12.1	9	8.0	12	15.4
3. House, parlour, service-room	7	7.7	6	5.4	3	3.8
4. a. House, parlour, service-room, chamber	13		25		10	
b. House, parlour, service-room, 2 chambers	2	27.4	7	34.0	7	35.9
c. House, parlour, 2 service-rooms, chamber	3		4		7	
d. House, parlour, 2 service-rooms, 2 chambers	7		2		4	
5. a. House, 2 parlours	—		2		4	
b. House, 2 parlours, service-room	4		1		—	
c. House, 2 parlours, chamber	5		2		—	
d. House, 2 parlours, 2 chambers	—		5		1	
e. House, 2 parlours, service-room, chamber	8		7		5	
f. House, 2 parlours, service-room, 2 chambers	3	37.4	9	36.6	2	29.5
g. House, 2 parlours, 2 service-rooms,	2		—		—	
h. House, 2 parlours, 2 service-rooms, chamber	5		3		4	
j. House, 2 parlours, 2 service-rooms, 2 or more chambers	4		8		6	
k. House, 2 parlours, 3 service-rooms, 3 or more chambers	3		4		1	
6. House, 3 parlours, etc.	5	5.7	5	4.3	—	
7. House, 4 parlours, etc.	—	—	1	.8	—	
Totals	91	100.0	112	100.0	78	100.0

Riding forms a transitional zone, in which lowland standards diminished and highland customs took over. Holderness, with its strong boulder clays, resembled clay regions farther south and supported quite wealthy farmers with houses of medium size in the east Midland style: hall house, two parlours, or two butteries and one or two chambers upstairs for stores. The Ouse valley as far north as York was an extension of the Isle of Axholme and Trent valley. The chalk wolds carried a relatively thin population, and it is no coincidence that three farmers from Wetwang whose inventories have survived were small yeomen or husbandmen living in two-roomed houses.[1]

In the smallest houses, the same priorities were observed as in the Midlands a generation earlier, and the long, single-storey building was still the point of departure for new work. There is no evidence of the single-roomed house, though its survival could not be denied; only one labourer's inventory turned up in a sample of more than one hundred, and the poorest element is certainly not included in the review. A carpenter's house at Pudsey in 1666 consisted of one room with a chamber over it. He was a small farmer as well, with a barn, some arable and livestock. This is the only example of the type which has come to light.[2] The two-roomed cottage may well have been the commonest single type. Anyone who wanted a third room was rather more likely to make a chamber over the parlour, for storage, than to make a service-room downstairs. If a service room could be contrived, a milkhouse or a buttery was somewhat more popular than a kitchen.

The peculiarly northern features can be seen in larger houses, and the most striking is still the popularity of the parlour-bedroom and the multiplication of parlours, which were usually unheated. No other county had so many houses with two or even three parlours. They amount to two out of five in this sample. Phrases like 'the parlour where he died',[3] or 'the Bed Parlour' familiar in midland inventories a generation or two earlier, still come from the pens of Yorkshire appraisers. Some of these parlours are explicitly said to be new. Edward Bright, vicar of Pickering and quite a wealthy parson,[4] had enlarged his parsonage house. It was already reasonably comfortable, but he had built a new house alongside it with two parlours, so that he now had three.[5] In one house, that of Ann Brooke, widow, of Gateforth, there was a kitchen parlour, presumably for servants; it was not a matter of making the servants sleep in the kitchen,

[1]York Registry, inventories of Wetwang prebend: Jacob Chambers (1664), William Cole (1668) and William Moore (1668).

[2]York Registry, Manorial Court of Crosley, etc., 1600–1700.

[3]Inventories of Robert Seadlocke, yeoman, of Acomb, 1661, and Richard Topper of Tockwith near Wetherby, 1666.

[4]His goods were worth £110, compared with a median value of about £63 in Yorkshire at this time, and he had land of his own as well as his glebe.

[5]Deanery Peculiars, bundle 1661.

for that was a separate room. Her house had three rooms upstairs, one of them with a bed in it but the others were only used for storage.[1] She really had four bedrooms: three parlours downstairs and a chamber above. Some houses show how the long house tradition might affect new development. William Taire, yeoman, of Bramham, had a parlour 'adjoining the Firehouse' and another 'beyond the kitchen'.[2] William Topham of Norton in the Clay was a wealthy yeoman, engaged in mixed farming on a large scale. His home consisted of a hall-house with the usual three service-rooms (kitchen, milkhouse and buttery), two parlours and three chambers. The parlours were at either end of the range of building—'on the West end of the House' and 'on the East end of the House'. The three chambers were over the hall and the two parlours. The chamber over the hall had blendings (mixed corn), salt flesh, hemp yarn and bread in it; that 'over the east end of the house' had wheat, rye and blendings and a bedstead; the third, upon the west end, was a bedroom proper, with a fireplace and two bedsteads in it.[3]

Although the Yorkshire parlour of this age sometimes had sitting-room furniture in it—a table with a carpet, or a desk, a couple of buffet stools—the hall living-room tradition was really unshaken, as common terminology shows. Half the people still called it the house, or in very few cases, the housebody, the housestead or the dwelling house. Most people in and near Bradford spoke of the housebody. A quarter of them spoke of the hall or the hall house, and those who used the name hall were, if anything, the wealthier sort. The remaining quarter used the term firehouse or forehouse, indifferently. They were by no means the lower ranks of Yorkshire society; that is, the widow and the heir who led the appraisers from room to room were not offended to hear the term firehouse used, even if they did not use it themselves.

There is one more traditional element in this pattern of northern home life: the service end of the house. Wealthier farmers and their wives were content to have buttery, milkhouse and kitchen at the most. No doubt cooking was being moved to the kitchen, since the hall was still a living room. Very few people wished for more elaborate arrangements than that; brewing and baking gear were kept in one or other of those rooms, no one had a brewhouse, and a boulting house or a washhouse was almost unheard of. The reverse aspect of this simplicity is that the unspecialized service-room had not yet disappeared. It appears in several houses, in the north-east and north-west of the county rather than in the Vale of York.

[1] Selby Peculiars, Box B.
[2] Dean and Chapter Peculiars, 1665.
[3] Leeds City Library, Deanery of Richmond, AP/1/T, 1659.

It is in fact retreating to the highland parts proper. In most cases it is the 'low end of the house', the 'nether end', or 'the low house'; in the rest 'the backend'. These houses have no service-rooms other than a milkhouse at most, and in some the low end might as well, from its contents, be called the buttery. In a few it is still part of the farm rather than the dwelling. John Crakehill, yeoman, of North Milforth in Kirkby Wharf, had a plough 'in the end of the house', and Christopher Sharrow, yeoman, of Ample-forth, kept a cart 'in the low end'. The simplest pattern of forehouse, parlour and 'backerend' occurs in only one house, that of William Tindall of the Spittle in Fangfoss, where the back end was used for ladders, racks, scythes, a gate and other wood.

Most of these features can be summed up in the house of Thomas Woodwith of Grimston in the parish of Kirkby Wharfe, who died in 1660.[1] He was a wealthy yeoman, with goods worth about £200, and his farm was mainly arable. The firehouse was simply furnished, but was clearly the living-room, for neither the greater nor the inner parlour had any chairs or stools. The kitchen was used for brewing. What was called the lower house was a buttery, with a cupboard, various wooden tubs, barrels and measures, and also oddments like pack saddles, pillion sheets and empty corn sacks. There was a range in it, however, and another room called the lowest room had beds in it, so the two probably comprised a small house downgraded by new buildings. There was a chamber over the firehouse with a trundle bed and a chaff bed, but otherwise used for implements which may have been made on the farm: twelve plough heads, four axle trees, a plough beam and 'certain ox bows and stees' (ladders). The only other chambers were over the low parlour and the old house; and both were 'laid loose': that is had floor boards laid without fixing on joists which could also be removed, in order to get bulky stores upstairs.

Among the wealthier clothiers round Bradford the practice of having the looms upstairs had unmistakably set in. One of them, John Hodgson of Allerton had a shop downstairs, with three looms in it, but Samuel Willson, clothier of Pudsey, had a loom chamber so called, with 'one pair of broadlooms with bartrees, damsels, iron broithes and one pair of gears and one pair of shuttles'. The loom chamber was probably over the sun parlour or the north parlour, or both; the only other chamber, over the house, was full of wool and cloth 'unmilned'. William Whitlay of Pudsey, who was called a yeoman, had a loom in the chamber over the house.[2] These

[1] York Registry, Wetwang Prebend.
[2] York Registry, Manorial Court of Crossley, Bingley and Pudsey, 1600–1700: i.e. the continuation of the series printed by the Bradford Hist. and Ant. Soc. (see p. 121 above).

men were above average in wealth, and poorer weavers still had the loom in the parlour (see Appendix, p. 287).

There is a remarkable contrast between Yorkshire and Derbyshire by this time. The textile industry in the West Riding enabled farmers there (for the weaver or clothier still had his land) to reach the same standard of wealth as men in other parts of Yorkshire where land was of better quality and more plentiful; but the lead industry made no equal contribution to Derbyshire economy. The Derbyshire farmer was therefore much poorer, and miners were among the most impoverished members of a backward community.[1] In general development followed midland and northern lines, but in this later stage of the housing revolution the impact of ideas from outside produced some unusual houses. This is nothing new in the archaeological record of Derbyshire, but it is an impressive fact that even in modern times the Pennines should still have monuments as difficult to classify as those of the Bronze Age.

One of them is a farmstead called Long Lee, in the hamlet of Rowarth, and just in Derbyshire; it stands high on the western slopes of the Pennines overlooking the Lancashire plain from which the early settlers had come to clear these bleak slopes. After the Restoration the property was acquired by John Hyde, gentleman. By 1661 he had rebuilt the house (see pl. XXIa). In 1679 he put up a new barn and shippon combined, in the highland style: taking advantage of the sloping site, he built the barn or hay house over the cowplace, and on the upward side there is a round opening through which hay was forked into the loft. At the same time he put up another small farm building also of two storeys, and built, like the shippon, in coursed rubble masonry with quoins and lintels of gigantic proportions. He died in 1703, for his tombstone has survived—not, as one would expect, in the churchyard, but in one of the farm buildings.[2] His best monument is this extraordinarily impressive group of buildings overlooking the hollow in which the hamlet of Rowarth began. The house has two storeys but a very primitive plan (see fig. 32): a hall and cross wing design, with a kitchen in the wing and a parlour behind it. There were good chambers over all three rooms. The interior has been somewhat altered, precisely because by 1800 the design was unsatisfactory. The house part was then divided and a new staircase put in, which involved blocking the old fireplace and making another, and also doing away with

[1] Birmingham Registry, Lichfield Peculiar, bundles B1663–5. The median value of 63 inventories is £41, compared with about £60 for Yorkshire, and the median of 7 miners' inventories is £14 8s.

[2] I am indebted to Miss M. M. Anderson, the present owner, for her kindness in letting me examine and prepare a record of the house and buildings.

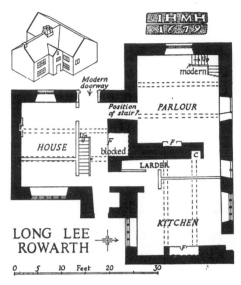

FIGURE 32. Long Lee, Rowarth, Derbyshire, rebuilt in 1679 by John Hyde, gentleman, after he had completed the rebuilding of the barn and other buildings of his remote farmstead. Modern alterations have made the original plan obscure, especially the position of the stairs used before the eighteenth century staircase was inserted in the hall or house part, but the simplicity of the design, and of John Hyde's way of life, are very evident. See pl. XXIa.

the old staircase. At the same time a 'front' door was made, which leads only to a very bleak little garden. The cellar under the parlour has been filled in, and a larder made by taking part of the kitchen. Even so, the house lacks service-rooms by seventeenth century standards, and in that it reflects Lancashire standards, rather than those of the eastern side of the Pennines.[1]

Yew Tree Farm in the hamlet of Sowerbutts Green and the chapelry of Samlesbury, north-east of Preston, must be of similar or slightly later date, and was of equally primitive design, for it had no parlour.[2] It had (see plan and elevation, fig. 33) a living-room or house part with gable end fireplace and the entrance at that end; the further half contained a kitchen, a larder and a framed staircase to the first floor, with its three chambers. The chamber over the house had small closets at either side of the chimney breast, each lighted by a small round-headed window. The other windows

[1]There is now a (modern) scullery at the north-east corner entered from the kitchen.

[2]The house has been demolished, but was carefully recorded by H. Ogle in *Trans. Lancs. and Cheshire Hist. Soc.*, 100 (1948), 45–54. I am indebted to Mr. Ogle for lending me his original drawings.

YEW TREE FARM, SAMLESBURY

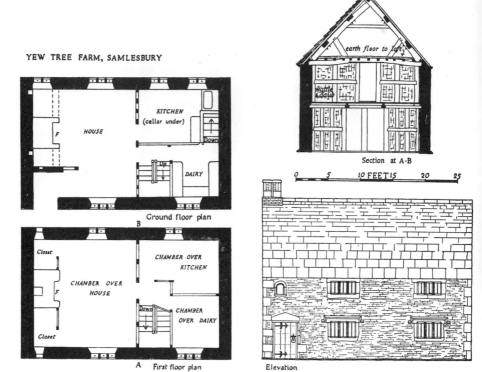

Section at A-B

Ground floor plan

First floor plan

Elevation

FIGURE 33. Yew Tree Farm, Salmesbury, Lancashire, a small stone house of the late seventeenth century, extremely well built but of very simple design, for it has no parlour. The entrance at the end of one side, giving on the speer, is common in the north at this time. The closets upstairs, each with a small window, are a new and widespread feature of the age. The cellar under the kitchen is probably not original. (After H. Ogle.)

are of two or three lights with stone mullions, and those downstairs have angled hood moulds. The quality of the mason craft is throughout of a high order, and the house is important for its combination of good workmanship with simple standards. Even if the date suggested for it is too early, which is quite possible, it constitutes a valuable item in the meagre catalogue of houses which link the single-roomed dwelling with the non-parlour house of modern times. Since the northern parlour was only a bedroom, a man who put up a two storeyed house could dispense with it. In regions such as Lancashire and Lincolnshire, where medieval standards were low, these new stone houses are descended from the simplest types, without a parlour, or without the cross passage.

These two houses are not only outside the tradition of Lancashire and the Pennines; they are still far from typical. A wider conspectus of

Lancashire houses now comes into view in the terriers returned by the clergy of the diocese of Chester in 1663.[1] They show marked similarity in standards and conventions to Yorkshire. The rector of Ashton under Lyne had a house of six bays, 'built cross wise and 2 out aisles'. The hall was open to the roof and the rest of the house chambered over. The vicar of Eccles had four parlours: a 'kitchen parlour' next to the kitchen, and presumably for servants; a great parlour and two little parlours, one of them 'in the side of the passage leading from the body of the house (i.e., the hall) to the great parlour'. In contrast to such large houses, most of the other houses which happen to be described because they stood on church land were of between two and four bays, and no doubt some of the three bay houses which still abound in the Fylde belong to the period 1650–1725. Nearly all the farmhouses in the terriers had their buildings separate from the house, but in Radcliffe near Bury the parson owned two properties each consisting of 'house and barn under the same roof, one of two bays and the other of three'. The parson at Brindle near Chorley made in his return that distinction which still eludes us, between firehouses and cottages. The former were larger, of three or four bays; two of them were farmhouses, with a barn, stable and a shippon, but the others were in fact cottages by status, since they had only gardens attached. The cottages so called were occupied by a shoemaker and a blacksmith, two innkeepers, a husbandman and three widows. The last naturally had the smallest homes: '1 bay of building', or '1 bay with another little building for a coalhouse'; '1 bay for a house and a small bay for a chamber but formerly a shop'. The largest cottage was one used as an inn, with '3 bays and 2 End Aislings': that is, with a lean-to at each end.

Whitaker, writing of Whalley in 1801, said that many cottages in the older part of the town were 'single apartments without chambers, open to their thatched roofs and supported upon crucks'.[2] They must have been survivals from the seventeenth century. Another survivor to the present day which fits perfectly the context of seventeenth century records is the cruck cottage of three bays at Bispham known as Ivy Cottage, which has the date 1686 in painted wall decoration.[3]

c. Cumberland and Westmorland

A closer study of the Cumberland coast, especially from Whitehaven or Maryport towards Carlisle, would show that it is essentially one with the

[1]Those for Lancashire are now in the Lancs. R.O. at Preston, DRM/3 and DRB/3.
[2]*History of Whalley* (1876), II, 574.
[3]R. C. Watson in *Trans. Lancs. and Cheshire Hist. Soc.*, 109 (1957), 63.

Lancashire coast. Single-storey cottages of a style rare inland are still to be seen. Building in clay was still the common medium until *c.* 1700, and at least one clay house, Lamonby Farm, still stands.[1] It belongs to the long house tradition, with a wall between the cross passage and the byre; the separation of the two parts and the crudeness of the cruck trusses suggests a date about 1650–1700. The outer walls have cobble foundations and are so low that the ground floor ceilings are little more than six feet high. There are two dwellings as well as a byre in the range. One of them has two rooms (house and parlour), the other only a house part and a small service-room. Each house has only one loft or chamber, in the roof; it is almost dark and the headroom is cut off by the collar of the cruck truss. It is not surprising that inventories of this period make so little of the rooms of a house, if standards were as simple as this.

There is a marked contrast between these regions of clay building and the stone areas of Westmorland and Cumberland; it must reflect different social conditions. The typical farmer of the Lake District was the 'states-man', the customary tenant who in Elizabeth's time had obtained the right to bequeath his land by will and paid only a small money rent.[2] Now, just a century after he had attained it, his house begins to reflect that security of status. No region in England has so many small farmhouses of a period, and of so stereotyped a design.[3] To some extent this activity must reflect a change from mud to stone building. They are built of rubble, and the walls are constructed in the traditional fashion of outer and inner leaves, with an earth core and through stones to bond the two. Lime mortar was not used originally; Celia Fiennes spoke of seeing houses built with dry walling. From this time onwards farmers began to finish them with a thick coat of rough cast, lime washed, so that the white farmhouse flanked by farm buildings in dark stone now began to be a characteristic sight.[4]

The type plans in fig. 34 show that the statesman found the traditional design as satisfactory in 1660–1720 as it had been for his superiors a

[1] *T.C.W.A.A.S.* 53, (1953), 156–9. The main house may be older than the byre and cottage.

[2] See H. S. Cowper, *Hawkshead, the Northernmost Parish of Lancashire* (London, 1899), 99–103, 155–6; R. W. McDowall, 'The Westmorland Vernacular', *Studies in Architectural History*, ed. W. A. Singleton, II (1956), 131.

[3] See R. W. Brunskill. 'The Development of the Small House in the Eden Valley 1650–1840', in *T.C.W.A.A.S.*, 53 (1953), 160–89. Of 993 houses examined, 27 per cent of the small houses were of the type described as the statesman plan, and most fell between 1660 and 1710. Examination of the records of the Hist. Mon. Comm. for Westmorland gives similar results. See also W. M. Williams' study of Gosforth parish in *T.C.W.A.A.S.* 54 (1954), 248–64.

[4] Aydon White House, co. Durham, was rebuilt in 1684 and so called from the beginning; H. L. Honeyman in *Arch. Aeliana* XXXI (1953), 144–6.

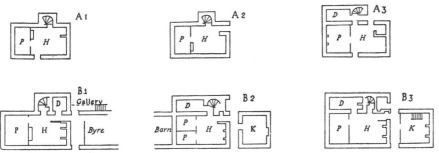

FIGURE 34. Westmorland statesmen's houses 1660–1715. They fall into two groups. Of the first with two rooms, A1 is dated 1677 over the front entrance; A2 has gable end entrance; A3 with a dairy in the outshot is dated 1694. The second group, of houses with a cross passage and a third room, contains houses with a more complex history. B1, with cupboards dated 1678 and 1701, was built alongside an older byre, and has a spinning gallery on the north side. B2 consisted originally of house and barn, and had a kitchen added c. 1700. B3 has the date 1693 over the door. (R. C. H. M., *Westmorland*, 30(31); 38(13); 39(22); 29(14); 31 (56); 38(14).) The third room was often known as the *down house*.

century earlier. The essential elements—house and parlour, cross passage and byre or low house (called the downhouse in Westmorland) are unchanged. The upper storey, now essential to the highland vernacular, is reached by a staircase on the back wall of the house, which is either a newel stair starting in an outshot, or a ladder within the main structure. Little attention was paid to the quality and convenience of the staircase. The house alone was heated, by a hearth taking up a quarter or a third of its space with a timber-framed hood making a large half pyramid in the chamber over. The hearth was large enough for chairs by the turf fire and sometimes there is a separate 'fire window' lighting it. In the chimney was fixed the rannel balk or cross beam at the level of the loft floor, and from it hung the racken crook, a chain with hooks for pots to hang at the desired height. By the fire stood the brandreth, an iron tripod used to support the girdle plate on which haver bread was baked. The original timber and plaster hoods have been replaced by stone chimney flues, and the oak mullions, which were never common, by sash windows.

The novelties in the house are the fittings, which reflect the pride and solid sense of craftsmanship of a stable and successful peasant community. The partition between house and parlour was framed with moulded posts and panels, and a cupboard, used principally or originally to store bread, was built into it. Occasionally the cupboard faced both ways, but usually little expense went into furnishing the parlour, since it was no more than the bedroom of the master and mistress. To the house side the cupboard presented two or three tiers, with carved panels and rails, often bearing the date. In the wall near the hearth was another small cupboard, usually called a spice cupboard (see pl. XVb). An aperture in the wall in a warm dry place was the traditional place for salt, but these spice cupboards are made decorative; the doors are carved and often dated. Most of the dated bread cupboards fall between 1670 and 1700 but the spice cupboards come a little later, between 1680 and 1710.[1]

The statesman's house has been described as though there were dozens of examples of one date and build, but it is rare to find one so. Even if a date on a doorhead appears to indicate a complete rebuilding, masonry from an earlier one is often incorporated. A porch might be added, or a down house. Cupboards were put into old houses. Many of the cupboards which have found their way into antique shops and so been dispersed all over England must have come from clay farmhouses now demolished. Whatever the detailed history of a particular fell side farmhouse, it falls into a pattern which obviously filled the mind of the statesman and his wife. It is remarkable how often a single parish may contain half a dozen houses with dates which show that building work was going on at the same time.[2] The demand for fitted cupboards was as insistent as that for a television set or a washing machine today. The difference was that the compulsion came from within the community, not from advertising media outside, and it shows how close knit this highland society still was.

However satisfied with its own standards, it was a society which was also receptive of improvements. Two were immediately possible: first, to improve the entrance to the dwelling and to separate it from the working part; second, to make easier access to the chambers. The first of these fell in line with the current conventions of lowland Britain, particularly the idea of a main entrance in the front giving on to house and parlour, and a balanced arrangement of door and window openings. Foulsyke in Nether Wasdale, Cumberland, (fig. 35) is an example, possibly from the first half of the eighteenth century, of the 'double fronted' house, which began to appear before 1700.[3] It may be thought of as descended from the two-unit house, or as a radical departure from the cross-passage plan. The other improvement, a better staircase, is also to be seen in Foulsyke. The commonest way of providing it was in an outshot which usually contained a service-room or two as well. Foulsyke has a back wing, making an L plan. The cow byre alongside is of one build with the house, extended later at

[1] R. W. Brunskill, *loc. cit.*

[2] E.g. houses in Holme dated 1676, 1686, 1693, 1695, 1698 and 1708; in Shap 1671, 1680, 1687, 1691 (2), 1694, 1696, 1704. R.C.H.M. *Westm.*, 113, 205.

[3] R. W. Brunskill, *loc. cit.*, 180–5. I am indebted to Mr. H. Ogle for lending me his drawings of Foulsyke.

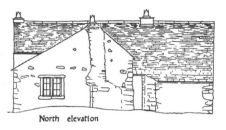

North elevation

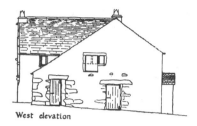

West elevation

FOULSYKE, NETHER WASDALE,
CUMBERLAND

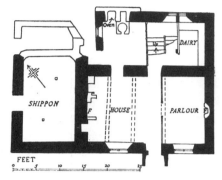

SHIPPON

HOUSE   PARLOUR

DAIRY

Oven

Up

FEET

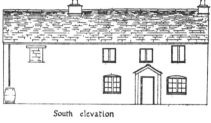

South elevation

FIGURE 35. Foulsyke, Nether Wastdale, Cumberland; a developed form of the types shown in fig. 34, for the house has a symmetrical front, and there is a storeyed cross wing instead of an outshot at the rear. The chamber over the shippon has been turned into a hay loft, the shippon itself has been extended, and a kitchen or scullery has been made in the rear wing. (After H. Ogle).

the back; the chamber over the byre has been turned into a hayloft. The parlour now has a fireplace and a room in the wing has become a scullery.

Now that the Lakeland farmer had at last become house-conscious and had satisfied his immediate wants by a whole-hearted adoption of medieval ideas, further wants could not be stemmed, and in the course of the eighteenth century the stages of development which we have already traced for lowland England were repeated. But that stage is beyond the scope of this book.[1]

There is no clear-cut distinction in type or size between the statesman's house and that of a wealthier farmer. The one merges into the other, with a more useful range of rooms in the outshot and cooking or brewing facilities in the third room. The fashion for ornamental plaster work, started by the highland gentry a hundred years earlier, reaches the level of quite small houses at this time. One of the unusual features of this age was

[1] R. W. Brunskill, *loc. cit.*, deals with the later stages in 185–9.

the 'spinning gallery'[1] an open balcony at first floor level, built of wood and sometimes furnished with turned balusters. Access is usually from outside. There has been much speculation about the origin and purpose of the spinning gallery, and attempts have been made to give it a Scandinavian origin, but this is unlikely since none of these galleries are earlier than this period. They must simply be an outcome of local conditions—a heavy rainfall, lack of storage space, and a readiness to build at two levels, as when a barn or hayloft was built over a cow byre. Most of the galleries face north, and cannot have been intended to catch sunlight. They were certainly used for hanging yarn to dry, and for spinning.

In a very few cases the parlour was fitted with box beds: that is beds which in the daytime were concealed as in a cupboard. They were common in Norway, and their rarity in northern England shows that Scandinavian influence no longer had any strength. The cupboard doors in a house at Waitby dated 1690 have openings at the top filled with turned balusters,[2] and that way of providing for the ventilation of a cupboard or buttery was not uncommon in 1650–1700. These Waitby beds are in the parlour. The point of beds in a cupboard was to make more space in the day time, as with the trundle bed which pushed under a standing bed. The only other examples which have come to notice are in the house of a shoemaker of Pocklington, Yorks., in 1696.[3] They were still to be found in a single-roomed cottage at Egton in Cleveland c. 1870[4], and they have of course remained common in Scotland.

[1] See R. W. McDowall, *loc. cit.*, 132.; J. Walton, 'Upland Houses' in *Antiquity*, 30 (1956), 145–7, where fourteen examples are listed, and H. S. Cowper, *Hawkshead*, 157. There are surviving examples at Bampton, Low Hartop near Patterdale, Mardale, Troutbeck and Windermere.

[2] H.M.C. *Westm.*, 234 and pl. 59.

[3] York Registry, Deanery Peculiars, bundle 1697, Thomas Linton, whose goods included 2 beds in the cupboard in the house', i.e. in the living-room.

[4] J. C. Atkinson, *Forty Years in a Moorland Parish* (1923), 19.

Conclusion

In the generation following the Restoration the contrast between high-land and lowland zones is even more pronounced than at earlier times. In both, the amount of new building is at least as great as before. In the lowlands, however, the traveller through time is conscious of having crossed a watershed and caught his first glimpse of a modern social land-scape. He sees a rural society on the move, both physically and meta-phorically, to a degree that was new and modern. The new inns that now lined the main roads have been referred to. They must have accommodated the gentry, passing from country house to London residence, and church-men about diocesan business; brickmakers and masons, plumbers and glaziers, painters and joiners on the way to a new job, and tailors and shoemakers on a round of farmhouses, with their rolls of cloth and baskets of boot lasts. All these travellers carried new ideas of living and spending.

Farming on a larger and more productive scale was thrusting more and more yeomen and husbandmen out of the lower levels of the social pyramid into its middle tiers. Social status and economic means were no longer tied so closely to houses of a particular size and style, for new wealth might come more rapidly than a taste for a new way of life. It was no longer unusual to find a wealthy yeoman living in a small house or a poor husbandman in a large one.

Two aspects of this nascent modernity are particularly apparent. One is a readiness to adopt new habits: to have a house built of brick instead of timber; to smoke tobacco, and to buy imported foodstuffs such as sugar which had hitherto been a luxury only for the wealthy. The other is the greater gulf between the ways of rich and poor even within the limited range of the rural community. Among the rich the service-rooms are still being made more convenient for the family and for entertainment. The divergence shows best in the status of the parlour. In better-off farm-houses, especially in the south east, it was at last becoming a room in which the family sat and took its meals. In more remote areas and in cottages everywhere it was still and long remained the principal bedroom.

In the north the growth of new houses sprang entirely from medieval roots. That was no less true in the West Riding, where the woollen industry was putting more money than ever into the pockets of farmers, than it was in Westmorland, where there was virtually no industry of any kind, or Durham, where the coal industry had no direct links with agriculture. We shall see in the next chapter how distinctively northern houses of William III's time reveal their highland ancestry, but in the main the contrast between north and south was due to disparities of wealth. The differences can be put into monetary figures derived from contemporary estimates.[1] They show that if a Kent householder was assessed to pay 9s. in taxation on a particular occasion, the corresponding figure for Cumberland was 8½d. When the counties of England are arranged in order of wealth, the result is also a geographical order, with south eastern counties at the head of the list and Durham and Cumberland at the foot. The only exceptions are Dorset, Somerset and Devon. The figures are not necessarily real, but they give striking confirmation, out of contemporary ideas, of what has been said about lowland wealth and highland poverty, and also of the exceptional position of the South-Western counties.

[1]See V. F. Snow, 'Parliamentary Reapportionment Proposals in the Puritan Revolution' in *E.H.R.* (1959), 406–36. Thorold Rogers, *History of Agriculture and Prices*, V, 120–1.

Part Five

THE DEATH OF THE VERNACULAR TRADITION

Introduction

THERE are several reasons for rounding off this survey with a review of conditions in the years 1690–1725. The first is that there was less new building from 1725–60 than at any time since 1550, to judge from the number of dated houses. In some regions at least there was a minor agricultural recession and in the lull which that caused, the vernacular styles of the sixteenth century quietly disappeared. The innovations which began in the Tudor period have now won general acceptance, and no newer ones made any significant impact on the lowland village until the later years of the eighteenth century. Then the final enclosure of open field systems set off another major phase of building which must await another chronicler.

The types of dwelling popular in the sixteenth and seventeenth centuries because they met widely felt needs were displaced in popular esteem by the products of a new, literate type of builder, who could reproduce in miniature or diluted form the features which, for want of a better term, are called the Renaissance style. The first guide of that kind was Moxon's *Mechanick Exercise,* published in 1682. There was a flood of such works in the Georgian period, and the farmhouse and cottage were, to one degree or another, modified to fit their mould. Under the influence of such fashionable and bookish styles, whose impact varied from class to class and region to region, the local styles of the seventeenth century everywhere succumbed sooner or later. The most drastic change was in those parts where the regional style had developed out of a medieval tradition, such as that of the cross passage, or the hall and cross wing plan.

In these circumstances a regional survey of lowland England in the time of Anne and George I has less to commend it than before. Social distinctions, between rich farmer and smallholder, are more important than differences between one county or another. The accumulation of land in the hands of fewer farmers, and the dispossession of the small proprietor, had by now set a similar mark on rural society throughout the counties south of a line from the Wash to the Bristol Channel, to a degree that seems more significant than any differences between any of them.

243

Another practical reason for disregarding county or regional boundaries is that the documentary material is now too plentiful for summary treatment. Several counties about which nothing has been said in earlier chapters, such as Dorset, East Sussex, Hereford and Middlesex have collections of inventories beginning between 1660 and 1700. They await study, and it would be foolhardy to treat this much more voluminous material in summary fashion.

The distinctions which remain valid, and important, are between lowland and highland England, and between those two and an intermediate zone on either side of their common frontier. Ways of life and standards of wealth were still more different than any variation from region to region within either zone. The time lag between the two parts which had been a significant factor ever since the Stone Age was never more remarkable than now, for the great rebuilding reached its peak in Westmorland in the years 1680–1725, a century later than in the lowlands. For all these reasons the last phase will be described in two sections: the lowland and the highland zones.

CHAPTER ONE

The Lowland Zone

AFTER 1660 the population had recovered from whatever check it received in the previous half century, and one of its aspects must have been increasing longevity. The housing of old people was no new problem for the rural community, but by the end of the seventeenth century the aged formed a much more distinct element than ever before. Apart from the establishment of almshouses, such as the charming group built in Denton Park, Lincs., by William Welby in 1653 (see pl. XXIIa), or the combined school and almshouses at Clifton, Notts., built in 1709, the smallest cottages in the village served an increasingly useful purpose in housing them. Some almshouses were single-storey buildings such as the group at Chilton Canteloe, Somerset, and the Well Almshouses at Clifton, Notts., or those at Benington, Lincs., built in 1728. The Willoughby Almshouses at Cossall, Notts., founded in 1685, are of two storeys in the local brick style, and most were no doubt on that scale, with one room downstairs, with a larder perhaps under the stairs, and one chamber above. The one-roomed house, chambered over, was the standard adopted for them because that was the minimum acceptable to the village at large.

Almshouses, like schools of this age, often strike a new architectural note, because the founder was usually a member of the gentry and not a member of the classes which maintained the vernacular tradition. Welby's building at Denton is of stone with elaborate gables in a style not approached in any farmhouse near by; the almshouses at Clifton and Cossall have architectural pretensions in their design, though the detail is traditional.

When the parish officers had to build for the poor, the cheapest traditional methods were good enough. The village of Saleby, Lincs., built in 1686 a cottage for an old man who had kept the alehouse there for fifty years. Sentiment reinforced legal obligation, but the cottage only cost £19 14s. It was of mud and stud, and two bays, for the account included six bay stones to place below the principal upright timbers. They were only poles, and fifty were used in all. The other material included straw for thatching and rush rope to bind it, and 6s. 10d. worth of nails. Bread and ale were provided, as usual, when the house was raised, and then Goodman Young was paid £1 18s. 6d. (the largest single item after the £2 2s. 6d. for carpenters' work) 'for the earth making and the house walling and the chimney'. 'Making' the earth meant mixing it; another man had spent four days with a horse and cart 'drawing up earth' from a suitable field.[1] Many villages still possess cottages built by the parish for its poor, sometimes on the manorial waste or common,[2] and they usually belong to the late seventeenth or to the eighteenth century. For such purposes, methods and materials remained unchanged from the end of the Middle Ages to the end of the eighteenth century.[3] When open fields were enclosed and a new pattern of farmsteads was created, new cottages were also needed, and traditional methods received, for a short time at least, a new lease of life. Arthur Young, writing in 1799, recommended building in mud and stud because of its cheapness. 'They will at Frieston build a cottage of mud and stud for £30. Mr. Linton showed me four he had built . . .; one set of mud and stud and thatch, the other brick and tile; the two former cost £40, the two latter £60.'[4]

The comments of the travellers who, following Celia Fiennes and Daniel Defoe, began to publish descriptions of England, reflected this duality in the visual appearance of the villages of eastern England. They remarked on the contrast between the older houses of mud and stud and thatch, and the new ones of brick and tile.[5] The brick-built farmhouse must have been a commonplace by the early years of the eighteenth century, but before about 1775 the distinction between brick and older materials was largely a social difference, between farmhouse and cottage.

Hitherto in our account the steady dispossession of smallholders and

[1] *Lincs. N. and Q.*, XVIII (1925), 30.
[2] E.g. at Lambourne, V.C.H. *Essex*, IV, 85.
[3] E.g. accounts of repairs at Owersby, Lincs., in 1684 include the cost of daubing the walls; L.R.O., Monson Accounts 10/3/21/3. The Overseers' Accounts of Brant Broughton, Lincs. include in 1788 the cost of 'a load of clay leading to Widow Vickerstaf's house' and 'to daubing Pen Freake's house'; Poor of Broughton Book 1785–1815.
[4] *General View of the Agriculture of . . . Lincoln* (1799), 35–36.
[5] E.g. the (rather inaccurate) comments of Celia Fiennes (*Journal*, ed. C. Morris, 7–13); those of Thomas Quincey in 1772–4 (*Short Tour of the Midland Counties* (1775), 26).

the engrossment of land has been no more than an implicit element. It must have been a very powerful factor in the great rebuilding from Tudor times, for, as has recently been pointed out, engrossing was as great an evil as enclosure to Tudor legislators.[1] Its consequences were twofold. The growing demand for larger farmhouses, with more room for dealing with and storing agricultural produce from larger farms, has been our main theme. The other side of the medal is that dwellings which had been farmhouses became cottages; their barns and cowhouses were allowed to decay, and small farmhouses became cottages let at rent to men who now sought employment for a wage. The housing of the farm worker was provided either by his own effort, in building on the waste—and that sort of self help only ceased in the Victorian age—or by his renting a house from his employer or another property owner. At some stage the large farmer must have found that he could not get or keep his labour force without building cottages for them. This stage, the beginning of the tied cottage, is of great social importance, but is singularly difficult to date from documents. When one searches through any southern or midland village, the problem is to distinguish between rows of cottages built as such, and houses, barns or other buildings converted into cottages. It is usually difficult to put a date to such conversions, beyond saying that it was perhaps done in a particular century. An example from Nottinghamshire is a barn at Lenton, built in 1696 and neatly converted, by quartering, into four small houses. The blocked great doors and ventilation slits reveal that it started as a barn. It was converted c. 1800 and demolished in 1959.

Most rows of cottages belong to the later years of the eighteenth century, like the row at Bletchingdon, Oxon., dated 1794. There are thirteen cottages in it—too many for a single farmer, one would think, and perhaps put up as a speculation when housing was peculiarly short. A semi-detached pair at Alvington, Somerset, dated 1706, must belong to a significantly early phase of this development. They are built of Ham stone, in the local vernacular style; that is, with mullioned windows (all with hollow chamfer mouldings except one which has ovolo moulding) and one hood mould embracing all the ground floor openings. They are of two storeys. In eastern England there is a row of about eight cottages at Boxworth, Cambs., south-east of the Golden Ball Inn, probably c. 1730 or soon after (see plate XXb). Unlike the Alvington cottages these are of one and a half storeys only (like those at Bletchingdon) with dormer windows in the thatched roof. Their most dateable feature is the treatment of the brick gables, which have tumbled copings, and a gable-end window with imposts and hood in raised bricks; they belong, that is, to the last phase of ornamental brickwork in the

[1]Joan Thirsk, *Tudor Enclosures* (Hist. Ass., 1959) 12.

eastern counties. Another row at Litlington, Cambs., is of much the same period.[1]

Three examples are a slender basis for a generalization of such importance, but it seems safe to say that building cottages to let was rare before 1700. This coincides with other evidence. The farm worker only needed a cottage when he married. Till then it was cheaper and more convenient for his employer to have him living in. We have met yeomen's houses with chambers or parlours for servants from the Elizabethan period onwards, but they become much more common after 1660. The enclosure of Norfolk open fields, which represented the final phase in the dispossession of the small landholder, began to assume significant proportions at that time.[2] The inventories from Writtle, Essex, contain only two instances between 1635–40 and 1658–71, but in 1672–90 there are fifteen.[3] By 1690 nearly every Kentish yeoman's house had a servants' chamber, though they were rare in 1660.[4] What accomodation the farmer needed for his workers depended on his special line. Sheep farming was economical of labour, but arable farming needed ploughmen and boys, dairy farming needed maids to milk and make cheese. In the Trent valley the great growth of dairy farming in the early seventeenth century was reflected in the appearance of men's parlours and maids' parlours in inventories of wealthier yeomen and husbandmen. Flora Thompson described in *Lark Rise* an Oxfordshire village of c. 1875 in which every boy and girl left home for service in a country house or a farmhouse. That pattern of life was imposed by population and employment conditions from the seventeenth century onwards, and particularly after c. 1675. It collapsed with the change in the relations of town and country two centuries later. Much that has seemed characteristic of rural life sprang from it: the relationship between classes; high standards of housewifery; festivals when the young people returned home for a few days' holiday; entertainments such as mumming and plough boys' plays—and a high rate of illegitimate births.

[1] I understand that the Hist. Mon. Comm. investigators have found pairs of semi-detached cottages of the seventeenth century in the same county. It may be remarked that in the older inventories published by the Commission (e.g. for Essex, Bucks. and Hunts.) in days when only buildings earlier than 1714 were included, no rows of cottages are mentioned.

[2] K. J. Allison in *Agr. Hist. R.*, 5 (1957), 28–29.

[3] E.g. the Men's Chamber in the house of Abraham Brecknock, yeoman (no. 74); the Maids' Chamber in one house of Francis Taverner, yeoman and a Maids' Chamber as well as a Men's Chamber 'in his farm called Reads' (no. 79); *Essex Inventories*, 123, 128.

[4] Maidstone R..O, PRC 11/54; nine of the eleven inventories of men with goods valued at more than £170 had at least one servants' chamber. In a sample dated 1663 (PRC 11/21) there are only three instances in the twenty wealthiest homes.

In these circumstances the farmer and his wife found it more necessary to use the garrets for sleeping as well as for storage. Jacob Aldrich, a rich yeoman of Walberswick, Suffolk, who died in 1685, had a bed in his vance roof[1]—no doubt for a servant—and so had William Garnon of Brant Broughton, Lincs., in 1672 (see Appendix p. 280). From about 1700 onwards farmhouses in the eastern counties often have small dormer windows high in the roof. They may be seen as far north as the Lincolnshire Fens, but in the rest of Lincolnshire they are rare before 1775, and never common. They reflect the growing labour needs of large scale arable farming. Equally characteristic of East Anglia is the mansard roof: that is, the pitched roof in two slopes, the lower nearly vertical to give more headroom. It is the latest borrowing by the country builder from Flemish sources, and it occurs as far north-west as Stamford, but not beyond. Nearly every farmhouse in the east Midlands has evidence that the garrets were used as bedrooms at some time: for instance a Jacobean fireplace moved into the attic of Manor Farm, Stretton, Rutland, or the underside of the rafters plastered and a few glass pantiles inserted at the Old Hall, North Muskham.

To the observers of *c*. 1800 the main distinction from the point of view of social conditions was between those villages which were open, where land could be bought or rented for building, and those which were closed, belonging to one owner who could control building. From the early years of the eighteenth century the closed village began to assume the uniform pattern of one owner, employing masons or brickmakers. The practice may well have spread from East Anglia since the Norfolk landlord had accepted responsibility for repairs since at latest the early seventeenth century,[2] and Walpole was one of the first landowners to rebuild houses and cottages on an extensive scale. By the 1730's however several landowners were following his example: Lord Howe at Langar, Sir Thomas Parkyns at Bunny and John Emerton at Thrumpton, all in the one county of Nottinghamshire (see fig. 36).

In the open village those who could afford to do so employed a builder, and others built for themselves, as they always had done. The squatters' cottages of turf which could be seen in counties south of the Thames a hundred years ago have now disappeared. There still remain cottages built on the newly allotted freeholds of the nineteenth century enclosures, in the manner that George Bourne described.[3] Writing of a Surrey hamlet

[1]Suffolk Public Library, Archdeaconry Inventories, N6/5/2.
[2]See W. Marshall, *Rural Economy of Norfolk*, I, 66. Bailiff's accounts for East Rainham 1637–43 include various payments for repairs (Norwich Public Library).
[3]*Change in the Village* (1955 edition) 85, describing the effects of the enclosure of the common in 1861.

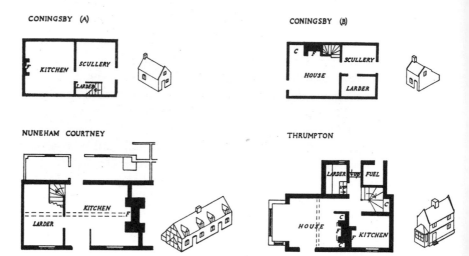

FIGURE 36. Detached and semi-detached cottages. Coningsby (A) stands on the edge of the Lincolnshire fens and is probably *c.* 1700; (B), further into the fens, is perhaps *c.* 1800. Nuneham Courtney, Oxon. (after D. Portman), is part of the rebuilding of the village early in George III's reign. Notice that the gable ends are still timber-framed. The cottage at Thrumpton, Nottinghamshire, is part of the rebuilding of that village by John Emmerton, and is dated 1735. It has the lofty proportions of midland brick building.

half a century ago, he was the last discerning witness to the qualities of self-reliance and self-respect which had formerly been the mark of the village community. The chance to take a pride in craftsmanship had vanished with the loss of land and opportunity. The mud-walled and thatched cottages which can still be seen in parts of east Dorset, scattered in a modern field system, are traditional in scale and materials; but their interiors are quite devoid of the workmanship and finish of, say, houses of similar size built in Monmouthshire in the seventeenth century.

So much for the economic changes of the years after 1675 and their effect on building. Within the house, the living pattern which had developed during the seventeenth century shows no sign of modification, although in some regions new names for rooms were supplanting the old. The principal social distinction was between houses with a parlour and those without. How common the latter class was in any county in the period from 1688 to 1775 only further research could show. The new rows of cottages were usually of that type: one room wide with a second small service-room, made within the usual depth of 18 feet or so (see pl. XXIIb), or else at a later stage in an outshot. A pair of semi-detached cottages at West Mudford, near Yeovil, dated 1728, built of lias limestone

XXIa. A part of Long Lee, Rowarth, Derbyshire, showing John Hyde's initials and the date 1661 over the porch, and mullioned windows typical of Pennine houses. See p. 231.

XXIb. Such farmhouses as this at Little Horton Green, Bradford, Yorks., with a house and barn in one range, became common *c.* 1750 and must be derived from the long house. Note the opening over the barn door for loading hay into the loft.

XXIIa. Almshouses built in 1653 for Sir George Welby in the park at Denton, Lincs., by an unknown architect. See p. 215.

XXIIb. One of the earliest known rows of cottages, at Boxworth, Cambs. The date must be *c.* 1730, to judge from the treatment of the gable end (note the tumbling) but the history of the row is unknown. See p. 247.

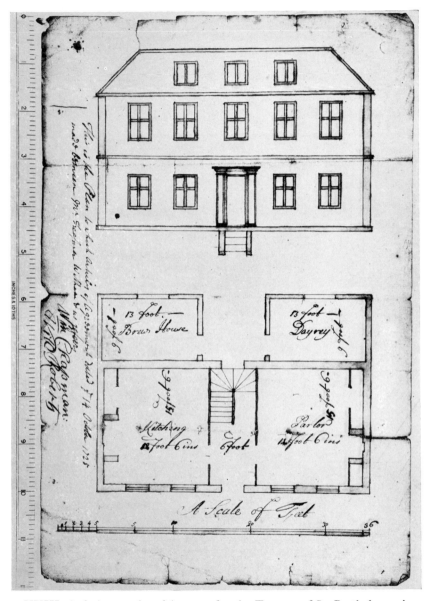

XXIII. A design produced in 1725 for the Trustees of St. Bartholomew's Hospital, London, for erection on their estate at Bottisham, Cambs. The elevation is more imposing than the simple plan, which has only hall (now called kitchen, and divided from the entrance lobby), parlour and two service rooms. The estimated cost, with farm buildings, was £417.

XXIVa. Single storey cottages of stone at Silloth, Camb., of the 18th century or even later.

XXIVb. The change from mud building to stone in west Cumberland signalised by the name of Stone House Farm, built at Moorhouse in 1706. The barn beyond still has a gable wall of mud, though the side walls have been rebuilt in stone.

with lofty mullioned windows in Ham stone, has a hall-kitchen in front
and a scullery behind; the two houses share an axial stack. The easiest
way to improve this design was to make it deeper from back to front, and
during the course of the eighteenth century that was done by reducing the
pitch of the roof so that rafters of the same length would span a larger
building. That in its turn depended on the use of lighter and more im-
pervious roofing materials: clay tile instead of stone or thatch.

Even the double-fronted cottage may in fact have only a hall-kitchen
with a service-room at the other side of the entrance. During the eighteenth
century, the village of Nuneham Courtney, south-east of Oxford, was rebuilt by Earl Harcourt farther away from his new mansion, and fig. 36
shows the plan of one of the semi-detached cottages which line the new
village street. It had originally only two rooms, with two small bedrooms
over lighted by dormer windows. In 1809 these cottages were thought 'just
what they ought to be, comfortable but unostentatious'.[1] Their accommodation matches the house of John Hunt, labourer, of Kirdford, Sussex,
described in an inventory of 1685: Kitchen (i.e. hall), drinkhouse and milkhouse, with chambers over kitchen and milkhouse.[2]

The non-parlour type of cottage is common in the Lincolnshire Fens;
although one calls them cottages because they are rarely accompanied by
a barn or other typical farm buildings, they were the homes of smallholders, and new ones have been built in this century simply because they
belong to a mode of life still viable on that rich soil. There is one of *c.*1700
at Coningsby Moorside: that is, on the very edge of the peat fen (see fig.
36). Most of them are *c.* 1820 or later. They have a living-room and a small
service-room either under the main roof (in the earlier example) or in an
outshot. The contrast between such smallholders' dwellings and the average farmhouse was so obvious to contemporaries that a two-storey farmhouse of c. 1725–50 nearby was named High House Farm.

By 1700, East Anglian labourers and craftsmen living in such houses
had ceased to use the medieval term hall for their living-room. A few spoke
of the 'low room', an appropriate name for a cottage of the kind described
in the previous paragraph. Richard Swallow, yeoman, of Filby, had only a
low room, a buttery and a chamber. The term 'low room' was much used
by Yarmouth people living in the single-unit, storeyed houses in the Rows,[3]
and no doubt spread from there to the country districts. A few others still

[1]W. Mavor, *General View of the Agriculture of Berkshire* (1809).

[2]G. H. Kenyon 'Kirdford Inventories 1611–1776' in *Sussex Arch. Coll.* 93
(1955), 134.

[3]See H.B. St. J. O'Neil, 'Seventeenth Century Houses in Gt. Yarmouth,' *Arch.*
95, (1953), especially figures 1–4.

called it the fire-house or the fire-room, again people who had single-unit houses with a bedroom upstairs. One of them was Robert Mingay, weaver, of Ditchingham, but the inventory fails to make clear where his two looms were. Another was Edward Calton, husbandman, Attleborough: useful proof that this tiny house was not confined to labourers, mariners and craftsmen. With a family of any size, someone had to sleep in the firehouse. Richard Mingay had two bedsteads upstairs in the chamber and a third downstairs.

South of the Thames and in Essex the term hall was still in common use, but in Norfolk and Suffolk it had virtually disappeared by 1700 among all classes. Instead of hall and kitchen, we meet kitchen and backhouse, or even kitchen and back kitchen.[1] The parlour is the room of highest status, and the appraisers were taken into it first. When they found themselves in a farmhouse in which the parlour was still used as a bedroom, they were at a loss, and called it the bed house.[2] In these years after 1675 the whole range of medieval terminology for parts of the house is disappearing, except for the parlour. The milkhouse has gone, and dairy taken its place. The buttery is still there, but the name pantry occurs sometimes. The chamber used for sleeping becomes a bedroom.[3]

We have commented on the appearance of inns as a symptom of the collapse of rural isolation and also as a new element in rural building. Another new amenity in the village was the retail shop. Hitherto the countryman had been content to go to the market town for those needs which could not be met by his wife's skill, his own ingenuity or by the village craftsman. After 1660 the shopkeeper appears, sometimes in the most unlikely neighbourhood, and stocking the remarkable range of goods which, until the advent of the bus and the private car, made him an essential member of the community. His appearance had no direct effect on village building, but he set in train a revolution in living standards and domestic comforts, and so contributed to new modes of thought and behaviour in which medieval survivals could not flourish. It was worth his while to set up shop in a village because there was more money in the pocket of the average farmer; after 1660 the increase in the value of goods and

[1]Out of twenty-eight inventories dated 1674–92, one mentions a hall (Archdeaconry of Norfolk Collection, Norwich Public Library, case 33, shelf D, bundle 1674–92). The back kitchen occurs in the inventories of a Norwich clothier (1692), a butcher of Gaywood (1693) and a mariner of Bungay (1727).

[2]Norwich Consistory, inventory of Thomas Cooper of Felthorpe, 1727. The inventory includes the bedhouse, the kitchen and the chamber, the last used for ripening cheeses.

[3]The earliest example of bedroom noted is dated 1727, in the inventory of Hannah Watson of North Runcton.

chattels, as reflected in inventories, outpaces very distinctly the trend of prices.

Joseph Clarke of Roxwell, Essex, grocer and draper, is a good example of the new phenomenon.[1] When such men died, their executors naturally needed to know the precise value of their goods, and so there are scores of such inventories, in local collections, from which one can see what the villager thought he needed, and what luxuries he was beginning to be aware of. The shop at Roxwell had the usual range of mercery, haberdashery and grocery. At Kegworth, Leics., a large industrial village, Thomas Morrison kept a much more interesting shop, in the last years of the seventeenth century. He had crockery: large jugs and small, porringers, 'white pots'. He could supply the home cobbler with small hobnails (11,000 of them!), or with large, with sprigs or 'sparables'; for the housewife he had various lines in haberdashery—buttons, ribbons— as well as mercery—serge, crepe, ticking, fustian or black printed calico. He had got a stock of books for the pupils at the grammar school: Testaments, Latin grammar books and the like. There was ironmongery (fireshovels and tongs), spices of many kinds, tobacco for the smoker and 'dust' for the snuff taker, castle (Castile) soap, washballs and tallow for the housewife, 'horse spice and jollop' for the farmer: everything in fact for the everyday needs of the community. These village shopkeepers are descended from the medieval chapmen (see inventory of a chapwoman, dated c. 1672, in Appendix p. 280).[2] Now there was sufficient demand for them to stay at home and carry a much wider stock of goods.

In this age when the products of the Old and the New Worlds could be bought over the counter of any village shop, the village builder could not, even if he would, keep at bay the new fashions which were invading his sphere. He had to make two innovations. First, the farmer who wanted a new house expected it now to have a symmetrical, two-storey elevation. Hitherto the Renaissance idea of symmetry had gained virtually no hold, except that, in the stone belt, masons had long been ready to arrange the windows of a gable end in symmetrical tiers, reducing the size at each storey. But even he made no concessions as far as the façade was concerned, since the three unit plan, with a cross passage, threw it out of balance. After 1700 farmhouses began to spring up with a balanced façade, especially with a doorway flanked by two windows on either side, and five

[1] *Essex Inventories*, 213.
[2] The inventory of Ursula Thomson of Gt. Limber, Lincs., dated 1649, included mercery and haberdashery, but she was called 'petty chapman' which means that she had a travelling business as well as a shop (L.R.O., inventories 155/103). There were such chapmen still in eighteenth century Sussex.

windows on the first floor (see pl. XXIII). Not many of them have been planned, but one type, of which there are examples as far apart as Lincolnshire and Monmouthshire,[1] both dated c. 1700, had only two rooms in the main range, hall and parlour. The entrance was to the hall, which thus occupied three-fifths of the range. Such an arrangement called for either a double plan (as in fig. 31), with a parallel range of rooms behind, or a wing at right angles. Vanbrugh designed the manor house at Somersby, Lincs., as a double house,[2] and all these three are socially at the top of the scale we are concerned with. Before the eighteenth century was more than a quarter gone, the symmetrical façade, with or without a double plan, was becoming a commonplace for larger farmhouses. In south Nottinghamshire alone there are half a dozen examples, all of double plan. That at East Leake is dated 1715 on one gable and 1728 on the other; a house at Langar, now the Unicorn's Head, is dated 1717, and Manor Farm, Ratcliffe on Soar, is 1715. The earliest in the county is the school at South Leverton, founded in 1691.

The second innovation at this time arises from the general desire to have a framed staircase without the necessity of building a wing for it. With an axial stack taking up much of the centre of the house this was impossible. The alternative was to move the fireplaces, and so the eastern tradition of the axial stack gives way, and fireplaces are placed at the gable ends. Manor Farm, Grassthorpe, Notts., had that arrangement in 1697. By the 1730's small farmhouses were being built with a symmetrical façade of three bays (i.e. central doorway flanked by one window on either side), with hall and parlour with gable end fireplaces, and between them a staircase rising opposite the entrance. Plate XXIII shows the plan and elevation of a house which St. Bartholomew's Hospital proposed to build at Bottisham, Cambs., in 1725, for £417.[3]

A third change is not so much an innovation as the culmination of a long process. The kitchen had by this time become a necessary part of the house. Although plenty of detached kitchens still stood, and were no doubt still being used,[4] it is very doubtful if any new ones were built after 1700.

[1] Manor Farm, Somersby, Lincs.; a house at Fulbeck, Lincs., and Treworgan, Llandenny, Mon., illustrated in *Mon. Ho.*, III, 103, fig. 60.

[2] Although the house may be thought outside the range of this book, it is in fact no larger than many a farmhouse, and Vanbrugh's details (battlemented parapet, vaulted ceiling to the hall, etc.) are quite out of proportion. See L. Whistler, *Sir John Vanbrugh, Architect and Dramatist* (1938), 300.

[3] The specifications as well as this plan, are preserved among the archives at St. Bartholomew's Hospital, Box 11, bundle II, No. 38.

[4] Parsonage terriers refer to detached kitchens at Thurcaston, Leics. (1709), Oakley, Beds. (1708), and no doubt other examples could be found.

Even so, the habit of thinking of the kitchen as distinct from the house persisted into the eighteenth century. A contract was signed in 1729 for rebuilding a farmhouse in Gosberton, Lincs., on a site already known as Monk's Hall.[1] It was a small farmhouse, and was to have two 'low' rooms (i.e. ground floor rooms), the hall and the parlour. The parlour was to have a cellar under it. The fireplace in each room was to have a closet on either side—another common feature by this time. The chambers over were to have fireplaces, and the garret, the full length of the front, was to be lighted by three 'lucarn' (lucerne or dormer) windows. Transom windows were specified for the main rooms, four downstairs and five above: that is, the house was to be of the new symmetrical, five-bay design, with dormers in the East Anglian manner. One imagines that this is all, but the contract then goes on: 'And to erect and build another room for a kitchen . . . to adjoin to the front building and to have a communication therewith . . .' William Sands, a well known local architect of Spalding,[2] provided a 'plan or form', and this farmhouse must be one of the first in which a known architect can be shown to have had a hand.

So much for the new designs which emerge out of the new needs shaped in the seventeenth century. Travellers riding through the villages of lowland England saw them as made up of new (brick) houses and old, but if they had looked more closely they would have observed every variety between. This comes out clearly in descriptions of parsonage houses. Broadly speaking the parochial clergy had had little part in the rebuilding of the later part of the seventeenth century. Their needs as married men had been borne in on them sharply at first, and once they had built a family house most of them were content with minor improvements. There are of course exceptions in every decade. The parsonage house at Worlaby, Lincs., was burned down in 1674 and was promptly rebuilt in brick. At Epworth the rectory, 'of mud and plaster', from which young John Wesley was rescued, was replaced by a brick house costing £400.[3] The vicarage at Westbury, Bucks., was rebuilt in stone in 1661, and that at Lathbury was described in 1709 as 'a new house built with brick and stone and covered with tile'.[4] Other parsonage houses came down in the world if there was no resident vicar. That at Ancaster, Lincs., a stone house of four bays in 1605, was in 1822 'a small old cottage, having been occupied by Mechanics and Labourers time immemorial'. There was no resident parson at Alkborough, near the Humber, because by 1709 'the vicarage house is

[1]Appendix p. 272. The house has been rebuilt again.
[2]See H. M. Colvin, *Dictionary of English Architects*.
[3]*Ass. Arch. Soc. Reports and Papers*, 18 (1885–6), 19.
[4]L.R.O., Terriers 19; H. M. C. *Bucks.* II, 315.

dilapidated and all the materials whereof it was built removed many years since'.[1]

A series of terriers for Bedfordshire and Buckinghamshire provides a detailed description of nearly every parsonage house in each county[2] (see map fig. 37). There had been little change in materials in the stone region at the north-west of the two counties, but elsewhere the invasion of brick is clearly shown, particularly in Buckinghamshire. Very few houses were yet built entirely of brick, but the older houses, variously described as built of timber, studwork, stud and clay, timber and clay, were in many instances now patched or filled with brick—whether original or a renewal one cannot always tell from parsons' words. At Battlesden, Beds., there was 'a framed building the walls filled up with brick'; at Hockliffe the house was 'of timber (oak), the walls some brick some clay, the covering tiles'; at Totternhoe it was 'built partly with brick and partly with timber with clay walls'. The rector of Farnham Royal, Bucks., told the archdeacon that 'the house is a timber frame and the lath and plastering being decayed I have brick panelled it all over'. Even if few parsons saw the need to rebuild their residences, replacing the old filling—described as clay, earth, loam, or 'whitearth' (a Buckinghamshire dialect word, commonly 'witch-ert') or 'tearing' (another local word)—was a matter of routine which could now be done best in brick. Those who expressed dissatisfaction with their official residence could not afford to do anything about it. The vicar of Shitlington, Beds., included 'one cottage, vulgarly called the vicarage house', in his return of 'all that Papa-Caesareo Diabolical Sacriledge has left to the vicar of Shitlington'.[3]

In Lincolnshire the use of brick had made less headway, and since houses of mud and stud commonly had the frame embodied in the walling and not exposed, there was no question of panelling with brick. Instead the old walls were cased in brick, either throughout their height or up to window sill height. Others were 'groundsealed' or 'footed' with brick, or the chimneys were 'headed' with brick.[4] Just as in the southern Midlands some panelling is an original feature of new houses of this period, so in the

[1] Unless otherwise stated, these Lincolnshire examples come from unbound terriers, L.R.O.

[2] Those for Bedfordshire are at the Bedford Record Office, bound in two volumes, ABE 2, and transcripts were made by Mrs. Brenda Hull. I am indebted to Mrs. Hull and to the archivist, Miss Joyce Godber, for depositing the transcripts at Nottingham for my benefit. It is much to be hoped that the Bedfordshire Historical Record Society will one day publish them. The Buckinghamshire terriers are in L.R.O., Terriers 19.

[3] L.R.O., terriers 15, 1703.

[4] L.R.O., terriers of Barrow on Humber (1693), S. Ferriby (1707), Theddle-thorpe St. Helens (1707), Cumberworth (1709).

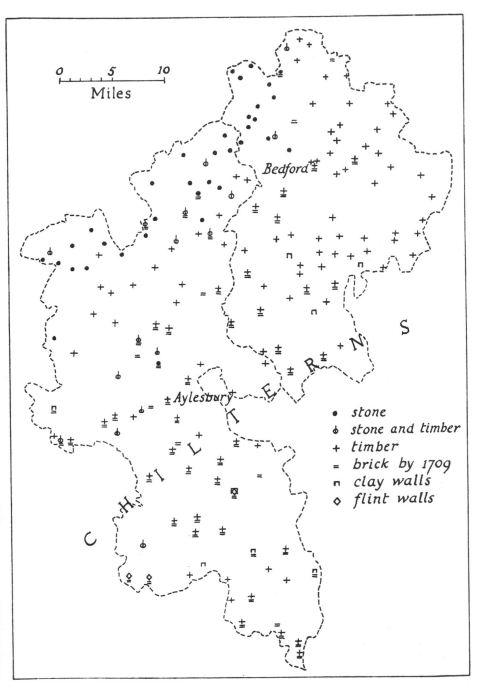

FIGURE 37. Map of Buckinghamshire and Bedfordshire showing building materials in use in the seventeenth century according to parsonage terriers.

east Midlands new houses were erected with brick walls to sill height or thereabouts and mud and stud above.[1]

These contemporary comments are a useful reminder that the transition from timber to brick walling was a gradual process. The cottages at Nuneham Courtney, Oxon., display a stage reached *c.* 1730–40. The side walls are one brick thick (i.e. 9 inches), and the gable walls only half a brick (4½ inches), with a rather slight timber frame as an essential, and not merely ornamental, part of their construction.

In Bedfordshire and Lincolnshire we are able to see how rooms were floored in Queen Anne's time. Earthen floors were still very much the rule rather than the exception; in either county, but especially Lincolnshire, some houses could be found with nothing else, and most houses still had a few rooms like that. The next best thing was brick, and about half the Lincolnshire houses had one room so paved. It was usually the hall. In Bedfordshire the majority of halls were paved, and so were about half the kitchens. Occasionally a parson had decided to have white bricks,[2] very much a novelty in 1700, for they only came into widespread use for building after 1730.[3] In the stone region, bricks were out of the question, for none were made locally, so it was a matter of either earth or stone paving. A few houses still had cobbled floors in a kitchen or a brewhouse.[4]

Earth or brick floors, however hard and clean, were at best cold and no doubt often damp. The one room in which a warmer, drier floor was fashionable was the parlour, and about two houses in three had a boarded floor there. In some cases it was boarded because it had a cellar under. A boarded floor also kept out damp, and the country builder was already used to laying boarded floors in barns for that reason. The idea of wainscotting the parlour was just reaching the social level to which the village parson belonged. In Bedfordshire some downstairs rooms were ceiled, particularly the parlour: that is underdrawn with plaster, so that warmth did not escape upwards. In Lincolnshire that precaution was unnecessary, because most chamber floors were still of earth or plaster, which were

[1]T. L. Marsden, 'Minor Domestic Architecture of the Lower Trent Valley, 1550–1850', (Manchester thesis 1952), 33–34. I am indebted to Mr. Marsden for allowing me to read his thesis.

[2]E.g. Caddington, Upper Stondon.

[3]S. D. T. Spittle, *op. cit.*, 44–9. They were known to Moxon in Kent in 1682, and Wren recommended that white (or grey) bricks from Ely should be used. They became, during the course of the eighteenth century, a standard product in the region stretching between London and Cambridge, with an outlying area on the north bank of the Humber, and were probably all made from the Kimmeridge clays.

[4]E.g. Fulletby, Gunby St. Peter and Minting in Lincs., and Bedford St. Mary and Little Staughton, Beds.

recognized to be inferior as floors but certainly provided good insulation. In the region where lime was cheap the vogue for plaster floors was not threatened, and, like mud and stud, was recommended by the Board of Agriculture in Arthur Young's time.[1]

We may then picture the average parsonage house, and hence the average farmhouse, as having earth or brick floors downstairs, except in the parlour, and boarded floors there and in the chambers, although, in the region from Lincolnshire and Nottinghamshire south-eastwards, floors upstairs were often of lime or gypsum plaster. Walls were white-washed, for wall painting and painted cloths had gone out of fashion, and farmers and parsons could not afford the flock wall-papers which were now beginning to be made.[2]

A discreet reference occasionally to the 'necessary house' reveals that it was among the outbuildings of the better parsonage houses. The out-buildings at Little Barford, Beds., comprised a 'brewhouse and wood-house 1 bay each, a stable, haybarn and a boarded barn of 5 bays, a small granary and a necessary house, all timber building thatched'. At Southill there was 'a barn of 2 bays with a lean-to which serves for a stable and a privy house'. It is difficult to believe that any parsonage house lacked a necessary house, though in the middle of the nineteenth century, cottages without any privy at all were still exceedingly common.[3]

[1]See J. Lawrence, *The Modern Land Steward* (2nd ed. 1806), 201, for a receipt for plaster floors. They were to be made of one third lime, one third coal ashes, one third loamy clay and horse dung. After tempering to a 'tough and glewy' consistency, the mixture was to be laid by treading and beating with a rammer. Upon an upper floor the trowel only could be used, and the plaster had to be allowed to dry slowly to prevent cracking.

[2]The terrier of Raithby, Lincs. (1707) says: 'the hall is whitened with a chimney . . .; the parlour is boardened and whitened. . .' etc. For wall-paper, see C. C. Oman, *Catalogue of wall-papers* (V. and A. Museum, 1929). The earliest type was flock paper, which evolved out of the painted cloths of the sixteenth century, and was a monopoly of the Company of Painters and Stainers. One of the earliest known flock papers was found at the Manor House, Saltfleet, Lincs., a brick house rebuilt in 1673; the paper is of that time.

[3]Loudon, *Encyclopaedia of Agriculture, Supplement* (1843), 1333.

CHAPTER TWO

The Highland Zone

a. The frontier counties

MUCH has been said of Lincolnshire and Nottinghamshire as though they belonged to the lowland zone. In other respects their affinities were with the north and north-west. In looking for social differences one discovers not only the pure contrasts between highlands and lowlands, but an intermediate zone which has some features of both. Soil and climate made much of the highlands inexorably poor. Even today it is reckoned that the productivity of agricultural capital deployed on marginal soils, such as Exmoor, is only half that of soils of ordinary quality elsewhere, and whether modern farming methods have reduced the contrast or increased it, it was a much more potent fact in pre-industrial England than we can easily recognize. There are areas of poor soil within the lowland zone, but since they were small their farming methods and living standards were part of the larger region within which they lay. Similarly within the highland zone the richer pasture lands carried farm buildings of better quality, not different type; the carpenters' work in timber houses of Devonshire or Monmouthshire is a reminder that highland building is not necessarily inferior to that of the lowlands. It preserves a distinct tradition.

On this broad pattern imposed by climate and soil, human activity imposed local variations. In particular, the movement of farmers and craftsmen, within the orbit of a few market towns and seldom from familiar conditions to those completely unfamiliar, blurred the junction of highland and lowland zones. The medieval cruck tradition had survived in the west Midlands and the south west as well as in Wales and the north. In 1700 the frontier between those who still called the living-room the *house*, in the

northern fashion, and those who used the southern word *hall,* ran through
south Lincolnshire, Leicestershire and Staffordshire. Similarly the north-
ern·house with two or three parlours is just as characteristic of those
counties as of Yorkshire. Both came from the single-storey dwelling but
had become part of the storcycd house.

The new fashion for a symmetrical façade and a spacious staircase
could be fitted into the traditional arrangement of an axial chimney stack
opposite the entrance. Manor Farm, Coddington, built in 1714, has this
blend of old and new, in the lofty style which the builder in brick could
achieve (see fig. 38). The draughty hall with its six openings recalls Mme.

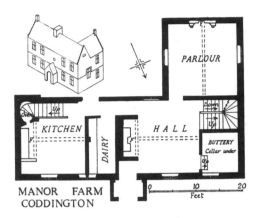

FIGURE 38. Manor Farm, Coddington, Nottinghamshire, built in brick in 1714.
Notice the lofty proportions, the symmetrical front, the buttery off the hall with a
cellar under and the old-fashioned relation of the hall to the rest of the house.

de Maintenon's complaint about Fontainebleau: because Louis XIV held
that screens destroyed a room's proportions, 'I must perish symmetrically'.

In the Midlands brick farmhouses continued to display a few Gothic
tags as late as 1730. The angled hood mould over windows persists till
that date. In Cheshire the vogue for elaborate brickwork only appeared
after it had vanished in eastern England. A farmhouse at High Leigh,
Cheshire, built for Robert and Anne Dewsbury in 1731, has the popular
hall and cross wing plan, with a moulded brick string course and the
parlour gable filled with a lattice pattern in protruding headers on a lighter
background. Both the hood mould and the lattice or diaper pattern,
essentially medieval, have their vogue in the north and west Midlands long
after they had disappeared in the south-east. The use of brick, though it
reached the Fylde before 1700, was most in evidence after 1725. Culver
House, Newent, dated 1693, is probably the earliest brick farm house in

the Forest of Dean. In the construction of barns, and probably in houses as well, carpenters were now using the upper cruck: that is, curved principals which rested on a tie-beam at wall plate level instead of going down to the ground.[1]

The north midland style of living then has two aspects. One is the late reception and the persistent use of ideas from the south-east. The other is an equally persistent reflection of highland modes, for the movement of people and habits was not merely in one direction.

b. The West Country

The mason's supremacy and his conservatism were hard to break down in regions where good stone was easily got. Hence the persistence, through much of the eighteenth century, of the mullioned window in Somerset houses round the Ham Hill quarries. The window becomes loftier, and the moulding was reduced to a mere fillet on the angle, but a division by mullions and a casement type of opening remained usual. One of the more obvious marks of eighteenth-century windows is the stone frame protruding from the wall face. Where ashlar was rare, timber lintels and frames are to be found. The use of brick remained very rare. A farmhouse at Drayton, Somerset, dated 1733, has the traditional three unit and cross passage plan and mullioned window of traditional proportions; but its brick walls are about half as lofty again as those of its neighbours in stone— a familiar effect of the new material.

Another farmhouse called Darbole in East Coker shows the local mason's idea of how to produce the double plan. He achieved it in the only way possible, with a single span roof: by making the house so lofty that the outshot along the rear could be nearly as wide as the main rooms. In the plan, which measured 35 × 30 feet, he put four rooms, a hall and a parlour, and two service-rooms, in the outshot. One of the service-rooms is identified as a dairy, by having had the word painted over the window at the end of the eighteenth century to show the village constable that it should be exempt from window tax. Thus in the new houses of c. 1700 and after, the local tradition is more potent than the incoming novelty, and easily absorbs it.

In the Dartmoor region the local tradition is scarcely altered. One of the most attractive houses in the county is Higher Tor, in the parish of Widecombe, built in 1707 (see pl. XIXb). In this final form of the long-

[1] E.g. a barn at Lea Fields Farm, Shutt Green, Brewood, Staffs. (V.C.H. *Staffs.*, V, 24); a brick barn at Sowerby Hall, near Preston, Lancs., and probably the house itself (ex. inf. R. Watson).

house tradition there are separate entrances to house and shippon—two cross passages side by side—and the house entrance has a storeyed porch (see plan, fig. 17). There was originally a doorway from the house passage into the shippon. The house itself has two rooms, hall and parlour, with an outshot dairy. Close to the porch is the well house with open front.

Although plans and construction had changed little, Devonshire, to judge from its parsonage houses, was as receptive as any other region of minor improvements within. The parlour almost invariably had a boarded floor, or 'planched', in the local idiom. The other rooms usually had earth floors. The local material for the plaster floor was called lime ashes, since it was mainly the waste of the bottom of the lime kiln, but it was not common as yet.[1] If quarry stone or paving was available, it was used in the kitchen because that floor was the most likely to get wet. A few houses had a kitchen or dairy with a cobble floor, and cobbles continued to be used into the nineteenth century. Floors upstairs were invariably of wood, and as yet were very rarely plastered underneath, so that curious children in bed could hear conversations not intended for their ears, and even see what went on downstairs through cracks between floor boards.

When cross walls downstairs were of stud and plank construction only the outside walls could require wainscotting. At Beer Ferrers the hall was 'wainscotted inside the table as high as a man's breast': that is, the wall against which people leaned while at meals was panelled so that the lime wash of the stone wall did not come off on clothes. No Devonshire parson had yet any wall-paper in 1680.

c. The northern counties

The table printed on p. 226 above shows the strength of the single-storey tradition in the north at the end of the seventeenth century, and it was not entirely dislodged in the eighteenth (see pl. XXIVa). In the main street of Wibsey, one of the townships of Bradford parish, there is a substantial stone house built by Benjamin Kitching in 1776. The roof of stone slates has a very low pitch, which gives considerable depth from back to front. The doorway has a plain ashlar frame, and the windows are large and equally plain mullioned openings.

The new device of a sash window, double-framed and sliding vertically, had not found its way into many farmhouses of 1700, but some ingenious Yorkshireman had devised a simpler form which dispensed with weights. The Yorkshire sliding sash, in which one part of the frame moves sideways behind the other, was obviously more suited to low houses with windows

[1] B. W. Oliver, 'The Devonshire Cottage', *Trans. Devonshire Ass.*, 81 (1944), 44.

wider than they were high. It spread over the Midlands as well as the north—another example of the interchanges between the highlands and the lowlands (see pl. IXb). Moss Farm, Moss, near Doncaster, was built in 1705, and is one of the earliest dated examples of this new type of window.[1] It must have originated in a region of brick building with wooden window frames, and not of stone.

Round the clothing towns of the West Riding the growing population demanded much more beef and butter than local farms could produce, and farmers near to such an insatiable market could afford new buildings. By the middle of the eighteenth century they were putting up a long and lofty range, with house and all the farm buildings under one roof: obviously a derivative of the medieval long house. The dwelling at the end was of two full storeys, and the lathe had a wide doorway lofty enough to drive in a wagon loaded with hay (see pl. XXIb). The lathe contained hay barn, stable and cowshed or mistal. These hillside farms were naturally sited on a spring or stream, and the water supply was channelled through a trough in front of the house and used both for the house and for cooling milk. Law Farm, Thornton, near Bradford, is of this type and is dated 1750.[2] Edge End, Overden (see above p. 174), near Halifax, was rebuilt to the same design at about the same time, and many others can still be seen.

By the time of Queen Anne the church authorities were once more tackling the problem of the adequacy, or inadequacy, of the parochial clergy. Schemes for new churches in London and for improving clerical stipends are one side of this campaign, and diocesan inquiries about parsonage houses, such as those of bishop Wake in the diocese of Lincoln, are another. William Nicolson, bishop of Carlisle, made a personal survey of his diocese in 1703, and his notes[3] show a great contrast between the few houses well maintained or rebuilt by the incumbents, and the rest. At Beaumont there had been 'a pitiful clayhouse . . . but the walls are now laid flat and the timber is a nuisance in the church'. The house at Irthington 'lies in most scandalous ruins. It fell in the time of the present vicar, who is the wretched and beggarly father of ten children'. The vicar of Ainstable did not reside in his house, which was 'extremely ruinous, but chiefly at a little alehouse kept (by the side of the road to Brampton) by his wife or daughters'. The bishop was acute enough to see that the vicarage house was neglected when the parson was either too rich, and

[1]*Ex. inf.* T. L. Marsden.
[2]The best description of the farms round Halifax and Bradford is in W. B. Crump, *The Little Hill Farm* (London, 1951). I am indebted to Mr. John Wilson for obtaining for me a copy of this now rare book.
[3]Ed. R. S. Ferguson, 'Miscellany Accounts of the Diocese of Carlisle etc.' (*Cumb. and Westm. Ant. and Arch. Soc.*, 1877).

lived elsewhere, like the squarson of Barton, or too poor; he thought both conditions equally unfortunate. Even houses reasonably well cared for might be 'low, moist and smoky' (Brough under Stainmore) or 'very mean and cottage-like' (Deerham). Most needed rebuilding, or complete modernization. The parson of Plumland was busy putting his house 'in a more modish frame, in his apartments, windows, staircases, etc.' Some others earned the bishop's praise, even for improving such a house as the 'long row of low buildings of clay' at Kirk Andrews on Eden.

When Celia Fiennes travelled through Cumberland in 1698 on her way to Scotland she saw cottages 'daubed with mud walls', and later travellers echoed her observations.[1] The business of building a cottage was still a communal matter in which the young man who wished to marry and set up house could rely on neighbours to join him in building it.[2] The difference between north and south lay not in the materials used, but in the survival of communal action in building. Today the cottages and farmhouses of 'clay daubin' have nearly all vanished, although they were common in Westmorland in 1775,[3] and there is inevitably some uncertainty about how they were built. Some had stone foundations and cruck trussed roofs, like Lamonby Farm; others are said to have had a framework of laths. It has even been suggested that shuttering was used,[4] but this seems unlikely. A few clay-walled buildings still survive,[5] and the field worker still has a chance to solve a problem which the historian cannot touch.

The first alternative to mud construction was to use stone. Even in St. Bees, Cumberland, where good sandstone is available on the hill behind the village, a new farmhouse built in 1712 was called Stone House Farm. Another of the name at Moorhouse is dated 1706 (pl. XXIVb); the clay barn referred to belongs to it. These names are proof enough that stone houses were unusual in these parts at the time when they were erected. Brick was the other possibility, and it was used in rebuilding the parsonage houses at Orton and Aikton at this time.[6] The use of brick in the coastal belt of Cumberland is another link with the Lancashire coast, and no doubt the brickmakers had moved northwards. The brickwork seems of poor quality, to an observer familiar with the Midlands or East Anglia, but in detail

[1]*Journey through England*, ed. C. Morris (1947), 196–204.

[2]C. L. M. Bouch in *T.C.W.A.A.S.* 53 (1953), 152, refers to a ballad published in 1805, called 'The Clay Daubin', describing the process and celebrations.

[3]A. Pringle, *General View of the Agriculture of Westmorland* (Edinburgh 1794), 84. Not a single mud walled farmhouse was found in Westmorland in the 1930's by the Historical Monuments Commission.

[4]By W. G. Collingwood in *Records of Holme Cultram*, 240.

[5]In August 1959 the writer noticed a clay barn at Moorhouse, four miles west of Carlisle.

[6]R. S. Ferguson, *loc. cit.*

these brick houses of the eighteenth century show the familar cycle of relations between the highland zone and the lowland beginning over again. Lowland practices arrived very late, and were adopted with some decline in standards; features such as the bolection moulding for a door frame were retained long after they had gone out of fashion farther south.

But, as we have seen already, it would be wrong to imagine that the culture of these remote settlements was incapable of originality. This is most apparent in the development of the double house in the north. In the midland counties, it was adopted for the small manor house by *c.* 1725 but not so far for any simpler dwelling. It appeared in Cumberland and Westmorland just as early, and in more modest houses. Stone House Farm, St. Bees, has an almost square plan with house and parlour in front and kitchen, dairy and staircase behind. The single-storey cottage, like that mentioned at Wibsey, would not have survived if it had not had two rooms, one behind the other. In these double houses, whatever their size, the roof is very flat in pitch, giving both depth of plan and suitable support for the heavy stone slates. One wonders how timbers long enough for the roof truss could be found. The truth is that there is no truss; the rafters are supported on purlins running from gable to gable, or gable to internal dividing wall,[1] and such a flat roof has little thrust.

The double house was not merely an import, but an independent merger of old and new ideas. In one sense its ancestry lies in the aisled hall tradition, with the radical innovation at some stage of an internal division into more or less equal, instead of distinctly unequal, parts. Because of that tradition the northern farmer took over the double plan from his superiors more readily, and earlier, than his midland counterpart. The examples were certainly there[2] to be copied, and they were less distant in scale from a farmer's standards than were houses of similar style in the Midlands or the south.

The regional distinctions which have been drawn from seventeenth century evidence were still apparent to observers in the years 1790–1840, and their comments confirm our analysis.[3] North of a line between the Humber and the Dee, the East Riding was the only region where a labourer's cottage was usually of two storeys, with house and parlour below, and two bedrooms above. If Strickland had looked more closely when

[1] I am indebted to Mr. Frank Atkinson for this simple but fundamental point.
[2] E.g. Mansion House, Eamont Bridge, Westmorland, built in 1686; R. W. Brunskill, 'The Development of the Large House in the Eden Valley, 1350–1840', in *T.C.W.A.A.S.*, 57 (1957), 90–1.
[3] They provide the material for J. H. Clapham's first chapter, 'The Face of the Country', in *An Economic History of Modern Britain: The Early Railway Age 1820–50* (1926).

collecting data for his *East Riding* (1812) he would have found a number which had no chambers: survivors of the rebuilding of the seventeenth century. The best Cheshire cottages might have chambers, or else what were now call 'bed cabins', downstairs, for the name parlour had at last gone out of use. Farther north, and increasingly as one neared the border, the one-roomed cottage became more typical. Even in 1850 many Northumberland labourers still kept the cow and the pig in the house. In the North Riding the box bed in a single-roomed dwelling was said to be as common as in Lowland Scotland. It had not been common two centuries before, so that we can see it as an improvement of Georgian times and later, rather than as a primitive survival.

The extreme contrast between living standards of the gentry and yeomanry, on the one hand, and the labourer on the other, which was a characteristic of lowland England in the later Middle Ages and of Yorkshire and Lancashire in Elizabethan times, was now the most striking feature of border communities. Cobbett described the farmhouses of Northumberland and farther north, 'big enough and fine enough for a gentleman to live in', and nearby the bothies or sheds for unmarried labourers and the single storey barracks of stone for the married. Even in the north the new rows of cottages built for miners in the early years of the nineteenth century were better than that, for they usually had a bedroom in the roof space. All over England when millowners or pottery manufacturers had to provide housing for workers, as the Strutts did at Milford and Belper in Derbyshire and the Wedgwoods at Etruria, they adopted the minimum standard, the one-roomed cottage, since it gave the greatest housing density, but they built two storeys, or even two and a half. Better housing was one of the magnets which drew the farm worker and his family into the industrial town.

The last of the houses built by Josiah Wedgwood at Etruria were demolished about 1958—without, alas, being properly recorded—but Milford remains as the most impressive example of how the industrialists turned tiny farming villages into industrial communities. Much thought and ingenuity went into the design of the new community, from the construction of the mill to reduce fire risks to the design of gutter brackets on the houses and their cast iron casement windows, made in Strutt's own foundry. So well built and carefully maintained have the houses been that they have a good chance of survival, in this age of slum clearance and redevelopment. One hopes they will long remain as historical monuments, for they form a valuable link in the sequence of social and economic changes which the English house has undergone.

Conclusion

THE essence of the vernacular tradition was the satisfaction of certain human needs, basic in character but limited in scope—the need for shelter for a family, and for a building from which farming could be carried on and those ancillary operations which required cover—out of the resources of the village community. At no time was the village immune from outside influences, or unwilling to adopt new ideas of design, whether they came from higher social levels or from more advanced craftsmen. As long as the result was more than a copy of the model, the vernacular tradition could be said to live. The movement of ideas from the sources of patronage in architecture to the farmer and the village craftsman was not a mere matter of giving and taking. It was a complex interplay of tradition, social pretension and practical considerations. A new idea might reinforce and give wider currency to an old form, such as the double house in the north of England. An ornamental feature might be seized on for practical reasons; the band of protruding bricks on the outer face of a brick wall, making an ornamental feature, provided on the inside a ledge on which ceiling joists rested. The sliding sash window was presumably an ingenious native adaptation of the imported Dutch sash, rising vertically and counter-weighted.

Even the advent of machinery and the application of mass production methods to building construction did not always and everywhere put an end to vernacular features. The use of power in the timber yard ensured the persistence of weather boarding as a cover for timber framed houses and barns.[1] When William Strutt wished to make cast-iron (and hence fire-proof) window frames for his mills, and also for the houses of his workers, the only design he could cast was one with a casement opening. A hunt for survivals in the nineteenth century, or even in the twentieth, would produce countless instances of traditional practices still used

[1]The first saw mill, driven by wind, was erected in Limehouse in the 1760's. Samuel Bentham was a pioneer of steam driven saw mills, for the use of the navy, in the 1790's. See B. Latham, *Timber* (1957).

by builders, either self-consciously, through habit or for convenience.[1]

It is clearly impossible to make any pronouncement on the date of the disappearance of the vernacular tradition in domestic building. Equally, most of the domestic habits described in these pages could still be found surviving in some part of the country or other. Nevertheless, the last of many fine distinctions must be drawn. It is that by the eighteenth century so many inroads had been made by economic and cultural changes in the way of life we have studied that it then ceased to be characteristic of the countryside. To the architectural historian, the reception of the Renaissance was complete by the early Georgian period at the latest. The ultimate source of the traditions of the jobbing builder today is not medieval Gothic, but the pattern books of the eighteenth century. To the economic historian, the transformation of the medieval landscape was completed in the same century with the final enclosure of open fields. When these links with the medieval past were finally shattered, the farmhouses and cottages which we have inspected and entered were no longer a current reflection of family life and working habits. They became part of an historic past whose wealth is still untold and ought not to be squandered.

[1] A report of the Building Research Station entitled *A Study of Alternative Methods of House Construction* published by the Stationery Office in December 1959 stated that 'in general, economy in house building can best be sought in the evolution of traditional processes rather than in the introduction of radically different principles of construction'.

Appendix of Select Documents

A. EXTRACTS FROM COLCHESTER TAX ASSESSMENT

Translations of extracts from assessment of Colchester for a tax of one fifteenth on personal property, 1301 (*Rotuli Parliamentorum*, I, 243, 263).

Roger the Dyer had in treasure 1 silver brooch worth 18*d.*; 1 bowl of maple wood (*mayer*) worth 18*d.* In the Chamber 2 garments 20*s.*, 2 beds worth 6*s.* 8*d.*, 1 piece of cloth and 1 towel worth 2*s.* In his Hall 1 laver with a bowl worth 14*d.*, 1 andiron worth 8*d.* In the Kitchen 1 brass pot worth 20*d.*, 1 brass posnet worth 8*d.*, 1 tripod 4*d.* In the Brewhouse 1 quarter of oats 2*s.*, wood ashes 6*s.* 8*d.*, 1 large dying vat 2*s.* 6*d.* Then 1 cow 5*s.*, 1 calf 2*s.*, 2 pigs worth 12*d.* each, 1 sow 15*d.*; billets and faggots for the hearth 13*s.* 4*d.* Total 71*s.* 5*d.*; tax payable at a fifteenth 4*s.* 9¼*d.*

Alice Reyner had on the said day 1 poor robe worth 2*s.*, 1 brass posnet worth 12*d.*, 3 bushels of barley worth 13½*d.*, 6 bushels of oatmeal worth 15*d.*, or 2½*d.* a bushel, 1 pig worth 2*s.*, tubs and troughs worth 12*d.*, a tripod worth 3*d.* Total 8*s.* 9½*d.*; tax 6*d.*

B. PETITION FOR LICENCE TO BUILD A COTTAGE

Letter to Sir Thomas Kitson, Kt., at London. (Bury St. Edmunds and West Suffolk Record Office E3/15.7/4.3); 28 March 1598.

Sir—Thomas Rodger the younger—an honest true labouring man in his trade of plowright & one that hitherto has had his dwelling in the town of Fornham all Saints—But now there being no house for him to bestowe himself in, neither can he provide himself elsewhere, but ready to lye in the street, hath made his humble suit that we would in his behalf be humble suitors to your worship that it might please you to give him licence to build himself up a cottage or poor dwelling-place upon a piece of the common next the east end of your pasture called the Mare Close, and that he might by your worship's good means have authority to enclose for the situation thereof ½ rood of ground by your ditch of the said pasture, in such manner and form as your steward by viewing same thinks both convenient and meet.

But because many have interest of common in that plot of ground, as well as in the rest adjoining, and amongst those many, the poor man fears he shall not get all their consent before your worship's good liking thereof may be had. And to the end that your worship may be advertized whose consents are already given, And who they be that humbly sue in his behalf—the underwritten have severally subscribed name or mark.

(*11 names follow*)

Endorsement My master was pleased to grant this request, & to give him a load of timber & two loads of bricks towards the same house—Condition—he

271

to hold it for the lives of himself & his present wife, paying 2/- p.a. and keeping the pale in sufficient repair, in . . . for the ditch next all the side of the Meare close next the said common and his said cottage. And that the longer liver of them both shall leave the said house now to be built sufficiently repaired fit and meet to serve for another of his quality or otherwise as best shall please Sir Thomas or his next successors to dispose or appoint there.

Note: Rodgers piece of ground is 10 foot in breadth at the N. end

In length 19 pole 2½ feet

In breadth at the south end—2½ pole 2½ feet

C. BUILDING CONTRACT, 1729

Lincoln Record Office, Tennyson D'Eyncourt Collection, G/6/2.

Articles of Agreement . . . between John Farnham of Weston in the County of Lincoln Gent. for and on behalf of Christopher Clayton in the said County Esq of the one part and John Proudlove of Kirton in the County of Lincoln Carpenter of the other part as followeth—

Imprimis The said John Proudlove . . . doth Agree to & with the said Christopher Clayton . . . that John Proudlove shall forthwith begin to Erect & Build a Dwelling House in Gosberton . . . on a certain piece of ground there called Monks Hall according to the Form . . . specified viz: The Front of the said Building to be forty feet in length from out to out And the width from out to out 16 feet and an half and to contain two Low:Rooms an Hall and a Parlour the Parlour to be made Fourteen Feet square and to be a Cellar under the Parlour as large as the Dimensions of the said Parlour will admitt The Cellar Floor to be laid with Brick and to be Six Feet high from the Floor to the Trasons And the Timber for the Floor over the Cellar to be good Oak & of a sufficient thickness To make a Chimney in each of the Low:Rooms And Closets on each Side of the said Chimneys. To raise the Floor of the said two Low:Rooms two Foot above the Ground and to make a sufficient Number of Stone: Steps to ascend into ye Same. To build two Chambers over the said two Low: Rooms and to make a Chimney in each Chamber with Closets on each side of the Chimneys to make the Chambers Square and Regular and to build a Garrett over ye said Chambers the full length of the Front The two Low: Rooms to be divided from each other by a Brick Wall which is to be carried up as high as the Garrett to divide also the two Chambers. To put four Transom Windows in the Low:Rooms five Transom Windows in the Chambers and three Lucarn Windows in the Garrett. The Frames of the said Windows and all the Door:Cases to be of Oak:Wood. To draw the Walls and Ceilings of the sd. Front Buildings with two Coats of Mortar the one black the other white And the said Low:Rooms and Chambers to be Eight Foot and a half high from the Floors to the Ceilings. The Timber for the Chambers & Garrett Floors to be good Elm:Wood & sufficient to the Judgement of any Workman And the Roof of the Front Buildings to be made also of good Elm:Wood . . . And to Erect & Build another Room for a Kitchen Twenty Six Feet in length from out to out and Sixteen Feet and an half in Width from out to out with a Chamber and Garrett over ye same Which Building is to adjoin to the Front:Building and to have a Communication therewith And the Roof thereof to be carried as high as the Roof of ye sd. Front:Buildings To make a large Chimney in the sd. Low:Room and also a Chimney in the Chamber over the same To put one large Transom:Window in the sd. Low:Room one Transom:Window in the Chamber and a Lucarn Window in the Garrett The Window Frames and

APPENDIX OF SELECT DOCUMENTS

Door:Cases of this Building also to be made of Oak:Wood . . . Walls to be drawn with black and white Cement & ye Rooms to be as high as the Rooms in the Front:Building To Carry up a large handsome Staircase with an Handrale & Bannisters to serve all the sd. Chambers . . . And also to build a Walch or Out:Shot to adjoin to the Back Building or Kitchen Twenty Feet in length . . . and Seven Feet wide . . . with a Door & Window convenient for ye same The Frame and Case thereof to be made of Oak Wood And the Roof of the said Walch or Out:Shot to be made of good Elm:Wood The whole Building to be thatched with Reed And the Front Back:Building and Outshot to be built according to a plan or Form drawn by Mr. Willm Sands. (Consideration: £200)

D. EXTRACTS FROM PARSONAGE TERRIERS

1. *Bedfordshire* (Bedfordshire County Record Office ABE 2.)

Battlesdon (1710). Parsonage house is a fram'd building, the walls fild up with Brick, all tiled except two Rooms lying to the north west called by the name of the wash house & sink drink house. It contains six Rooms & a Pantry upon the first floor, three of them, the Wash house the Kitchen & Drinkhouse, floor'd with earth or clay; the hall floord with Tile, the Pantry with Brick, the Parlour and Inner Room with Boards. The Barn and Stable . . . are the only outhouses.

Carlton (1707). Parsonage house built of stone & covered with thatch. 3 bays, divided into a Kitchen Hall & parlour with Buttery Pantry & the like convenienceys whereof the Parlour is floored with stone & the rest with earth there are also ffour chambers & a Study over the porch & one garrett all floord with boards but ye garrett is floor'd with loose moveable boards Also one barn of seven bays built with stone . . .

Oakley (1708). Vicarage house built in some part with stone, the other part Studwork & covered with Tiles containing two roomes with Earthen floors over which are two Chambers floord with boards & one of them ceiled a Kitchen of one bay at a little distance from the dwelling house built with Stone an Earthen floor a Chamber over it a Barn of one bay. . . .

2. *Buckinghamshire* (Lincolnshire Record Office, Terriers 19)

Farnham Royal (1707). Dwelling house 6 rooms upon a floor, one story high with garretts all in good order, I having layd out upon ye house &c. 220 li. One parlour and Study are new wainscot'd 3 floors new laid with Cristiana deales. a Brewhouse & woodhouse new built of Brick. The house is a timber Frame & ye lath & plastering being decay'd I have Brick pannel'd it all over, Put up new doors & windows where decay'd new lay'd & fenced ye Gardens with handsom Pales & Palisades in ye front of ye House, w'ch before was only enclosed with an Hurdle Hedge, built up a new Carthouse, w'ch was wanting.

Woughton (1707). 5 bays . . . straw & tile divided into a Kitchen with an Earthen floor a hall with a stone floor 2 Parlours with boarded floors, a Pantery with an earthen ffloor a Sellar pitched with pibbles a Milkhouse with an earthen ffloor, 2 Chambers o're the Kitchen, the first cieled the other not cieled A chamber o're the sellar & Milkhouse cieled, a Chamber o're the hall 2 o're the Great Parlour not cieled a little dark Room o're the little Parlour a Garrett a Closet a Study.

273

3. *Devonshire* (County Record Office, Exeter Castle)

Alphington (*c.* 1601). There are 4 houses: hall and parlour under one roof, kitchen and malthouse under another, the third a barn, the fourth a shippon with a new stable and a corn chamber, which I have built.

    (*c.* 1679). 1 parsonage house, part of which on the west side of the inner court, in it 1 parlour ceiled round, floor planched; 1 Hall ceiled over the bench, a buttery, 2 small rooms under 2 pairs of stairs, 2 cellars, 1 small room by the great cellar door; all floored with earth. 2 entries laid with quarry stone, one between the hall and parlour and one between the hall and buttery; one entry from the hall to the great cellar paved. One parlour chamber with a ceiled portal. Seven more chambers, 2 closets, 1 apple loft, all covered with shindle. The other part on the east side of the inner court, in it one kitchen, pastry, brewhouse, (in it a furnace) all paved; 2 chambers, 1 malt dry, 1 little woodhouse at stair head, one linney fenced from the court with pale (at the end of it a pump) all covered with thatch. One parlour garden, one hall garden (in it one house or office divided into two parts floored and covered with boards, walls timber and plastering), this inner court all paved except a green plot . . . All walls are of earth, footed with quarry stone except that all the chimneys and 3 walls of the parlour and parlour chamber are throughout quarry stone.

Combeinteignhead (1679). Parlour wainscotted and laid with board, and a little room [i.e. a buttery] within it. Hall partly laid with board, rest earth. Entry which parts said hall and other rooms. Three rooms then adjoining called the cellar, inner and outer dairy. Parlour chamber and a study within it. Chamber over and a hall chamber. Apple chamber. Porch chamber. Broad chamber. Inner chamber and a little chamber within it all these within the dwelling house. Without the house are one kitchen, one house within it called the middle room, and a little room within it called the larder. Malthouse chamber over, and a chamber against it. Barn. Pound house at south end of it. These are houses of parsonage enclosed with walls, besides hogsties. Most of these houses from the foundation are built with stone about 6 foot and then mud laid on it to the roof.

4. *Leicestershire* (Leicester Museum)

Great Dalby (1690). A house and Parlour: with Chambers over them containing too bayes of building: a lean too adjoining to the house for a small room. A barn . . .

Lockington (1638). The vicarage house stands southeast from the Church, on the left hand on the entry of it is an hall with plaistered walls, with a chimney in it, over it is a chamber wherein is a garner to lye in corne.

Item on the east side of the hall is a buttery & all this makes one bay of building.

Item Two little parlours one whereof has a study in it on the north side of the hall. With two chambers over them containing two bayes of building.

Item on the right hand of the entry is a kitchen with an oven in it almost a bay of building.

Item Southward from the house is a barn for corne . . .

Thurcaston (1709). Parsonage house 9 bays built from ye foundation about three foot high with stone, from thence to ye wall plate with stud and mud faced partly with lime & partly with plaster & ye Roof cover'd with slates. The ground Rooms are a large Hall open to ye Top. Two Parlors, a cheese Room, Dairy, Cellar, Coal & Wood House & at a small distance, a Kitchen & Brewhouse. A convenient Room under ye Hall Staircase, another in ye old Staircase behind ye great Parlour, in all twelve on ye ground floor. Upon ye second floor are four chambers at ye North end of ye House, & two closets, one of ym in ye great parlor Chamber wherein my late Lord Keeper Wright was Born. At ye South end of ye house in ye same story are two chambers & two more over ye Kitchin & Brewhouse. in all Ten. And over the said Chambers at north end of ye house are four Garrets.

Dovehouse 2 bays tith barn 5 bays. Hay barn 2 bays Stable 2 bays A Hovel, Cowhouse. Kill Barn 2 bays all these except ye kill barn stand round ye fold yard.

(Lincolnshire Record Office, Terriers 6, 160)

Hungarton (1611). Imprimis the hall conteineing twoe bayes & also twoo parlers with chambers over them of two bayes
Item one kitchen conteininge twoe baies
Item one neathouse & Stable twooe bayes
Item one barne conteininge five bayes . . .

5. *Lincolnshire* (Lincolnshire Record Office)

Alford (1708). Walls of clay or mud only there are two brick chimneys. 3 small lower rooms, floors of earth or what's as bad, having the like number of Garrets over them, floor'd indeed with boards but exceeding meanly.

Bicker (1606) . . . covered with reed, containing v bayes whereof the hall conteyneth ii bayes, i parlor & a kitchen cont iij bayes, with a double brick chimney & having ij chambers over them, the parlour chambered with boards, the kitchen chamber with earth.

Candlesby (1605). 5 little bays, built of timber & earth & covered with reed & some straw (whereof 3 bays have been founded and builded by the nowe Incumbent) one of the old bayes chambered over with a fastened chamber of a somertree joists and boards, the other old bay having a somertree and joists fastened but the boards loose and moveable all' the rest boarded over with Chambers moveable made of timber and earth.

Cumberworth (1625). 3 bays built all of wood and walled with earth covered with reeds & rushes, 2 bays chambered and boarded over at both ends. 8 rooms— hall, 2 parlours 2 chambers, buttery, milkhouse, coalhouse. Item one Kitchen consisting of 2 bayes.
(1709) . . house with 5 low rooms with clay floors, two chambered. Built with timber & walled with clay and thatched with straw the chimneyes headed with brick.

S. Ferriby (1707) . . built of brick from the ground to the windows, the west side brick to the eaves or pan and two gable ends to the top brick the rest of the wall sand and mortar the roofs covered with thack it hath a kitchen to the east floord with stone flaggs, a hall in the midst paved with brick and a parlour to the west boarded a little Buttery to the north of the parlour and 3 chambers over them.

Fulletby (1707) . . . is an old Clay House covered with straw, containing at present these rooms: hall, parlour, kitchen, brewhouse, dairy, buttery, pantry, a passage & a study. Hall kitchen pantry & passage were floored this year with paveings & bricks. Dairy & buttery are earthen floors. Parlour & study have been floored with boards but they are very much decay'd, broke up, and gone. Brewhouse is pav'd with coggles. There are 4 chambers & 2 closets, but all are decay'd & mean, and indeed the walls & roof are almost everywhere ruinous.

Minting (1606) . . . consists of 3 bays walled with clay & covered with Strowe or Thatched as we call it. Having 3 rooms, one Hall, one Parlour, one Kitching. The Hall & the Parlour being Chambered over & floored with Clay.

Risby (1606). 2 bays built of stone & mortar, covered with thatch, chambered over with mortar. Hall and parlour.

Swaby (1606). 3 bays covered with thatch the whole building being contrived into Hall, 2 parlours, 3 chambers etc. Item a kitchen of one bay and an oxhouse.

S. Willingham (1606). 3 bays built with strong timber & well covered with thatch, all the bays being chambered over, some with boards & some with clay. Three rooms—parlour, hall kitchen, the same house having also two chimneys of brick in height about three yards.

E. PROBATE INVENTORIES

1. *Derbyshire*

a. (Birmingham Probate Registry, Lichfield Peculiars, A 1562–1709)

A true and perfect Inventory of all the goodes cattels & chattels of William Aston of Monnyash in the Countye of Derbye myner, late deceased. 1637.

Imps his purse and apparrell	I	3	4	Item two wheels	o	2	o
Item one cowe and a calfe .	4	3	4	Item one hatchet	o	j	o
Item two chaf-beds 2 bed coverings 3 blankets three bolsters and 4 little pillowes	i	o	o	Item one washing sive with the rest of the grour tooles .	o	iiij	o
Item fower payer of sheetes two towels 2 pillowbeares & 8 napkins . . .	j	5	o	Item one little grate pot racks pot hooks and two little payer of tonges .	o	ij	o
Item fower little coffers	o	vj	viij	Item one backstone & back sprittles	o	o	viij
Item Two little boxes . .	o	j	o	Item fuel	o	j	vj
Item one Cubboard a dishbord & a shelfe. . .	o	3	o	Item four shearing hooks .	o	o	iiij
Item a board a little fall board, & 2 tressels . .	o	j	vj	Item three Rakes . .	o	o	iij
Item Two churnes 2 barrels one dashon with all ye rest of the wooden ware . .	o	viij	o	Summa totalis 9 18 vij			

Tho: Penton

Thomes Boam   These being prizers

b. (Birmingham Probate Registry, Lichfield Peculiars, B 1569–1665)

A true . . . Inventory of all . . . ye goods . . . of Henry Bagworth late of Bakewell . . . taken . . . ye seaventh day of January 1664./

	£ s d		£ s d
Imprimis in his Purse 38s in silver and eleaven shillings in gold, Coate Doublett Breeches a wastcoate twoo hatts 1 per of hose and shooes . . .	02 = 16 = 08	Shovell one Pitchfork one settle two packe saddles .	00 = 15 = 02
Item in ye further Parlour one Seiled Bed with red Curtaines and Vallance, 3 sheets, 3 bed hillings 3 blanketts, 2 featherbeds 2 pillows and bolster one little table Cloath one Pillowbere & 3 napkins . . .	03 = 02 = 06	Item in the neere Parlour a per of bedstocks & Coard one Cupboard a longe table; a foarme beyond the table, one buffet foarme at Eliza Burrows, one old Churne one Kitt, a shelfe a broken Chaire & old wood under bed . .	00 = 19 = 00
Item one trunke, two old Chests, one Chayre one round stoole one great table one little table one fourme one Kymnell with Oates in it one Axe one		Item in ye house a longe table a foarme one Settle two Chests one Chaire one hand Iron & Gallowes two throggs one hetch doore one little table Old wood & two shelves .	00 = 18 = 06
		Item In the Chamber one per	

of Bedstocks one Press one Chest one little Churne one old featherbed 3 loose boards over ye Entry ore doore on the Staire Case.   .   .   . 00=11=00

Pewter brasse one Posnett 8 Pewter dishes two salts, one Candlesticke 4 brass Potts one Paire of Cobberds one lead Dripping Pan and an old Bible.   .   .   . 02=00=00

Item in the Barne one & twenty strike of Oates .   . 01=08=00

Item a per of Cart wheeles 1 per of old Sills & threshing floore   .   .   . 00=05=00

Item one Mare & two Stacks of Hay   .   .   . 06=10=00

Item twenty thrave of Oats unthrest   .   .   . 01=03=04

20=09=02

John Eyley Gervase Midleton
ffrancis Burton Richard Chared

2. *Kent*

a. (Maidstone Record Office, PRC/28/2, no. 127)

The Inventory of all the moveable goods and cattell of Thomas Wyhall late of the parishe of Bowghton Bleane deceased made and praysed by John Elstewe and Philip Corinxe (?) the xviij th day of June in the yere of our Lorde gode 1569.

In the Hall

Item a table a forme iij chayers iij cosshens iij paynted clothes	vjˢ
Item in the parler ij Cobards iij chestes ij ioyne stoles a rounde table ij hampyers .	xiijˢ iiijᵈ
Item in payles platters dysshes trenchers spones temses and boules	ijˢ
Item a bedstedell a flocke-bedde one blancket a shredd coverlett	ijˢ
Item pyllowes a flocke bolster iiij paynted clothes . .	xˢ

Item a payer of potte hangers a payer of potte hooks a spytt a cobyron a trevell a garden rake a spade . . .	iijˢ iiijᵈ
Item in brasse . . .	xˢ
Item iij latten candelstykes	xxᵈ
Item iij pewtar . . .	xvˢ
Item iij paynted clothes .	iijˢ iiijᵈ
Item his aparell . . .	vjˢ viijᵈ
Item in his pursse . .	xxᵈ
Item in lynnen . . .	xxxvjˢ viijᵈ
Item in lomber . . .	vˢ

Summa totalis } vˡⁱ xvjˢ viijᵈ
Inventarii

b. (Maidstone Record Office, PRO28/17, no. 246)

A true and perficte inventorie of all and singuler the moveable goods Cattell Chattells debts and readie money of Robert Allison late of Lidd in the countie of Kent husbandman deceased seene and apprised by us whose names are hereunto subscribed the ninth day of Aprill in the yeare of our Lord 1632.

Imprimis his purse girdle and ready money in the house .	vjˢ
Item his weareing aparell linen and wollin with other necessaries . . .	ixˢ
Itim in his lodgeing Chamber one old standinge bedstedde with a feather bedd furnished with two olde chestes and one olde Chayre. prised at . .	xxˢ vᵈ
Itim in the fire roume one ioyned Cupbord two smale ioyned tables wt frames and one smale foorme a Cradle and three smale Chayres. prised at	xiijˢ viijᵈ
more three brand yrons a fire slice a payer of tongues a	

gridiron and a payre of pot-hangers	ijˢ iiijᵈ
Itim in the buttery one brass panne three brass kettells two brasse potts a brasse stuppente and a brasse Chaffindish prised at	ixˢ vjᵈ
more of peauter seaventeene pieces of all sorts . .	viijˢ vjᵈ
more one double selte and two Candlestickes . . .	jˢ
more two tubbs fouer keelers one beare	ijˢ
more five dishes seaven trenchers a ladle and three wooden spoones . . .	iiijᵈ
Itim in the milke howse thirteene smalle bowles .	jˢ

more one yron potte . . j^s vj^d

Itim in the chamber over his lodgeing Chamber a standinge bedstedle two feather pillows and a matte . . . vj^s viij^d

more fouer payre of sheets seven table cloathes one dousen of napkins a payer of pillow coates and one hand towell . . . . viij^s

Item more two chestes and a smale rounde table . . l^s ij^d

Itim in the Chamber over the butterie a wollin trendle and a linen one two old tubbes and pillion . . . . j^s

Itim in the Chamber over the fire roume a trundle bedstedle a solte slacke a pike and hed peace a sworde two sithes with creates three yron wedges and a packsaddle . . . iij^s iv^d

more an olde flocke bed a boulster and one blanket . viij^d

Itim smalle thinges which happelie may be forgotten and not seene . . . . l^s ij^d

Sume totalis   iiij^s xj^s viij^d

Will Yornhall   John X ffryshewell
Richard Glover   his mark

c. (Maidstone Record Office, PRC 11/21)

Jan 23 1662

An Invintory of the goods and Chattalls and Cattall of Bartholmawe Burch latt of Shaddoxhurst in the County of Kent Labarer deceesed Taken and aprised by us whose names are hereunto subscribed the day and yere above written:

Item in the hall one tabel one cubord one Kneeding trofe tene chayer a payar of pothanggeres: a payer of tongs: a grid ierne a salt Box 0 6 6

Item in the Milke house five tonges sixe bowes (sic) three plattares a payer of scalls . . 0 4 0

Item in the hall chamber one beed and beedsteedell there Bolsters fower blankets one Coverlett one truckell beedstall one linin trendell one wollin trindell fowr Chestes . . 1 0 0

Item in the drinke hows three tubes tow Barralls and other old lomber and a Chayrne . . 0 5 0

Item one hay Cutter one hand saw and other old[ ] and a mattock 0 4 0

Item Bords and Shelfes and old Lomber 0 2 6

Item with out dores wood and heye and Botts (?) . . . 2 0 0

Item three Cowes . . . 9 0 0
Item one hoge . . . 0 7 0
Item one Birding peece . . 0 7 0
Item things un seene and forgott 0 3 0
     13 19 0

Nathanell Manering   Thomas Yates

3. *Leicestershire* (Leicester County Record Office)

Inventory of William Lillye of Diseworth . . . yeoman . . . 5 November 1635

In the hall house

IMPRIMIS his purse girdle and apparell 2. 6. 8
Item one presse Cubboarde . 0. 8. 0
Item table with a forme two joyned foormes two little buffet stooles and two Cheyres. . 0. 15. 0
Item the sealeinge behinde the Table 0. 4. 0
Item twoe brasse pots and a posnet 0. 16. 0
Item one broad brasse pan one great Caldron three kettles two skillets and a skimmer . . 2. 0. 0
Item foure spits one paire of Cobyrons 2 Cressets and a fryinge pan 0. 10. 0
Item one woolen wheele, one

peire of cards one piggin one spade, two stools and twoe quishins 0. 2. 0
Item 9 platters twoe pewter Candlesticks 2 brass Candlesticks twoe double salts one single salt one pestel and a morter 2 basons 4 smal dishes and one quart pott. 1. 10. 0
Item one woodden morter and an yron pestell . . . 0. 0. 10
Item one old bible and the practise of pyetie . . . 0. 4. 0

In the parlour in the west end of the house

IMPRIMIS one bedstead with a tester one Truncke 2 chests and one presse Cubboarde. . . 2. 10. 0

Item one fetherbed, one mattries two Coverlids two blankets one peire of Curteynes one peire of sheetes one boulster and three pillowes 5. 0. 0

Item one Twiggin Cheyre and five quishins 0. 4. 0

Item 4 table Cloathes one peire of flaxen sheets one peire of harden 2 Towels three flaxen napkins and one hand Towell . . 1. 6. 0

Item one pewter Candlesticke 2 platters one brasse Candlesticke one sawcer and a longe quishin . 0. 8. 0

Item two dozen of Trenchers . 0. 0. 8

[In the other parlour]

ITEM one bedsted with a tester one fetherbed twoe Coverlids one boulster one pillowe one-peire of flaxen sheets and one of hempen one pillowbeer and a Coffer 3. 15. 0

Item one mattrice one boulster one pillowe three blankets and one Coverlid 1. 0. 0

Item two barrels and a Churne . 0. 5. 0

Item milke vessels & chielves in the milkhouse . . . 0. 5. 0

In the chamber over the house and parlors

ITEM 2 bedsteds with beddinge and one cheyre . . . 1. 0. 0

Item 2 Tables one planke 2 linen Wheeles one peire of blades & foure bottels 0. 10. 0

Item one Coffer, one Cheese-cratche, with chielves and certeine wooll & other Implements 1. 10. 0

[In the kitchen]

ITEM one boulting arke with kneeding troughs one mouldinge board one strike with all other valuables in the kitchen . . 0. 16. 0

In the chamber over the Kitchin

ITEM one bedsteed one mat-trice & other beddinge with secks, bags, window cloathes sieves & skuttles . . . 1. 10. 0

ITEM three kyne . . . 7. 0. 0

Item one other cowe and a yerelinge calfe . . . 2. 10. 0

Item one sowe 2 hogs & 3 weaninge pige . . . 2. 0. 0

Item the Timber in the yearde & one ladder . . . 1. 10. 0

Item the hovel Timber with al the Timber fences . . . 2. 0. 0

Item one fillye . . . 2. 0. 0

Item two sheepe . . . 0. 5. 0

Item the barlye peaze haye & wintercorne 13. 6. 8

Item twoe hives of bees . . 0. 10. 0

Item Certejne bricke & quarrell 1. 18. 0

Item pullin 0. 4. 0

Item one foulde of old fleakes & a planke 0. 7. 0

Summa tot—62. 15. 10

4. Lincolnshire

a. (Lincolnshire Record Office, 175/100)

A true and perfect Inventory of all ye goods and chattells of William Garnon late of Brant Broughton in ye County of Lincoln gent Viewed valued and apprized ye Eighteenth day of July in ye yeare of our Lord one thousand six hundred seaventy two by us whose names are hereto subscribed

Imprimis His purse and appar-ril . . . . . £ s d
20.00.00.

In ye Hall

Imprimis One table 6 stooles 4 chaires one little table . . 01.06.08.

In ye Best parler

One Table and one carpit Eleven chaires 2 stooles and one hand iron . . . 05.00.00.

In ye little parlor

One Round table 3 Stooles . 00.10.00.

In ye Kitchinge

One Table 3 chaires pewter Brass hand Iron Fire Shovell Tonges pott hookes and other thinges there . . . 06.00.00.

In ye chamber over ye best parlor

One diper table clothe with Napkins to ye same 7: paires lininge sheetes 1: holland sheete 1 callicoe Sheete table Cloathes and Napkins 1: Chist 3: trunckes 09.06.00.

Coarse Sheetes and Napkaines 01.06.00.

Six Silver Salts 6: Silver Spoones and one Silver Cuppe. 03.10.00.

In ye Greate Chamber

One Bedstead with Bedinge Thereto belonginge . . 07.00.00.

One little table and other things there . . . . 01.10.00.

In ye littell Chamber

Two Bedsteads with Bedinge.

thereto belonging and one cubboard . . . 05.06.08.

In ye Kitchinge Chamber £ s d

Two Bedds with Bedinge Two Chists one Chaire Two peeces of New Cloth . . . 03.03.04.

In ye Garretts

One Bedstead 4 Wheeles Barley Cheeses one Iron Beame and other things there . . . 01.12.06.

One parsell of Wool . . 25.00.00.

In ye yard and field

One wayne and harrows . 02.00.00.

Fencing for Stakes and cheeses hooks . . . . . 01.10.00.

Eightyone old Sheepe and Eighty Lambes . . . 105.00.00.

Eight Cowes and Twelve

Young Beasts Five calves . 44.10.00.
Six horses and Mayres . . 018.00.00.
Swine . . . 04.00.00.
Oakewood . . . 03.00.00.
Two Troughes . . . 00.13.04.

In ye Sellers

Six Barrolls . . . . 00.12.00.

In ye Dairy

Milk Vessell and Shelves . 00.12.00.

In Brewhouse

Leade and Brewing vessell . 01.13.04.

Things not Seene and things forgott . . . . 00.06.08.

Some . . . . 272.13.06.

Tho Moore George Ridder
Geo: Langworth Edm: Ankersalls

b. (Lincolnshire Record Office, 172/274)

A true and perfect Inventory of all ye goods of Elizabeth Lawrence Chapwoeman (as folleweth) of Donington deceased [c. 1672]

Purse & aparrell with a boxes of wearin Lining . . . 3 13 0

Item too Trunks too Chests one boxe with some corse linning. a dish binch 1 13 4

Item one bedstead with a fether bed & beding . . . 3 10 0

Item one bed-stead more too Coverlids three blanketts . . 1 0 0

Item one fether-bed with a bolster & too pillows & to blanketts 2 6 8

Item in ye Cithing too plancks with fewell & other housell-ments 1 3 0

Item Pewter & brass . . 2 9 4

Item in ye Hall one Cubord too tables with other housellments . 1 10 0

Item In ye Chamber Corne . 7 0

Item In biendings . . . 6 0 0

Item In blacke browne & collered thredds. 5 10 0

Item In White thredds . . 4 0 0

Item In Pinnes . . . 6 13 0

Item In Cottons & buttons . 2 0 0

Item In Cottons inckles & Tayes 3 0 0

Item In White & collered Inckles 4 0 0

Item In Points & leather lases . 1 0 0

Item In thredd lases . . 1 0 0

Item In broken ware . . 2 0 0

Items In Combs, Needles & other broken ware . . . 1 10 0

The Sum 56 5 4

5. *Norfolk*

a. (Norwich Diocesan Records, Inventories bundle Goodram, 1633, no. 5)

Richard Coliard, a yeoman of Thornage near Holt (the formal heading is omitted).

In primis his apparel . . xlv^s

In the parlor

In primis, a posted bedsted of ioyned worke: one fetherbed & twoe pillowes twoe bolsters one rugge & blankets & curtaines and three curtaine roddes . iiij^s lid

Item one Trundle bedsted one pillowe one flight bed and bolster one Coverlet one blanket with two mattes and cordes xv^s

Item one small frame table one

chaire of ioyners worke one framed forme & two stooles ioyners worke . . . xiij^s iiijd

Item one deske one litle boxe a windowe curtaine & rodde . ij^s 6d

Item one paire of dogge irons & a paire of tonges . . . vj^s viijd

In the kitching

In pr one framed table with a shorte forme & a chaire & 2 litle ioyned stooles . . xv^s

Item one cupboard of ioyners

worke one liverie cupboard a
planke with trussles & an old
cheste . . . . xx^s
Item a litle caldron three
kettles ij litle skillets a chafing-
dish a chafer a brass candlesticke . . . . xxj^s
Item xxix peices of pewter
small & great . . . xx^s
Item twoe lacthpans of iron
three spittes twoe hakes a paire
of dogge yrons a firepan a greed-
yron 2 frying pans a paire of pot
hookes a trevet an iron barre . x^s
Item an alestoole a chyrne
three small beare vessels a
powdringe Tubbe a standill 2
killers 3 stooles a paile nine
boules 10 wooden dishes ij
dozen trenches and a pinte
with spoones a reele . . x^s
Item an olde bible and service
booke . . . vj^s viij^d
Item 6 quishions ij pillowes and
a cradleclothe . . . x^s
Item a lether Jacke a childes
chaire of wicker a flasket a
basket a paire of bellowes &
earthen pots & glasses . . ij^s vj^d

In the Chambers
In pr in linnen 6 paire of
sheetes 6 pillowe bearers 18
table napkins 3 board clothes
4 towells . . . . xl^s

Item twoe bedsteds one fetherbed one bolster one blanket ij
olde coverlets with matte &
corde . . . . xxx^s
Item an olde trunke an olde
musket an old head piece ij
swordes a paire of tables . xv^s
Item mixtlin 6 bushells barly 1
combe . . . . xxiij^s iiij^d
Item 10 yardes of blanket . xv^s
Item a wheele & a paire of
cardes a cloke bagge an olde
minginge troughe ij sackes a
poke with a bushel of woole . v^s
Item 2 bacon flickes . . xiij^s iiij^d
Item one hooke one hatchet ij
pichforkes one shovell ij rakes
one sythe & an olde colde & an
olde cheese presse one mucke-
forke . . . . vj^s viij^d
Item woode in the yarde . x^s
Item compasse . . . iij^s iiij^d
Item ij neate whereof one is
olde and weake & cannot rise iij^{li}
Item ij swine . . . xv^s
Item iij geese . . . iij^s
Item olde yron & olde lumber iij^s iiij^d
Item a paire of harrowes iron
& cartsadle & j ladder . . vj^s

Total £26. 6s. 8d.

Thomas Martyn   Roger Bailie
his marke

b. (Norwich, bundle Goodram 1633, no. 278)

The inventory of the goods and cattells of Edward Bell of Boughton in the county
of Norff labourer deceased made . . . this 16 daye of June . . . Anno Domini:
1633:

	s				s	
Imprimis in ready money .	j	o	Item his labouring tooles of all			
Item his apparell . . .	8	o	sortes	8	4
Item in ye fire house one stand-			Item a fryen pann, a speete, a		
ing bedstead with a stand bed		d	payer of Dogg irons a hale and		
upon it furnished as it is . .	13	4	a payre of tonges . . .	3	4
Item his small lynen with			Item the dishes spoones with		
sheets and pillowbearers and			other trifles unthought of .	5	o
other things	8	o	Item one sow with 5 piggs .	10	o
Item 2 little tables, a seat with			Summa totalis 4^{li} 11^s 8		
4 feets, 2 chaires and 2 stooles .	3	4			
Item in brasse and Pewter .	1^{li} 3	4	John Inglebright Thomas x Curlington		
Item one cubbard and 3 chests	10	o	his mark.		

c. (Norwich, bundle 1668, no. 12)

An Inventorie Indented made the three and twentyeth day of October 1665 off all
the goods Cattle Chattles household stuff Moveables or other personall Estate that
Thomas Waynforth late of Roydon in the County of Norff Maultster & Brewer
deceased dyed seized of valued & prised by ffrancis Waynforth and Wm Cammell
as followeth.

Imprimis

In the hall	li	s	d
One long Table two forms & one great Cupboard . .	01:	00:	00
One Keepe & a Livery Cupboard . . .	00:	12:	00
Two Joyn'd chaires . .	00:	05:	00
Seaven Chaires & Stoles .	00:	07:	00
A strikeing board & a plate candlestick . . .	00:	03:	00
A paire of Cobirons a paire of tongs two hakes two box irons	00:	10:	00
One Curbine a paire of Bellowes & other lumber .	00:	10:	00

Item   In the Parlour

	li	s	d
his library . . .	00	10	00
one long fram'd table . .	00	14	00
One Table Carpit . .	00	02	00
One press for Cloathes .	00	10	00
Six leather Chaires and fower leather Stoles . .	00	12	00
A Box table & ye Carpet .	00	06	00
A glasskeepe & fouer cushions	00	10	00
A Brazen Clocke . .	01	10	00
Two Muskequets furnished .	01	10	00

Item   In the Kitching

	li	s	d
A Copper one table & one Cheesepress . . .	02	00	00
One Cowle for brass & peulter	00	02	06
All the peulter . . .	03	00	00
All the brass . . .	05	00	00
Two iron potts & pothookes .	00	15	00
A brazen iacke & three speits an iron dripping pan two hakes a paire of Cobirons firepan & tongs & other lumber	01	00	00

Item   In the dayry

	li	s	d
An old milke tray & salting tray & a Cheese tubb . .	01	00	00
Eight Cheese fatts fower breds	00	10	00
A Butter Killer & five other Killers	00	08	00
Eight old Bowles and three traffling (?trassling) dishes .	00	02	00
A frying pan a brass bottim & other Lumber . .	00	06	08
A Barrel Chirne . .	00	06	00
	24	01	02

Item In the Storehouse	li	s	d
A Keepe & five dozen trenches	00	10	00
three poudring tubbs . .	00	10	00

Item   In the little Butteries

A Boulting hutch & killers two old sives & other Lumber	00	08	00

	li	s	d
A paire of scales and eighty three pounds of leading weights	00	15	00

Item   In the Hall Chamber

A feather bed boulster pillows bedstead matt & line Curtins Curtin rods Valance blankets as it standeth .	03	10	00
A little old table & a Chaire a Cushion a paire of Cob-irons tongs & bellowes .	00	10	00

Item   In the Parlour Chamber

Silver Plate . . .	05	00	00
A featherbed bedstead a Boulster pillowes & blanket Rugg mat & line as it standeth	04	00	00
A Trundle bedstead mat & line	00	04	00
A great Chest . . .	00	07	00
A press for Cloathes three Chaires a Stoole & two Cushions	00	15	00
Linning. Twenty fower paire of sheets two dozen pillow beers fower dozen napkins & other linning . .	13	00	00
three Riding sadles and furniture	01	00	00
A hanger a looking glass a basket & other things there .	00	13	04

Item   In the little Buttery Chamber

Sixty fower pounds of lead & old Iron	02	00	00

Item   In the servants' Chamber over ye Kitching

two beds as they stand with some other things there .	03	00	00

Item   In the Vauns Roofe

Lining Yarne . . .	03	00	00
hempe & other things . .	02	00	00

Item   In the Kitching Chamber

A posted bedstead & feather-bed Coverlet boulster pillows & blankets Curtins Matt & line	03	10	00
A Chest of Trammel a spinning wheele a wicker Chaire & other Lumber . .	00	10	00

Item   In the two little Chambers over the Buttery.

three feather beds three bedsteads blankets & other things as they stand .	09	00	00
Some old lumber there .	00	05	00
	54	07	04

Item   In the Vauns Roofe over the old hall

Wheate & Rye . . .	03	00	00
Cheese	02	00	00

Item In the old hall			
A Bulting hutch & backiron.	00	10	00
Item In the Cole house			
A parcell of Coles . .	13	00	00
Item In the Barne			
Barley	16	00	00
Item In the Shopp			
A Cupboard & lumber .	01	00	00
Wood in the yards . .	04	00	00
Eight Cowes . .	22	00	00
five Calves three Bullocks & a Colt	09	00	00
hay upon the stakes . .	14	00	00
A Boore . . .	00	15	00
A grindlestone & two Swath-Rakes	00	10	00
Item In the Brew house			
Eight Score Barrels twelve halfe Barrels the Mill and all things thereto belonging & all the brewing vessels .	50	00	00
hopps	08	00	00
Item In the Mault Chamber			
A Screen & skoppits . .	01	00	00
A paire of stryses & exeltrees	01	10	00
A parcell of hempe in the steele boords peeces of timber & other Lumber .	05	00	00
Item In the little house in the fore-yard			
A Bed & bedstead & other lumber . . .	02	10	.00
Brakes & fireing for the Mault house . . .	02	00	00
Barley bought & paid for .	45	00	00
ffouretene working horses & three Colts. . . .	45	00	00
Two Brew Carts & ye Carr two Roade carts the tumbril an old cart three ploughs & three paire of harrows .	15	00	00
Twenty fower hoggs . .	10	00	00
harness for Cart horse & ploughhorse & sacks . .	04	00	00
In debts desperate .	58	00	00
part of a Shipp at Sea .	25	00	00
his Apparell . . .	10	00	00
Ready Money in his purse .	05	00	00
Posts & Rayles & other lumber at Stradbrook .	02	00	00
In good debts . . .	70	00	00
twenty Barrels of beer .	10	00	00

454—15—00

ffrancis Waynforth Willm: Cammell

6 *Shropshire* (Birmingham Registry, Worcester diocesan inventories, bundle 1661–2, no. 309)

A true and perfect Inventory of all . . . the goods . . . of Richard Mucklowe late of Lappall in the parishe of Halesowen & County of Salopp yeoman deceased taken . . . the thirtyeth day of Aprill Anno domini 1662 before us whose names are subscribed.

	li	s	d		li	s	d
Imprimis his purse & money & wearing Apparell . .	2.	10.	0	Item two Coffers & all the rest of the goodes in the Parlour	0.	13.	4
Item one table board & frame & fower stooles .	0.	13.	4	Item Barrelles & benches & all the goodes in the two little Buttereyes . .	1.	0.	0
Item one Cubberd Shelves Benches and stooles and other goodes in the Hall Howse .	0.	6.	8	Item for Barrelles & shelves & all in the dayhouse . .	1.	6.	6
Item one Backe one handiron & drippen pann one paire of Bellowes Cobberdes & Broaches	1.	10.	0	Item one Joyned Bedd in the Soller over the Parlour three Coffers three shelves one Board	3.	5.	6
Item Gailes & pothookes fyer shovell & Tongs & Salte barell	0.	3.	6	Item in the Soller over the dayhouse two Beddes & all that belongeth to them one Chest & one Coffer Shelves & other Goodes . .	3.	10.	0
Item for Beefe and Bacon .	2.	2.	0	Item all the goodes in the Soller over the Hall . .	2.	0.	6
Item one Bedsteed & Bedd & all belonging to it in the Parlour	4.	10.	0	Item one Mault mill one donge Vessell one dresser and Washeloome & all in the Kitchine . . .	2.	10.	0
Item one presse & Cubberd in the Parlour . .	0.	16.	0				
Item one Truckell Bedd in the Parlour . . .	0.	10.	0				

Item one warmeing pan one Morter & one paire of weights	0.	13.	0
Item tenn dishes of pewter two flaggons two Cannes one Bole two Candlestickes two Saltes Spoones Chamber pottes and all the rest of the pewter	2.	10.	0
Item one Brasse pan ffive kettles two Brasse pottes one Iron pott & all the rest of the Brasse	3.	3.	4
Item two Bedsteads & some bedding in the Soller over ye Entry	0.	13.	4
Item three Little wheeles one greate Wheele . . .	0.	13.	4
Item three pailes two gaunes	0.	5.	0
Item Tenn paire of weareing sheetes two Boulster Cases and Bedd and Bedding unmade	4.	2.	0
Item for Yarne made of Toe .	1.	2.	0
Item Toe Hurdes and fflaxen Yarne	2.	4.	0
Item Table Clothes Pillowbeeres towelles and table napkins & sheetes . .	4.	2.	6
Item one Waggon one Carte two Tumbrelles . .	7.	10.	0
Item three plowes three paire of Irons . . .	0.	15.	0
Item one Oxx Harrowe & one paire of small Harrowes .	1.	3.	4
Item Motthooks spades Sheppikes one Wayne Ropp			

Corses beetle & wedges & one Ringer . . .	0.	10.	0
Item for timber and Boardes	3.	4.	0
Item Horsgeeres & all manner of implements belonging to Husbandry .	1.	10.	0
Item fower acres of Muncorne of the ground . .	8.	0.	0
Item Tenn acres of Oates and Pease . . .	13.	6.	8
Item five acres of Barley .	10.	0.	0
Item Corne unthreshed in the Barne	2.	0.	0
Item Mault in the Howse three strike . . .	0.	15.	0
Item ffive Cowes att 3^{li} 15^s a Cowe	18.	15.	0
Item fower yeere Olds att j^{li} 6^s. 8^d a peece . . .	5.	6.	8
Item seaven Horses & Mares and Coltes	20.	0.	0
Item fower weaneling Calves	2.	10.	0
Item two store pigges . .	1.	10.	0
Item all the Manure about the Howse . . .	2.	0.	0
Item Tewtawes and Brakes and all the Goodes lefte unapprized . . .	0.	10.	0
	145.	11.	0

Richard Mucklowe   Thomas Hadley
Elizabeth Hadley

7. *Staffordshire* (Birmingham Registry, Lichfield Peculiars, A, 1562–1709, no. 1678)

A true Copy of the inventory taken ye 14th day of february Anno Dom 1677 of all the whole Estate of John Addam [yeoman][1] of Copnall in ye County of Stafford lately deceased

imprim in ye house one table one forme & too Cheeires .	1—0—0	
In the parlor one bed too blankets and one Coverled .	3—0—0	
one Cofter one box & warming pan	0—10—0	
in bras & pewter . . .	2—0—0	
barells & all Loumeary ware .	0—5—0	
one grate fire shovell & tongues	0—5—0	
too sping wheles . . .	0—3—0	
in ye over Chamber one bed with all belonging to it . .	2—0—0	
Corn & hay in ye barne . .	3—0—0	
his wearing aparell & mony in purse	2—0—0	
in Chees & bacon . . .	1—0—0	

Corn upon ye ground . .	1—0—0
five Cows & one Calf . .	16—0—0
part of a lease of tyth . .	5–10–0
debts due upon bond one from Robert Talbot of Kerbridge .	20–12–0
due from Mr Edward Chumley upon bond	10–6–0
due from John Scillam upon bond	2—1—2
pultry & any thing els that may be forgotten . . .	0–10–0
the Some	71—2—2

a true copy taken per me Humphrey Caule

[1]He describes himself as a yeoman in his will.

APPENDIX OF SELECT DOCUMENTS

8. *Sussex* (Chichester Record Office, Ep I/29, Box 1662)

An Inventory taken the Eleventh day.of August.1662 of.the goods & chattells of Henry.Summersell of Warneham in the. County of. Sussex husbandman . . .

In the. Chamber

Imprimise 5 payre. of sheets	.	01	5 00
Item 4 pillowes	.	00	05 00
Item 3 featherboulsters .	.	00	16 00
Item 3 blancketts	.	00	15 00
Item old bedds .	.	00	12 00
Item old blancketts	.	00	02 00
Item 2 old bedstedds	.	00	10 00
Item 3 Chests .	.	00	13 00
Item wearing clothes	.	01	10 00
Item 2 hatts	.	00	04 00
Item Chests & A box .	.	00	9 00
Item 2 wedges & A sledge	.	00	6– 6
Item 2 dencher plowes .	.	00	5 0
Item 2 Axes .	.	00	2 0

In the. Buttery

Item 5 small drinke tubbs	.	00–	7– 6
Item A Cuubbord	.	00–	4– 0
Item 3 tubbs .	.	00–	6– 0
Item 3 trayes .	.	00–	1– 6
Item A Bottle a fryingpann & a searcher. . . .	.	00–	2– 0
Item for trenchers dishes A peck & Jett. . .	.	00–	2– 6
Item shelves & other things	.	00–	1– 0

In.the.Hall

Item pewter 8 peeces .	.	00–13–00
Item A fflaggon & quart pott .		00– 3– 0
Item 2 kettles & a skillett	.	00–11– 0
Item 2 Iron potts & A kettle	.	00–10– 0

Item 2 potthangers 2 smooth-ing Irons fire shovell tongs an

AndIron GridIrons & A spitt .		00 06– 0
Item A Cleaver & Shreding knife . . .	.	00–01 03
Item A Table & forme .	.	00 06 00
Item An Ironfoote a Skimmer & sheepsheers & A fleshhooke .		00 01–06
Item 2 payles . .	.	00 00 08

In an Outlett

Item 2 keelers & 3 tubbs. .	00 10–00
Item prongs a gardenrake a dencher Shovell A dencherrake a dencher Matthooke. a a spitter & A hop pitcher .	00 06 0
Item A Cross Mathooke .	00 01 6

Abroad

Item hoppoles . .	.	01 00 0
Item Cordwood . .	.	01 02 0
Item a Grinstone & winch	.	0 03 0
Item a shoote . .	.	0 14 0
Item a Lymecourte & wheeles & things thereunto belonging .		0 12 0
Item Ladders . .	.	0 03 0
Item 2 Lyme Shovells .	.	0 01 0
Item an Anger & wimble	.	0 02 0
Item a sythe a saw a hammer a Chizell & Iron Hooke .	.	0 01– 0
Item apples & pease .	.	01–00 00

Sum total . .	.	17–08–05

William Reefer John Parr
Exhibitum fuit . . .

9. *Warwickshire* (Birmingham Registry, Worcester diocesan inventories, bundle 1613–4, no. 3289)

An inventory of all the goods . . . of William Windle of Samborne in the parish of Coughton in the countie of Warwicke husbandman . . .taken . . . the fowrth day of Maye in the yeare . . . one thousande six hundred and fowerteene . . . as followeth.

Inprimis In the Hall one cubborde, ix^s, a Table borde & ij formes, ij benches, iiij shilves, iiij stooles, one loome, ij payles, one great wheele, a ladle & dishes a piggin & other Implements in the said Hall, v^s iiij^d, iiij Brasse kittles, one skellet, one skimer, one chafingdishe, xvij^s, iij Brasse potts, xv^s, a Brande Iron, a payer of bellowes, pott hookes, & pott links ij^s a mattock, one axe, ij bills, iij^s all praysed to } li^s iiij^d

Item In the romme or soller over the chamber, x pewter dishes or platters, x sawcers, ij saltes, a counterfet dishe, a candlestick praised at xij^s, iiij brasse candlesticks, xxz^d, vj quoffers, one Box, a Bedstide and a forme, xiij^s iiij^d, one fetherbedde, iiij flocke bedds, xxx^s, iiij bed hiilinges, ij blankets, v canvasses, xlvj^s viij^d, iiij boulsters, v pillowes, x^s viij^d } vl xiij^s viij^d

285

Item In Lynnen, vij payre of sheetes, and one dossen of table napkins, ij towells, ij pillowbures, a table cloath } li^s

Item In the Chamber, a Table borde on trestles, and a forme, iij^s iiij^d, one cubborde, a chiste, iij^s iiij^d, iij fryinge pannes, ij paire of scales, a paire of great ballance iiij^s, a plate, hammer & pinsons, iij quishions, iij^s } xvij^s

Item In the house beyond the halle, ij skeeles, one cheese presse, ij spitts, iiij wedges, & all other Implements in the said howse } xx^s

Item One cowe, xl^s, iiij sheepe, xx^s, ij stalles of bees, x^s } iij^{li} x^s

Item Milke pannes, woole cardes, & earthen potts } xij^d

Item iij hennes & some chickins } ij^s

Item parte of a flitchen of Bacon } iij^s

Item flaxen & herden yarne vj^s viij^p

Item a shoole & a spade xvj^d

Item Haye in the Barne, ij lathers, & other things there } xiij^s iiij^d

Item In woode praysed at xx^s

Item corne one the grownde that is to say Barley sowed } xl^s

Item His Purse and his girdle, & all his wearing apparell, praysed at } xx^s

Total [£23 8s.]

witnesses hereof, John Woodwarde, George Geaste, George Greene, Richard Tomes, George Wrigget.

10. *Yorkshire*

a. (York Registry, Dean and Chapter Various)

True & perfect Inventory of . . . Marke Scawbye of Acombe Labourer . . . Aprill the 29th 1674

	li	s	d		li	s	d
Imprimis							
His purse & Apparrell . .	1–	5–	0	Item in the Lower end of the house one parcell of Hay one Ladder 2 old Sythes wth other odd huslem^{ts} . . .	o	8	6
Item in the Parlour one half headed bed & bedding belonging it	o	16	o				
Item more there 4 litle old Chists	o	6	o	Item one white Mare one horse & one ffilly	05	10	–00
Item more there 6 yard of Harden Cloath 2 little Basketts & a Tempse . . .	o	5	o	Item 2 Kyne one Calfe & a stirke	05	06	–00
				Item unthreshd Rie . .	o	12	o
Item more in the ffire house Pewder & brasse . . .	o	11	6	Item a small parcell of Barlye .	o	6	o
Item wood vessell there . .	o	4	4	Item 3 rood of winter Corne newly sowne. . . .	01	06	08
Item one Cupboard a litle Table & hencaule (?) . .	o	12	o	Item more ware corne sowne .	o	16	o
				Item Manure . . .	o	6	8
Item Chaires & stooles wth a litle Hall table . . .	o	3	o	Item one Cart betwixt Robte Wilkinson and Marke Scawby his parte	01	05	o
Item one Iron range & Tongs Reckon & Gallow balke .	o	3	o				
Item one Hatchett & 2 Spades.	o	1	8		li	s	o
Item plucked Wooll . .	o	8	o	Total	20	11	8

b. (York Probate Registry, Dean and Chapter Various, B 10)

Part of the inventory of Alice Squire, widow, of Bramham, 1675.

	£	s	d		£	s	d
Item her purse and apparell .	10	00	00	Item 3 pewther Dublers 1 Candlestick 3 chaires & sawcers	o	4	10
In the fire house							
Item 1 great table 2 formes & a buffer stoole. . . .	00	12	00	Item one Jron Rainge & Rekkon fire shovell & Tonges .	o	7	8
Item i Liveray Cubbort; 1 pott & 3 brasse pannes . .	00	17	08	Item I frying pann with other house holdments . .	o	2	00

APPENDIX OF SELECT DOCUMENTS

In the Parlor

Item 2 stand bedds & 1 Chest .	01	15	00
Item 2 Coverlitts 2 Blankitts 2 paire of course Sheets & 1 linin sheet . . .	1	2	4

In the Chamber over the Parlor

Item 1 Cimlins 1 Dough Tubb with other houslements .	0	6	8
Item 2 Bushells of Mashelshon 5 hennes & a Cock . .	0	10	00

In the Barne

one Hay mew 2 Ackres of Corne (viz) 1 Ackre of Hard Corne & another of waire Corne	3	10	00
Item Two Kine . . .	3	7	8

Debts amounting to £23 10s.

c. (Reprinted from Yorks. Arch. Soc. Record Series, *Miscellanea*, VI, 57.)

A true and Perfect Inventory of all the goods & Chattels of John Bancroft in the Paroch of Barnoldswick Latley Deseased Judged and a Priced by us whoas Names are under writ the 13th Day of Octobr 1719

Imprimis his pors and aparell £1 1s.; in the body sted of the Hous one taible Long setl two Chists six puder Dishes one Dreser fouer Chears one /?/ Baxton one frying pan two pans one /?/ Coral pott, £1; in the parler one Bed and beding three Boxes one Deske one Chest, £1; Law parler one pear of Loums and 3 springs wheels, 12s.; House Chamber one Bed & beding one Chist with wool & yarn in, £1 2s. 6d; Parler Chamber one Chist one Arke with meall in one wheelbarrow, £1 1s.; two Cows, £5; one Mare and Coult, £3 10s; in the Barn Corn and Hay, £3; Husborney gear wheels Carte, £1. /Total/ £18 6s. 6d.

Will: Mitchell, Christopher Hudson, Robertt Stringer, James Varley

287

Glossary of Building Terms

ARCADE PLATE. A horizontal timber in the roof of an aisled hall, supported by the piers of the arcade and supporting the lower ends of the rafters of the nave roof. Its being placed in the same plane as the piers distinguishes it from the purlin (q.v.) which is in the plane of the rafters.

BAY. A unit of building, its length determined by the distances apart of the principal uprights or of the window openings. The length is commonly 16 feet but may be as little as 9 feet.

CHAMFER. The surface made by cutting off the square angle of a ceiling-beam or of the opening for a door, window or fireplace. The chamfer often ends with a carved feature (the chamfer stop), which with the form of the chamfer itself may have chronological significance. The chamfer may be, for instance, plain, hollow (i.e. concave) or ovolo moulded (i.e. convex and forming approximately a quadrant).

COLLAR PURLIN. A horizontal timber along the axis of a trussed rafter roof, supported by the crown-post and supporting the collar to each pair of common rafters.

CROWN-POST. A short post standing on a tie-beam and supporting the collar-purlin; it should be distinguished from the king-post, q.v.

CRUCKS. Pairs of large timbers inclined inwards from the line of the outer walls and meeting at the apex to support the ridge-beam.

GABLET. The small gable formed at each end of the main ridge of a hipped roof by bringing the rafters of the hip up to a point below the crest. The triangular opening so formed was left open for smoke to escape, or (in a barn) for ventilation.

HEADER. A brick so laid that its end, or head, appears on the face of a wall.

HIPPED ROOF. A roof with sloped ends instead of vertical gables. In a half-hipped roof the slope begins about half way between eaves and ridge level.

JETTY. The overhang of an upper floor in a timber framed house.

JOISTS. Timbers laid across from wall to wall, or to an intermediate beam, to support the floor boards of an upper room. Their size, cross section, spacing and moulding may be a clue to their date. They were usually visible from below in farmhouses of the seventeenth century or earlier: that is, the room beneath was not ceiled.

KING-POST. A vertical timber resting on a tie-beam and supporting a ridge-beam (see crown-post).

LOUVRE. An aperture in a roof for the escape of smoke from an open hearth.

MULLION. A vertical bar, in stone or wood, dividing a window opening.

NEWEL STAIR. A stair turning round a central post or newel; i.e., a spiral or winding stair.

PANTILE. A clay roofing tile, S shaped in section, of Dutch origin.

PARGETTING. The plaster rendering of the outside of a timber-framed building. The term is mainly East Anglian, though the practice was more widespread.

PURLIN. A timber running the length of a roof, intermediate between wall plate and ridge, supporting the common rafters.

SPEER. A screen to exclude draughts from a doorway.

STRETCHER. A brick so laid that its side appears on the face of a wall.

STRING. A horizontal band, in stone or brick, projecting from the face of a wall between floor levels. In brick houses the ledge so formed inside the wall usually supported the ends of joists.

STUD. A vertical timber in a wall of a timber-framed house, or in an internal partition.

SUMMERTREE. A tree or beam used as a 'summer', a horizontal bearing beam; called a breast-summer or bressumer when on the face of a building.

TIE-BEAM. A horizontal timber across a building, resting on the top of walls and tieing them together.

TRANSOM. A horizontal bar, of stone or timber, in a tall mullioned window to strengthen the mullions.

TRUSS. A triangular arrangement of timbers in a roof, either of common rafters with a collar, or of larger timbers at intervals forming the principal members, as in a cruck truss, hammerbeam truss, speer truss, etc.

TUMBLING. A gable in brick with a series of triangular wedges of brickwork laid at right angles to the line of the gable, so as to make a smooth finish to its edge; of Dutch origin.

VANCE ROOF. An East Anglian term for the roof space of a house elsewhere termed the garret. In manuscripts (e.g. in probate inventories) it has sometimes been confused with *vauce* (i.e false) roof, but vance (occasionally *vannce*) was certainly intended.

Index

Note. This is mainly a subject index. Reference to particular houses will be found classified under the various types (cottages, farmhouses, etc.), arranged in alphabetical order of counties and places.

291

symmetry in design, 72, 74, 98–99, 115, 157, 178, 213, 219, 236, 253–4, 261

terriers, parsonage, 91–95, 221, 255–7
Thetford, Norf., 6, 13
toftstead, 88
towhouse, 75
town houses, 19, 42
tradesmen, 44, 59–60, 62, 64, 75, 281
Treswell, Ralph, 87, 89

Valentine, Henry, 87, 88
vance roof, 72, 144, 198–9, 249, 282, 290
villages, open and closed, 249–50

washing facilities, 36
water supply, 223–4
Waynforth, Thos., 198, 281

Wealden house, 26–31, 32, 34, 42
windows, casement, 267, 268
  closet, 231
  dormer, 63, 72, 106, 249, 255
  fire, 112, 232, 235
  glazed, 61, 70, 113, 115, 150
  mullioned, 106, 112, 225, 262
  transom, 225, 255, 272
  storeyed bay, 98, 99, 216, 217
  Yorkshire sliding sash, 263–4
'withdrawing room', *see* parlour

yard, 14
Yarmouth, 199–200, 251
yeomen, 40, 41, 44, 47–48, 58–59, 60, 62, 64, 66, 67, 73, 75, 84–85, 90, 103, 105, 113, 120, 135–6, 143–4, 149–50, 152, 153, 155, 165, 168, 171, 172, 173, 185, 186, 196, 198, 211, 229, 239, 251, 267, 278, 280, 283, 284